All of the People,
All of the Time

PETER LANG
New York • Washington, D.C./Baltimore • Boston
Bern • Frankfurt am Main • Berlin • Vienna • Paris

Carl Cavanagh Hodge

All of the People, All of the Time

American Government at the End of the Century

PETER LANG
New York • Washington, D.C./Baltimore • Boston
Bern • Frankfurt am Main • Berlin • Vienna • Paris

Library of Congress Cataloging-in-Publication Data

Hodge, Carl Cavanagh.
All of the people, all of the time: American government at the end
of the century / Carl Cavanagh Hodge.
p. cm.
Includes bibliographical references and index.
1. United States—Politics and government. 2. Democracy—
United States. I. Title.
JK271.H69 973—dc20 95-37856
ISBN 0-8204-3019-6

Die Deutsche Bibliothek-CIP-Einheitsaufnahme

Hodge, Carl Cavanagh:
All of the people, all of the time: American government at the end of the century /
Carl Cavanagh Hodge. –New York; Washington, D.C./Baltimore; Boston; Bern;
Frankfurt am Main; Berlin; Vienna; Paris: Lang.
ISBN 0-8204-3019-6

Maps of the Electoral College courtesy
of *Congressional Quarterly Inc.* and *Election Data Services*

Cover photo: Paul Strand, *Wall Street, New York,* 1915.
Copyright © 1971, Aperture Foundation Inc., Paul Strand Archive.

The paper in this book meets the guidelines for permanence and durability
of the Committee on Production Guidelines for Book Longevity
of the Council of Library Resources.

Printed in the United States of America.

To Jane, who loves politics

If you once forfeit the confidence of your fellow citizens,
you can never regain their respect and esteem.
It is true that you may fool all of the people some of the
time; you can even fool some of the people all of the time;
but you can't fool all of the people, all of the time.

-attributed to Abraham Lincoln

Table of Contents

Preface

This book was provoked by questions, questions posed by students, colleagues, and fellow enthusiasts of American politics. I could not answer all the questions; in fact, I found that I was not able to answer most of them to my own satisfaction. I noticed, however, that most of the questions shared the assumption that there is something wrong with the manner in which public affairs are currently conducted in the United States. "What", they asked, "is wrong with the American political system?" As soon as the issue was framed in this way, as the discussion moved from politics to government, I found myself on firmer ground. I was able to answer that in fact very little is wrong with the government of the United States and that anyone with Thomas Paine's appetite for common sense would realize this if they were to take the time to appreciate American government for the durable work of intellectual balance, the monument to human ingenuity that it is. The United States has survived and triumphed in a terrible century. It is today a more vital and vigorous place than it has ever been . . . after more than two hundred years of living with the same constitution.

Yet one of the great growth industries of our time, indeed the past forty years, has been lamenting, or celebrating, the alleged decline of the United States, while slandering as naive or arrogant the American mission in the world, that of democracy and individual enterprise. The people who have been professionally dedicated to this position cannot be converted. But they have been, I will argue, decisively refuted by the direction of recent history. Both free enterprise and democratic self-government are today more universally popular than ever before. Perhaps it is the Puritan heritage that makes Americans themselves the most frequent critics of their own foibles, but it is incontestable that they lead the pack in alleging hypocrisy and corruption in the elected leadership of the United States. I want to emphasize the word *elected*, because a central theme of this book is that the United States is the most genuinely and comprehensively democratic country among the nations qualified to lay legitimate claim to parliamentary tradition. To the extent that Americans damn their politicians, they damn themselves; at the heart of political divisions in the United States is the fact not that Congress and the President fail to represent the aspirations of the voting public but rather that they represent them all too well.

The single greatest contribution to the malign spirit infecting American public life today is a widespread belief that almost any problem has a political dimension and a political answer. The founding generation of the American republic assumed exactly the opposite, namely that a civilized and tolerant people will want to keep ninety-five percent of all human endeavor beyond the ambit of express governmental authority. They dedicated the United States to a contractually limited government that places enormous expectations in its citizenry to govern itself without resort to any form of public authority whatever. The gap between what Americans expect of government and what the Constitution of the United States will concede they have a right to expect is the root explanation for popular discontent with Washington today. Americans want liberty and security in equal measure, yet their system of government is rightly founded on the principle that there exists an invisible threshold where the pursuit of the latter becomes a threat to the former. The Constitution is a conservative defense of classical liberal values.

This book is to a significant extent a history of American political parties. This is unavoidable, because democracy over the past two hundred years, in America and elsewhere, has been a party affair. And for all the quaint talk of interconnectivity and direct democracy, political parties will no more disappear from the project of steering public policy or the effort to win public office than will the human instinct to collude and coalesce in the furtherance of parallel interests. The Democratic and Republican Parties, moreover, have for the most part done a worthy job of brokering the influence of popular sentiment on government and debating between them the legitimacy of demands on government with reference to the principles of the Constitution. There is no doubt, admittedly, that party competition in the United States is today at something of a crossroads, but a review of the American electoral past will show that populist rebellions against the two-party system are a recurring habit of American public affairs and not at all a symptom of any failing vitality. If there is a critical difference between former phases of partisan flux and that of the 1990s, it is that the conduct of party competition in the United States is now more open and democratic than it has ever been, though not necessarily more civil or satisfying for that fact.

Lastly, this book attempts to portray the domestic and foreign affairs of the United States as inseparable parts of the same story. The teaching of government and foreign policy as discrete categories is an organizational convenience for professional academics, but intellectually it is less justified in the case of the United States than for any other established democracy. The Constitution deliberately involves the executive and legislative branches in a competition over the spirit and conduct of American diplomacy, and the post World War II superpower status of the United States has meant that American domestic affairs and international commitments routinely impinge on one another. Very few of the initiatives the United States undertakes in the world are fully understandable in their form and content without reference to political conditions at home, and no nation's foreign policy is more representative of its people. The most obvious feature of American diplomatic history to anyone who will contemplate it soberly and without prejudice is that it has been preponderantly adroit and successful. Its setbacks have been few, temporary, and, with some exceptions, due to factors not solely attributable to the political leadership of the United States. This book will further argue that American diplomacy has always been more pragmatic and realistic, less ideological and idealistic, than is usually conceded. Its treacheries are outnumbered by its noble gestures and flashes of brilliance.

Inside the United States and abroad, American politics has its own vast constellation of devotees, those who follow the public affairs of the Great Republic but who also love politics generally. They know democratic politics to be, for all its grime, a wholesome pursuit. For their help in conjuring the idea for this book I would like to express my gratitude. More particularly, I would like to tanks those who have contributed to the book's progress, above all my wife Jane Everett, Douglas Everett, Cathal Nolan, Owen Lancer, Trumbell Rogers, and the many colleagues and students with whom I have had the great pleasure to talk politics. It has been a privilege.

Carl Cavanagh Hodge –Hyattsville, Maryland, 1997

Abbreviations

AAA	Agricultural Adjustment Act
ABM	Anti-ballistic Missile (Treaty)
CBO	Congressional Budget Office
CEA	Council of Economic Advisors
DNC	Democratic National Committee
EEOC	Equal Employment Opportunity Commission
ERA	Equal Rights Amendment
ERP	European Recovery Program
Exim	Export-Import (Bank)
FAP	Family Assistance Plan
FTA	Free Trade Agreement
GATT	General Agreement on Tariffs and Trade
GOP	Grand Old Party (Republicans)
ICC	Interstate Commerce Commission
IMF	International Monetary Fund
INF	Intermediate-range Nuclear Forces (Treaty)
LSG	Legislative Study Group
MFN	Most Favored Nation
NAFTA	North American Free Trade Agreement
NIRA	National Industrial Recovery Act
NRA	National Recovery Administration
NSC	National Security Council
NWRO	National Welfare Rights Organization
PAC	Political Action Committee
PLO	Palestine Liberation Organization
PPA	Progressive Party of America
RNC	Republican National Committee
SALT	Strategic Arms Limitation Talks
SDI	Strategic Defense Initiative
START	Strategic Arms Reduction Talks

TVA	Tennessee Valley Authority
UN	United Nations
UNRRA	United Nations Relief and Rehabilitation Administration

PART I
DEMOCRATIC AMERICA

Chapter One

The Spirit of
American Republicanism

The institutions now made in America will not wear wholly out for thousands of years. It is of the last importance, then, that they should begin right. –John Adams, *A Defense of the Constitutions of Government of the United States of America*

The republic is old. The United States, a nation in which the theme of national renewal is as constant as the rhythm of the political seasons, is a venerable democracy. In the two hundred years since the Philadelphia Convention, America's contemporary in the radical democratic experiment of the nineteenth century, France, has gone through four republics. The Soviet Union has come and gone. In the late 1980s the United States emerged triumphant from the greatest test of character in its two-hundred year history and is today more secure from foreign attack than at possibly any time this century. The past fifty years have featured none of the catastrophes of the first half-century, two world wars and the Great Depression, due primarily to the services rendered by the United States to the maintenance of international peace. The Cold War confrontation with the Soviet Union, from the outset endowed with the potential to make everything preceding it seem trivial, ended without the principal participants ever coming to blows. So the story of the United States is one of success. At the most fundamental level this success can and should be traced to the quality of the American people, but it also owes a debt to the resilience of the nation's political institutions, founded as they were on the thousand-year genius of Western civilization and science of government.

The effectiveness of American government has lately come under strain. Cynicism erodes popular faith in the integrity of national institutions and political officeholders alike. The English Tory Edmund Burke once cautioned that any constitution that had served "in any tolerable degree" deserved reverence rather revision.[1] The founding document of the United States is widely regarded as, at the very least, tolerably ingenious, so it is today fair to assume that the American people are dissatisfied with their government not because the formula of 1787 was critically flawed. Rather, the evolution of the United States into a world power and then a superpower has imposed contradictory pressures on its populace and tested the national consensus on the ends and means of government both at home and abroad. In the twentieth century the relationship between president and Congress has changed fundamentally. At the same time, partisan competition for the loyalty of the electorate has eroded public appreciation of the founding principles of the Republic. Few Americans would challenge openly the principles on which their government is based, yet most have come to expect more of government than they care to admit. For this reason above all Adam's words represent an appropriate point of departure. Americans today often fail to appreciate that in 1787 the institutions did begin right, while fooling themselves about the fundamental assumptions on which those institutions were founded.

It is therefore important to remind ourselves of the maturity of American democracy and the trajectory of its history in order think soberly about the nature of politics and the realities of contemporary problems in American government. It is above all instructive to go back to the authors of the Constitution and to measure their broad intentions for the working of Washington's institutions against the true nature of those problems. Why? Because, the authors of the Constitution understood their task to be that of establishing a system of governance *for all time.* They thought of human nature as more-or-less demonstrably unchanging and beyond debate: *we hold these truths to be self-evident.* For the student of American government at the end of the twentieth century who accepts that the principles of the Constitution are sound, it is irrelevant that the founding document was written by 'dead white males' of the eighteenth century. The legitimate expectation of any constitution built upon a universalist concept of human nature is that the citizenry conforms itself to the constitution, not the reverse.

Government and Self-government

The Constitution of the United States is about *liberty*. To found a government on the principle of liberty, of course, is something of contradiction. So much of the energy of government, any government, is committed to the maintenance of *order*. But fundamental to the entire logic of the *Constitution of the United States* is the conviction that a government properly constituted must at the very least preserve that with which its citizens were born and to which they have a right by virtue of their very birth, individual freedom. They otherwise owe its laws no obedience. The idea is nowhere more eloquently expressed than in the words that first made explicit the American claim to sovereign statehood, the *Declaration of Independence* itself, where Thomas Jefferson declares the necessity "for one people to dissolve the political bands which have connected them to another," in defense of the self-evident and inalienable rights of life and liberty of which colonists had been deprived by the abuses of imperial Britain. The Declaration goes on to itemize twenty-seven specific transgressions, for which Britain's subjects in America had unsuccessfully sought redress. Considered together they reveal that the signatories sought liberty first in a negative sense. Beyond the grievances of taxation without representation and mercantilist impediments to foreign trade, the colonists sought a more general freedom from the British crown's interference in the attempts of New Englanders simply to govern themselves. Indeed, the very first charge against George III is of withholding assent to laws "the most wholesome and necessary for the public good."

Long before independence the American colonies were in many respects already self-governing, endowed with representative assemblies that initiated legislation, levied taxes, and set appropriations. The revolutionary generation was nothing if not confident in its intellectual capacity and moral right to govern itself. Its leadership understood themselves to be in-

volved as much in an act of preservation as of rebellion, defending the rights of free-born Englishmen against the excesses
of an imprudent, nay impudent, king.[2] Equally, the colonists
never conceived of *revolution* as a bloodbath of class revenge.
On the contrary, they used the word in reference to a procedure for change both legal and, so far as possible, peaceful.
From the very outset they were at pains to justify their actions
with what the Declaration called "a decent respect for the opin-
ions of mankind." When the French Revolution degenerated
into the Terror, many of them concluded that only the descendants of Englishmen knew how to make a revolution. Ever
mindful of the forces they unleashed by renouncing obedience
to the British crown, the Founders sought to replace its might
as completely as possible with another kind of authority. Hence,
the exalted status they gave the written guarantee of their liberties and in the sovereignty they took from a monarch and
invested in their constitution. At its core the Constitution's
defense of liberty was based on a fairly rigorous understanding of *limited* government. In so far as the government of the
United States was to confine its actions to the strictures of the
founding document, so too were its citizens to conform their
expectations of that government to the same parameters.

Between the conception of political independence in 1776
and the constitution of an independent government in 1787,
however, lay six years of military struggle and another four to
contemplate how best, as the Constitution finally expressed it,
to "secure the Blessings of Liberty" while "insuring domestic
tranquillity." Freedom with order. With the *Peace Treaty of 1783*
and the rather generous terms conceded by Britain, the revo-
lutionaries secured the former, but the *Articles of Confederation*
of 1781 hardly provided for the latter. Until the Philadelphia
Convention of 1787 the newly independent states of America
represented a league of friendship without either the blueprint
or the most rudimentary scaffolding of a political union. Shays'
Rebellion, an uprising of debt-ridden farmers from central and
western Massachusetts in 1786 against the merchants, banks,
and courts of Boston, touched on fears for elementary security and unity in a way that made the need for a truly national
government as obvious as the musket fire that ended the rebellion itself.

On the one hand, the revolt represented the infant republic's first open tax revolt; on the other, it was a threat to the rule of law so audacious that the British press promptly celebrated it as evidence that America was weary of independence and incapable of self-regulation. At Philadelphia the Founders transformed it into a catalyst for history's most extraordinary achievement in conception and design of representative government.[3] The document they drafted, *The Constitution of the United States of America,* was and is a hybrid of liberal political philosophy, classical republicanism, and protestant theology.[4] The Founders saw themselves as "enlightened friends of liberty." Yet, contrary to much of the folklore of the revolution, they held ambivalent views concerning *democracy* as the guarantor of liberty. For many the word had pejorative connotations, and yet within a generation its use was interchangeable with *republic,* so that Jefferson's Republican Party became the Democratic Party without so much as backward glance. The Founders agreed that a *republican*[5] form of government incorporating constituent states into a federal union would best ensure the "internal tranquillity of states" against the kind of insurrection whose violence in Massachusetts represented a mortal threat to the very possibility of liberty.[6] Indeed, many were openly sceptical that there existed any inherent virtue in a democratic form of government. John Adams, a Massachusetts Yankee whom Jefferson once praised as "the Colossus of Independence," argued that "there never was a democracy yet that did not commit suicide," and added that "it is vain to say that democracy is less vain, less proud, less selfish, less ambitious, or less avaricious than aristocracy or monarchy".[7] It is a strong statement, yet also very representative of the measure of democracy taken by the first generation of American leadership. The architects of American nationhood were a literate and propertied elite, who had no intention of delivering the government of their hard-won independence into the hands of a rabble whose uninstructed understanding of freedom could lead, as the Founders saw it, only to anarchy.

And yet they planted the seed of democracy. More precisely, they installed a democratic element at the very heart of republic of 1787. If a democracy in the contemporary sense is to be measured both in terms of the ability of citizens to elect their government and also to influence its deliberations and policies between elections, then American government remains today easily the most democratic on earth. From the start, the implications of 1787 exceeded the physical dimensions of the little republic. The "grave and substantial men" who convened at Philadelphia inaugurated the human experiment whose goals form the very core of our understanding of modernity, an experiment so radical that many of them came to despair of their handiwork.[8] They reasoned that no republic would remain a wholesome environment for liberty if its government consistently and systematically excluded the people, in the larger sense, from deliberation on the public good. They noted that this had been tried in Europe with calamitous results. In some degree at least, the Founders concluded, *all* of the people must be self-governing. So that republican government might survive and prosper, meaningful concessions would have to be made to the *demos*. The most important concession was to institutionalize democracy at the very heart of government, and to then balance the potential of democratic excess with an American version of aristocratic privilege. It is today the stuff of elementary instruction that American government is based on an especially intricate system of checks-and-balances, but it is little appreciated in what a highly integrative and coherent fashion such checks and balances actually work.

Balancing the goal of representative democracy against their legitimate horror of rampant majority will, the Founders shaped the institutional structures of American government around the fundamental principles of separation of powers and federalism. The checks-and-balances of the Constitution are designed to provide for popular representation in national government while guarding against a "tyranny of the majority" that could arise should popular passions be allowed to determine the policy and actions of Congress unqualified by either the veto of the executive branch or by the constitutional test of judicial review. Representation itself, moreover, was understood to have a particular meaning. Allowing for the republic's authentic democratic concerns, its Congress was intended to be a deliberative assembly whose ultimate interpretation of the public good would add up to a sum much greater than its constituent parts. A common contemporary misunderstanding of representative democracy is that which holds that Congress ought to reflect the social, ethnic, and gender composition of society before it can claim to be a truly representative democratic forum. Aside from the prejudicial assumption that elected representatives automatically think and vote in certain ways because of their social status, cultural heritage, or gender, representative government is not based on the assumption that such efficient representativeness is either desirable or possible. One commentary notes that in any parliament:

> the percentage of people of *very* high or *very* low intelligence will be *lower* than in the general population: the very low very obvious reasons;the very high, for reasons only slightly less obvious: they get involved in other time-consuming pursuits. For similar reasons mystical contemplatives (rare anywhere) and artists will be underrepresented in Parliament. The shy, the unambitious, the self-doubting: Will there be *any* of them? I think not. Neither will there be any of those who have absolutely no interest in politics and regard all politicians as incompetent and dishonest. It follows that Parliament is seriously unrepresentative and will remain so until elections are replaced by random selection.[9]

An overstatement of the case, but also a wholesome reminder that in electing a representative for public office, voters are at one level (that of political talent) wise to choose somebody quite *unlike* themselves. It makes no more sense to elect a Congressman who possess no knowledge of government, based on the assumption that in ignorance is innocence, than it does to hire a plumber with no skill in plumbing, due to the fear that an expert plumber will undertake unnecessary repairs. Representative government in the American tradition demands that members of Congress be parliamentary advocates for the interests and concerns of their constituents. The comparative lack of party discipline in Congress reflects the fact that, relative to British MPs, the American system affords its citizens a greater variety of opportunities to express either satisfaction or annoyance at the effectiveness of their congressional representation. But the end of that very representation is to define a public good and, when necessary, to legislate in its interest.

The great democratic chamber of the United States Congress is the House of Representatives. It should be remembered that until the ratification of the Seventeenth Amendment in

1913 the Senate was an appointed chamber and that the six-year term to which Senators are elected today still gives them greater insulation from the electoral censure of a public whose sentiment may be out of sympathy with the chamber's actions. Where Alexander Hamilton observed that the representatives of the people "seem sometimes to fancy that they are the people themselves and betray strong symptoms of impatience and disgust at the least sign of opposition from any other quarter,"[10] he obviously thought that it ought not to be so. As regards the logic of the constitution on the organization of the two houses of Congress, certainly, it ought to be so least of all in the Senate. In his own time Alexis de Tocqueville commented on the contrast between the Senate and the House, the latter peopled with "village lawyers and tradesmen," the former featuring "a nobler and more beautiful shape" that, he supposed, only the refinement of indirect election could achieve.[11] The Senate today remains the chamber assigned more explicitly with the definition of the national interest, and it shares with the president a brief in the conduct of the nation's foreign affairs. The 435 members of the House, by contrast, have license to be more unapologetically narrow in the representation of their constituents' concerns, and their two-year terms go a long way toward guaranteeing that they will be.[12]

The six-year term of senators, moreover, exceeds both the four-year presidential mandate and the two-year tenure of representatives, making it the less vulnerable than either to democratic veto of its policy. Given the ambit of the Senate's responsibilities, its inherently conservative function is therefore meant to impinge both on domestic and foreign affairs with a stabilizing effect. With regard to the latter, James Madison argued on behalf of "a due sense of national character" that such a select and stable branch of government could provide; otherwise, the esteem of foreign governments so important to successful diplomacy would be forfeited "by an unenlightened and variable policy."[13] Because the Founders furthermore did not provide for direct election of senators, it is obvious that they intended the chamber to be immune from any direct electoral interpolation of its actions. So the constitutional requirement that the president work with the Senate in foreign affairs has always been serious and substantive.

The Senate is also an assembly of the states, the structure and functions of which effectively make the states an integral part of the federal government. Like all federalist arrangements the American system is in principle designed to decentralize political power while integrating the country territorially. There is something much more substantive than theory, furthermore, in the notion that the vitality of the republic depends on popular involvement in state and local affairs. De Tocqueville concluded that the lack of administrative centralization in the America of the 1830s provided an important check on the tyrannical use of national majority will. He explained that "municipal bodies and county administrations are like so many hidden reefs retarding or dividing the flood of the popular will," so that if a law were oppressive "liberty would still find some shelter from the way the law is carried into execution." It was also his judgment that the love of meaningful participation in public affairs, which in New England occurred most routinely in the townships, represented the real source of patriotism that Americans rightly regarded "as a sort of religion strengthened by practical service."[14] Though the nature of American government has since changed profoundly, the reverence with which political localism is regarded has not diminished. Even incumbent members of Congress, should they wish to remain incumbents, make great efforts to show their electors that the opulence of the marble corridors has not gone to their heads and that they remain, first and last, citizens of their home districts.[15]

Over the past two centuries the balance of American federalism has clearly shifted in favor of much greater federal authority. The United States remains, nonetheless, a true federation, in that certain powers remain unique to the states while others are Washington's sole prerogative. Any comparison of the United States with other federated states, ranging from Switzerland at one extreme to the Federal Republic of Germany at the other, will also reveal that the American system is an overwhelming historical success in answering the requirements of both decentralization and national cohesion. The states enjoy not only the capacity for bilateral bargaining with Washington in those areas where they retain substantive competence; they also have direct representation in and are party to the deliberations of the federal government through their membership in the Senate. Here is where federalism and the separation of powers combine with special effectiveness. For there is no doubt that most Americans think of senators as *national* politicians, and yet the fact that each state has two Senate seats—regardless of the obvious differences in size and importance between California and, say, Rhode Island—reflects the fact that the republic consists, after all, of *these United States*. Whatever imbalances are created in the Senate by the voting equality of states with vastly different populations and resources, is offset in the House of Representatives by the allocation of congressional districts according to the nation's demography.

The document of 1787 made the two houses of Congress the center-of-gravity of national politics in the United States. In the twentieth century the balance of political power between Congress and the president has changed significantly, both in terms of the authority the executive branch actually wields and with respect to popular expectations of presidential leadership. Before 1900 assertive presidential leadership in national affairs was the exception to the rule of congressional dominance, and powerful presidents were the product of a mixture of personality and extraordinary circumstance. It took more than one hundred and fifty years of political development for the White House to replace Congress in the hearts and minds of Americans as the focal point of public affairs. In the early years of the republic the presidency was generally regarded as little more than a celebrated clerk-in-chief. There are countless nineteenth-century presidents remembered for nothing in particular or forgotten altogether. That the Founders thought of Congress as the heart is worthy of special emphasis. Jefferson referred to the legislature as *first among equals* in the tripartite arrangement of government, and enumerating the powers of Congress is the business of Article I of the Constitution. Even where Madison considered checks against the possibility of congressional overreach, he did so because he understood that so much of the business of government in a republic is necessarily the business of its congress.[16]

An understanding of the original intent of American government therefore focuses first and foremost on Congress. Today, as in the last century, a presidential election is something of a plebiscite on the national mood, but the constantly shifting partisan balance in the two houses offers an infinitely more detailed cardiograph of public sentiment as it changes. Set against the authority of Congress elaborated in Article I, the powers of the president are outlined in the much more ambiguous contours of Article II. The contrast represents not negligence but a compromise settlement of the Founders' conflicting ideas on the imperatives and peril of executive power. What emerges from a careful reading of Article II, nonetheless, is that the Constitution intends the presidency to be an office of *delegated* authority. So, where the president is mandated to *take Care that the Laws be faithfully executed* (Article II, 3), he can uphold only the laws that Congress passes. Hamilton's explanation of the executive office repeatedly goes out of its way to contrast the qualified powers of an American president with the absolute powers of a British monarch.[17] Viewed from the contemporary context, the presidency of the United States defined by the Constitution appears a surprisingly modest office deserving little of the attention that today is lavished on it daily. This is why the real and perceived effectiveness of the executive branch depends so much on the skills of its occupant. For if the president has few positive powers at his disposal, his responsibility to be the president of all of the people necessarily elevates him above sectional and territorial interests and gives his every utterance a weight greater than that accorded the pronouncements of any other politician. It is most appropriate to say that a sitting president has assets at his disposal, which, if used skilfully and with a mind to opportunity and circumstance, can be converted into awesome authority. A president today can make a hero or a heel of himself with a single action; whatever he does, he acts with an enormous national and international audience looking on.

The differing terms awarded presidents, senators, and representatives; the scheduling of the elections themselves; and the punctuation of national politics by gubernatorial contests mean that in the United States something is happening electorally all of the time. Because, in Madison's words, the content of the public good is too often determined not by the rule of justice but "by the superior force of an interested and overbearing majority,"[18] the intention of the Constitution is clearly to frustrate any consistent application of majority rule. The "advantageous superiority" of the American system of representative government, Madison added, was to consist in *"the total exclusion of the people in their collective capacity* from any share" in governing.[19] Yet the actions of government in Washington are also more transparent than in any other democratic system. The government's very structure is an invitation to the interested public to observe, understand, and participate in the great game of politics in which the possibilities of winning and losing are very real, but in which victories and defeats are never complete and absolute. The vitality of American government depends like no other on the calculation that the most active and informed citizens will not only play the game but come to love it as a calling that, for all its perfidies, represents a fundamentally wholesome pursuit in which the promotion of their self-interest can and should be squared with a collective benefit. There is for political man, as much as for any other, the right to moral indignation when the machinery of government is turned entirely to cynical purposes, but such indignation is never sufficient justification for walking away from politics altogether. In this sense, a sincere hatred of politics is arguably un-American. It is certainly unrepublican.[20]

The Founders considered a principal object of a republican order and of civic mindedness to be the vigilant protection of private property. It is only a modest exaggeration to say that they considered liberty and property to be much the same thing; what distinguished the citizen of a liberal republic from the subject of even the most benign feudal order was the untrammeled right to the accumulation of material wealth, the control of which was beyond the ambit of government. Understanding property to be both the source of all real liberty, they also made it a qualification for citizenship.

In constituting the first government of the United States they had wilfully to overlook the fact that for a good many of them the right to property meant the right to own other men, for in 1787 they could address the moral blot of slavery only by destroying any chance of political union. Indeed, slavery eliminated any need for a large white landless laboring class that would have complicated the acceptance of republican principles at Philadelphia. The most capable minds present at Philadelphia understood that the spirit of liberty that had animated the colonies' struggle with Britain could never be squared with the fact of human bondage in their midst, but they were concerned with the confederation that was possible as a preliminary step to the ideal. By 1800, after all, slavery had been banned throughout New England, so in principle there was reason to hope that it would melt away elsewhere. In meantime, the *Three-fifths Compromise* not only sanctioned slave-holding, it went so far as to reward slaveholders politically. That is, it withheld from slaves any hope of citizenship and voting rights, yet counted them as people rather property in order to enhance the strength of the southern states, which were home to the vast preponderance of the slave population, in the House of Representatives. It was a moral and political compromise the full cost of which by 1865 amounted to more than 600,000 Union and Confederate dead, but in 1787 "it probably kept the South from unanimously rejecting the constitution."[21]

At the time of the Declaration of Independence there existed in the states a variety of property qualifications for electoral enfranchisement, along with stiffer property requirements for officeholding.[22] The conviction that a material stake in society necessarily colored a citizen's patriotic commitment to its defense and the standards of it administration excluded not only slaves but also paupers, vagabonds, and all those without visible property from full membership in the ranks of The People.[23]

But there was more to property still, so much in fact that it figured prominently in the *Federalist Papers* and in the cause of winning the states' approval of the constitution. Shays' Rebellion, after all, had been essentially about the security of property. So when James Madison addressed the destructive implications of "factionalism" for a self-governing people, he cited as the most common source of faction "the various and unequal distribution of property."[24] In what was perhaps his most important contribution to the logic of the Constitution, Madison reasoned that liberty could be preserved from both threats to and the abuse of property by a system that set interest against interest and in which ambition was made to counteract ambition. Any government that attempted to remove the sources of factionalism from society would also destroy all liberty, that of the civic-minded and cynical alike, in the attempt. The goal therefore was to constitute political liberty in such a fashion as to establish an "umpired strife," to permit the self-interest of citizens to a have the fullest possible expression, to contend with each other for public influence and its attendant benefits.[25] The Constitution calculates that human nature can be domesticated by the political system partly by the rough-and-tumble of participation itself. Properly umpired, crude human greed can actually quicken the wits of the republic without shattering its stability. It umpires political strife along a number of dimensions: federalism to decentralize authority territorially; distinct executive, legislative, and judicial branches to do the same functionally. Popular elections to see what the people want. The separation of powers to see that they don't get it . . . unless, of course, the people's desire for a specific kind of political good motivates them powerfully enough to elect both a Congress and a president who will champion its passage. The Constitution otherwise places the benefit of the doubt with the classical liberal sentiment that the best government is the least government and reserves for the Supreme Court to say whether what the voting populace wants, the president will propose, and Congress will pass is in fact "American" as the spirit and letter of the Constitution define it.

From the preceding it should be obvious that the Constitution and Bill of Rights are also based on high expectations of the active citizenry. These documents furthermore interpret the pursuit of happiness as an overwhelmingly private undertaking, in which it is manifestly beyond either the capacity or the legitimate authority of government to influence decisively the outcome. In exchange for a guarantee of certain inalienable liberties and the ability to change the personnel of government, the contract of liberal democracy demands that self-governing citizens be self-reliant and to look rarely, if ever, to Washington as the appropriate address of their hopes or frustrations. The constitution expects, furthermore, that the citizens of the United States will conduct their lives in such a manner as to achieve goodness as a society.[26] A true republic is of necessity a delicate construct, because its survival and prosperity depend on extraordinary moral character in its people. Madison warned the Virginia Assembly in 1788 that "to suppose that any form of government will secure liberty or happiness without any virtue in the people is a chimerical idea".[27] For the Founders republican *virtue* meant upright intentions; the cultivation of moderation, based on the knowledge that reckless promotion of personal gain in the present almost certainly imperilled its retention in the future; the pursuit of wisdom; a self-sacrificing love of the republic and its institutions. For Benjamin Franklin, whose *Autobiography* is widely thought to represent the most vivid tribute to the moral spirit of the Constitution, it was overwhelmingly in private pursuits of the individual citizen that such qualities were nurtured and in the citizen's intermittent contact with public affairs that their presence accrued to the benefit of the polity.[28]

Governmental institutions themselves, the Founders reasoned, had a vital role to play, both in the husbandry of virtue and in the preservation of the public interest whenever civic-mindedness was in short supply. Whether in voting or in holding public office, the individual who was called upon to act with lofty intentions would usually attempt to rise to the occasion. The experience of participation and the encounter with competing interests would meanwhile support the conclusion that only in compromise is a quantum of political fulfilment. Whereas Hamilton supposed that even the noblest men may not be moved by the love of republican virtues so much as by the reward of esteem obtained by demonstrated adherence to them, Madison concluded that republican virtue had not been in sufficient supply in the prerevolutionary republics and proposed that in the greater pluralism of a large republic the pressures favoring moderation and accommodation would sustain disinterested leadership committed to the public good. Like a good many of the leading Federalists, Madison accepted that "the mass of the people" had both the right and sufficient virtue to make responsible use of free elections, yet doubted that they possessed the requisite experience or wisdom to exercise responsible leadership themselves. For his part, Hamilton cautioned that there were occasions when "the interests of the people are at variance with their inclinations," and concluded in much the same way as Burke that "it is the duty of the persons they have appointed to be the guardians of those inter-

ests to withstand the temporary delusion in order to give them
time and opportunity for more cool and sedate reflection."[29]
What Hamilton was defending was an ethos of political *trusteeship* for elected officials, an ethos that is today little favored
by the public's expectations of Congress, but which was an
important aspect of the logic of the Constitution.

Inherent in the call to self-government is the expectation
that citizens will govern their own affairs with sufficient self-
discipline that elected officials are not required to invent new
laws to preserve a civil society. The Second Amendment to
the Constitution, ratified in 1791, is a case in point. Currently
an issue of enormous controversy, the right *to keep and bear
arms* is widely considered an embarrassing artifact of early
constitutional development wholly out of step with an understandable concern to arrest the rampant misuse of firearms. A
popular interpretation of the amendment is that it is based on
a now outdated provision for the raising of a popular militia
for the emergency defense of the young republic. The
amendment's very wording invites such a conclusion. The un-
comfortable historical truth is that the amendment rests both
on a long legacy of English law and the various state bills of
rights, and also that it was intended to sanctify a connection
between the right to arms and the very possibility of liberty.[30]
Madison observed that European governments were rightly
afraid to trust their people with arms, and among the founding generation it was accepted that Americans were by contrast of sufficient civilization to justify such trust. Considered
from this perspective, it is clear that the Second Amendment
is closely joined with the very republican identity of the United
States.[31] The Founders could not have anticipated the horrors
of firearm abuse in modern urban America, but equally the
debate about firearms ought not to focus on a false controversy about their intentions in 1791. The real issue is whether
in their ownership of arms Americans have since demonstrated
sufficient civilization to justify continued respect for the
amendment. It is not difficult, certainly, to guess at the likely
verdict of its authors.

Another current debate revolves around the claim that the
American body politic is a "Christian Nation", a notion as intellectually lazy as it is mischievous. The Founders were after

all the descendants of refugees of religious persecution. They understood that when one religion attempted to marry the state something akin to cultural civil war was inevitable. The First Amendment's separation of church and state was not only a guarantee against religious persecution but a calculation that citizens could conduct moral lives without feeling the need to flay their fellow citizens with moral absolutes. While the cohesion of New England society was rooted in Christian values, the notion that individual spiritual enthusiasms required the sanction of government was rejected. If anything the Revolution cultivated an appetite for republicanizing Christianity rather than christening the Republic. The churches America inherited from Europe soon fragmented and citizens became their own theologians. The Constitution, De Tocqueville noted, did not stop Americans from being deeply religious, but "for most people in the United States religion, too, is republican, for the truths of the other world are held subject to private judgment."[32] Self-restraint is at the core of honoring the very rights the Constitution recognizes, in pleasure, in comfort . . . in faith and security.[33] Living up to a document such as that of 1787 is not easy, nor was it intended to be.

The Republic, Great or Small

Where Madison lamented the periodic want of virtue in the prerevolutionary republics and advocated a larger, more consolidated, and truly national body politic, he set the tone for the greatest debate of the first generation of American independence. He argued simply that in a large republic a greater heterogeneity of interests would tend to render majorities more fluid and hence more benign in terms of their potential for tyranny and the systematic abuse of liberty.[34] This idea suited Hamilton perfectly, but for different reasons. Hamilton wanted to subordinate the states to federal power and create a much more centralized republic than did Madison or, more importantly, Thomas Jefferson.

The philosophical differences between Jefferson and Hamilton conformed, albeit imperfectly, to the conflict between the Federalists and the Democratic-Republicans during the early phase in the development of political parties in the

United States. Dominated by the personality and vision of Thomas Jefferson, the latter party believed that republican government could survive only where it existed in close contact between citizens and elected representatives. Speaking above all for the concerns of wealthy southern landowners, the members of this party argued that political power should be located not with a central government but rather in the smaller units of the states, where elected officials could deal more directly with a relatively homogeneous electorate and hence understand their electors' concerns and grievances more thoroughly. The Federalists, by contrast, reflected the ambitions of northern merchants whose enthusiasm for wider and more cohesive, and therefore a more centralized, union brought them at Philadelphia into direct collision with delegates from the South. As it turned out, the Federalists were the better prepared and more united camp in the constitutional debate. By the time the rhetorical smoke had cleared, they had gained the upper hand of the argument and were the preponderant influence on the Constitution.

But not without the kind of bitter opposition from anti-Federalists that gave victory more of the feeling of exhausted relief than of celebration. For the anti-Federalists had thoroughly legitimate arguments on their side, arguments that cut right to the core of the whole cause of American statehood and which, even after Philadelphia, retained enough vitality to require the debate to be taken up again some eighty years later on the battlefields of the Civil War. Among them was a question posed at Philadelphia by Patrick Henry, first governor of the state of Virginia. What right had the Federalists, he wanted to know, to say "We the People, instead of We the States?", thus pushing to the fore the matter of whether each of the thirteen colonies had gained political sovereignty by armed struggle or whether there existed such a superseding American sovereignty as was implied by making the People rather than the States the authors of the Constitution.[35] Other anti-Federalists ventured also that a republican government on a continental scale was folly, capable of unity only at the price of becoming an empire and debauching republican freedoms. At the time Federalists brushed aside Henry's defense of states' rights as one of the more trivial criticisms of the Constitution.

But Henry had, in fact, touched upon a fundamental issue that would not go away. In 1825 Jefferson himself composed a declaration of protest against what he considered an invasion of state and local democracy and a threat to "life, liberty, and property" by the encroachment of central authority.[36] By the 1850s the southern states were prepared to defend their property rights, which included the holding of slaves, under the banner of states' rights, so the debate as to which of the Constitution's fundamental principles was most fundamental moved from Philadelphia to Antietam, Gettysburg, and finally Richmond for a truly definitive answer.

The American Civil War, an event that from the retrospective of the late twentieth century stands out as one of the truly monumental events of modern history, was partly a product of the territorial expansion of the United States. The war cannot be understood without reference to it. The same could even be said of independence itself. It should be remembered, after all, that in the 1760s the British parliament had frustrated the territorial ambitions of the American colonies with obstacles such as the *Proclamation Act* of 1763 and the *Quebec Act.* Certain of the Federalists had not the remotest sympathy for Jefferson's agrarian utopia huddled on the eastern seaboard of the great continent. Hamilton once confessed to Jefferson's dismay that of all the great men of history Caesar was among his personal favorites. And as compelling as aspects of the anti-Federalist position were, the constitution of Philadelphia passed by the narrow margin of 88 to 80 votes for reasons not directly related to the merits of the arguments themselves. The balance ultimately tipped in the Federalists' favor, due to the concerns of delegates from the Alleghenies, the Shanandoah Valley, and the upper Ohio, whose sympathies would normally have been with Henry and his allies. They voted for a strong union for reasons of elementary security, in the hope that it would more quickly clear their territories of Indians.[37]

Clearly, Henry and other another anti-Federalists interpreted accurately something of the motivations behind Federalist constitutional designs. Madison and Hamilton in particular regarded such sovereignty as the individual states possessed a weakness rather than an asset, and they sought above all to subordinate the states to national authority.[38] On this issue,

Madison's position that an expansive republic could preserve liberty was designed, and for the most part it succeeded, to refute head-on the kind of objections raised by Henry. Since in a republic elected representatives rather than direct democracy articulated the popular will, the fundamental task of election, he argued, was to find the most trustworthy guardians of the public interest. The broader pool of political and administrative talent available in a larger polity, therefore, inevitably improved the odds that the electorate would find the cream of the available talent standing for public office. He reasoned additionally that it would be more difficult for unworthy candidates to ply the vicious art of bribery in the great open arena of national politics, arguing in effect that the kind of invisible reefs of municipal or state authority cited by de Tocqueville might equally protect local vested interests and the petty tyrannies that might otherwise come into conflict with federal authority. Madison added to this the *pluralist* prediction that the variety of interests found in a great republic would undermine the possibility that "factious combinations" of citizens could systematically and consistently abuse the rights of others.[39]

Hamilton's proposals regarding the utility of centralized administration both to its citizens and the place of the republic in the world, went further still. In fact, Hamilton regarded the authority of the individual states as all but useless except for the most mundane of administrative tasks, and, as Washington's Secretary of the Treasury, he sought to underpin national prerogatives in the political sphere with a central bank to supply investment for the growth of manufactures in the economic sphere. Additionally, Hamilton was not so enthusiastic as Madison to put into practice the free trade doctrine outlined by Adam Smith in *The Wealth of Nations* or to wait for American agriculture to mature fully before launching the nation into large-scale industrialism.[40] Instead, he sought protection for young industries and an array of measures to promote their vitality, including government subsidies and the utilization of child labor. Hamilton's bank policy amounted to little less than an economic plan based on the priority of building national economic power according to a blueprint that so suited dynamic north-eastern manufacturing and financial interests that anti-Federalists hardly knew where to start with their criticisms. Unwilling to leave American economic maturation to the growth promised by untrammelled free trade, Hamilton sought to move the United States away from dependency on agricultural exports toward the introduction of advanced manufactures via substantial government subsidies.

Opposition was both constitutional and ideological. Where Hamilton cited congressional power to *provide for the Common Defence and General Welfare* in justification of a vigorous regime of public finance, critics recoiled at the vision of an unrestrained legislature undermining separated powers and stretching the contours of limited government. A consolidated system of public finance, moreover, would represent an Anglicization and corruption of the political economy to the extent that a rapacious pursuit of private wealth would replace forever the republican virtue of austere civic-mindedness.[41]

The issue precipitated a rupture in the Hamilton-Madison constitutional alliance, although Madison's energies at the time admittedly were also diverted to the drafting of a *Bill of Rights* in order to answer some of the demands of anti-Federalists who now wanted a second constitutional convention. But Hamilton's ambition for American commercial power and federal authority was in any event much more in tune with the spirit of the coming century. Until the 1850s, when economic and territorial expansion itself transformed the controversy from a constitutional and ideological debate to a forthrightly political crisis, the vast potential of Hamilton's prescription remained relatively obscured. Yet even in its infancy the conflict was existential in nature, because it touched on fundamental principles of the Constitution. Civil war was the appropriate vehicle of its resolution.

There is a definition of the State formulated by the German sociologist Max Weber and employed routinely in contemporary political studies. In it the state is *a human community that successfully claims a monopoly on the legitimate use of force in a given territory.* Hamilton never bothered with his own definition, but it is clear that he considered the United States a single national community, and that he had no doubt as to where the legitimate force to ensure its cohesion ought to reside. His writings and deeds reveal a Whig mercantilist and in some

respects an authentic conservative, who believed that "the American People should be governed by a sagacious elite, chosen by popular election, acquainted with the needs of their compatriots, and qualified by education and experience to discern the long-term good of all".[42] His legacy is enormous, employed by partisans of the left and right at critical phases in national development.

The Jeffersonian vision was clearly more idealistic and more forthrightly democratic, but in the last century it influenced primarily the spirit of American politics rather than the evolution of American government itself. Jeffersonian values routinely percolate to the surface of American public life—in Waldon Pond and in the affectations of the 'post-material' lifestyles'—and they are ever-present in the symbolic gestures of public figures: witness Jimmy Carter's walk down Pennsylvania Avenue to the Capital building on inauguration day 1976 in the footsteps of Jefferson in 1801 and Bill Clinton's pilgrimage to Monticello on the day of his own swearing-in. Rare, in fact, is the public figure who does not claim some morsel of Jefferson's legacy. The most eloquent of the Founders can be quoted "on every side of every question" and American history has at times "seemed a protracted litigation" on the meaning of his memory.[43]

The Supreme Court of the United States played an early pivotal role in influencing the struggle between these competing philosophies of early American government. By the nature of its decisions, and the art of its argument it simultaneously staked out the authoritative terrain of the federal judiciary. In the 1803 case of *Marbury v. Madison* Chief Justice John Marshall struck down for the first time an act of Congress (the Judiciary Act of 1789) as unconstitutional. He could easily have botched the decision and compromised the potential of the Court, by attempting to use the powers the congressional act had given to the very seat he occupied, powers granted to the Court nowhere in the Constitution. Instead, he drew from Hamilton's prescription for the Court in *The Federalist no. 78*, specifically that the judiciary by its nature has "neither force nor will but merely judgement," and upbraided Congress for passing such a law and the president for signing it. He declined a specific power and established by precedent a vastly more comprehensive one, judicial invalidation of congressional action.[44] Marshall's decision is properly understood as a landmark victory for the tradition of judicial review. It did not represent as innovative a piece of constitutional thinking as is frequently assumed, but its discretion adroitly skated around what Hamilton called the "natural feebleness of the judiciary" (its inability to initiate), while making the most of judicial political independence, not to make law itself but to interpret for the other branches of government the substantive meaning of the fundamental law of the land. With the Marbury decision the Court acquired a majesty not given to by the Constitution, yet not at all at odds with it. Had Marshall handled the Marbury case less skilfully, it is doubtful whether the Court could have spoken with the authority it brought to bear in *McCulloch v. Maryland* in 1819.

In the latter instance Marshall returned a decisively federalist Court sanction to the legitimacy of congressional (and therefore national) authority to charter a national bank, while denying Maryland (and therefore any state) the right to tax such a bank. It was a nation-building decision of the first magnitude, resting on the Hamiltonian argument that some powers not prescribed by the letter of the Constitution are nonetheless implied by its intentions. Marshall observed that the authority of the national government of the United States "proceeds directly from the people" and that inherent in its very purpose was "to form a more perfect union," the economic aspect of which was indeed served by the establishment of a national bank.[45] In *Gibbons v. Ogden* the Marshall Court then amplified national supremacy further in the congressional authority to regulate interstate commerce. Having invoked the authority and established the prestige of the Court in Marbury, in other words, Marshall emphatically sanctioned by precedence a particular course for American economic and political development: One People, One Market. In the 1820s it was a course whose full-implications for American nationhood and republican government were not yet fully apparent, but which by the 1860s ultimately drove the nation to a more comprehensive definition of Americanness than the Founders of Philadelphia had dared to articulate.

It was not the Great Unmentionable of slavery alone that kept them for doing so. For many, the ideals of Jefferson and Henry were ideologically compelling in their own right, whereas Hamilton's consolidated economic system seemed as horrifying in principle as in application. With Andrew Jackson's election to the presidency in 1828, both anti-Federalist sentiment and the Jeffersonian heritage had a champion of the first rank: a hero of the Revolution and the War of 1812, a Tennessee gentleman who at sixty-one was as close to a living legend as anyone since Washington. This was a critical advantage, because the 1828 ballot occasioned the tentative emergence of genuine party politics in the United States, a process which by 1850 stripped away most property and religious qualifications that had constituted, in part, the voting rights of white males. It also established the conditions for genuine national two-party system, setting Jackson Democrats against federalist Whigs, in which presidential aspirants sought the support of growing state and local party organizations rather than congressional caucuses. The Democrats took the initiative in advancing suffrage reform. Whigs sneered to themselves that the republic would now "go down upon all fours" but declined to openly oppose a change that resonated so clearly with the Constitution and the radical inheritance of 1776. The development of national party competition in a distinctly American mold also moved the nomination and election of the president out of the House of Representatives and into the country, thus making the separation-of-powers more substantively real than it had ever been.[46] In other words, elections became more democratic, and it is worth noting that in America, as in every country with a claim on a democratic tradition, political parties were the vehicle by which any notion of government by the people was rendered meaningful. Those who insist that in the electronic age parties have outlived their usefulness ought to reflect soberly on the historic and universal connection between the vitality of democratic government and the instinct for humankind to seek a home for their political aspirations with some form of party organization.

Of course, there were accompanying developments of less noble purpose. A corollary to the growth of the parties was Jackson's increased use of the "spoils system" of political patronage, rewarding political supporters with government positions. Many a quietly competent public servant lost his job to some deserving Democrat. Jackson maintained that government work was so simple, anyone could do it. Perhaps a more

Machiavellian logic told him also that only well-maintained political constituencies followed present support with future support.

While Jackson's politics were Jeffersonian in pedigree, they were distinctly populist in flavor. More a chieftain of popular democracy than a genuine crusader for the poor, Jackson combined rough-cut simplicity with reliable political intuition. His appeal was strongest in the West and the South, as well as in the less prosperous farming regions of Pennsylvania, New York, and Massachusetts. In 1827 Jackson's supporters in the House had only 104 of 213 seats; by 1829 they had a majority at 113; and in 1831 a full 136. Their strength ran from western Maine in the northeast, along the Canadian border through most of western Pennsylvania to Illinois. It covered Tennessee, Kentucky, and the Deep South, but claimed three districts in Manhattan as well. The Jacksonians played upon popular fear and resentment of banks, corporations, eastern merchants, and Yankee wealth. All of these the Jacksonian Democrats labelled "aristocratic," the natural enthusiasts of Hamilton's Second Bank of the United States and therefore the natural enemies of the common man. Shays' Rebellion through the ballot box.[47]

Jackson, a personality of heroic dimension and violent prejudices, turned the Jeffersonian ideal of the yeoman farmer into a "rhapsodization of the unschooled mind" as the a central principle of campaigning and governing. "State a moral case to a ploughman and a professor," he once said, "the former will decide it as well, and often better than the latter, because he has not been led astray by artificial rules."[48] Jacksonians attacked the Whigs as Tory-by-any-other-name. Democracy did not tie its hair in a queue, they jeered, the "Modern Wig" was a "a cover for bald federalism."[49] Their success bequeathed to electoral politics in the United States two traditions: the Democratic Party's identity as the party of the bottom-dog, and a more diffuse populist inclination to associate political amateurism with incorruptibility. Today, the former is experiencing hard times; the latter is perhaps more powerful and unpredictable than ever, playing little or no role in one election but deciding the next.

Jackson's skill enabled him to use presidential power aggressively, to polarize debate over a renewed charter for the Second Bank of the United States as a contest of aristocracy versus democracy, vested interest against *laissez-faire* and the majority will of self-made men. Presidents cannot circumvent the separation of powers or nullify the legislative sovereignty of Congress. But Jackson demonstrated how, in the right hands, a presidential message that resonates with the populace can intimidate Congress and ally congressional careers to presidential authority, thus momentarily overcoming the inertia built into the Constitution. In 1833 Jackson armed himself with the approval of majority opinion in the country and destroyed the Second Bank of the United States. The bank's business had been conducted well for the most part, and Jackson's methods would doubtless have horrified Hamilton, Madison, and even Jefferson. But the bank had also meddled in politics. Jackson could possibly have lived with a compromise, conceding a recharter for the bank in exchange for a reduction of its administrative discretion. Instead, he shattered the association of the corporate form of business with monopolist privilege, and he thereby liberated enterprise in the United States during a period of rapid expansion, not at all an illogical convergence of policy with circumstance. The bank episode is just one of the many ways in which Jackson made an enormous contribution to the prestige of a strong executive, using the veto to refute the doctrine of executive restraint inherent in the Constitution while using a quasi-monarchical confidence of leadership, somewhat paradoxically, as the expression of popular will.[50] Considering Jackson's presidency together with Marshall's service at the head of the Supreme Court, one conclusion is inevitable: the *de facto* balance of power of the three branches of government is a product both of the *de jure* authority the Constitution awards to each and the determination of capable officeholders at critical points in American political development that they and their branch will be the vehicle of change. Ambition to check ambition.

To eulogize Jackson (authentic man of the people) or defame him (shameless opportunist) is irrelevant to my purpose here, because most successful politicians are thankfully a little of both. Jackson advanced the cause of popular democracy, yet drew power to the executive branch with the authority of his own popularity. Jackson was both a reflection and an agent of the republic's growth and maturation. Even in Jackson's time, however, it was a disfiguring maturation. By 1850 there were more than three million slaves in the United States, and the growth of the Union was such that neither a Missouri Compromise[51] nor any other could paper over the fundamental contradiction between the promise of the republic's constitution and the squalid facts of cotton culture in the South. Admittedly, Jacksonian Democrats didn't see it that way. Indeed, many of them used the word 'slavery' to caricature the plight of the most disadvantaged whites without so much as a blush at the institution of black slavery in their midst. To others the cause of abolition, which since the 1830s had gathered momentum and moral fervor, was a mischievous subversion of democracy by way of an attack on property rights and majority rule. Abolitionists, they charged, were either the unwitting dupes or willing allies of northern "blue light" federalists, bankers, and monopolists bent on inciting open conflict in order to restore elitist rule.

In southern states such as Virginia, moreover, popular support for democracy via suffrage extension had a bizarre twist. The aborted slave rebellion led by Nat Turner in 1831 made many Virginians view suffrage reform as a means of creating greater unity among all whites for the preservation of the southern way of life, against both slave revolts and the mounting criticism of slavery in the north.[52] De Tocqueville noted the degenerate effect on commercial ambition imposed by slavery in Kentucky relative to the free state of Ohio. Not surprisingly, a resident of the latter, Salmon P. Chase, interpreted the stark differences between two state economies in terms of two inherently antagonistic socioeconomic systems struggling for control of a single political system. At the fore of the antislavery forces in Congress, Chase charged that slavery was a violation of the principles of the Constitution; that its spread westward would inevitably subvert republican government with aristocracy; and that "slavery was sectional and freedom national."[53]

The new Republican Party, which by the mid-1850s replaced eastern Whigs and western Free Soilers, had its own interpretation of the relationship of both sectionalism and nationalism to liberty. Against the growth of northern industry and the increasing economic strength of the western free states, the failure of the South to keep pace with the rest of the nation could be traced to its slave economy, an institution that divorced the price of labor power from the energy of acquisitive self-interest. Slavery's extension westward would rob the nation of a market-centered internal development based on industry and homestead agriculture. Slavery, in short, was anticapitalist. Adam Smith had said as much in the year of the Revolution.[54] Those who could appreciate the threat that growing sectionalism posed to the Union struggled mightily to prove that it was not so, the Great Compromiser Henry Clay the most prominent among them. Clay was a Hamiltonian who advocated federal aid for roads and canals, a national bank, and protective tariffs. During his long career in the House and Senate he sought to bind the industrial Northeast with farmers in the West by promoting the ideology of the "American System" over regional antagonisms. But when the Supreme Court, under Chief Justice Roger Taney, returned its decision in the case of *Dred Scott v. Sanford* in 1857, the nation could see that the clock was fast running out for compromise. The decision declared the Missouri Compromise unconstitutional by stating that Congress had no authority to exclude the use of slave labor from the territories and ruled further that a black man could not become a citizen of the United States. Republicans pounced on the decision as evidence of a conspiracy of slave-owning political power to extend slavery to the territories on the strength of the Court's constitutional blessing, with dire implications both for the maintenance of industrial tariffs for the northeast and the spread of small-scale farming in the West. There was something to the charge, too, given that an influential coterie of southerners, headed by Jefferson Davis, William Yancey of Alabama, and Robert Toombs of Georgia were demanding that Washington should now be prepared the take action against any territorial legislature that passed antislavery laws of its own. While the Democrats split over the question of the rights of citizens in the territories to reject slavery in their midst, turning the doctrine of states' rights into knots of tortured logic in the process, the Republican Party built unity and fervor on the basis of confining all slavery to its present borders. At the party's Chicago convention, its principal rivalries for the presidential nomination of 1860,

Abraham Lincoln of Illinois, William Seward of New York, and Salmon Chase of Ohio, were of one mind on this at the very least. So when Lincoln triumphed at Chicago, a divided Democratic Party and the electoral college combined in 1860 to put him in the White House.

The isolation of the south over the issue of slavery seemed to turn on its head the reasoning of Madison's *Federalist No. 10* which at Philadelphia and after had been so crucial to the argument that a larger union offered stronger protection against the abuse of minority rights, understood by white southerners to mean the rights of a minority of *states*. But by 1860, of course, southerners were in no position to get over-wrought about minority rights. From another perspective Madison's reasoning had been prophetic: the gentlemen politicians of Old Virginia had taken a desiccated conception of liberty with them to Philadelphia in 1787 and come away with the assurance that their rights, including their property right to employ other human beings as draft animals, would not be threatened by the new constitution. The best of them knew that the institution of slavery mired them in moral depravity. And the fantasy could hold no longer once the feudal economy of the South began to threaten the prosperity of the industrial east and the mixed agriculture of the west. Ultimately, both the claim to the right of secession and the maintenance of slavery were rejected by the national body politic as the mischief of a "factious combination" of citizens. Moreover, in the 1850s the stars of change aligned themselves in a way that is extremely rare in politics: the moral crusade of antislavery suited perfectly the requirements of the northern economy and the political cause of saving the Union. The student of politics should strive to remember that interest motivates, principle legitimates. In the case of slavery, Seward, now Lincoln's Secretary of State whose territorial ambitions for the Union are well-recorded, could invoke the nation's "divine purpose" in spreading the rule of democracy and holding the Republic to the spirit of its constitution, while crushing the South and the doctrine of states rights along with it. If hitherto all the lofty talk of liberty, from Philadelphia to the present, had no substantive meaning to slaves, quite suddenly the very political heavens were revolving.[55]

As president, Lincoln's policy was straightforward. He sought the preservation of The Union against the secessionist fever now gripping the South—at whatever cost. He also insisted that only the Confederacy could decide the cost by initiating armed hostilities itself, if and when Southerners decided there was no escape from the impasse. Once the Confederate guns opened up on Fort Sumter, however, Lincoln called upon Congress to invest full war powers in his administration. Immediately following the Union's first battlefield humiliation at Bull Run, Congress added to this the *Crittendon Resolution*, declaring a state of insurrection and demanding the maintenance of the full supremacy of the Constitution for the goal of preserving the Union "with all the dignity, equality, and rights of the several states unimpaired."[56] Thereupon Lincoln acted swiftly with an expansive definition of the war powers of the presidency in a national emergency, ultimately assuming an authority independent of Congress that exceeded that of both Presidents Wilson and Roosevelt in the world wars of the next century. Since the struggle with the Confederacy was viewed from the Union perspective not as war with another sovereign state but the an existential trial against the forces of treason, the administration's authority to deal with disloyal actions during the war exceeded the normal bounds of civil justice. Lincoln suspended *habeas corpus* rights; when antiRepublican secret societies formed, Secretary Seward established an organization of confidential agents; summary arrests were numerous; persons discouraging enlistment or resisting the draft were subject to martial law. In a situation for which there was no precedent, in other words, Lincoln made the executive branch the command center of the whole Union and extended presidential prerogative into areas neither recognized nor anticipated by the Constitution. And yet he never attempted to dissolve Congress, stack the Supreme Court, or suspend the rights of the political opposition. The people retained the right to fire him from office in the election of 1864, and Lincoln half expected they would. In the circumstances of the gravest imaginable domestic crisis, Lincoln stretched the limits of the Constitution without debauching its republican essence.[57] Try to imagine this in any other nation.

After 360,000 Union and 260,000 Confederate dead in four years of fighting that at its worst anticipated the horrors of war in the twentieth century, Union armies secured the triumph of the social system of the North over that of the South, of Hamiltonian federalism over states rights, of the expansive capitalist ideology of the Republican Party over the Democrats' use of honorable Jeffersonian and Jacksonian ideals in a dishonorable cause. While a good many prominent Republicans never considered blacks the equal of whites, the essence of their argument was that any system that afforded constitutional legitimacy to the subordination of blacks was as demonstrably backward as it was immoral. In one fundamental sense, in fact, debate about equality was irrelevant. Lincoln said as much in his celebrated debates with Stephen Douglas during their Senate race of 1858. No matter how one regarded the abilities of any black man personally, he maintained, "in the right to eat bread, without leave of anyone else, which his own hand earns, he is my equal and the equal of Judge Douglas, and the equal of every living man."[58] The Republicanism of Lincoln's time did not set out to purge American society of racism, nor did it concede that it was within the capacity of any government to do so. Instead, the Thirteenth, Fourteenth, and Fifteenth Amendments ennobled the bloodiest conflict of American history, fought over the constitutional question of the right of the Confederacy to secede, by redefining slaves as Americans; making them members of the national body politic; and recognizing that the achievements of the republic were to be "almost wholly the result of the dignity and opportunities which it offered the average working man".[59]

To Democrats the Fifteenth Amendment appeared a conspiracy to promote black equality and transform the confederation of states into a centralized union. They were half right. Whereas the Union's armies had carried the day for Alexander Hamilton's philosophy of government, the amendment itself said nothing about the right of black citizens to hold office, nor did it make voting practices uniform across the nation.[60] But the Civil War was no less a great victory for liberty as defined in the Declaration of 1776. Triumphant Republicanism was entirely consistent with the concept of limited government that Lincoln understood to be the animating spirit of the Constitution, namely that "the legitimate object of government is to do for a community of people, whatever they need to have done, but can not do, at all, or can not, so well do, for themselves—in their separate and individual capacities."[61] The twentieth-century redefinition of the purposes of American government came to focus on the dignity Republican governments denied the working man, but in the meantime the party's ideology was instrumental in making the United States the most enterprizing society on earth.

The American Way in the World

The German Chancellor Bismarck once said that the policy of the King of Prussia could only be carried out through blood and iron. Lincoln found that the same was true of the Union cause, that the American republic could be reborn only through a contest of blood and iron, the outcome of which ultimately had international consequences every bit as profound and certainly more wholesome than the triumphs of German militarism. Before 1865 America remained for Europeans a frontier fiction by James Fenimore Cooper rather than a diplomatic force to be reckoned with. *Uncle Tom's Cabin*, by Harriet Beecher Stowe, afforded middle-class households an invigorating exercise in moral outrage, but few Europeans appreciated the deeper causes of the conflict or the wider implications of the Union's salvation. The Union victory of 1865 was disturbing to British Conservatives who resented and feared American success in egalitarianism and universal suffrage. Westminster Liberals were predictably elated. Anyone with the requisite curiosity could observe that American manufacturing output in 1861 exceeded Germany and Russia and was about to overtake France. For the time being, of course, neither Britain nor any other European power had anything to fear from the United States. Still, mixed among Lincoln's words at the dedication of the ground at Gettysburg, the hope that freedom *shall have a new birth* reflected an awareness that the American experiment was no longer so experimental. The issue as to whether the republic or any other government so constituted *can long endure* had been answered as unambiguously as any political conflict of modern times.[62] The debate about founding principles had been concluded definitively, and something incomparably more vital and worthy of respect was emerging from the ashes of the Civil War. The Union's particular advantages between 1861 and 1865 and its pursuit of final victory had also established something of an American way of war, namely the mobilization of massive industrial and technological assets to crush an enemy.[63] In the twentieth century both Germany and Japan were crushed by American technology, the victims of leaders that had never comprehended the consequences of provoking dormant American might.

Today, few Americans fully appreciate the relationship between how they conceive themselves as a nation and how they see their place in the world. This is in part the product of a tendency in the teaching of American government toward completely divorcing domestic politics from foreign affairs. Specialists in one field seldom have anything to do with specialists in the other, and students of American government encounter texts that immerse them in the dynamics of legislative-executive relations, the evolution of federalism, the travail of civil rights, the rise and demise of the welfare state, before turning in their eighteenth or twentieth chapter to the fact that the United States is the most powerful nation in history whose affairs effect profoundly those of scores of other states. This feature of American studies, admittedly, is partly the product of a thoroughly common-sensical determination to organize the conveyance of new and old knowledge into digestible chunks. Still, our understanding of American politics can be enriched significantly by a determination to view the domestic and foreign affairs of the United States as interdependent parts of the past two centuries' national experience.

The very creation of the United States of America occurred in part due to crises in the international relations of the eighteenth century: conflicts involving the New World colonial ambitions of Spain, France, and Britain and the outrage of New England colonists at attempts by Britain to tax them for the costs of their defense during the 1754–1763 war.[64] Moreover, while there exists a well-established school of thought maintaining that American diplomacy was instinctively isolationist and had greatness "thrust upon it"[65], it is an historical fact of record that Americans have always been an extrovert and gregarious people with a good many outward-looking national aspirations. "Our plan is for commerce", wrote Thomas

Paine, the English radical whose pamphleteering promoted the cause of independence, thus expressing a sentiment about the "business of America" a century and a half before it occurred to Calvin Coolidge. Among the many other charges brought against George III in the *Declaration* is that of "cutting off our Trade with all parts of the world," while many of Paine's contemporaries advocated a cosmopolitan and commercial spirit for the foreign policy of the United States that might liberalize international trade.[66] Only a trading world was one in which Americans could prosper in security. Henry Clay once claimed that commerce was for Americans a "passion" as unconquerable as any with which nature had endowed them, "you may attempt to regulate—you cannot destroy it."[67]

The field of more formal foreign affairs, moreover, has been critical to the development of American political institutions from the outset, just as the prestige of the contemporary presidency is inseparable from the status of the United States in the international arena; indeed, the rise of the modern presidency is directly parallel to the acquisition of that status. While the Founders could scarcely have anticipated the trajectory of twentieth-century history, the checks and balances of the Constitution quite deliberately made the field of foreign affairs one of conflict between presidency and Congress in a fashion that clearly reflects both a confidence that the United States was to become much more than the sum of its thirteen parts of 1787 and a concern that American greatness not be a threat to American liberty. Hence, the president's role as *Commander and Chief* checked by congressional authority to declare war and to *raise and support Armies*; the executive's prerogative to *make Treaties* and *appoint Ambassadors* yet only *by and with the Advice and Consent of the Senate* (Article II, 2).

Congress and President Washington first clashed over foreign policy before the United States had even made it safely into the nineteenth century. This occurred in 1793 when Washington decided to receive Edmond Genêt as emissary of the revolutionary government in France, thus in effect interpreting the president's authority to receive foreign ambassadors as tantamount to the power to extend American recognition to new foreign governments.[68] Aside from the divisions of opinion over whether the United States had some natural ideological kinship with the French republic—Jefferson thought it did,

Hamilton disagreed—Washington's proclamation of official American neutrality in France's war with Britain was attacked by James Madison as a mischievous violation of congressional authority in foreign relations. Ultimately, Genêt abused American hospitality to the breaking point, just as the Jacobites in France abused republican ideals in the murderous pursuit of their enemies. The controversy was influenced throughout by conflicting sentiments concerning whether the French Revolution was so out of control as to justify American dissociation from it (it was) or whether the British were treating the United States like a pipsqueak (they were). For our purposes the storm over America's policy toward the French Revolutionary wars is important for the precedents it set. Washington established a high executive profile in foreign relations by maintaining a hard line with Congress and invoking *executive privilege* in his refusal to submit to the House of Representatives papers pertaining to diplomatic negotiations with Britain, while the congressional clamor surrounding ratification of the *Jay Treaty* agreed with Britain in 1794 so unnerved him that he was moved to include in his 1796 Farewell Address to the nation a warning on foreign relations that became the first article of the tradition of isolationism.[69] Washington cautioned against "permanent alliance with any portion of the foreign world," but specified further that "Europe has a set of primary interests which to us have none or a very remote relation". Though the word *isolationism* itself did not enter the jargon of American foreign relations until the early twentieth century, it is worth noting that in Washington's day and ever after its spirit was essentially Europhobic. The United States has in fact always been more cosmopolitan in its approach to foreign affairs than is commonly assumed, yet successive generations of American leadership have held to the conviction that they could only lose in diplomatic entanglements with the jaded cunning of the Old Continent in particular. Robert Taft, a champion of twentieth-century isolationism, himself conceded that, if isolationism was to be defined as a determination to remain aloof from European wars, then he was pleased to count himself among the isolationists.[70]

Washington's parting message was emphatically not based on the assumption that the United States could or should avoid power politics altogether, but argued the pragmatic point that involvement in European affairs was especially dangerous to the young republic. Composed in part by Hamilton, who was himself unconvinced by an intellectual vogue of the time according to which republican government and international commerce would underwrite permanent peace between nations, the Farewell Address recommended instead that the United States steer clear of European rivalries and concentrate its diplomatic energies on achieving hegemony in the Americas.[71] But even the Atlantic Ocean was an imperfect moat. In his own inaugural Jefferson dwelled on the great advantages Providence had bestowed on the United States, yet found himself issuing threats to France once Bonaparte's successes forced Spain to cede Louisiana and the Floridas to Napoleonic presumption. Even misadventures such as the War of 1812 ultimately contributed to a sense of unified purpose. Despite the war's many military disasters, after the 1814 *Treaty of Ghent* European powers were aware that their American colonies were less secure than ever against the territorial designs of the United States. As American attention turned to westward territorial expansion, it was animated both by insecurity and opportunism: puzzled apprehension toward the future of British North America to the north, temptation regarding Spanish possessions in the south and the native population to the West. From the latter "unfortunate people," observed De Tocqueville, the United States acquired by treaty, purchase, or deceit "whole provinces which the richest sovereigns in Europe could not afford to buy."[72] Equally massive acquisitions proceeded at great cost to Spain: led by the military panache of Jackson (then acquiring the reputation that later made him a political force) and the aggressive diplomacy of Secretary of State, John Quincy Adams, the United States secured all of Florida and its first formal territorial rights to a Pacific coastline.

Relations with Britain required more circumspection. Adams calculated that, since it was in Britain's interest to see Spain's empire dissolve, peace with Britain could further American interests if British naval power could keep Spain out of Latin America. In the north, meanwhile, he reasoned that US policy should content itself with *containing* Britain in Canada until American commercial power could absorb it. Adams' statecraft was thus composed of remorseless logic and was appropriately crowned, in his time and afterward, with stunning victories. He was largely responsible for the doctrine first enunciated by President James Monroe in 1823, according to which the United States opposed the extension of European colonialism anywhere in the Western Hemisphere. On the face of it, the Monroe Doctrine was an exercise in breathtaking presumption, but, on closer examination, it reveals itself as an early exercise in the calibre of cool pragmatism concerning means and ends by which American diplomacy has been so vastly successful. Because British merchants were prospering from trade with the newly sovereign Latin American republics, London was as concerned as Washington to exclude France, Russia, and Spain from the American hemisphere. Adams reasoned that, as long as British naval power kept other European powers out of Latin America, the United States would not have to back its strong words a with a power it did not yet possess. Initially, Britain wanted to make an Anglo-American declaration on the issue, but Adams rejected the notion because it would in principle preclude American acquisition of Texas and Cuba. In other words, geography alone had handed the United States some very strong cards. The fact that Britain itself could ill afford hostile relations with the United States if it were to dispose simultaneously of its European commitments was measure of America's emergence as a force to be reckoned with. In this the United States shared an advantage with Russia: each could pose something of a nuisance to the Great Powers, yet both enjoyed a certain "invulnerability conferred by their distance from the main European battle zones."[73]

In late Jacksonian America the distances and dimensions of territorial expansion were such that it was often impossible to say just where domestic politics left off and foreign policy began. Under Presidents John Tyler and James Polk (1841–1849), the United States doubled its territory and captured the Spanish borderlands from Mexico. Democrats in particular were skilled in articulating expansionist policies in terms of Jeffersonian and Jacksonian values, justifying the acquisition of land to the west as vital to domestic welfare and stability. By matching the nation's population growth and industrialization with the opening of a broader frontier of economic possibilities, they thought, the country could offset the tendency toward class stratification and realize Jacksonian egalitarianism. Foreign powers had no cause for concern. In his inaugural address Polk recommended that they instead appreciate the true character of the Union as a confederation of independent states whose policy was peace with the world. To enlarge the limits of the union, he advised, "is to extend the dominions of peace over additional territories and increasing millions."[74] Thus, when John O'Sullivan wrote in 1845 of America's *Manifest Destiny* he was as much describing as prescribing a policy in which domestic and foreign affairs were closely linked. That policy was to promote the settlement of the soil by "productive men of simple habits" until every acre of the continent was occupied by citizens of the republic. Failure to do so would amount to a betrayal of the mission undertaken in 1776. It would exclude the people from the soil just as had George III and the other monarchs of degenerate Europe had done.[75] Texas, a prize as large a Germany, was acquired in 1845; Oregon joined in 1846; a massive Mexican cession that included California followed in 1848. The language of Jefferson and the populism of Jackson were mobilized in the service of a design of truly Hamiltonian grandeur.

A biproduct of the period, and of any period in American development in which foreign affairs come to the fore, was an extension of executive prerogative along with the reach of the republic. The Jacksonian Presidents—Jackson, Van Buren, W.H. Harrison, Tyler, and Polk—were generally bold and skilled in their use of their inherent powers as commanders-in-chief. Polk's war with Mexico secured the backing of Congress in part because his use of U.S. troops prodded the Mexicans into a belligerent act. Congress indulged his policy in so far as it avoided national humiliations. In the south Polk was aggressive with the beleaguered Mexicans because he could afford to be aggressive; in the north he was cautious with the British because a more strident approach could easily have been disastrous.[76] In the years preceding the Civil War British industrialists who traveled in the United States returned to England with stories of the enormous potential of the American system in manufacturing and the adaptability of American workers. The gap between America's territorial ambitions and its capabilities would be closed soon enough.

Whatever the practical impediments the advocates of expansion had few doubts about the nature and rectitude of America's territorial rights. Geography, indeed geology, spoke to them. Of Cuba, Seward claimed in 1859, that "every rock and every grain of sand in that island were drifted and washed out from American soil by the floods of the Mississippi."[77] And on the issue of expansion the border between the nation's foreign policy and its domestic constitution was erased entirely. Writing to Seward in early 1861, Lincoln pointed out that if the Republican platform and manifest destiny of the United States were ever to be realized, slavery could have no part in the realization.[78]

At the time of the founding, of course, commercial internationalism was hardly the guiding sentiment of the authors of the Constitution. Nor were foreign relations generally their dominant concern. But it is worthwhile remembering that, from the outset, there was a vision of the United States competing against that of an agrarian utopia huddled on the eastern seaboard of a great and unexploited continent. If early American foreign policy had more than a dash of imperial logic, furthermore, it distinguished itself from European tradition by way of its much more genuine sense of moral rectitude. In the earliest phase of its history the U.S. Navy refused to ransom sailors captured by pirates on the high seas. In its own small way this was a first installment in a tradition of principled diplomacy that was fated to reconstitute international relations in the twentieth century by way of an American national mission to improve the material and moral lot of all humankind.[79] Between the end of the Civil War and emergence of the United States as a major power in the early twentieth century lay four decades of economic and political maturation, the story of another chapter. For the moment it suffices to note simply that domestic and foreign affairs of the United States have always featured a delicate interplay, and that the appropriate place of America in the world has always been an issue of existential contention.

Notes

1 Burke wrote that "it is with infinite caution that any man ought to venture upon pulling down an edifice which has answered in any tolerable degree for ages the common purposes of society, or on building it up again without having models and patterns of approved utility before his eyes." Quoted from *Burke's Politics: Selected Writings and Speeches of Edmund Burke on Reform, Revolution and War*, Ross S.J. Hoffman and Paul Levack, Eds., (New York: Alfred A. Knopf, 1959), p. 305.

2 Gordon S. Wood, *The Creation of the American Republic, 1776-1787* (New York: W.W. Norton, 1969), pp. 3-255.

3 Peter S. Onuf, *The Origins of the Federal Republic* (Philadelphia: University of Pennsylvania Press, 1983), p. 37, pp. 177-179; Neville Meany, "The Trial of Popular Sovereignty in Post-Revolutionary America: The Case of Shays' Rebellion," in Neville Meany, Ed., *Studies on the American Revolution* (Melbourne: Macmillan, 1976), pp. 151-216.

4 Wood, *Creation of the American Republic*, pp. 46-124; Thomas L. Pangle, *The Spirit of Modern Republicanism: The Moral Vision of the American Founders and the Philosophy of John Locke* (Chicago: University of Chicago Press, 1988); Garret Ward Sheldon, *The Political Philosophy of Thomas Jefferson* (Baltimore: The Johns Hopkins University Press, 1991), pp. 41-82; Drew McCoy, *The Last of the Fathers: James Madison and the Republican Legacy* (New York: Cambridge University Press, 1989), pp. 39-83; John Murrin, "Religion and Politics in America from the First Settlements to the Civil War" in Mark Noll, Ed., *Religion and American Politics*, (New York: Oxford University Press, 1990), pp. 19-43.

5 Under *republic* two assumptions about the purpose and form of government were common to all the Founders. First that the sole legitimate purpose of all government consisted in securing the public good (*res publica*), the safety and prosperity of the community, and second that the only authentic sovereign power resided with the citizens of that community, yet was exercised through elected representatives who were responsible to the citizenry. Thus, citizens in a republic were self-governing not in the direct sense but rather in their natural right to elect and recall those who disposed of the functions of government.

6 See Alexander Hamilton, *The Federalist, No. 9*, and Richard Hofstadter, *The American Political Tradition* (New York: Vintage, 1954), pp. 3-17.

7   Letters to John Taylor of Caroline, Virginia, in *The Works of John Adams, Second President of the United States*, Vol. VI, Charles Francis Adams, Ed., (Boston: Charles C. Little and James Brown, 1851), p. 484. Also quoted in, Adrienne Koch and William Peden, Eds., *The Selected Writings of John and John Quincy Adams*, (New York: Alfred A. Knopf, 1946), p. xxxii; see also Wood, *Creation of the American Republic*, p. 198; Manning J. Dauer, *The Adams Federalists* (Baltimore: The Johns Hopkins University Press, 1953).

8   Paul Johnson, *The Birth of the Modern: World Society, 1815–1830* (New York: Harper-Collins, 1991) pp. 904–905; Gordon S. Wood, *The Radicalism of the American Revolution* (New York: Alfred A. Knopf, 1992), pp. 347–369.

9   A.W. Sparkes, *Talking Politics: A Workbook* (London: Routledge, 1994), p. 47.

10   Sotirios A. Barber, *On What the Constitution Means* (Baltimore: The Johns Hopkins University Press, 1984), pp. 113–115.

11   Alexis de Tocqueville, *Democracy in America*, Vol.1, Part 2, Chap. 5, Trans. George Lawrence, Ed. J.P Mayer, (Garden City, N.Y.: Doubleday, 1969).

12   "If we consider the situation of the men on whom the free suffrages of their fellow citizens may confer the representative trust, we shall find it involving every security which can be devised or desired for their fidelity to their constituents", wrote Madison in *The Federalist, No. 57*, adding that "All these securities would be found very insufficient without the restraint of frequent elections."

13   *The Federalist, No.63* .

14   De Tocqueville, *Democracy in America*, Vol. I, Part I, Chap. 5, Part II, Chap. 8.

15   Richard Fenno, *Home Style: House Members in Their Districts* (Boston: Little, Brown and Co., 1978).

16   Thomas Jefferson, *Notes on the State of Virginia* (New York: Harper Torchbooks, 1964), pp. 110–124; *The Federalist, Nos. 49 and 51*.

17   *The Federalist, No. 69.*

18   *The Federalist, No. 10.*

19   *The Federalist, No. 63*. The emphasis is Madison's.

20   See E.J. Dionne, Jr., *Why Americans Hate Politics* (New York: Simon and Schuster, 1991), who recognizes the currently popular hatred of

politics in the United States for a very real threat to its democracy. Much more problematic is John Diggins', *The Lost Soul of American Politics: Virtue, Self-Interest and the Foundation of Liberalism* (New York: Basic Books, 1984), which places too much stress on the Calvinist strain in the American political heritage and overestimates the importance of Christian morality to the republican spirit.

21   Donald Robinson, *Slavery and the Structure of American Politics, 1765–1820* (New York: Harcourt Brace Jovanovich, 1971), p. 201; David Brion, *The Problem of Slavery in the Age of Revolution* (Ithaca, N.Y.,: Cornell University Press, 1975).

22   Chilton Williamson, *American Suffrage: From Property to Democracy, 1760–1860* (Princeton, N.J.: Princeton University Press, 1960), pp. 3–39.

23   Henry Steele Commager, *The Empire of Reason* (Garden City, N.Y.: Doubleday, 1977), pp. 150–154; Williamson, *American Suffrage*.

24   *The Federalist, No. 10.*

25   *The Federalist, No. 51*; Hofstadter, *American Political Tradition*, p. 16.

26   Barber, *On What the Constitution Means*, p. 115.

27   Wood, *Creation of the American Republic*, p. 68; Madison quoted in Pangle, *Spirit of Modern Republicanism*, p. 45; see also *The Federalist, No. 55.*

28   *The Autobiography of Benjamin Franklin*, L.W. Labaree, Ed., (New Haven: Yale University Press, 1964), especially Part II; Paul A. Rahe, *Republics Ancient and Modern: Classical Republicanism and the American Revolution* (Chapel Hill: University of North Carolina Press, 1992) pp. 251–254, pp. 651–653; Wood, *The Radicalism of the American Revolution*, pp. 104–105.

29   The classic expression of political trusteeship is Burke's speech to the electors of Bristol, in which he maintained that "your representative owes you, not his industry only, but his judgement, and he betrays, instead of serving you, if he sacrifices it to your opinion." See *Burke's Politics*, p. 115; also Pangle, The Spirit of Modern Republicanism, p. 110; Madison, *The Federalist, No. 51*; Charles S. Hyneman, *The American Founding Experience: Political Community and Republican Government* (Urbana: University of Illinois Press, 1994), p. 232; Drew McCoy, *The Last of the Fathers*, pp. 59–64; *The Federalist, No. 71.*

30   Joyce Lee Malcolm, *To Keep and Bear Arms: The Origins of an Anglo-American Right* (Cambridge: Harvard University Press, 1994); Robert E. Shalhope, "The Ideological Origins of the Second Amendment," *Journal of American History*, Vol. 69, No. 3, 1982, pp. 599–614.

31   *The Federalist, No.45*; Joel Barlow, *Advice to the Privileged Orders of the Several States of Europe* (Ithaca, N.Y.: Cornell University Press, 1956), pp. 16–17, and 45–46.

32   De Tocqueville, *Democracy in America*, Vol. 1, Pt. 2, Bk. 10; Wood, *The Radicalism of the American Revolution*, pp. 331–333.

33   Barber, *What the Constitution Means*, pp. 113–115.

34   *The Federalist, No. 10*.

35   Quoted in R.D. Meade, *Patrick Henry, Practical Revolutionary* (New York: J.B. Lippincott, 1969), p. 350; Wood, *Creation of the American Republic*, pp. 526–527.

36   Sheldon, *The Philosophy of Thomas Jefferson*, pp. 88–94.

37   James MacGregor Burns, The *Vineyard of Liberty*, (New York: Alfred A. Knopf, 1982), p. 55.

38   Edward Millican, *One United People: The Federalist Papers and the National Idea* (Lexington: University Press of Kentucky, 1990), pp. 31–32.

39   *The Federalist, No. 10*; Millican, *One United People*, pp. 117–118.

40   Alpheus T. Mason, "The Federalist–A Split Personality," *American Historical Review*, Vol. 57, No. 3, April 1952, especially p. 639; Drew R. McCoy, *The Elusive Republic: Political Economy in Jeffersonian America* (Chapel Hill: University of North Carolina Press, 1980), pp. 148–152; Bray Hammond, *Banks and Politics in America* (Princeton, N.J.: Princeton University Press, 1957).

41   McCoy, *Elusive Republic*, pp. 69–75 and pp. 152–162.

42   Millican, *One United People*, p. 78.

43   Merrill D. Peterson, *The Jefferson Image in the American Mind* (New York: Oxford University Press, 1962), especially pp. 445–446. See also Douglas L. Wilson, "Thomas Jefferson and the Character Issue," *The Atlantic*, November 1992, pp. 57–74.

44   Robert Lowry Clinton, *Marbury v. Madison and Judicial Review* (Lawrence: University of Kansas Press, 1989), pp. 192–233; Kermit Hall, *The Supreme Court and Judicial Review in American History* (Washington D.C.: American Historical Association, 1985), pp. 11–13; Gerald Gunther, *Cases and Materials on Constitutional Law* (Mineola, N.Y.: Foundation Press, 1980), pp. 30–35.

45   *McCulloch v. Maryland, 4 Wheaton 316 1819*; Gerald Gunther, *John Marshall's Defense of McCulloch v. Maryland*, (Stanford: Stanford University Press, 1969), pp. 3–4.

46   Williamson, *American Suffrage*, pp. 260–299; Epstein, *Political Parties in the American Mold* (Madison: University of Wisconsin Press, 1986) pp. 86–87.

47   J.M. McPherson, *The Battle Cry of Freedom* (New York: Oxford University Press, 1988), p. 30; Glyndon G. Van Deusen, *The Jacksonian Era, 1828–1848* (New York: Harper and Row, 1959) pp. 26–46.

48   Quoted in Richard Hofstadter, *Anti-Intellectualism in American Life* (London: Jonathan Cape, 1964), p. 55; Michael P. Riccards, *The Ferocious Engine of Democracy: A History of the American Presidency* (Lanham: Madison Books, 1995) pp. 117–120; Peterson, *The Jefferson Image*, pp. 69–87.

49   Robert Remini, *Andrew Jackson and the Course of American Democracy, 1833–1845* (New York: Harper and Row, 1984), pp. 137–138.

50   Edward Pesson, *Jacksonian America: Society, Personality and Politics* (Urbana: University of Illinois Press, 1985), pp. 322–323.

51   When in 1819 Maine and Missouri applied for statehood, there were 22 states in the Union, evenly split between free states and slave states. Because the population of northern states was growing faster than that of southern states, the South looked to its sectional representation in the Senate to offset the preponderance of the North in the House, and became especially concerned with the legal status of slavery in Missouri and all territory west of the Mississippi. The congressional debate between abolitionists and the defenders of slave labor was temporarily defused when House Speaker Henry Clay brokered a compromise admitting Missouri as a slave state and Maine as free state, but forever banning slave labor from the territory acquired by the Louisiana Purchase north of the parallel 36° 30'.

52   Williamson, *American Suffrage*, pp. 231–241; Lawrence Frederick Kohl, *The Politics of Individualism: Parties and the American Character in the Jacksonian Era* (New York: Oxford University Press, 1989), pp. 21–62.

53   De Tocqueville, *Democracy in America*, Vol. 1, Pt. 2, Chap. 10; Eric Foner, *Free Soil, Free Labor, Free Men: The Ideology of the Republican Party Before the Civil War* (New York: Oxford University Press, 1970), pp. 73–102.

54   Richard Franklin Bensel, *Yankee Leviathan* (New York: Cambridge University Press, 1990), pp. 42–43 and 66–67; Adam Smith, *An Inquiry into the Nature and Causes of the Wealth of Nations*, 2 vols., W.B. Todd, Ed., (Indianapolis: Liberty Classics, 1976) Bk. 3, Chap. 2, par. 12; Frederick Blue, *The Free Soilers: Third Party Politics, 1848–1854* (Urbana: University of Illinois Press, 1973).

55   Glyndon G. Van Deusen, *William Henry Seward* (New York: Oxford University Press, 1967) pp. 104–105; Burns, *Vineyard of Liberty*, p. 537.

56   J.G. Randall and David Herbert Donald, *The Civil War and Reconstruction* (Lexington, K.Y.: Heath, 1969) pp. 278–280.

57   Randall and Donald, *The Civil War and Reconstruction*, pp. 293–309.

58   Quoted in McPherson, *Battle Cry of Freedom*, p. 186.

59   Foner, *Free Soil*, p. 11.

60   Eric Foner, *Reconstruction, America's Unfinished Revolution, 1863–1877 (New York: Harper & Row, 1988), pp. 446.*

61   "Fragment on Government," *The Collected Works of Abraham Lincoln*, Roy P. Basler Ed., (New Brunswick N.J.: Rutgers University Press, 1953), Vol. II, p. 221.

62   Even at the beginning of the war Lincoln's messages to Congress anticipated the spirit of the Gettysburg address where he asked "is there in all republics, this inherent fatal weakness? Must government be too strong for the liberties of its own people, or too weak to maintain its own existence?" Randall and Donald, *The Civil War and Reconstruction*, p. 279.

63   Paul Kennedy, The *Rise and Fall of the Great Powers* (New York: Fontana, 1989) pp. 228–234; Ernest May, *Imperial Democracy: The Emergence of America as a Great Power* (New York: Harcourt, Brace & World, 1961), p. 47.

64   Jonathan R. Dull, *The Diplomacy of the American Revolution* (New Haven, Conn.: Yale University Press, 1985), pp. 3–39.

65   Most notably, Ernest May dates the reluctant emergence of the United States as a great power to the McKinley administration of the 1890s. *Imperial Democracy*, pp. 263–270.

66   *The Life and Works of Tom Paine*, 10 vols. William M. Van der Weyde, Ed., (New Rochelle N.Y.: Thomas Paine Historical Association, 1925), Vol. II, p. 129; Felix Gilbert, *To the Farewell Address: Ideas of Early American Foreign Policy* (Princeton, N.J.: Princeton University Press, 1961), pp. 44–56; McCoy, *Elusive Republic*, pp. 86–90.

67   Quoted in Wood, *The Radicalism of the American Revolution*, p. 326.

68   In a sense the philosophy of the Declaration of Independence left him little choice. See: Thomas Bailey, *A Diplomatic History of the American People* (Englewoood Cliffs, N.J.: Prentice Hall, 1980), p. 84.

69   Robert Rutland, *James Madison, The Founding Father* (London: Macmillan, 1987), pp. 140–143; Harry Ammon, *The Genet Mission* (New York: W.W. Norton, 1973); Idem., "The Genet Mission and the Devel-

opment of American Political Parties," *Journal of American History*, Vol. 52, No. 4, 1966, pp. 725–741; James Thomas Flexner, *George Washington, Anguish and Farewell (1793–1799)* (Boston: Little, Brown, 1972) pp. 292–307.

70   Quoted in Klause Schwabe, *Der amerikanische Isolationismus im 20. Jahrhundert, Legende und Wirklichkeit* (Wiesbaden: Franz Steiner, 1975), p. 3.

71   Gilbert, *To the Farewell Address*, pp. 111–136.

72   De Tocqueville, *Democracy in America*, Vol. 1, Pt. 2, Chap. 10.

73   Kennedy, *The Rise and Fall of the Great Powers*, p. 120; Frederick Merk, *The Oregon Question* (Cambridge, Mass.: Harvard University Press, 1967), pp. 122–124.

74   Thomas R. Hietala, *Manifest Design: Anxious Aggrandizement in Late Jacksonian America* (Ithaca, N.Y.: Cornell University Press, 1985), pp. 95–131; Polk quoted in Henry Steele Commager, Ed., *Documents of American History* (New York: Appleton-Century-Crofts, 1948), pp. 307–309.

75   Hietala, *Manifest Design*, p. 115.

76   Riccards, *The Ferocious Engine*, pp. 115–170, especially pp. 163–165; Charles A. McCoy, *Polk and the Presidency*, (Austin: University of Texas Press, 1960), pp. 92–96.

77   Albert K. Weinberg, *Manifest Destiny: A Study of Nationalist Expansionism in American History* (Gloucester: Peter Smith, 1958), p. 66.

78   Frederick Merck, *Manifest Destiny and Mission in American History, A Reinterpretation* (New York: Alfred A. Knopf, 1963), p. 213.

79   Johnson, *Birth of the Modern*, p. 61.

Chapter Two

The Great Republic under Party Democracy

Nobody ever did anything very foolish except from some strong principle. –Lord David Cecil, *The Young Melbourne*

The period bounded by Union victory in the Civil War and
American entry into World War I accounts for the ripening of
the American political nation and the emergence of the United
States as a Great Power. The maturing of American diplomacy
took somewhat longer, for between the Treaty of Versailles and
the late 1930s, Washington declined a role in world affairs either commensurate with American economic power or fully
cognizant of the nature of American interests. It is to this latter interregnum of nervous aloofness from European affairs
in particular that the term *isolationism* most appropriately ap-
plies. Before Versailles American diplomacy was fundamentally extrovert, reflecting the unmatched dynamism of American industrial and commercial growth. The terms of this growth
itself were conditioned by the general dominance of the Republican Party and the determination of its leadership before
World War I to expand the powers of active and effective government.

The progressive movement of the early twentieth century
simultaneously placed the issues of democratic reform and
social justice high among the priorities over which Democrats
and Republicans competed for electoral advantage. While the
parties adjusted more or less successfully to the challenge of
brokering the grievances of new and established interests, there
were also new tensions between branches of the federal gov-

ernment. These tensions were partly the product of the forthright use of executive powers by Presidents Theodore Roosevelt
and Woodrow Wilson to achieve the ends of American national
policy abroad. After World War I the respect commanded by
the United States in foreign capitals, particularly European,
was not sufficient to bring about a peace in Europe reflecting
American values or protecting American interests. By the 1920s
the Republican Party was clearly no longer the dynamic force
it had been at the turn of the century. The social coalition that
elected Harding, Coolidge, and Hoover believed that the business of America was business itself, yet the commerce the
United States conducted in the 1920s was no longer neatly
divisible from the vitality of European economies in a new
age of upheaval. Americans nevertheless remained ambivalent
about elaborating a leading role in the international arena.
The nation's diplomacy of the 1920s fell back on the comfort
of its geographic distance from the terminal crisis of democratic government in Europe.

A decade that began with the failed diplomacy of Woodrow
Wilson at the Paris Peace Conference ended with the collapse
of the New York Stock Exchange in 1929. American government suddenly appeared neither active nor effective enough
in dealing with the onset of economic depression. The dominance of the Republican Party itself then came to an end, with
the failure of the government of Herbert Hoover to return the
economy to health. The message of a new decade appeared to
be that, despite the enormous changes wrought by the Progressive Era, the future security of the Republic and its democracy would require a new interpretation of the long-standing principles of American governance and diplomacy.

Populists, Progressives, and Party Competition

The story begins with Reconstruction. Reconstruction refers
generally to the reintegration, roughly between 1865 and 1877,
of the defeated South into the Union after the rebels' surrender at Appomattox. At its best it crowned the Union's salvation and commemorated Lincoln's death with the passage of
the Fourteenth and Fifteenth Amendments to the Constitution. At its worst it featured the emergence of violent reaction-

ary movements in the Old Confederacy egged on by the self-righteousness of radical reconstructionists in the North. Lincoln's policy had been a lenient peace based in part on the hope that the Republican Party could build a base in the South starting with the political loyalties of southern Whigs who had been unenthusiastic secessionists. Armed with the power of executive order, he began with Southern reconstruction long before the war was over. As early as 1862 he installed military governors in the occupied territories of Virginia, Tennessee, Louisiana, and Arkansas, calculating that they might later become the nucleus of legitimate government. In December 1863 he issued a *Proclamation of Amnesty and Reconstruction*, offering a pardon to former Confederates who would take an oath to the Constitution of the United States. He offered further to recognize the government of any state in which 10 percent of the voting populace would submit to such an oath.

When Congress passed the *Wade-Davis Bill* in 1864, requiring more stringent criteria for the reestablishment of democratic norms, Lincoln let the bill die the slow death of a pocket veto. He had thought it providential that Lee's surrender came while Congress was adjourned, wanting above all to make progress, free of the pressure for vengeance, toward reanimating postwar government in the North and South before Congress reconvened in December. But his assassination lent such new zeal to Northern vindictiveness that Reconstruction began and ended as a "long, drawn-out tragedy of misunderstanding."[1] It didn't help the policy of a moderate peace either that Lincoln's successor, Andrew Johnson, was a Democrat with a history of only qualified hostility to slavery.[2] Johnson mismanaged almost every aspect of his relationship with the legislature, losing the political initiative and very nearly the presidency itself to congressional impeachment. After a strong showing in the congressional elections of 1866, radical reconstructionists went on the offensive in setting the terms for the South's reintegration, while reclaiming the constitutional terrain of legislative supremacy it had lost to Lincoln during the war. The Old Confederacy responded in kind. When Congress, led by Charles Sumner of Massachusetts and Thaddeus Stevens of Pennsylvania, demanded that southern states accept both the Fourteenth and Fifteenth Amendments, yet encountered embarrassing resistance to the amendments even in the North, emboldened southerners thumbed their noses at ratification. When Congress placed the South under military control and imposed carpetbagger governments, white southerners formed clubs and secret societies—the Young Men's Democratic Club, the Knights of the White Camelia, the Ku Klux Klan.[3]

Violence and intimidation were used to keep black citizens from the polls, as white southerners beavered away at reviving as much of their former way of live as could either escape the attention of the law or outlast the will of Congress to apply its letter. The Democratic Party meanwhile undertook to "redeem" southern and border states electorally for the cause of white supremacy and legal segregation of schools, theaters, and hotels. Democrats consolidated their popularity by imposing state poll taxes and property qualifications designed to disenfranchise the black population and protect white southerners from Republican Washington's legislated revolution. The Klan and kindred organizations acted as a military force serving the extralegal interests of the party, occasionally to the extent of wholesale assault on Republicans and sympathizers.[4]

Not until after the election of 1876 was it fully obvious that the radical reconstruction of the South had been a dismal failure. The newly elected Republican President Rutherford B. Hayes withdrew the troops from the South and declared Reconstruction over. He would have had difficulty continuing with it in any event, for he occupied the White House during period when initiative in the federal government was shifting decisively back to Congress after the exceptional circumstance of the Civil War. The Democrats captured control of both the House and the Senate in the elections of 1874 and promptly refused to pass appropriations bills needed to keep federal troops at southern polling stations.[5] By that time the Democrats had all but finished their reconquest of the Confederacy. For decades the South remained an electoral bedrock for the Democratic Party, where local interests bore no relationship to those of the party nationally; for longer still the constitutional rights of black citizens in Dixie remained a political fiction.

Not that Republicans in 1876 had any special claim on moral authority. The outgoing administration of Ulysses Grant had been a carnival of graft and malfeasance. A degree of corruption was a more or less inevitable by-product of the rapid growth of the national economy in the decades between the Civil War and the 1890s. The conflict itself, after all, had accelerated the growth of heavy industry, the exploitation of natural resources, the building of railroads, all the while multiplying the opportunities for transforming profit into public influence. Party competition intensified and altogether new political cleavages emerged over controversies that did not look back to 1865 but forward to territorial expansion, maturing industrialism, and the market price of foodstuffs. The partisan organization of electoral loyalty in the United States went back to the very infancy of the Republic. Tammany Hall, historically the most infamous of the great urban patronage machines, was in fact founded as a benevolent and patriotic society shortly after Washington's inauguration. At a time when so many of the founding generation prudishly debated the malignant influence of parties and "partyism," the rudimentary ligatures of the some of the most durable and effective constituency organizations in American political history were going into place under their noses. By the 1870s, however, economic progress in the country was outstripping the ability of Republicans and Democrats to respond to the satisfaction of emerging industrial interests. Entrepreneurs often saw in the nature of electoral competition too much ritual combat and not enough demonstrated relevance to their daily concerns. They acknowledged the democratic legitimacy and stabilizing features of party competition, yet sought reliable organizational vehicles for influencing policy rather more directly than through membership in the broad social coalitions on which responsible party government depended. So they founded organizations such as the Railway Managers' Association, the National Association of Manufacturers, and the Iron and Steel Institute, interest lobbies tasked with financing concerted legislative lobbying along with a variety of political activities including the funding of election campaigns.[6]

Part of their impatience with the apparent stagnation was indirectly a product of the narrowness of partisan competition itself. Particularly after the 1874 electoral choice was closely split between Democrats and Republicans, the presidential dominance of the latter obscuring the fact that the av-

erage margin of victory between 1874 and 1892 was a sliver of
1.4 percent of the popular vote. In fact the Democrats bested
Republicans in the presidential ballots of 1876 and 1888, but
lost in the electoral college. When the going was narrow the
parties were inclined to caution, more concerned with electoral costs of an error than inspired by the theoretical gains of
a leap of the imagination. There were, moreover, profound
regional differences within each partisan camp, and the parties responded above all to particularist concerns.[7] Business
lobbies represented the best organized but not the sole critics
of party government. The Noble Order of the Knights of Labor was established in 1869, while splinter parties found a home
among other socioeconomic groupings. Greenback, Grange,
Equal Rights, and Anti-Monopoly third parties in the 1870s
and 1880s culminated in the formation of the Peoples' Party
and mobilization of rural protest in the 1890s.

There was more going on within the established parties,
admittedly, than was evident to the uninitiated. Highly competitive elections required special attention to party organizational efficiency in mobilizing the vote and to holding electoral loyalty between elections. While the formal function of
Tammany Hall and other urban clubs like it was to help nominate and elect officeholders, their energies between elections
were devoted to the elaboration and maintenance of a patronage network that bound voters and their dependents materi-
ally through employment, public contracts, kickbacks, to the
party machine and its political families. The complexity and
efficiency of machine politics in democratic America was one
of the phenomena foreign students of the republic regarded
with a mixture of horror and awe. In his own study, *The American Commonwealth,* the Englishman James Bryce credited
Tammany Hall with building through the Jacksonian spoils
system a little empire in which some 40,000 New Yorkers employed by city authorities represented only the hard core of
the electoral garrison of the Democratic Party. George Washington Plunkitt, the ward boss under whom Tammany Hall
reached the zenith of its power, was for its critics the very personification of urban corruption.[8] But Tammany was only the
most notorious of the urban political machines whose legacy
to American public life is more ambiguous than the time-hon-

ored caricatures of "bossism" will concede. Tammany and other clubs like it were also microcosms of the ethnic and social melting pot America was fast becoming, a ruthless meritocracy in which Catholic and Jew, merchant and tradesman together transformed the United States into the capitalist metropolis of the twentieth century. In a predominantly market society the machines provided services for which there was an obvious demand but which were inadequately answered by legitimate government.[9] The emergence of the modern Democratic Party was in part a product of the lasting social coalitions fashioned by its urban bosses with political imagination and graft.

Still, the enemies of machine politics can be forgiven for failing to appreciate in their own time the peculiar ways in which machine politics facilitated future American greatness. The urban political clubs were frequently also the home of stultifying conservatism. Plunkitt was a firm believer that all politics was essentially a business and patronage its hard currency; primary elections he deemed dangerous, women's suffrage "unAmerican."[10] The state of Wyoming hadn't seen it that way in 1869 when it introduced voting rights to its female populace. It was in the farming states of the West that the pulsebeat of democratic reformism was the quickest and enmity toward eastern money and political corruption the most virulent. Whereas the efficiency of American farmers increased by leaps and bounds over the decades following the Civil War, their terms of exchange deteriorated steadily due to factors well beyond their influence. Selling wheat cotton or beef in a world market, the price of their labor was determined in Liverpool, while the cost of their household goods and machinery was set by American industrial trusts and protective tariffs. Mortgage indebtedness compounded their problems. Many farmers believed further that their government's attachment to the gold standard—rather, Congress's refusal since 1873 to purchase or to coin silver—was killing them. If silver were restored and all of the available supply were minted, they reasoned, the value of money would fall and the prices they could command would rise in proportion.

With the founding of the Patrons of Husbandry in 1867 and the National Farmers' Alliances between 1879 and 1884, farmers took the first organizational steps in potent political coalescence. As the movements ignited local brushfires of populist resentment, an effort was made to unite the grievances of agriculture and labor behind the leadership of the People's (Populist) Party. In Nebraska the plight of marginal agriculture united farmers across ethnic lines that once divided them; smashed established party loyalties; pushed Populists and Democrats into an electoral coalition; and placed regulation or outright government ownership of the railroads on the state's political agenda. Populism's appeals resonated well with the poorer farmers in the South as well. Among its most remarkable champions there was Tom Watson, a direct descendent of slaveholders, who in the heart of rural white supremacism attempted to build a reform electoral alliance that included black tenant farmers and sharecroppers. Still, the real fire of the movement was in the West. The Populist Party held its first national convention in Omaha in 1891.[11] Basing its strength in economic issues, yet drawing from other causes, such as female suffrage, Populism obviously had enormous potential to bring grief to the established parties.

This was demonstrated in the congressional elections of 1890. Populist alliances reached out to labor organizers, socialist, "single-taxers," and the advocates of the women's suffrage to create the most serious challenge to Wall Street Republicanism the Grand Old Party had ever seen. Republican electoral losses were due mostly to popular outrage at tariff protection. The consumers and producers of the nation's staples blamed trade protection for higher prices. Mary Ellen Lease, a suffrage reformer, union organizer, and temperance advocate form Kansas, ignited her state with the indictment that "Wall Street owns the country. It is no longer a government of the people, by the people and for the people, but a government of Wall Street, by Wall Street and for Wall Street. The great common people of this country are slaves, and monopoly is the master. The West and South are bound and prostrate before the manufacturing East. [. . .] The parties lied to us and the political speakers mislead us".[12]

Lease's sentiment, nonetheless, spilled over the brim of the movement itself and actually influenced the strategy and fortunes of the Democratic Party in the most immediate sense. When in 1892 Populists polled over a million votes in the presidential election, it was the Democrat Grover Cleveland who went to the White House. Cleveland's was a well-intentioned administration, but his party was essentially riding the Populist tiger with little hope of ever controlling it. As president he based his policy on the conviction that the market would correct itself and alleviate accompanying miseries without silver coinage or vigorous remedial legislation, aside that is from tariff reduction. His mobilization of federal troops in the Pullman Strike of 1894 so angered the legions of wage-labor voters who had supported him as to spell the general decline of his economic philosophy among a good many urban Democrats, while rural radicals were even more damning in their caricature of Cleveland as an overfed dupe of eastern corporate interests. Cleveland was a Bourbon Democrat who believed that government interference in the economic laws of supply and demand constituted a check on the march of human progress, a march that was led by the entrepreneurial energy of small business. This philosophy was conversant with that of the Republicanism that had triumphed in the Civil War, with the important difference that Bourbonism rejected protective tariffs and was often openly hostile to the interests of farmers and labor. In the economic circumstance of the early 1890s, it was an ideology courting electoral disaster; what it offered Populists with one hand it took away with the other. Had Democrats been able to hold onto the gains they made electorally from the Populist surge, they would have been in a position to dominate national politics. But Cleveland's policies cut across the grain of the movement's whole direction, and Democrats booked huge losses at the local, state, and congressional level in 1893–94.[13] Thus, by the middle of the decade there was a good deal of partisan flux in American politics, but the jury was still very much in doubt as to whether either of the major camps was to profit decisively from it.

The Populist revolt was often propelled by visceral sentiment, but its impact on the parties was rather diffuse; the diverse social groupings that gave it political life did not form the kind of narrow clientelist relationships with political parties that were routine in continental Europe and disastrous for European democracy. Lease's rhetoric was often laced with the dark denunciations of Jewish bankers in Eastern cities, but rural anti-Semitism in the United States never congealed into the reactionary nationalist lobbies that ultimately formed the base of Nazism in Germany.[14]

The Democratic Party, with its Jeffersonian and Jacksonian traditions of the liberty-loving yeoman, was in some respects a natural political vehicle for the Populist protest. The Nebraskan Democrat William Jennings Byran certainly thought so, and urged his party to fuse with the Populists. And if it was the cause rather than its organization that really mattered, the Populists could have no better national champion than the charismatic Bryan, armed with the moral rectitude of a crusader for the producing masses and extraordinarily gifted in the art of peroration. It was Bryan's imagery of Wall Street money men crucifying mankind on a cross of gold that congealed the various strands of Populism into a potent political mass, and it was the agility of the Democrats in shrugging off the memory of Cleveland and hijacking the Populist cause that enabled them to stake a claim on American social democracy in the next century. The urban-based progressive movement that set the agenda of American politics after 1900, after all, drew both inspiration and strength from the Populist cause and provided both the platform and the broadened social base that in the 1930s made the Democratic Party an electoral powerhouse.

Progressivism was as much an amorphous social phenomenon as a purposeful political movement. It too was ideologically ambiguous, composed of a spectrum of interests in uneasy and wary political coalition. By 1890, for example, women accounted for some four million of the nation's wage earners, but the most articulate female advocates of reform were less than radical in the cause of suffrage reform. Outside their own circles the upper middle-class members of the Federation of Women's Clubs, founded in 1890, were regarded by their critics as the wives of wealth with rather too much time on their hands. Though the contribution of female wage earners to the industrial economy grew steadily, trade unionists resisted their integration into the labor movement. At the turn of the century the enormous potential of their energies awaited another two decades of political ripening. In the meantime, their activities ranged from labor organization to temperance, from mother-and-child protection laws to education, from aesthetic improvement of cities to birth control.[15] Progressivism based its strength of numbers on the urban counterpart to Populist grievances, of industrial wage earners and urban consumers seeking a better return for their labor and cheaper loaf for their table. The urban middle class of the 1890s felt "assaulted economically and socially from above and below", from the rise of corporate power on the one hand and labor power on the other, yet remained fundamentally confident about the future and the potential of an alliance with the laboring populace.[16]

And yet there were remarkable limits to the progressive imagination, especially compared with the reformers of the decade preceding the Civil War. In May 1896 the Supreme Court handed down a decision in the case of *Plessy v. Ferguson*, holding that "separate but equal accommodations for the white and colored races" on passenger rail coaches in the state of Louisiana did no offence to the Constitution of the United States. The doctrine of separate but equal, in the judgement of the lone dissenting vote of Justice John Marshall Harlan, was a thin disguise for obvious legal perfidy, validating a wide pattern of racial segregation in housing, schools, transportation, and recreation. The decision reduced at a stroke the citizenship rights guaranteed black Americans under the Fourteenth Amendment to a pious goodwill clause. Compounding the juridical outrage was the fact that in 1896 it elicited no chorus of popular protest.[17] The *New York Times* reported the *Plessy* decision on page three among other items of its Tuesday column on railway news. The fact that a decision of such fundamental constitutional magnitude failed to ruffle the conscience of a nation otherwise consumed by new issues of social justice reflects only that the Court's majority stood on a bedrock of popular racialist conventional wisdom. In the 1890s segregation was common in the Old Confederacy and beyond, and it rested on an assumption of negro inferiority so pervasive that the rights of black Americans counted for nothing among the aspirations and calculations of the larger body politic. The amendments of 1865 and 1868 had made black Americans citizens in the formal sense, but the project of making such rights fully substantive had hardly begun and would now

be more difficult. Because the *Plessy* decision had merely transformed *a de facto* racism that had become widely institutionalized and was supported by legal precedence in the states into
de jure racism, its deeper implications slipped by progressives
unacknowledged. It did not affect them. The plaintiff in *Plessy*
rightly argued that the American Constitution necessarily
embodies the principles of republican government and that it
therefore categorically rejects the recognition of race before
the law. But the Court in essence had decided to hold the Constitution to the People rather than the reverse, and it was not
until the 1950s that it decided to correct its error.[18]

The great election 1896 was another kind of reckoning, one
in which the Republican Party got the better side of the issues
of the decade along with the better part of the electoral dividend. Given the increasing cost of money and the terms of
their indebtedness to eastern finance, farmers had just cause
to rally to the Populist banner. But in its personification in
William Jennings Bryan Populism ultimately worried more
people than it inspired. Catholics and immigrants in the cities
were put off by his revivalism and nativism, while farmers in
the northeast and midwest, where agriculture was both highly
capitalized and prosperous, had no time for Bryan's determination to do away with the gold standard. Many wage earners,
who otherwise might have seen Bryan as a champion of the
working man, instead feared that his election to the presidency
would mean the closing of their factories. In certain instances
their employers went so far as to tell them so; in others, the
working class vote was determined by a gut awareness that jobs
as well as profits huddled behind protective tariffs.[19] In 1896
the coalition of eastern industry and western agriculture
formed under the Civil War banner of Free Soil, Free Labor,
Free Men was strong enough to resist the obvious corollary of
Free Trade and get away with it.

This was due in no small part to the calibre of the Republican presidential nomination for 1896, William McKinley. As a
veteran of six terms in the House, McKinley was a champion
of those congressional ballots that kept industrial tariffs in
place; as a seasoned politician he was also well-studied in the
art of making Republican nationalism legitimate to mass opinion and palatable to the ever-widening industrial constituency.

In tactical terms, the McKinley Republicans took an unequivo-
cal stand on the gold standard, which in effect wrote off those
states where advocacy of the free coinage of silver had a
grassroots constituency. They sought at the same time to consolidate support from manufacturing interests and the finance
sector, while enlisting the votes of large numbers of industrial
workers. On election day the GOP carried the ten largest cities in the country with working-class, middle-class, and upper-
class votes. In rural New England they compensated losses in
the West with the votes of Yankee Democrats who converted
to McKinley Republicanism.

As an independent political movement Populism came away
with a bloody nose. Many of its enthusiasts cursed as fatal the
decision to fuse with the Democratic Party, but in this they
were mistaken. Neither the arithmetic of the electoral college
nor the complexities of majority-building in Congress favor
the survival of any agenda that will not submit its demands to
brokerage of a national party. The election of 1896 was one of
critical realignment, in which tensions in American society not
adequately answered by either the organization or platforms
of the established parties forced themselves to the surface of
national affairs. Partisan loyalties broke down; new
sociopolitical coalitions emerged; the frontiers of the politically possible were revised. In short, the electoral universe was
redefined. Over the two decades following the Civil War, presidential elections in the United States had been a clash of traditions, Republicans and Democrats in ritual combat over issues
essentially settled. But when the Democratic Party absorbed
the Populists, they also appropriated the defense of silver
money; the cause of Eugene Debs and the Pullman strike; and
popular outrage at high court decisions, such as *The United
States v. E. C. Knight & Company*, favoring corporate trusts and
the wealthy. In so doing, the party began a long process of
redefining its role in American politics in a way that eventually brought it massive advantages. In the 1896, however, the
Republican strategy sufficed to strengthen traditional GOP
support in Pennsylvania, Illinois, Michigan, Wisconsin, and
Iowa, while cutting into Democratic support in Connecticut,
New Jersey, New York, Indiana, California, Delaware, and West
Virginia. Both the unwieldy nature of the Democrats social

coalition and the radicalism of the party platform transformed more-or-less balanced party competition into GOP dominance. Challenged to overthrow the Republican constitution for the American economy, the People instead turned the GOP into the POG, the natural party of government.[20]

It was also the first national skirmish of a more general conflict over the constitution of American capitalism in which progressivism had yet to make its major contribution. That contribution was essentially to divide thinking on the U.S. economy in the political world into three schools of thought, all of which made major contributions to twentieth-century politics: a partly state-directed corporate capitalism championed by Theodore Roosevelt; a new vision of the regulatory state associated with Woodrow Wilson; and the minimalist, laissez-faire philosophy of William Howard Taft.[21]

After 1900 the Populist revolt and Progressive movement blended into one great political weather system. Democrats and Republicans appropriated and blended themes from both and brokered their impact on American public life on a bipartisan format. But while Populism reflected in spectacular fashion a persistent cultural characteristic of American politics, the weight of which could tilt rightward or leftward depending on the specific conditions of time and place, progressivism represented an ideological mutation in middle-class attitudes, which, like Populism, was felt over the long-term preponderantly by the Democratic Party. Bryan's "cross of gold" speech at the 1896 convention was really the first shot in the Democratic Party's transformation into a much more potent force in the middle decades of the next century. Lyndon Johnson grew up in the hill country of Texas where Bryan became the stuff of political legend and New Deal liberalism later acquired the strength of political religion.[22]

Immediately after the victory of 1896, however, McKinley directed American energies outward rather inward. Although popular enthusiasm for some form of American response to uprisings in Cuba against Spanish rule was set aside momentarily for the election, in 1897 it reemerged newly invigorated. It was as if the moral fervor of populist and progressive causes had been deflected by the domestic settlement of 1896 to foreign affairs and come to focus quite suddenly on a single is-

land in the Caribbean. At an increasing rate newspaper reports of real and imagined Spanish atrocities against Cuban
subjects whipped up outrage and bellicose patriotic insistence
that a blow be struck in Cuba for liberty. Anti-Catholic nativism
was rampant in parts of the country, and, although its target
was more usually new immigrant minorities, Spain was the
ideal enemy for a popular war. The wonder was not that the
McKinley administration went to war with Spain over Cuba,
but that it resisted until 1898 the demand of the most vocifer-
ous public opinion that it either do so or face an electoral
drubbing in 1900. A jingoistic press and bellicose Congress
told McKinley that if the administration failed to act in Cuba,
the Democratic Party would add Free Cuba to the slogan of
Free Silver and ride a progressivist majority to the White House.

The idea that the war was merely a product of externalized
domestic tensions or that in Cuba the United States had imperial greatness thrust upon it, is in both instances an exercise in
caricature.[23] If the McKinley administration was of a mind to
mobilize public opinion behind a project in territorial acquisition in the tradition of the astute opportunism of John Quincy
Adams, however, then Cuba was perfect. The anticolonialist
chord resonated with 1776, while confrontation with Spain fit
the extravagant claims of the Monroe Doctrine without subjecting the as yet limited military capacity of the United States
to humiliation. In terms of the doctrine the United States had
as strong a case against British imperialism in Venezuela as it
did against the Spanish variety in Cuba, yet both public sentiment and diplomacy opted for the adversary with fewer battle-
ships and facilitated America's emergence as a great power at
a minimal cost. In his war message to Congress McKinley
named the interest of humanity and the threat to both Cuban
and American property and commerce in justification of military action, citing the mysterious destruction of the U.S. battle-
ship *Maine* in Havana harbor almost as an afterthought. On
the one hand the Cuban adventure initiated a tradition of sporadic U.S. interventions in Latin America over the following
century, in which the region claimed a role in the national
consciousness somewhat akin to a neglected backyard subject
to imperfect and ill-tempered cleanups. On the other hand,
Spain relinquished all sovereignty over Cuba and ceded to the

U.S. Puerto Rico and other islands in the West Indies along
with Guam in the Marianas. The United States also acquired
possession of the Philippines and with it a commercial door to
and military outpost in the Western Pacific. Considered together with the annexation of Hawaii in 1898 and an agreement with Germany over Samoa the following year, the step-
ping stones of an American presence in Asia fell into place
with remarkably little effort. Whereas the *New York Herald* had
as recently 1892 recommended the abolition of the State Department because it had so little to do, within months of the
Cuban conflict Washington was insisting on a say in the affairs of China. The historical enigma of McKinley's personality does not justify the conclusion that Machiavellian machinations in and of themselves projected the United States into the
Caribbean and the Western Pacific, but the Spanish-American
conflict and the president's decision to annex the Philippines
does fit nicely into earlier episodes, particularly the cost-effective application of force in broadening American horizons.[24]

The European powers were surprised, both by the ease and
completeness of the American victory over Spain and by the
self-assurance with which Washington relieved the Spanish of
their overseas possessions in the *Treaty of Paris*. They might
have drawn more from the episode than mere astonishment.
Though in theory the Monroe Doctrine applied equally to the
presence of Spain and Britain in the Caribbean, the United
States had emerged as world power in part by choosing both
the right opponent and the right opportunity to assert itself.
American victory was underwritten by vast resources and growing industrial muscle, the full potential of which had scarcely
dawned on most Americans, just as the treaty itself reflected
the boundless commercial ambition of those to whom it had.
There were problems, of course. In terms of overall military
preparedness, the United States was hardly among the first
rank of nations; the war exposed profound weaknesses that
years of parsimony and neglect had imposed on the army in
particular. Still, the nation had matched its aspirations to its
capacity, and neither the circumstance nor the outcome of the
war with Spain testify that the republic was thrust blushing
onto the stage of world power. The cause and the outcome,
lastly, were popular, as popular, indeed, as wars ever get.[25] From

the outset McKinley assumed from the responsibility inherent in his status as commander-in-chief the capacity to coordinate and direct the American war effort. He established a war room in the White House complete with new telegraph and telephone communications; involved himself routinely in military decisions; expanded the authority of his office; and emerged as something of an "imperial tutor to the American people."[26] Neither he nor his people, however, accepted for an instant the idea that their goals had been merely imperial.

The Progressive Republic and World Power

McKinley was not the last of the pre-World War I presidents to view the White House as a platform for national moral leadership. In the two decades between the election of 1896 and American involvement in World War I, progressivism in the United States was driven by two equally popular perceptions. One said that America's emergence as a global diplomatic force was merely a tribute to the status that the United States, a dynamic and productive society, had earned. The other conceded that Americans were preponderantly better off than their contemporaries in Europe, but maintained that the expansion of national material wealth was not accomplishing a proportionate expansion of opportunity and prosperity. If the pursuit of happiness was the birthright of American citizenship, then it was being compromised. In Europe a parallel advance of science and industrial technology were throwing up issues of wealth distribution and turning wage laborers toward trade unions and socialist politics. In the United States the pressures for change were more diffuse but just as powerful. Starting with the farmers of the Midwest, it had centered on breaking the hold of eastern economic privilege; in the industrial and commercial realm it meant rolling back the power of the trusts; in politics it focused on broadening the definition and deepening the participation of the People, on making the republic more democratic. Whereas in Europe the political cause of working people was monopolized by socialist parties, in the United States both Democrats and Republicans faced fundamental redefinitions in the face of the mass politics of the industrial age.

There were important differences, however, in the way that change swept over and transformed the parties. In the cities, where the extremes of wealth and poverty were most profound, the patronage machinery of the bosses became a principal target of political reform. In cities such as New York, Chicago, and Cleveland progressives and municipal populists fashioned reform coalitions. Middle-class progressives regarded the working immigrant populations of the cities as all too easily manipulated by the bread crumbs of city hall beneficence and resolved to mobilize the ethnic vote behind an agenda for "good government" and "expert public administration." In terms of cleansing urban politics of corruption, the results of their efforts were mixed at best. The machines remained, but the challenge to their ascendancy facilitated cross-class and interethnic political alliances. As garrisons of partisan loyalty, the machines were improved by the progressive experience, because "no matter how much the bosses and their assistants might have enriched themselves, they maintained popular images as representatives of the great urban masses."[27]

While the tonic of progressivism filtered through the urban channels of the Democratic Party, transforming it in ways that were not fully appreciated for decades, in the Republican Party it was personified in Theodore Roosevelt in a style of direct import to the here-and-now of American politics in 1900. Roosevelt's sudden arrival in the White House was something of an accident of history produced by the McKinley assassination, but there never seemed to be anything but predestiny in Roosevelt's presidency. His inauguration marked the dawn of the Progressive Era, in which popular grievances reaching back beyond the electoral tremors of 1896 to the Populist revolt of the 1880s now wrote the script of public affairs. Of all the many qualities Roosevelt brought to the work of the Oval Office, none were so important as that of the utterly pragmatic and professional politician. He was an authentic democrat and a political realist, an American nationalist and faithful Republican. Himself a beneficiary of the Hamiltonian political economy erected by the Republican Party after the peace of Appomattox, his experience in New York State of the politics of labor strife and factory conditions convinced him that only enlightened conservatism could preserve it. A somewhat simplistic yet useful generalization is that there were two breeds of progressive, those who sought to reform business in the name of efficiency and those who advocated the same in the cause of social justice. Like no other contemporary, Roosevelt appreciated that in 1900 only wrongheaded statecraft would attempt to separate the two. With this rule written in his conscience he was poised to become the first of the great progressivist presidents of the twentieth-century presidents who set the general course of American public policy until the late 1960s.[28]

Applying without regret to the casuistry that is the daily bread of successful democratic politics in a period of reform, Roosevelt accepted generous funding from the trusts in his reelection campaign of 1904, and then turned on them with new regulatory power in the *Hepburn Act* of 1906 and the *Mann-Elkins Act* of 1910. Steel magnate Henry Clay Frick stormed that "we bought the son of a bitch and he didn't stay bought."[29] It is never easy for a president to rise above his party and still hope to achieve very much without its support. In the political atmosphere of the prewar years, however, Roosevelt understood that ostentatious independence was perhaps the key to electoral survival and legislative effectiveness. His regulatory initiatives, after all, inevitably alienated factions of the corporate sector to which the GOP had been wedded for decades; then there was the fact that, in even in the best of circumstance, far more Democrats than Republicans were in genuine sympathy with the content, if not the inspiration, of his reforms. "If I cannot find Republicans, I am going to appoint Democrats," he once warned, and a good many of his initiatives succeeded because the enthusiastic support of minority Democrats in Congress forced reluctant Republicans to contribute to a legislative majority.[30]

In and of themselves big business and economies of scale caused Roosevelt no offense. He was more concerned with business practices, economic efficiency, and the contribution of each to the national product, so his "trust-busting" policies were often highly selective and geared to his personal vision of America's economic future. This was especially true with regard to transportation generally and the railroads specifically. Though Roosevelt was interested in tariff reform as well, his political instincts told him that he could accomplish more by conjuring the bogey of tariff reductions to force conservative Republicans to yield acquiesce to the regulation of the railroads. When the GOP old guard in the Senate put up resistance to railroad regulation, he compromised in the interest of the legislation's passage yet salvaged sufficient bite in the bill to enable the Interstate Commerce Commission (ICC) to set maximum rail rates. He also buried provisions within the bill's text giving the ICC control of interstate oil pipelines.[31]

From the outset Roosevelt exhibited an instinct for the relationship between interstate and international commerce, and in 1903 demonstrated the point with his grandest initiative in transportation infrastructure. The canal treaty with the new state of Panama, a state itself created partly because of Roosevelt's encouragement of a Panamanian rebellion against Colombia, drew together the strands of strategic interest and the continental market. The canal promised to enhance the mobility of the U.S. Navy, a priority for Roosevelt ever since he had served as Secretary of the Navy under McKinley, so it was partly with a mind to speeding its construction, as well as impressing upon Japan the new Pacific reach of the United States, that Roosevelt sent the fleet on a much-publicized world tour. Roosevelt believed that a strong navy and a demonstrated willingness to use it should be the cornerstone of national policy, a policy that required warships so that the United States might "take the position to which it is entitled among the nations of the earth."[32] The legitimacy of that position seems never to have cost Roosevelt a moment's doubt, and the confidence with which in 1905 he offered American conciliation in settling the Russo-Japanese War reflected the generally expansive mood of progressive America.

If many conservative Republicans had abhorred Roosevelt's progressivism from the very day of his very arrival in office, by 1910 their abhorrence was doubled by a speech he gave in Osawatomie, Kansas, in which he quoted Lincoln that labor was "prior to and independent of capital," and went on to denounce the influence of "swollen fortunes" and "special interests" in distorting the rules of the market economy.[33] Roosevelt's *Square Deal* concept of progressive reform expressed the traditional Republican ideal of open competition among a vast constellation of small producers, an ideal now seriously under revision by way of the merger boom restructuring corporate America. By 1912 abhorrence turned to contempt, and for Roosevelt the feeling was entirely mutual. Roosevelt's Osawatomie salvo was in reality the first article in the establishment of the Progressive Party in reaction to his disappointment in the presidency of William Howard Taft, whose succession at the head of the GOP Roosevelt himself largely engineered. Taft's appeasement of the party's conservatives at the expense of its progressive wing came at a particularly inopportune juncture, given the recurring popularity of Bryan in the Democratic Party and the very real danger that the GOP might lose the progressive initiative. Although the Democrats too were inwardly divided, Taft was a portly caricature of Republican complacency whose weak leadership promised to give the game away.

After having served nearly two full terms as a Republican president, Roosevelt declared the two party system so moribund that only the creation of a third force could push the nation forward. The founding of the Progressive Party was an attempt to do this on a platform that was both reformist and nationalist, to achieve the ends of Jeffersonian/Jacksonian democracy, if you like, with the means of the Hamiltonian state. Then as now, claims made on behalf of the third force were often arrogant in staking out a terrain supposedly above petty partisanship, but equally Roosevelt was motivated by a sense of dry rot in the GOP. He died before getting the chance to attempt a reconstructed Republican Party in 1920. Progressives in the party promptly split into factions supporting rival candidates and thus permitted the convention to nominate the dark horse Warren G. Harding, the favorite of the GOP's old guard. The 'Bull Moose' Progressives never found out what a redirected Republican Party could achieve, and, as it turned out, only decades later were Republicans to get another chance. Once Roosevelt was no longer the driving force of the Republicanism, there was very little drive left in the Grand Old Party.[34]

But Roosevelt had nevertheless left his stamp on the nation. In domestic affairs his presidency took its cues from both the Populist revolt and the rise of progressivism. He supplemented his trust-busting approach to business practices with the promotion of more democratic political procedures, direct primaries, initiatives, and referenda. He attempted, and partly succeeded, to reorder industrial society consistent with the apparent wishes of the people, yet staked out new regulatory terrain for Washington in the process. While the government and the electoral process could and should be renovated to accommodate more direct participation of the people in the nomination and election of the custodians of the public interest, he reasoned, the parameters of government itself could and should be broadened to enable it to facilitate the people's welfare. In foreign affairs he both consolidated and extended the gains realized in the McKinley administration's war in Cuba. The most forthrightly imperialist president in the history of the republic, he defined the Caribbean as an American lake and made the Monroe Doctrine substantive, most spectacularly in the construction of the Panama Canal, but also with interventions in Venezuela, Santo Domingo, and Cuba. He enunciated a policy of Open Door toward China to help to balance against a newly ascendent Japan and in recognition of American interest in the Western Pacific.

Roosevelt's presidency was also generally the most assertive since Lincoln. Like no other president since Lincoln he claimed the power of moral authority in national leadership for the executive branch. Though he applied such authority with equal confidence to both domestic affairs and overseas diplomacy, Roosevelt sought to make the presidency the head office of an extrovert foreign policy based on a strong army and navy, above all because these were concerns about which "the average American citizen does not take the trouble to think carefully or deeply".[35] Lastly, through presidential leadership in foreign affairs, Theodore Roosevelt sought to disabuse his countrymen of what he considered to be two of their most hallowed illusions: that a nation such as the United States could avoid deep involvement in the twentieth-century world's affairs and that the natural condition of such a world was one of peace. It was as if he could smell the cordite of the coming decades. The work he began was left for Woodrow Wilson to further.

It was the acrimony among Republicans in 1912 that facilitated Wilson's election to the presidency and the inauguration of a new chapter in progressive presidential leadership.

His nomination as the Democratic candidate was little short of a miracle, requiring Wilson's backers forty-six ballots and laborious factional alliance-building among the boss-controlled delegations at the party's brawling Baltimore convention in order to overcome the candidacy of Champ Clark, Democratic Speaker of the House. In an essentially three-way election race, Wilson was better positioned than any candidate. Though he claimed only a plurality (6,293,019) of the popular vote, the Republican camp split between Roosevelt and Taft to give Wilson a landslide in the electoral college: 435 to Roosevelt's 88 and Taft's 8. Republican fratricide also delivered both houses of Congress to the Democrats.[36] So strong was the progressive tide in the country, that every candidate laid claim to it in some form or another, and only Taft's claim was preponderantly fallacious. Moreover, a good many progressive initiatives percolated up from the state to the national level. By 1912 many states had introduced primary elections and twenty-nine were experimenting with various ways of electing their senators, so that the Seventeenth Amendment, providing for the direct election of the Senate was never really an issue of significant controversy. The peacefulness of the change was a measure of the republic's democratic confidence and a tribute to the power of the democratic ethos. The Founders, after all, had opted for an appointed Senate in part to offset the fiercely democratic nature of the House. For the progressives, primaries and Senate election were the political counterparts to government regulation of corporate monopolies, a generalized democratization championed by figures such as Robert "Fighting Bob" LaFollette of Wisconsin who defeated the Republican machine in his state to become governor, representative, and senator. In an address to the Grand Army of the Republic Wilson underscored the confidence of progressivism, by noting that the Constitution of the United States was once considered a noble experiment, but that since the Civil War Americans had shown that "a nation as powerful as any in the world can be erected upon the will of the people; that, indeed that there was a power in such a nation that dwelt in no other nation".[37]

Whereas Roosevelt had avoided the tariff reduction in recognition of trade protection's place in Republican tradition,

Wilson used his Democratic majority on Congress to express
national confidence with the first move toward revision in tariff schedules in fifty years. He moved with much the same dis-
patch on banking reform and the ever-nagging currency issue,
producing in the *Federal Reserve Act* a decentralized banking
system and conditions for liberalized credit. The *Clayton Antitrust Act* of 1914 forbade interlocking directorships, price-fix-
ing, and made corporate directors legally answerable for
breaches of antitrust laws. In the same year the *Federal Trade
Commission Act* gave Washington new powers to investigate
business operations and to hear charges of unfair practices.
All of these initiatives undertook to make the operation of the
national economy generally more open, supple, and competitive. The egalitarian sentiment of the time was powerful enough
to elicit a Jacksonian tribute from Wilson, to the effect that
the Democratic Party aspired to "a government in the world,
where the average man, the plain man, the common man, the
unaccomplished man, the poor man had a voice equal to the
voice of anybody else"[38] in the settlement of public affairs. From
the vantage point of the late twentieth century the shear optimism of Wilson's particular expression of the cult of the common man appears a quaint historical curiosity. But in the age
of socialism it was one of the great intrinsic virtues of the
American love of liberty that reform was directed toward more
political democracy and economic opportunity rather than
toward some bloodless collectivist concept of social harmony.
Ultimately, in fact, the democratic force was itself critical to a
reconstitution of capitalism that only in America proceeded
without a direct threat to or an outright debauch of the principles of property and personal freedom.

Politically, Wilson's reforms exploited the conflict between
conservative and reformist Republicans. But they also featured
a more intellectually satisfying blend of American political traditions. Reformers who were originally drawn to the Hamiltonian sweep of Roosevelt's proposals, recognized it again in
Wilson's emphasis on federal activism. Corporate capitalism
could be made to benefit the working man. The Wilson reforms involved bringing outdated government and law into
alignment with the natural evolution of free enterprize at the
beginning of new century, "to narrow the gap between

America's well-advanced economy and technology and her backward social and political institutions".[39]

This imperative, to synchronize change in the socioeconomic system with the advance of democratic reform, required a redefinition of *liberalism*. Hitherto the word had been used in America and elsewhere to denote a philosophical preference for strictly limited government. In Wilson's America it acquired a wholly different meaning, one not unique to but certainly preponderantly common to public discourse in the United States: *the positive use of public authority on behalf of the material security and personal satisfaction of individual citizens*, what the rest of the world came to call *social democracy*. From the retrospective position of 1908 Wilson criticized the *Federalist Papers* for their mechanistic and static concept of government. "Government," he maintained, "does not stop with the protection of life, liberty, and property," but rather "goes on to serve every convenience of society," its sphere of activity "limited only by its own wisdom."[40] By any measure, this was an extraordinary statement, considering the frequency with which congenitally unwise politicians were and are elected to office. The separation of powers, as provided for by the "static concepts" of the Founders, was based on the assumption that at some point elected politicians could be counted on to attempt some unwise but popular things. Wilson was going a long way toward saying that a decision taken democratically could never be wrong. When self-proclaimed conservatives employ the word *liberal* today only with an accompanying sneer, the more enlightened of them do so in the awareness that it has come to stand for theoretically unlimited government after having stood for the sanctity of precisely the opposite.

Progressive Diplomacy

Significant though they were, it was not for his domestic reforms that Wilson is remembered. Rather, it was under Wilson that American power and influence came first to assert itself precisely there, Europe, where historically it had been least inclined to do so. It was not the terms by which Wilson took the United States into World War I, but rather the terms on which postwar European peace was to be based that ultimately reinforced popular isolationist sentiment in America after 1919.

The official policy of neutrality to which Wilson held the country for two years was legitimate, above all because it reflected a popular determination to stay out of the conflict. At another level, of course, American neutrality was a fiction. If challenged concerning their attitude toward the belligerents, most Americans would have confessed a sympathy for France and Britain; whatever the achievements of German culture and science, something in the American republican soul recoiled at the spectre of warrior Prussia bullying Europe with its technology and soldiery in the service of medieval virtues. Yet until 1916, at least, Wilson saw no clear moral issue at stake for the United States in the conflict. The war was a collision of imperial interests in which the participants were more-or-less equally culpable. Behind the policy of neutrality was also a genuine desire to be recognized at the end of the conflict as a disinterested facilitator of a just peace. If participation in the war was the price to paid ultimately for a place at the table of negotiation, then neutrality followed by late and decisive entry to the conflict was a wholly pragmatic approach for American statecraft. This is an underappreciated fact of a diplomacy that is too often thought to be pathologically idealistic.

Moreover, Wilson understood that American participation in the war could only be defended domestically if it were justified in American terms, consistent both with the progressive spirit of the age and with the fact of the now-elected Senate's constitutional authority in the realm of treatymaking. He finally put his office behind the cause of American entry because the Century of Total War, exemplified in the German navy's conduct of unrestricted U-boat warfare, clashed with Age of Mass Politics. German submarines attacked civilian targets as well as military, and public opinion demanded an appropriate response to criminal behavior.[41] But German excesses did not relieve the other participants of an important quantum of responsibility. The war had been started by individual statesmen and the too-clever realism of their balance-of-power diplomacy. When their nineteenth-century wisdom failed them, they had mobilized entire populations and conducted a war of unprecedented carnage with breathtaking stupidity. Wilson therefore was determined to inscribe on the war a meaning, namely that it had become a "peoples' war," not at all wrong in terms of the burden of its prosecution, but also that its armistice should be ennobled with a particular meaning. Lincoln had done the same in the Civil War, a conflict to preserve the Union that had become a crusade for emancipation. American participation in the cause of the Anglo-French Entente would take place on these terms if it were to occur at all:

> By inscribing on its banners the sacred words Democracy and Freedom, the Entente aroused special sympathy in America. Since it was universally inspired, the language used by the Allied representatives was understood in every continent. A crusade to make the world "safe for democracy" was, so it seemed, of world-wide concern. What meaning had the defense of German *Kultur* outside of Germany itself? It was ideology that won over American opinion to participation in the war, arousing and maintaining the enthusiasm of a young nation.[42]

Franklin Roosevelt, who at the time was working in the administration as Assistant Secretary of the Navy, had himself little quarrel with Wilson's line of reasoning, but he brought an additional perspective to his duties. The conduct of the war confirmed the younger Roosevelt first in his long-cherished conviction that the United States should begin with the construction of a first-rate navy and then in the belief that early American participation in the Allied cause might be more prudent than Wilson's policy.[43] But politically Wilson was on the more prudent course. In the presidential election of 1916, after all, Wilson ran on his record of having kept the United States out of the war, yet cautioned that he would make no commitment to peace at any price. With that strategy he defeated the Republican nominee, Charles Evans Hughs. But it was a close race, with Wilson edging past Hughs 277 to 254 electoral votes on the strength, thought most post-election analyses, of Wilson's progressivism and peace. Wilson, in other words, waited for public opinion. By April 1917 the continued prodding of German submarine warfare had shifted it enough to permit a War Message to Congress.

Even if America's allies did not take the democratic cause fully seriously, they were to discover at the end of the war that the United States did. Wilson approached the issue of a postwar peace with two assumptions: that the United States could be the honest broker of a just settlement, since four years of bitter fighting had robbed Europeans of the ability to see what was in their own best interest, and that the peace should herald a new order of things, as Wilson put it, "the common will of mankind has been substituted for the particular purposes of individual states."[44] One of the more durable myths about Woodrow Wilson is that woolly-minded progressivism led him to expect from America's allies commitments to European peace that were simply unrealistic. In fact, Wilson was more realistic than any other signatory of the treaty in his understanding that only a Germany disarmed and pacified by republican government could eventually reenter a community of democratic and trading nations as a force for stability. The Americans at Versailles were far and away the best-informed delegation to the conference. Harold Nicolson, a British delegate at Versailles later wrote that "had the treaty of peace been safely drafted by the American experts, it would have been one of the wisest as well as the most scientific ever devised."[45] But Wilson was forced into compromises at Versailles due to the revanchist sentiments of the French and British governments, which were themselves enhanced by Berlin's less than repentant attitude to the conflict just concluded. And many of the same Europeans who admired the American delegation's thoroughness also reflected that it all might have turned out better if Wilson himself had remained in Washington. He was driven, in their view, by the conceit that his calling at Versailles was as "the representative of the Great Dumb People," a prophet of the rights of men whose principles the representatives of states could not legitimately oppose.[46] This self-appointed status made the European statesmen draw back. Wilson did not speak their language. The doctrines of self-determination and collective security "put European diplomats on thoroughly unfamiliar terrain"; for them "alliances were formed in the pursuit of specific, identifiable objectives, not in the defense of peace in the abstract."[47] The European leaders had come to this day on the fuel of their own folly, but the war had bled their nations white and they were in no mood for what seemed to them the inflated rhetoric of a puffed-up American schoolmarm.

And yet Wilson's responsibility for the conference's failings emanated less from a flawed vision of the future international relations recorded in his famous Fourteen Points than from critical mistakes in attempting to implement it. Before leaving for Europe he had given the provisional German government, headed by Prince Max von Baden, to believe that Washington would not back a settlement that was particularly punitive toward Germany. Yet at the same time his Special Envoy to the Allied Supreme War Council, Colonel Edward House, was in secret contact with the French and British governments, both of which expected comprehensive compensation for the costs of the war. Wilson never really addressed the yawning gap between the Allies' demands and the peace Germany had come to expect. Because a series of spontaneous revolts swept a republican government into power in Berlin in the meantime, the representatives of the democratic Weimar Republic faced in Paris much harder terms than were expected in the form of a *fait accompli*, and Germany's first democratic government bore the stigma, mostly unjustified, for having sold out the country to an Allied *diktat*. Both House, and Wilson's Secretary of State, Robert Lansing, were routinely distressed over their President's imprecision.[48] Compounding the diplomatic weak footing of the new democratic German government were the reparation payments heaped on by the Allies. Though Wilson thwarted France's demands for a truly enormous reparation bill, he compromised on the sum of reparations Germany was to pay and on provisions for their administration, when he should have opposed a financial indemnity altogether. Admittedly, the failure to bring home financial booty almost certainly would have hurt the reelection chances of the Allied governments in particular, but as it turned out the hobbling of the German economy in the 1920s undercut the political viability of the Weimar Republic and ultimately imperilled European peace at its strategic center. We don't know that Germany would not have turned to fascism anyway, but we do know that the Versailles settlement aided Nazi electoral fortunes immeasurably.

Wilson believed he could moderate the implementation of the Paris Peace and therefore the political consequences any agreements that violated the principles of the Fourteen Points, above all through American leadership in the League of Nations. Once it became obvious that continuing American involvement in the new order could not be assumed, Wilson's blueprint for European peace was altogether at the mercy of luck and the proven folly of European diplomacy. Wilson, in fact, was more of a politician than his many detractors assume. He made compromises at Versailles, above all because he understood that any treaty is a piece of paper the substantive meaning of which unfolds over time depending on the interpretation of the treaty's articles by its signatories. He expected passions in Europe to cool, so that what was not possible one day might well be the next. He came to focus his efforts on the League, because he deemed it to be the vehicle through which American leadership toward a just European peace could operate. Lastly, he expected to be around himself to provide that leadership.

The truly benighted idealists were to be found among American liberal commentators who rejected the half-loaf Wilson brought home as worse than no loaf at all. Isolationists, on the other hand, attacked the implied compromise of sovereignty featured in Article Ten, thinking themselves sober realists because they understood that the essence of effective foreign policy is self-interest. In their own way they were as immature as the Wilsonian liberals, because they in essence would not admit that in 1919 there was a power vacuum in Europe that was in part America's to fill. A determination to spread American ideals through engaged diplomacy was the better part of self-interest. To be sure, Wilson's own tendency to treat self-interest and morality as mutually exclusive categories, an unfortunate progressivist habit, reinforced the prejudices of both antitreaty camps. But his understanding of the condition of world politics in 1919–20 was fundamentally sound and in many respects more realistic than that of his critics.[49]

The most important defeat came at home, in the Senate's rejection of the Versailles peace and the whole principle of international organization. The tradition of isolationism had always been Europhobic, and the American perspective on Europe in 1919 seemed to confirm the veracity of Washington's Farewell Address. The Paris concessions to the complexities of European diplomacy alone offered Wilson's Senate adversaries numerous angles of attack. The treatment of Germany was too punitive. The treatment of Germany was too lenient. Why should the United States back Italy against the legitimate claims of Germans and Slavs? Could not the principle of territorial sovereignty be used by Britain to thwart the republican aspirations of the Irish? Was it not true that under Article Ten the United States was committed to preserve against territorial aggression the integrity and independence of all members of the League? Wilson argued that such a commitment was essentially moral, but even senators who defended the tradition of arbitration, conciliation, and codification of international law wanted neither a legal nor a moral amendment to the historical American refusal to enforce any of these processes. There was also sheer inflexibility and malice on both sides of the debate. Henry Cabot Lodge, Chairman of the Senate Foreign Relations Committee, personally detested the president and used the committee and its Republican majority as a podium for every form of denunciation, eventually conjuring a cruel list of Fourteen Reservations, the most important of which sought for Congress the right to second-guess any American move to defend a victim of aggression. At Lodge's side was a chorus of irreconcilables—James Reed of Missouri, Miles Poindexter of Washington, William Borah of Idaho, Frederick Hale of Maine, Albert Ball of New Mexico, Philander Knox of Pennsylvania—steeped in both ignorance and prejudice, who would likely have opposed the treaty in any form. Wilson himself contributed to the defeat with the combination of his failing health, which dulled his faculties and drained his energies, but also with the intellectual hauteur he carried with him at the best of times. In the country and in the Senate there was a potential majority for the cultivation, but Wilson never took up the task. Instead, he turned to the great vanity of progressivism, that of moral superiority, and dismissed even his more open-minded Senate opponents contemptuously as "bungalow heads" avoiding any discourse with them "for fear they might corrupt his ideas."[50]

So Wilson's best hopes were dashed at home and abroad, because "the people of Europe were more vindictive than [he] had anticipated and those of America less generous than he had hoped".[51] There's a lot to this. Yet the real flaw of the treaty was that it attempted too much at precisely the wrong time. For the Europeans the nineteenth century was in 1919 coming to its violent end, and alas all of them were losers. The continent was racked by sweeping economic dislocations and ideological dementia of every imaginable form, the direction of which was difficult to discern, much less influence decisively. The Europe Wilson approached with his reasoned blueprint for a stable international order was in state of political delirium. Even with a shorter list of principles, as one biographer sees it, he would have been attempting to harness lightning.[52] In other words, Wilson's plans were defeated, not deluded. The battle might have been rejoined even after the Senate rejected the treaty 38 votes to 53, but Wilson's health never recovered. For a generation neither did the idea that the enormous economic heft of the United States could be mobilized to defend free trade, stabilize German democracy, or better yet, remake the Old Continent in America's image.

Part of the Old Continent, of course, was already being remade by the Bolshevik Revolution. Between 1918 and 1920 Wilson had sent 10,000 troops to help the Allies in their attempts to topple Lenin's government, and a subtext of the Paris conference had been Western attempts to isolate the newly founded Soviet state by creating a *cordon sanitaire* out of Rumania, a recreated Poland, and the new states of Czechoslovakia and Yugoslavia. Diplomatic developments themselves put Lenin's government in a suspicious light. In the 1918 *Treaty of Brest-Litovsk* Russia and Germany reached a separate peace that conceded the latter victory in the east and allowed Berlin to commit more troops to Germany's western front. In the United States rumors circulated to the effect that Bolsheviks were in fact puppets of the Kaiser in a diabolical endgame to the war. Then the postwar domestic scene at home was rocked by labor unrest, strikes, and anarchist bombings, very few of which could actually be traced to Socialist or Bolshevik plotters. As the paradise of international socialism, however, the Soviet Union was cast in a sinister role of an ideological enemy. Though at the time many of the caricatures of the Bolshevik regime were overwrought, the popular conviction that the Soviet state was a living refutation of every American ideal was altogether accurate, and in due time Soviet socialism lived up to its reputation for brutality. In the meantime, it provided for the Red Scare, a brushfire fear that the country's social peace was being subverted by aliens and a nativist mania for associating individuals with foreign connections with "unAmerican" activities.[53] In terms of international relations and the domestic politics thereof, the United States was in 1920 experiencing a first instalment on the Cold War.

The scare subsided quickly enough but the same could not be said for the conviction that the war to make the world safe for democracy had been for nought. Apparently, democracy was more imperilled than ever. This alone helps to explain the desire to return to domestic concerns and leave Europe to stew in its corrupted peace. From the domestic perspective Wilson's plan seemed to radically alter the course of American foreign relations, so it was defeated by tradition and the separation of powers, then in final repudiation in the presidential election of 1920.[54] But the world had not heard the last of Woodrow Wilson. The principles he articulated at Paris have had an impact on American diplomacy and international affairs profound enough to qualify him as one of the great figures of the century now drawing to an end. The advocacy of free trade and international rule of law as foundations for global peace rank among the noblest contributions the United States has made in the name of global peace and the triumph of democracy.

From the retrospective of the 1990s, the same cannot be said for the principle of national self-determination, the legacy of which has been routinely pernicious with regard to respect for fundamental human rights and individual freedoms. Implicitly at least, Wilson envisaged the opening of European colonial peoples to the penetration of American commerce; their acceptance of liberal values; and their ultimate attainment of self-government. Even at the level of principle, however, national self-determination was always open to a variety of interpretations, and it is hard to disagree with Wilson's Secretary of State, Robert Lansing, that the ideal was then and is now "simply loaded with dynamite."[55] Self-determination has so often been drummed into the cause of ethnonationalist movements, with entirely sinister intentions and murderous results, that one wonders whether a resurrected Wilson would not prefer to see it struck from the business of Paris altogether.

With Wilson the progressive movement reached its high water mark with the American electorate, possibly with his very election in 1912. By the time Wilson's plans for European peace were thwarted his ballot base at home was in a state of serious erosion. He had accomplished a good deal. His reduction of trade tariffs represented a significant amendment to the protectionist policies championed above all by Republican administrations since the Civil War. In building a legislative coalition for the initiative in Congress, he rightly argued not only that tariffs were an immoral tribute to economic privilege but that the U.S. economy had outgrown protection in any event, that American enterprise and agriculture could compete successfully in open market. The *Federal Reserve Act* of 1913 was an especially coherent reform of the nation's banking system, blending public authority with private control. The *Clayton Antitrust Act* of 1914 was a real improvement on the *Sherman Act* of 1890 in that it made corporate officers individually responsible for the violation of business law; facilitated civil suit procedures for injured parties; and included a clearer definition of unfair business practices such as undercut the conservative Supreme Court's ability to interpret ambiguous wording to favor the trusts. Wilson pushed through overdue reforms on behalf of labor and agriculture; he gave rail workers an eight-hour day; he increased federal spending for highway and education.

His presidency witnessed some of the most laudible and most ridiculous of Progressive reforms. In 1920 the Nineteenth Amendment gave the vote to women, thus capping the efforts of generations of suffragettes to secure the most elementary passport to the nation's body politic. Before being rewarded with the vote for their own contribution to the Century of Total War, women's organizations had played a prominent role in the pacifist cause. It was almost as if they were finally recognized as full citizens only when they had diverted their energies from the prevention to the prosecution of military conflict. The Eighteenth Amendment a year earlier echoed the preference of some twenty-six states for moral renewal by denying Americans the right to drink. Just in time for the troops returning from Europe, federal lawmakers "swallowed without a murmur an act that challenged all the ancient war cries about individualism, personal choice, family responsibility, and local option."[56]

Denouement: The Death of the Grand Old Prosperity

The election of a Republican administration in 1920 was seen by a good many progressives as some form of mental lapse in the electorate. In fact the Republican Party of 1920 was a much more united force than it had been in over a decade, while the Democrats were in a confused state about how to deal with their faltering leader, before at last replacing him with James Cox in the forty-fourth ballot of their party convention. But there was also a widespread reaction to Wilson and Wilsonism, to New Freedom and internationalism. A cynic might have said at the time that the only thing more universally loathed than a politician who breaks his promises is a politician who attempts to keep them. The progressive movement itself was fragmenting at precisely the point where the public found itself resenting wartime regimentation and privation, postwar inflation then recession, Wilson's foreign policy for its demands and limited dividends. When the GOP's nominee, Warren G. Harding, observed that "America's need is not heroics, but healing; not nostrums, but normalcy; not revolution, but restoration; not surgery, but serenity," sixteen million voters, set against nine million for Cox, agreed. [57]

If Harding's election had been made possible by fissures in the progressive coalition combined with a general fatigue with Wilsonianism, his nomination in the first instance was a product of truce between the GOP's internationalist wing, personified in Herbert Hoover, and anti-League nationalists such as William Borah, Hiram Johnson, and Henry Cabot Lodge, all stewing together in the stifling June heat inside the Chicago Coliseum, where the Republican convention was held. Unable to decide for one of the frontrunners at the convention, GOP delegates retired to Suite 404 at the Blackstone Hotel, the "smoke-filled room" of American political folklore, to arrive at a compromise. They ruffled through the names of candidates, in the words of Harding's biographer, "like a deck of soiled cards" and finally agreed on Harding because among them he had the smallest number of dedicated enemies.[58]

There could hardly have been a better advertisement for open primaries. In Harding's defense it could be said that he had been at least astute enough to build a broad second-tier base of influence in the party and that he was as representative of the spectrum of GOP opinion as anyone. What's more, Harding appeared to strike the right note when he called for a return to 'normalcy' during the campaign, by which he meant "a regular steady order of things", but which his fellow Republicans managed to translate into a code word for prosperity and an antonym for Wilsonian progressivism. In substance normalcy came to mean economy in government expenditure, new tariffs, lower taxes, reduction of the national debt, restrictions on immigration, and the *Budget and Accounting Act* of 1921. But Harding's administration itself was beset by corruption, the Teapot Dome affair of 1921 representing only the most spectacular of a litany of scandals. More generally normalcy referred to a restoration of the ideal of limited government and the legitimacy of *laissez-faire*, and it was Harding's successor, Calvin Coolidge, who presided over its consolidation.[59]

In Coolidge's case the word "preside" has a special appropriateness. For it was in the 1920s that the Republican commitment to the strictures of limited government, in reaction to the claims of Wilsonian government, completed the GOP's transformation from the erstwhile champion of a Hamiltonian vision of the Great Republic and of Lincoln's victory of the Union over states' rights into the party for which the extension of federal authority was henceforth anathema to the unique vitality American individualism was thought to give to the economy of the United States.

Progressivism ground to halt during the Coolidge years, not because of any negligence or laziness on the part of the administration, but because Coolidge himself was candidly hostile to the idea that government should or could influence decisively the economic fortunes of the people. When he offered that the chief business of the American people was business itself, he merely echoed a sentiment that for the fathers of the Constitution was so self-evident as to require no discussion when they set about the task of drafting rules for the functions of government. Coolidge thought that the kind of activist presidencies Woodrow Wilson and Theodore Roosevelt had run were mischievous enterprises to convince the people otherwise. So in practical terms a good many of the antitrust regulatory norms recently established were either overturned or ignored in the mid-1920s. Whether or not Americans agreed with every article of the Coolidge "Work and Save" philosophy, in a booming economy they found it easy to vote for him in a landslide presidential victory along with a Republican Congress in 1924.

The same preoccupation with domestic prosperity that made the Coolidge administration popular also precluded creative American diplomacy. True, Coolidge was not predisposed to new international initiatives in any event, but he was less an unabridged isolationist than "too canny a politician to brave dominant bias of the day, a complete intolerance of advance contracts for collective action."[60] His instincts regarding America's relationship with the world were reinforced by irreconcilables in Congress who were much more impassioned about American separateness than himself. Moreover, progressives and liberal internationalists in the 1920s represented an inwardly divided political opposition that completely mismanaged the advocacy of their cause. They took their cues from Woodrow Wilson's worst moments and came to identify isolationism with every variety of reactionary sentiment and lowbrow nativism. In fact, it was a wholly logical outlook of the small-town environment in which it was based, where voters were not concerned with international banking or debt readjustment and had been given no good reason to abandon the notion that America was prosperous because of its separate peace. Most isolationist Congressmen merely articulated this fact. Others, who were not isolationist, thought it equally legitimate that they represent majority opinion in the country. "If the people want to stay out and take the consequences," confessed the internationalist Democrat Newton Baker on the issue of League membership, "I want to make common lot with them."[61] Beyond the hard reality that they lived in a democracy, lastly, Wilsonians often seemed oblivious to the fact that a good many of America's platforms had been simply unwelcome in Europe in 1919 and that Europeans could match Americans shrug- for-shrug in the habits of parochialism.

The Coolidge administration did undertake to reschedule Germany's reparations obligations by implementing the Dawes Plan in 1924, itself followed by the Young Plan in 1929. The Dawes Plan scaled back German reparation from $33B to $9B, which helped to improve the picture during the best years of the Weimar economy, 1923 to 1928, but there were limits on what the United States could or would do. Reparation had been set extraordinarily high in the first place because the Senate had refused to ratify the Treaty of Versailles, leaving the U.S. with no representative and no veto on the international reparations commission. Meanwhile both France and Britain used German reparations to pay off their own debts to the United States. Most Republicans agreed with Wilson that a healthy German economy was the best medicine for all Europe, but they refused to take the political risks to make economic diplomacy more effective. Instead, private bankers floated huge loans to Germany to help it through the reparations schedule, in effect loaning money to Germany that made its way via London and Paris back to Wall Street.

While Coolidge held to the faith that global commerce could provide the basis for lasting peace, he and other Republicans sought to keep business and politics apart. High-minded diplomacy was fine, but they balked at meaningful discussions in the tertiary zones of negotiations where the United States might be held to substantive commitments. The Washington Naval Conference of 1921 placed limits on the size of the navies of the United States, Britain, and Japan in ways that were advantageous to the United States and recognized America's dominant role in the Pacific alongside Japan. Republicans called it the greatest document for peace ever drawn, comforting themselves with the thought that the idea of arms limitation itself accomplished something for its achievement.

Turning to Europe specifically, American diplomacy opted again for high-minded half-measures in the 1928 *Kellogg-Briand Pact* (formally titled *The General Treaty for the Renunciation of War*). The agreement was the product of an initiative from the French Foreign Minister, Aristide Briand, who sought to draw the United States into a defense pact with France. It was also part of a step-by-step retreat from the terms of the Versailles settlement and France's disingenuous attempt to conduct an independent foreign policy during its military occupation of the Ruhr Valley in 1924, colored by a growing awareness that France, having miscarried its postwar diplomacy with the Weimar Republic, would need outside assistance for its defense.

Briand tried to limit the Coolidge administration's options of response through the use of open diplomacy, taking his message of peace and hope directly to the American people with the proposal that the two great democracies openly "outlaw" war. Politicians had made war, the People would make peace. It goes without saying that Coolidge wanted neither a defense pact and its attendant obligations nor to have to reject an idea of such unimpeachable wholesomeness. His Secretary of State, Frank Kellogg agreed, too that an agreement should stay clear of American neutral rights to trade with an aggressor. But the Republican Senate isolationist, William Borah of Idaho, matched Briand's cleverness with a set piece of Congressional cynicism and spared his president the difficulty of a choice. Borah transformed the Briand initiative into a multilateral declaration outlawing war, to which ultimately sixty-five states, including Italy and Japan, added their signature, that reserved the right to use of force in legitimate self-defense. Americans would happily smoke Briand's new pipe of peace, noted one congressional observer, once the Senate had ensured that "it would not interfere with the free use of tomahawks and hatchets."[62] Coolidge, understanding that under the terms of the final agreement the United States would remain obliged to nobody, defended American ratification and with other Republicans called it a *covenant*, a tribute to the sensibilities of progressives and internationalists. They had "outcovenanted" Woodrow Wilson.[63]

Their cleverness was all forgotten within months, with the onset of the Great Depression. It is a tribute to the cruelties of public life that Herbert Hoover, a man as qualified to be president as any politician of his time and who understood its problems better than most, was doomed to be identified with the disaster. He had worked for the Wilson administration during the war and subsequently headed the Commission for Relief, where he earned a reputation for concerted benevolent intervention on behalf of millions of starving European children. Because he was also militantly anticommunist and appreciative of the true potential of Bolshevism, he was furious at the continuing Allied blockade of Germany after the armistice of 1918 and its harmful effect for the economic environment into which German democracy was to be nurtured. Hoover had been a member of the American delegation at the Paris Peace Conference, where he was dismayed at the terms of the Versailles Treaty, said so, and was rewarded with Wilson's disdain for his efforts.[64] Undersecretary of the Navy Franklin Roosevelt, by contrast, thought Hoover so brilliant that he thought the United States could hardly have a better president.

As Secretary of Commerce in the Harding and Coolidge cabinets, he was clearly out of step with the spirit of his times, approaching his brief with an interventionist ethos and a belief in concerted government-business-labor cooperation that was in some respects similar to European corporatism.[65] His nomination to head the GOP ticket of 1928 was brought about mainly by the efforts of northeastern business and manufacturing interests who backed a platform in which tariff protection was still thought the font of all prosperity. Given the prosperity that accompanied the election of 1928, Hoover's easy win was no surprise, but the distribution of the vote revealed that the Democratic nominee, Alf Smith, the first Catholic to have that honor, had made serious inroads into metropolitan, industrial, foreign-born, and strongly Catholic constituencies. Because these changes positioned the Democratic Party so well for the electoral politics of the 1930s, the 1928 election can be considered a critical one with some of the structural features of an impending realignment.[66]

When the stock market crashed not one full year into Hoover's presidency, the full potential of realignment was hardly yet visible. Because the economy, in fact, did not collapse of one giant speculative hemorrhage, but seemed again and again about to be rescued by a series of aborted recoveries, the GOP actually won a vote of confidence in the 1930 congressional elections, even though losses in securities of every variety had by this time totaled in excess of $40 billion. Hoover convened meetings with leaders of the real economy—industry, labor, railways, utilities, and agriculture—and asked them not to cut wages or payrolls. When he maintained that the economy was fundamentally sound, he was clearly not just whistling in the dark. Although he considered the situation very grave, there were morsels of evidence in the winter of 1930 that he might be right. The adminstration expected the downturn to bottom out at some point in the summer of 1931.

When this did not occur, declining confidence in the basic strategy of attempting to maintain wages and hold employment was further damaged by an outflow of gold, rising interest rates, crashing bond prices and a run on the banks.

While it is true that Hoover ruled out direct relief, any description of his response to the crisis from this point on as *laissez-faire* is pure fantasy. He cut taxes drastically and increased government spending, running a deficit $2.2 billion in 1931 in an attempt to reflate the economy, and he initiated public works projects. In other words, he resorted to many of the stimulants that in the folklore of the New Deal were deemed revolutionary when Franklin Roosevelt tried them all over again. But with money tight and interest rates high, low confidence in the dollar spooked the government into shooting for a balanced budget in pursuit of confidence in federal credit and the currency. The 1932 *Revenue Act* witnessed the largest peacetime tax increase in U.S. history, which at a stroke made a hash of all Hoover's previous reductions. The best evidence that Hoover was too much the prisoner of Republican tradition to innovate his way out of the Depression, however, was his signature on the *Smoot-Hawley Tariff Act* of 1930, an act about which he had serious personal reservations. Small wonder given that it raised tariffs on dutiable items to an average of 60 percent and more than any other single act of policy essentially exported the depression to Europe, a more substantive form of isolationism than that undertaken in any court of high diplomacy. Combined with the other factors constricting demand, its effects were devastating. American exports to Europe dried up, business failures mounted, and unemployment soared to the nearly 25 percent in 1933. By that time Hoover had to face a reckoning with the electorate, and, though real wage rates had actually increased during his administration, it was the legions of those who had no wage at all that returned the verdict.

Just as the Democratic Party had been torn up by the issues of secession and slavery in the 1850s, the Great Depression was the shoal on which Republican dominance was wrecked for good, and possibly above all because Hoover allowed the party to reach just one more time for the policy that had once made it great, but that had become a fatal self-indulgence.

Notes

1 Robert Selph Henry, *The Story of Reconstruction* (Gloucester, Mass.: Peter Smith, 1963), pp. 4–5; J.G. Randall and David Herbert Donald, *The Civil War and Reconstruction*, (Lexington, Ky.: D.C. Heath, 1969), pp. 553–558.

2 Johnson was elected to the vice presidency in November 1864 by Republicans because they wanted to reward Southerners who had been loyal to the Union at the same time as they extended the Republican organization into the South.

3 John Hope Franklin, *Reconstruction after the Civil War* (Chicago: University of Chicago Press, 1961), pp. 150–169; Stanley Horn, *Invisible Empire: The Story of the Ku Klux Klan* (Montclair, N.J.: Patterson Smith, 1969).

4 Eric Foner, *Reconstruction: America's Unfinished Revolution, 1863–1877* (New York: Harper & Row, 1988), pp. 421–428.

5 Leonard D. White, *The Republican Era, 1869–1901* (New York: Macmillan, 1958), pp. 45–67.

6 James MacGregor Burns, *The Workshop of Democracy* (New York: Alfred A. Knopf, 1985), pp. 213–214; Joel H. Silbey, *The American Political Nation, 1838–1893* (Stanford, Calif.: Stanford University Press, 1991), pp. 227–229.

7 Silbey, *The American Political Nation*, p. 219 and pp. 227–228; Morton Keller, *Affairs of State: Public Life in Late Nineteenth Century America* (Cambridge, Mass.: Harvard University Press, 1977), p. 289; Samuel P. Hays, *The Response to Industrialism, 1885–1914* (Chicago: University of Chicago Press, 1957).

8 James Bryce, *The American Commonwealth*, 2 vols. (New York: Macmillan, 1911), II, pp. 112–113 and pp. 379–405; Oliver E. Allen, *The Tiger: The Rise and Fall of Tammany Hall* (New York: Addison-Wesley, 1993); William L. Riordan, *Plunkitt of Tammany Hall*, Terrence J. McDonald, Ed.(New York: Bedford Books, 1993).

9 James MacGregor Burns, *The Vineyard of Liberty* (New York: Alfred Knopf, 1991), pp. 83–84; Robert K. Merton "The Latent Functions of the Machine" and Joel A. Tarr, "The Urban Politician as Entrepreneur" in Bruce M. Stave Ed., *Urban Bosses, Machines, and Progressive Reformers* (Lexington, Ky.: Heath, 1972) pp. 27–37 and pp. 62–72.

10 Riordon, *Plunkitt of Tammany Hall*, p. 8.

11 Robert W. Cherny, *Populism, Progressivism, and the Transformation of Nebraska Politics, 1885-1915* (Lincoln: University of Nebraska Press, 1981) pp. 149-166; C. Vann Woodward, *Tom Watson, Agrarian Rebel* (New York: Oxford University Press, 1963).

12 Quoted from Harold U. Faulkner, *Politics, Reform and Expansion, 1890-1900* (New York: Harper Torchbooks, 1959), p. 115.

13 Silbey, *The American Political Nation*, pp. 232-234; Richard E. Welch Jr., *The Presidencies of Grover Cleveland* (Lawrence: University of Kansas Press, 1988), pp. 141-155; Horace Samuel Merrill, *Bourbon Leader: Grover Cleveland and the Democratic Party* (Boston: Little, Brown, 1957).

14 Richard Hofstadter, *The Age of Reform, From Bryan to FDR* (New York: Vintage, 1955), pp. 78-79. On Germany see Alexander Gerschenkron, *Bread and Democracy in Germany* (New York: Howard Fertig, 1966).

15 Burns, *The Workshop of Democracy*, pp. 275-286.

16 George E. Mowry, *The Era of Roosevelt and the Birth of Modern America, 1900-1912* (New York: Harper Torchbooks, 1958), p. 103.

17 Charles A. Lofgren, *The Plessy Case: A Legal-Historical Interpretation* (New York: Oxford University Press, 1987).

18 Lofgren, *The Plessy Case*, pp. 7-27 and pp. 196-208.

19 Faulkner, *Politics, Reform and Expansion*, pp. 208-209.

20 V.O. Key, *Politics, Parties, and Pressure Groups* (New York: Thomas Crowell, 1964), pp. 170-173; Walter Dean Burnham, *Critical Elections and the Mainsprings of American Politics* (New York: W.W. Norton, 1970) pp. 1-10 and pp. 71-90; James L. Sundquist, *Dynamics of the Party System: Alignment and Realignment of Political Parties in the United States* (Washington D.C.: Brookings, 1983) pp. 134-169.

21 Martin J. Sklar, *The Corporate Reconstruction of American Capitalism, 1890-1916: The Market, The Law, and Politics* (New York: Cambridge University Press, 1988), p. 35

22 Hofstadter, *The Age of Reform*, (New York: Vintage, 1955) pp. 132-135 and pp. 272-328; Idem, *The American Political Tradition* (New York: Vintage, 1954), pp. 186-205; Robert Caro, *The Years of Lyndon Johnson, The Path to Power* (New York: Alfred A. Knopf, 1983), pp. 32-39.

23 Variations on each are found in Robert Dallek, *The American Style of Foreign Policy: Cultural Politics and Foreign Affairs* (New York: Oxford University press, 1983), pp. 3-31; John Higham, *Strangers in the Land: Patterns of American Nativism, 1860-1925* (New York: Atheneum, 1966), pp. 77-87 and pp. 107-108; Ernest R. May, *Imperial Democracy: The Emergence of America as a Great Power* (New York: Harcourt, Brace & World, 1961).

24　H. Wayne Morgan, *America's Road to Empire:The War with Spain and Overseas Expansion* (New York: Wiley, 1965), p. 18; Ephraim K. Smith, "William McKinley's Enduring Legacy: The Historiographical Debate on the Taking of the Philippine Islands," in James C. Bradford Ed., *The Crucible of Empire: The Spanish-American War and its Aftermath* (Annapolis, Md.: Naval Institute Press, 1993), pp. 205–249; David F. Trask, *The War with Spain in 1898* (New York: Macmillan, 1981); Lewis L. Gould, *The Spanish-American War and President McKinley* (Lawrence: University of Kansas Press, 1982); Paul Kennedy, *The Rise and Fall of the Great Powers* (New York: Fontana, 1989), p. 318.

25　Joseph Smith, *The Spanish American War: Conflict in the Caribbean and the Pacific, 1895–1902* (New York: Longman, 1994), pp. 226–231.

26　Gould, *The Spanish-American War*, pp. 55–90.

27　Leon Epstein, *Political Parties in the American Mold* (Madison: University of Wisconsin Press, 1986), p. 140; J. W. Chambers II, *The Tyranny of Change: America in the Progressive Era, 1900–1917* (New York: St. Martin's, 1980), pp. 125–139; Kenneth Finegold, *Experts and Politicians: Reform Challenges to Machine Politics in New York, Cleveland, and Chicago* (Princeton, N.J.: Princeton University Press, 1995).

28　Sean Dennis Cashman, *America in the Age of the Titans: The Progressive Era and World War I* (New York: New York University Press, 1988), pp. 45–106; John Morton Blum, *The Progressive Presidents: Roosevelt, Wilson, Roosevelt, Johnson* (New York: W.W. Norton, 1980); Hofstadter, *The American Political Tradition*, pp. 206–237.

29　Quoted in Cashman, *America in the Age of the Titans*, p. 68.

30　Cashman, *America in the Age of the Titans*, p. 59; David Sarasohn, *The Party of Reform: Democrats in the Progressive Era* (Jackson: University of Mississippi Press, 1989), pp. 3–34.

31　John Morton Blum, *The Republican Roosevelt* (Cambridge: Harvard University Press, 1954), p. 86; Burns, *Workshop of Democracy*, pp. 335–336.

32　Howard K. Beale, *Theodore Roosevelt and the Rise of America to World Power* (Baltimore, Md.: Johns Hopkins University Press, 1956), pp. 38–39, 56–57 and 328–329.

33　Henry F. Pringle, *Theodore Roosevelt* (New York: Harcourt, Brace & Javanovich, 1956), p. 381.

34　John Allen Gamble, *The Bull Moose Years: Theodore Roosevelt and the Progressive Party* (Port Washington, N.Y.: Kennikat Press, 1978).

35　Blum, *The Progressive Presidents*, pp. 50–51.

36　Arthur Link, *Woodrow Wilson and the Progressive Era, 1910–1917* (New York: Harper & Row, 1954), pp. 22–24.

37   Woodrow Wilson, *The New Democracy*, 2 vols., Ray Stannard Baker and William E. Dodd, Eds. (New York: Kraus Reprint, 1970), Vol.I, pp. 371–372.

38   Quoted in Hofstadter, *The Age of Reform*, p. 262.

39   Ernst A. Breisach, *American Progressive History: An Experiment in Modernization* (Chicago: University of Chicago Press, 1993), p. 104; Sklar, *The Corporate Reconstruction of American Capitalism,* pp. 427–430; George E. Mowry, *The Era of Theodore Roosevelt* (New York: Harper & Row, 1958), pp. 234–236.

40   Quoted in Sklar, *The Corporate Reconstruction of American Capitalism,* p. 405.

41   Arthur S. Link, *Wilson: Campaigns for Progressivism and Peace, 1916–1917* (Princeton, N.J.: Princeton University Press, 1965) pp. 290–339.

42   Franciszek Draus, Ed. *History, Truth, Liberty: Selected Writings of Raymond Aron* (Chicago: University of Chicago Press, 1985), p. 67.

43   Frank Freidel, *Franklin D. Roosevelt: The Apprenticeship* (Boston: Little, Brown & Company, 1952) pp. 220–235 and 268–269.

44   Quoted in David Steigerwald, *Wilsonian Idealism in America* (Ithaca, N.Y.: Cornell University Press, 1994), p. 37.

45   Harold Nicolson, *Peacemaking 1919* (New York: Grosset & Dunlap, 1965), p. 28. Another British representative, John Maynard Keynes, thought that only Herbert Hoover had an understanding of "the true and essential facts of the European situation," which, had others in attendance shared, "would have given us the Good Peace." See *The Economic Consequences of the Peace* (New York: Harcourt, Brace, & Howe, 1920), pp. 54–55.

46   Nicolson, *Peacemaking 1919*, pp. 52–53.

47   Henry Kissinger, *Diplomacy* (New York: Touchstone, 1994), p. 222.

48   Arthur Walworth, *America's Moment: 1918, American Diplomacy at the End of World War I* (New York: W.W. Norton, 1977), pp. 117–118.

49   Robert Endicott Osgood, *Ideals and Self-Interest in American Foreign Relations* (Chicago: University of Chicago Press, 1953), pp. 298–304; Arthur S. Link, *The Higher Realism of Woodrow Wilson and Other Essays* (Nashville, Tenn.: Vanderbilt University Press, 1971), pp. 138–139.

50   Cathal J. Nolan, "Woodrow Wilson, German Democracy, and World Order," in Carl C. Hodge and Cathal J. Nolan Eds., *Shepherd of Democracy? America and Germany in the Twentieth Century* (Westport, Conn.: Greenwood, 1992), pp. 21–39.

51   Nolan, "Woodrow Wilson, German Democracy, and World Order," p. 37.

52   Kendrick A. Clements, *Woodrow Wilson, World Statesman* (Boston: Twayne, 1987), p. 212.

53   Higham, *Strangers in the Land*, pp. 222–233.

54   Burns, *Workshop of Democracy*, pp. 459–473.

55   N. Gordon Levin, Jr., *Woodrow Wilson and World Politics: America's Response to War and Revolution* (New York: Oxford University Press, 1968), pp. 247–249.

56   Burns, *Workshop of Democracy*, pp. 442.

57   Wesley M. Bagby, *The Road to Normalcy: The Presidential Campaign and Election of 1920* (Baltimore, Md.: The Johns Hopkins University Press, 1968), pp. 13–24; Donald R. McCoy, "Election of 1920," in Arthur M. Schlesinger Jr., et al., Eds., *The History of American Presidential Elections, 1789–1968*, 4 vols. (New York: McGraw-Hill, 1971), Vol. III, pp. 2349–2456.

58   Francis Russell, *The Shadow of Blooming Grove: Warren G. Harding in His Times* (New York: McGraw-Hill, 1968), p. 381 and pp. 355–396; also Randolph C. Downes, *The Rise of Warren Gamaliel Harding, 1865–1920* (Columbus: Ohio State University Press, 1970).

59   Robert K. Murray, *The Politics of Normalcy: Governmental Theory and Practice in the Harding-Coolidge Era* (New York: W.W. Norton, 1973).

60   Selig Adler, *The Uncertain Giant: American Foreign Policy Between the Wars* (New York: Macmillan, 1965), pp. 80–81.

61   Quoted in Steigerwald, *Wilsonian Idealism*, p. 103.

62   Robert H. Ferrell, *Peace in their Time: The Origins of the Kellogg-Briand Pact* (New Haven, Conn.: Yale University Press, 1952), pp. 66–83 and pp. 240–252.

63   Selig Adler, *The Isolationist Impulse* (New York: Collier, 1957), p. 214.

64   Arthur Walworth, *Wilson and his Peacemakers: American Diplomacy at the Paris Peace Conference, 1919* (New York: W.W. Norton, 1986), p. 394 and pp. 521–524.

65   Harris Gaylord Warren, *Herbert Hoover and the Great Depression* (New York: Oxford University Press, 1959), pp. 24–34.

66   Key, *Politics, Parties, and Pressure Groups*, pp. 530–531.

Chapter Three

New Deals at Home and Abroad

A disposition to preserve, and an ability to improve, taken together, would be my standard of a statesman. –Edmund Burke, *Reflections on the Revolution in France*

The New Deal was a revolution in the economy and government of the United States. The extended emergency of the 1930s itself brought new powers to the executive branch, to which the personal charisma and wartime diplomacy of Franklin Roosevelt added rising popular expectations of vigorous presidential leadership in public affairs. Such expectations, while wholly inconsistent with the reality of the President's constitutional powers, have ever since influenced profoundly the conduct of national public affairs in the United States. The Roosevelt era, 1932–44, also occasioned the emergence of the Democratic Party as the dominant partisan camp in American politics. At the polls a social coalition of multinational business and organized labor underwrote Democratic election efforts and pushed the United States toward the advocacy of global free trade after 1945. The 'business of America' was freed from the constraints of Republican isolationism and pre-Keynesian economic policy, and national government acquired a capacity in patronage and entitlement that it had never known before.

So runs a stock narrative of the presidency of Franklin Delano Roosevelt. As is the case with all durable narratives, there is a good deal of truth to these generalizations, but Franklin Roosevelt was both less and more that is commonly assumed. More specifically, the bald assertion that "Roosevelt's claim to greatness must rest on his achievements in domestic affairs"[1] is hard to square with the substance of his achievements in foreign relations before and during World War II. The New Deal did bring sweeping changes to American government. These changes were generally furthered and consolidated over the presidencies of Truman through Nixon. In the grim economic weather of March 1933, however, Roosevelt had little idea where to begin with the project of returning the nation to economic health. He knew that the political economy of industrial capitalism in United States and Europe was a shipwreck. He also understood that for Americans the blow to the national psyche was in many ways particularly profound, because free enterprise was a national article of faith, a badge of Americaness. The democratic instincts of his countrymen made them less vulnerable to Marxist utopianism and fascist cynicism than their European cousins whose spirit had been broken in World War I, but their confusion and despair was no less overwhelming because of their fundamental pragmatism. The very same pragmatism made Americans wary of involving their country in the deepening international crisis of the interwar years, but their President's political instincts ultimately convinced them to think differently. It turned out to be a sound match, the Depression generation and the aristocrat of Hyde Park. Together they made the United States a colossus among nations.

Initial Innovations

Of the half million congratulatory letters Roosevelt received after his electoral triumph, the one that offered that "people are looking to you almost as they look to God" was possibly the most accurate.[2] The most substantive measure of the popular bet placed on the new president was in the electoral returns of 1932. The Republican Party, whose preeminence had been the most prominent feature of the American political landscape since the Civil War, was cut off at the knees. Presiding over the rout of his party was Herbert Hoover, probably the wisest Republican of his generation. Any other Republican would have been thrashed just as thoroughly. Roosevelt received 22,821,857 against Hoover's 15,761,841 votes and captured 472 electoral votes in 42 states against 59 in 6. It was a breathtaking victory by any measure, all the energies of progressivism, populism, and just plain panic lifting the Democrats in one great tide. Americans did not yet know Franklin Roosevelt but had handed him an enormous victory. You could call it a probationary landslide.

On the day of his swearing-in it was Roosevelt's fervent hope that he could deal effectively with the economic crisis without being particularly radical. His economic philosophy, the starting assumption of which was that only limited government action to stimulate a market economy was legitimate, was in many respects much the same as Hoover's; even one of Roosevelt's most adoring biographers observes that the key difference could perhaps be found in the new president's combination of "fuzzy altruism and wide ignorance."[3] If in 1933 he had a broad blueprint for reform, it was at best sketchy. It was also carefully concealed in order to undercut the chances for preemptive critiques. But he was not without experience, and as a politician Franklin Roosevelt never yielded to the argument that one had to fully understand a problem before one could move against it. His great political strength, furthermore, was that he could convey a sense of movement. Whereas Hoover had been unable to give the populace a clear picture of what he was trying to accomplish, Roosevelt "was often able to suggest a clear line of policy when none in fact existed."[4] For Roosevelt it was the political moment, not the intellectual ripeness, that mattered. Too often academic students of politics use the word "opportunism" to suggest a lamentable lack of intellectual coherence or ethical principles in the conduct of political leadership. But opportunism is a primary ingredient of effective statecraft. Roosevelt was a shameless opportunist, and no less a responsible president for it. He had an agile mind, could turn an apt phrase, and he appreciated that, in the nation's current circumstance, national morale building had to figure prominently among his highest priorities. He also knew that plain bad luck had handed his predecessor an unusually harsh verdict and that winning the confidence of the People, by whatever means, was the prerequisite for ultimately accomplishing something substantive on their behalf.

Just what that something should be was a problem. Roosevelt did not arrive in the Oval Office with a briefcase of original ideas, and much of his early legislation consisted of warmed-over Hoover initiatives. The *Loans to Industry Act* and *Emergency Banking Act*, both of 1934, belonged to this category, as did the *Home Owners' Loan Act* of 1932, the *Sale of Securities Act* of 1933, the *Securities Exchange Act of 1934*, along with the banking legislation of 1933 and 1935. As governor of New York State Roosevelt had served an apprenticeship in depression crisis-management. Hoover's struggle with the crisis had told him not that the outgoing administration had acted according to the wrong principles, but that, whatever principles were applied, Washington would have to act with vigor and, in a sense, be willing to risk spectacular failure if it were to succeed at all.[5]

Much of what he tried did fail dismally. *The National Industrial Recovery Act* (NIRA), which in early 1933 established the National Recovery Administration (NRA), was declared unconstitutional by the Supreme Court in 1935, but by then its political support had broken down anyway. The NRA established committees of business leaders essentially to orchestrate the terms of market competition among themselves. It gave them government sanction for price agreements and production quotas, but differently situated business representatives found it difficult even to reach agreement in principle, while those agreements that were achieved proved impossible to enforce. At the same time, the Recovery Act seemed to move the country in the direction of more forthright recognition of labor representation, yet was so vaguely worded it provoked rather than placated trade unions. The Supreme Court's invalidation of the act had broader implications. In *Panama Refining v. Ryan, Perry v. the United States,* and *Railroad Retirement Board v. Alton Railroad Company* the justices had already returned predominantly negative verdicts on the constitutionality of many items in the New Deal's first wave of legislative initiatives. In a 9–0 vote against the government in *Schechter Poultry Corp. v. the United States, 295 US 495* (1935), however, both conservatives and liberals on the Court found that Congress could not delegate to the executive branch legislative powers on any scale approximating the provisions of the NIRA, and added further that the government's attempt to regulate working conditions in a poultry firm could not, in any event, be squared with the Commerce Clause of the Constitution.

The Court's narrow interpretation of federal authority to regulate commerce, in particular, struck at the trial-and-error logic of Roosevelt's approach to national economic recovery during the first New Deal. The positive impact of a visibly interventionist government on national confidence could sustain the administration only so long. At some point Roosevelt needed some indication of the substantive impact of his policies, yet it appeared the Court would not let any policy survive long enough to produce a discernible result. "The implications of this decision," intoned an aroused chief executive, "are much more important than any decision probably since the Dred Scott case," and thus declared war both on the Court and on its Jeffersonian philosophy of federal prerogative. In newspapers and press conferences he pounced on every opportunity to ridicule the Court's "horse and buggy" understanding of the needs of a twentieth-century economy and to denounce its attempt to thwart Washington's "effort to make a national decision based on the fact that 48 sovereignties cannot, in our belief, agree quickly enough or practically enough on any solution for a national economic problem or a national social problem."[6] The Court, of course, was only doing what is arguably the most important aspect of its job, holding Congress and president to the Constitution's understanding of limited government, according to which the popularity of a policy itself makes no case for its legitimacy. For his part, Roosevelt was making a whipping boy of the Court in in order to stir up an atmosphere of popular creative anger and thus deepen popular support for his administration. The nation was in a fight, and for its new president there was no political percentage in appearing to be less fed up than the average American. If the Court offered itself as a sparring partner, so be it. Whether or not they fully appreciated it, Roosevelt's reaction to the Recovery Act decision indicated that under this president the Democrats were about to transform themselves into Hamiltonians, advocates of powerful federal authority, just as the Republicans had under Lincoln, McKinley, and Teddy Roosevelt. Admittedly, this was no overnight development;

many of the foundations had been laid by turn-of-the-century progressivism and by the prewar agenda of the Wilson administration, but the metamorphosis was now in full momentum. Roosevelt himself didn't know where it was taking him. He was feeling his way.

Agriculture figured prominently in the first phase of this process. Roosevelt sponsored and Congress enacted the first *Agricultural Adjustment Act* (AAA) in 1933, which essentially insulated farmers from the market with an array of price-supports and production quotas. It belonged to the famous "First One Hundred Days" of the new administration and was motivated partly by the mythological status of the American family farm; also by the government's awareness of the volatile potential of rural penury since Shays' Rebellion and the populist revolts of the late last century; but not least of all by the conviction that by restoring a balance between agriculture and other sectors of the economy by enhancing rural consumption the government could provide American business with a more stable home market.[7] It raised food prices for the average urban consumer and may have actually delayed the general recovery, but the first New Deal was an exercise in choosing between risks and then dealing with their fallout. Massive public works projects such as the Tennessee Valley Authority (TVA) and rural electrification were also products of the first New Deal that were especially beneficial to the agricultural economy. The public-works approach to enhancing employment was not altogether original. The idea had acquired legitimacy among some economists in the 1920s, and Hoover had asked Congress for $100 to $150 million for public works in December 1930.[8] With Roosevelt public works came to provide the central thrust of the early New Deal, though Roosevelt himself never really planned it that way. Public works projects offered two critical poltical merits: they were the kind of high-profile government intervention that won votes, and they permitted the administration to proceed on an ad hoc basis and thereby keep its opponents off-balance, forever guessing at Roosevelt's next move even as he guessed himself. Beyond this, it was the task of financing public works that broke the president's strong philosophical attachment to the principle of budget-balancing. In the 1932 campaign, after all, he had attacked Hoover over his apparent abandonment of fiscal orthodoxy, and in 1934 he announced a balanced budget by mid-1936 to be a "a definite objective."[9] However, when in May 1933 Roosevelt asked Congress for $3.3 billion "to be invested in useful and necessary public construction and at the same time put the largest number of people to work," he set a new course for American fiscal policy and abandoned the symbol of the balanced budget as a categorical imperative.[10]

In the greatest industrial economy on earth, no political strategy that left labor at the margins of public policy could hope to succeed. The disastrous consequence of Germany's failure to square labor with business interest was by 1933 already sitting in the Chancellory in Berlin, while in Britain the trade unions had destroyed the Labour government of 1931.[11] The Democratic Party of the early 1930s profited at the polls primarily because of the disintegration of a Republican electoral coalition that had endured more or less since the election of 1896. It did not make substantial progress toward building an alternative Democratic majority until the mid-1930s, when Roosevelt combined landmark labor reform with social welfare and a free-trade platform that appealed especially to capital-intensive industries, discarding protectionism along with political support of many of labor-intensive industries it helped sustain.[12]

The signal for a leftward shift of the administration's policies came from the congressional elections of 1934. Just when key officials were resigning from a government they thought in total disarray, the voting public returned 322 House representatives from the president's party, up from 313 in 1932, and bolstered Democratic strength in the Senate from 59 to 69. Democrats captured a handful of governorships as well. The result defied the more usual electoral rhythm of American politics, according to which an administration can count on a loss of congressional strength at midterm. In 1934 Roosevelt's congressional base actually broadened despite the fact that he had achieved very little. Part of the explanation, surely, lay in the improved state of the economy late in the year, but equally important was the public's approval of Roosevelt's insistent optimism and of the many things their unremittingly active oresident *appeared* to be doing.[13] He had their attention, and they turned up the volume.

They had good reason. Roosevelt's rhetorical reaction to the Court's decision on the NRA had been to deride its understanding of interstate commerce as quaintly nineteenth century. His substantive reaction was to apply the whip to his congressional majority, telling the Democratic leadership that the passage of certain bills was simply imperative. Among them, the *National Labor Relations Act*, better known as the Wagner Act, represented a landmark in American labor legislation. Roosevelt himself was not particularly prolabor in his approach to industrial relations, nor was he warm to the substance of the labor reforms contained in the initial bill sponsored by Senator Robert Wagner of New York. But Wagner's initiative tapped into ideas most coherently expressed by Alexander Sachs, an economist formerly with Lehman Brothers, according to which the Depression had been in part a product of the failure of a corporate imagination made sickly by the doctrine of laissez-faire. The right to collective bargaining, Sachs reasoned, could introduce stability to industrial wages, while rising wages enhanced mass consumption and aggregate demand in the economy. Strikes across the country in 1934–35 had already shaken management's confidence in its right and ability to cope effectively with labor unrest, so the time had possibly come for Washington to broker a new understanding between capital and organized labor that strengthened the position of the latter while delivering more stable labor relations to the former. Wagner's bill passed the Senate in June 1935 by a surprising 63 to 12 margin and then cleared the House when Roosevelt changed tack and casually announced his support for it at a press conference.

Roosevelt's personal reputation as a champion of labor is somewhat ironic given his attitude toward the bill up to the very moment of truth, but the Democratic Party nonetheless began to realize political dividends immediately. Roosevelt had not wanted to commit the White House openly for the Wagner initiative in part because of the probable political costs of alienating business. Still, business opinion in 1935 was something of a disappointment. Although corporate America was still furious over the NRA reforms, Roosevelt reasoned that many of his early reforms had generally done more for business than either agriculture or labor, while economic indices in 1935 showed a healthy increase in industrial production. Business, he thought, should be more grateful. Ultimately, there was for the Democrats enormous potential in an electoral coalition of organized labor and international business, an alliance the party eventually was able to construct. But that was a long-term project, and in the heated atmosphere of 1935, with the reelection problem of 1936 already looming large, the incumbent obviously had to ask himself how many votes, after all, fit into a boardroom as compared to the shop floor.

Yet Roosevelt's reelection in 1936 was the result of much more than a cleverly reconstructed electoral coalition. In many respects the political weather of that year was even stormier than that of 1932, above all because of the nature and strength of conservative resistance to the New Deal reforms. Republican caricatures of the reforms as creeping socialism could be shrugged off; when Alf Landon, the GOP's presidential nominee, offered that he could answer the people's needs more effectively and cheaply than Roosevelt, New Dealers could as least interpret the remark as a Republican admission that those needs were legitimate. The Supreme Court was another matter. In January it voted 6 to 3 against the AAA crop control program, indicating again that it would accept economic regulation only from the state level of government. But the following June the Court foreclosed on that alternative, when it struck down a minimum-wage law in the state of New York. Justice Harlan Stone found himself on the dissenting side of both cases, and in the AAA decision counseled his colleagues to practice judicial forbearance. If the majority had merely wanted to underscore the majesty of the Court, they were perfectly within their rights to do so. If, on the other hand, they seriously sought to arrest the progress and political appeal of Roosevelt's reforms in election year 1936, they had committed a grievous error. When farmers in Ames, Iowa, hanged in effigy six figures in black robes,[14] Franklin Roosevelt was given a hint, both powerful and politically reliable as it turned, on how to approach the coming campaign.

The unofficial launch of his reelection bid took place at the rostrum of the House of Representatives with the 1936 State of the Union address. The speech is not remembered as one of Roosevelt's great occasions, but as a sample well-crafted

presidential rhetoric it is worthy of review. The incumbent
began by talking in grave tones about the deteriorating international situation. In anticipation no doubt of the coming demands on American foreign policy and a popular appreciation thereof, Roosevelt spoke in hemispheric terms about the
peace between the United States and its neighbors and then
warned that the time had come for the peoples of the Americas to acknowledge trends toward aggression and armaments
in both Europe and Asia. But foreign policy itself was hardly
at the center of Roosevelt's concern on that particular January
evening. Having warmed his audience, he then turned to domestic affairs and likened the machinations of power-seeking
minorities at home with the rise of totalitarian power abroad.
He invoked the memory of Jefferson, Jackson, Theodore
Roosevelt, and Wilson as crusaders against the claims of privilege, and then turned on the enemy of the moment, for whom
the Court seemed a willing errand boy:

> They steal the livery of great national constitutional ideals to serve
> discredited special interests. As guardians and trustees for great groups
> of individual stockholders, they wrongfully seek to carry the prop-
> erty and the interests entrusted to them into the arena of partisan
> politics. They seek—this minority in business and industry—to control
> and often do control and use for their own purposes legitimate and
> highly-honored business associations; they engage in vast propaganda
> to spread fear and discord among the people—they would gang up
> against the people's liberties.[15]

This form of take-no-prisoners class warfare was highly effective in 1936. There were, after all, still nine million unemployed
in the nation, and Roosevelt was soon to be judged on his own
performance rather than on the failure of the GOP. Although
much of the first New Deal had been badly conceived and in
some cases wrong-headed, national morale was on the upswing,
and reemployment was a statistical reality. Even those who were
sure that Roosevelt did not fully understand what he was doing, hardly thought it logical to reverse course in mid-experi-
ment. For many more there actually was something to fear
beyond fear itself, the Republican Party.

In 1936 the organizational assets of the Democratic Party
in the major cities began to pay serious dividends. The party's

urban coalition drew the support of new ethnic groups both for New Deal welfare measures and in gratitude for the astute dispensing of patronage. The high profile of Catholics and Jews among the administration's advisors relative to previous administrations, played well to two key components of the party's widening base. Catholic leaders in particular lauded the social conscience of the New Deal programs, while organizations such as the Lithuanian Roman Catholic Alliance of America, the Slovak Catholic Sokol of New Jersey, the Croatian Catholic Union of America, and the National Alliance of Bohemian Czech Catholics of America openly endorsed FDR's reelection. In 1936, moreover, the Democrats also made serious inroads into the black vote, largely a GOP preserve since the Civil War. The party that until 1924 had permitted no black American to participate formally in its functions now had black members in twelve of the state delegations. A forthright Democratic appeal to northern blacks was by 1936 in some respects more cost-effective electorally than an appeal to southern whites because of the big blocks of votes from northern cities now available in the electoral college, so the party was ready to accept marginal losses in the solid south of the Old Confederacy in order to reap benefits elsewhere. Landon's attempt to cut GOP losses came up against attacks on Republican states' rights principles by the National Association for the Advancement of Colored People (NAACP) and editorials such as that of the Baltimore *Afro-American* noting that "Abraham Lincoln is not a candidate in the present campaign."[16] The memory of emancipation alone could no longer justify the continuing Republican sympathies of black Americans, especially when so many of their constitutional rights had long since been stripped in a thousand ways of any meaning in the day-to-day conduct of their lives.

The election of 1936 consolidated the realignment of partisan choice inaugurated in 1932, and then some. Roosevelt took the entire electoral map save Maine and Vermont, an electoral vote victory of 523–8, based on the largest presidential vote to that date. The Democratic Party meanwhile captured the largest House majority since 1855 and the largest Senate majority since 1869.

The Modern Presidency and the Modern Economy

Emboldened by the fact and dimensions of his reelection victory, Roosevelt resolved to handle the Supreme Court in much the same way as he had handled the GOP. Two weeks after the annual White House dinner for the federal judiciary, he announced his intention to seek authority from Congress to appoint a new justice to the Supreme Court, up to a maximum of six, for every justice who declined to retire at the age provided for by the law. Some form of court-stacking initiative had been on Roosevelt's mind for at least two years. Now, with a fresh electoral mandate and a pliant Democratic majority in Congress, he turned his energies directly against the obstruction which separated powers and conservative legal tradition had placed in the path of the New Deal's progress. His plan had the potential to increase the membership of the Court from nine to fifteen justices and thus to alter entirely its overall philosphical complexion. Roosevelt chose the court-packing route in the interest of stealth. A constitutional amendment necessarily involved a challenge to the very principle of separated powers; it also entailed a battle for two-thirds majorities in both houses of Congress and agreement from three-quarters of the state legislatures. Congressional legislation, he reasoned, would take less time and cost less political capital.

On the last calculation he got it wrong. Congressional Democrats, as it turned out, took separated powers and the Supreme Court's integrity more seriously than Roosevelt's desire to inoculate the New Deal against judicial veto. The Republican leadership shrewdly instructed their members not to take a principled stand against the president's initiative; were the court-packing issue to acquire a partisan quality, they argued, Democrats might close ranks behind their president and deliver the majority he sought. As it turned out, the congressional debate was as often as not one among Democrats, and it came to center on indignation that Roosevelt's postelection hubris assumed congressional acquiesence while his circuitous strategy cited the Court's "inefficiency" as the source of presidential concern. Senator Burt Wheeler of Montana was particularly skilled in attacking the Court bill before the Judiciary Committee, where he produced a letter from Chief Justice Charles Evans Hughes refuting as fallacious any suggestion that

Court was not dealing well with its caseload. When Roosevelt then changed tactics, and attempted to reframe the struggle in terms of the Court versus the People, the justices delivered a direct blow of their own: they affirmed the constitutionality of the Wagner Labor Relations Act 5 to 4, when they found in *NLRB v. Jones and Laughlin Steel Corp.* that Congress had every right to promote industrial peace when a company's economy of scale gave a labor dispute the potential to disrupt interstate commerce.

By the time the decision came down Roosevelt was already losing the congressional battle, but the Court's refusal to strike down the Wagner Act removed any hope that newly aroused progressive Democrats might at last come to Roosevelt's aid. The adminstration could not muster the votes.[17] The Wagner decision therefore validated a regulatory capacity for the national government that it had never before known, and did so with language that allowed for a good deal of discretion in the interpretation. For the administration the decision was both a victory and a defeat. A major piece of legislation had passed judicial review, but Roosevelt's great congressional majority had refused his orchestration.

The counterpart to the Wagner Act in the realm of redistributive powers was the *Social Security Act* of 1935, the most comprehensive welfare legislation in the history of the nation. The act provided pensions for the aged, unemployment insurance, public health appropriations, benefits to dependent mothers and children. As in the case of the NLRB, social security was in 1937 challenged in the Supreme Court and upheld in the case of *Helvering et. al. v. Davis*, wherein the majority opinion invoked the general welfare clause in the preamble of the Constitution (reiterated in Article I, Section 8). It found further that "the conception of spending power advocated by Hamilton [. . .] has prevailed over that of Madison" and that "discretion belongs to Congress," while "the concept of welfare or the opposite is shaped by Congress, not the states."[18] Thus, the definition of the nation's general welfare lay with Congress, the judgment of whose members clearly trumped the separate definitions of the state legislatures and the restraint of which, barring clearly arbitrary uses of authority, depended entirely on the wisdom of the members of Congress.

It is possible to argue that Roosevelt's court-packing ploy had actually intimidated the justices sufficiently to save the labor relations and social security legislation. Still, at least two of its members, Chief Justice Hughs and Justice Owen Roberts, had by 1937 already gravitated away from unqualified hostility to New Deal reforms. Whatever the philosophical or political reasons for the Wagner decision, the Supreme Court emerged from the packing episode with its form and dignity intact. Franklin Roosevelt was chastened and somewhat bewildered. He has lost the Court battle yet secured a legislative breakthrough for American labor with very little effort. The New Deal, it seemed, had established its own momentum.

That momentum varied from one theater of public affairs to another. Roosevelt's contribution to macroeconomic management was more modest than in labor rights. His personal encounter with the Cambridge economist John Maynard Keynes, whose *General Theory of Employment, Interest, and Money* was published in 1936, left him less than impressed. This may have had more to do with Keynes scathing criticism of Woodrow Wilson's inattention to economic issues at the conference at Versailles than with the substance of their conversation itself. Still, Roosevelt was instinctively cautious with regard to deficit spending for the purpose of increased domestic consumption. He found Keynes spending targets fantastic and opted for much more modest stimulation, returning to fiscal orthodoxy in 1937 with cuts in federal spending in an attempt to bring federal expenditures into balance with revenue. Still, even Roosevelt's modest spending met with fierce conservative criticism. However, by 1938 he had in principle made the critical commitment to the use of government fiscal and monetary capacity to manage the overall performance of the national economy. Deficit spending was henceforth a legitimate part of any national discussion of economic issues and integral to any calculation of the political implications of economic performance.[19]

The disposition of New Deal economic policy on economies-of-scale, industrial efficiency, monopoly, and corporate corruption essentially endorsed a Hamiltonian vision at the expense of Jeffersonian and Jacksonian tradition, yet it did so in a manner that was politically circumspect, when not brazenly doubled-tongued. Fresh from the Court battle, Roosevelt shifted his focus on conservative opponents in the Senate. The struggle over New Deal liberalism, he said, was essentially "a war between those who, like Andrew Jackson, believed in a democracy conducted by and for a complete cross-section of the population, and those who, like the Directors of the Bank of the United States and their friends in the United States Senate, believed in the conduct of the government by a self-perpetuating group at the top of the ladder"; it was sound rhetoric, but it defended an expanded regulatory state that, in the name of greater equality, administered to its people.[20] At the outset the Depression was blamed in large part on ossifying effects of concentrated economic power. Roosevelt's inaugural address, with its resonating denunciation of "unscrupulous money changers" and "a generation of self-seekers", essentially accused Wall Street of such spectacular incompetence as to have robbed the common man of even the possibility of gainful employment, let alone wealth. By the late 1930s, however, large business units and a more extensive government organization of economic exchange were again associated with abundance and a popular rising standard of living. A political realignment of business saw capital-intensive industries in particular move to support Roosevelt in the 1936 election against Landon's Made in America trade policies and the Smoot-Hawley legacy.

The key to long-term recovery was in broader economic horizons. So, while Roosevelt took the counsel of Beardsly Ruml of the Rockefeller Foundation and instructed his Secretary of State, Cordell Hull, to promote reciprocal trade agreements, segments of the corporate community hitherto hostile to the New Deal rethought their options and applauded when the Council on Foreign Relations funded a symposium where the journalist Walter Lippmann opined that freedom itself would probably perish without free trade.[21] Roosevelt never attacked the *Free Soil, Free Labor, Free Men* legacy of nineteenth-century Republicanism, because its political potency remained largely untouched by its defeat in the economic realm. Americans sought a more efficient industrial system that provided jobs and material wealth, but also one in which economic opportunity and individual human dignity was real. The Democratic

Party was now the party of the People, of internationalism, and free trade.[22] So while the antitrust tradition was in large part a loser in the New Deal's reconstitution of the American economy, there were inconsistencies in the administrations's rationalization of the economy that spoke to the gap between the People's ideal and Wall Street's reality. Because Roosevelt appreciated the importance of balancing the imperative of liberty with the goal of security, he understood as well that the right measure of inconsistency was the key to electoral survival.[23] Contemporary spin doctors refer to this as "triangulation," but no multisyllabic label can change the fact that finding a center-ground between conflicting principles is the oldest rule in electoral coalition-building in democratic politics. When in 1936 Alf Landon attacked Social Security and Wall Street defended it, it was apparent to any informed observer that something seismic was under way in American political partisanship.

All these developments favored, to varying degrees, the growth of federal executive authority in almost every realm of public affairs. To begin with, there was an unprecedented enlargement of the very ambit of government generally. With the Wagner Act and AAA government claimed altogether new regulatory capacities. Projects such as rural electrification and the TVA enhanced the federal power of patronage, while Social Security typified a host of initiatives featuring an essentially redistributive thrust.[24] With very few exceptions these new capacities strengthened the federal government's hand relative to the authority of the states. Indeed, it is with respect to federalism above all that the Roosevelt years qualify as revolutionary, for until the 1930s the states retained preponderant authority in all issues ranging from hours of work to factory safety, education, prisons, and even conditions of suffrage. In less than a decade the New Deal reversed this situation comprehensively, nationalizing government and handing state prerogative its most sweeping defeat since the Civil War. There was a dose of irony in this turn of events, since many of the states, FDR's New York not least among them, had been laboratories of reform in old-age pensions and unemployment insurance. The conditions of national economic depression and the inability of all but a handful of states to deal effectively with the requirements of recovery and social stability, how-ever, turned federal *grants-in-aid* into a principal vehicle for the realization of national policy through state governments.

Simultaneously, the balance of authority between the execu-tive and legislative branches of the federal government shifted rather dramatically as well. The Supreme Court's refusal to be little more than a spectator to this development was symbol-ized by its thumbs-down in the Schechter-NIRA case. Among other things, the justices objected most strenuously to the del-egation of congressional legislative power to the White House and federal bureaucracy, which they quite rightly condemned as out of step with the letter of the Constitution and the estab-lished tradition of congressional prerogative. Yet while the 1935 ruling invalidated the NIRA, scores of other delegations of legislative authority proceeded without any appeal to or ruling from the Court. Of course the Congress was never for-mally divested of its powers under the constitution, and con-gressmen retained the capacity, from one case to the next, to decide whether or not to delegate legislative powers. However, Congress acquiesced in the Roosevelt administration's project of adding wholly new dimensions of administrative preroga-tive to the White House and federal bureaucracy beyond those that existed before 1932.

Considered together with Franklin Roosevelt's approach to presidential duties under conditions of national economic emergency, the rise of Washington over the state legislatures and the rise of the executive branch within the federal govern-ment meant that henceforth popular assessments of the suc-cess or failure of democratic government in the United States generally were to ride on the performance of the president. It is hard to imagine that this transformation could have been as spectacular as it was without the imprint of FDR, the charis-matic crisis manager for twelve years of depression and war. It is incontestable that since Roosevelt "everybody now expects the man inside the White House to do something about every-thing"; this, of course, is impossible because no president can cope fully with the breadth of the post-Roosevelt executive responsibilities.[25] And yet they all must in some degree attempt just that. Presidents today are at the very least expected to have something to say, preferably something moving, on ev-

erything from ballistic missiles to broccoli. In a nation constituted like no other on the doctrine of limited government, a
president may never confess that there are things of which he
has no knowledge or other things about which he does not
care.

The Tides of Partisanship

Party leadership, certainly, figured prominently among those
things in which Roosevelt took little interest. On the face of it,
this is somewhat surprising, because the New Deal's vindica-
tion at the polls of 1936 completely changed the partisan balance of power in American politics. It gutted the Grand Old
Party of McKinley Republicanism and gave the Democrats a
remarkably durable majority with which to set the agenda of
public policy in the United States for the next four decades.
The New Deal was also a defining moment for many of those
who served or opposed that agenda. A popular argument is
that the New Deal actually cleaned up the Democratic Party,
because the welfare programs it inaugurated and the professional social workers it employed promptly shunted aside the
party precinct captains who had controlled patronage. But this
argument is hard to sustain in the face of the obvious prosperity of many urban machines over the course of the New Deal
years. Boston, Memphis, New Jersey, New York, Pittsburg, Kansas City, and Chicago prospered by way of the now greatly increased patronage resources made available by the New Deal,[26]
and Democrats of real consequence served their political apprenticeship in supporting Franklin Roosevelt even as the
bosses supported them. Harry Truman was a protegé of the
Kansas City Democratic organization of T.J. Pendergast. It was
Pendergast who called upon Truman to first run for the U.S.
Senate in 1934, and Truman was one of those who rode the
Democratic tide to Congress. When he left for Washington
Pendergast told the newly minted Senator Truman "work hard,
keep your mouth shut, and answer your mail."[27] . In the Senate
Truman supported the *Farm Tenant Act* and the AAA; he voted
for low-cost housing and increased public works, and civil avia-
tion regulation. By the late 1930s he was also saying that the
U.S. should sell all the war-making materials it could to the

British Empire. Lyndon Johnson did not have a machine in Texas to equal the Pendergast organization. In part he built his own, but was helped by Richard Kleberg of the wealthy King Ranch family of southern Texas, who ran for the Senate, won, and appointed Johnson his secretary. Johnson was subsequently appointed at age 27 as a Texas director for the National Youth Administration program. So zealous was he in pursuit of his duties that Roosevelt made him something of a personal interest, instructing White House aide Thomas Corcoran to funnel help to Johnson's electoral ambitions. During the first Hundred Days Johnson worked to sign up South Texas farmers for the AAA. Thinking of the Democratic Party's special organizational assets in the big cites, Republican Senator Arthur Vandenburg likened the Roosevelt government's spending initiatives to an attempt to "Tammanyize the whole United States," while Barry Goldwater later called the New Deal the darkest chapter in American politics and a betrayal of the whole concept of limited government. Averell Harriman, who originally despised Roosevelt for his populist tirade against Wall Street moneychangers, subsequently helped to bring Wall Street into the Democratic fold and became the walking quintessence of Roosevelt's internationalist diplomacy.[28]

What Republicans had kept until Black Friday was the incumbent orthodoxy, a philosophically sound doctrine of limited government that was caught flat-footed and run over by the economic crisis. The GOP leadership offered the people no practical alternative to Roosevelt's policies, complained Republican Senator William Borah of Idaho; instead, "they have offered the constitution—but the people can't eat the constitution." [29] Once events appeared to have refuted the orthodoxy, the particular organizational assets of the Democratic Party came to bear in the electoral struggle in a way they never had before. Even as the ground shifted beneath them, very few Republicans had any measure of the enormity of the change now taking place. In the early phase of the New Deal too many of them interpreted the Democrats' new vitality as a product of unique and temporary circumstance, scarcely appreciating that the New Deal was reconstituting American government in ways that were to bequeath durable advantages to their rivals. Borah was in some respects one of the most progressive Republicans of his generation, but the fact that his Senate seat was safe with the voters of Idaho meant that he was often utterly inflexible on anything he considered an issue of principle. The progressivist legacy was clearly evident in his inclination to translate political issues into moral causes, and what has been observed of Borah—that he "seemed to think that a declaration of justice was equal to the realization"[30]—was in the 1930s and for many years afterward all too true of good many others in the bewildered Republican camp. They opted for trench warfare.

In one important respect, perhaps, they had little choice. Roosevelt's social democracy was a revolution, constitutional, institutional, political, of the relationship between citizen and government in the United States. It had little of the explicitly ideological baggage of European social democracy, and for that reason, among others, did not encounter the backlash to a center-left political economy that occurred in France, Britain, and Germany, and which in the latter case imperilled European democracy itself. The New Deal was held to consist of a series of wholly pragmatic solutions to the economic crisis. But in the great mass of the body politic it eclipsed any notion that government could never be more than a necessary evil and made it into a font of state beneficence. It corrected a good many past imbalances and injustices, particulary in the new legitimacy it accorded organized labor, and for those most positively affected by its programs the New Deal would be remembered as a tribute to human decency. But given its philosophical rooting in the progressive movement going back to the 1890s, it was based on a set of assumptions about equality and democracy that collectively gave it enormous ideological heft, and its implications for the future of limited government in the United States were open-ended. Its pedigree was progressivist, but "instead of relying on moral castigation and the penalization of a few rascals to promote the public weal," it expanded federal powers and wielded them confidently, opening up government to everyone in principle yet inevitably favoring those who had the will and organization to conduct a continuing dialogue with Washington problem solvers.[31] Measured against the Founders' spartan expectations of the rights and obligations of self-governing American citizens, it was a radical departure. The Great Republic was acquiring a Leviathan appropriate to the size and sophistication of the American economy. But could it remain a republic that would be at all recognizable to those who had first conceived it?

At the very least it was to become a very different republic. For Roosevelt had deep roots in the progressive movement, and, though he was hardly given to ideological exposition, his was fundamentally a social democrat's understanding of the requirements of responsible government in the age of industrial capitalism. As early as 1912 Roosevelt had delivered a speech to the People's Forum, in which he championed "the liberty of the community rather than the liberty of the individual," evidence of the powerful influence of an apprenticeship in politics spent in the prewar Wilsonian cause.[32] In the name of collective goals, the New Deal changed the manner in which the levers of government were manipulated, but more importantly it added entirely new levers of federal authority.

Viewed as a national political force, the Democratic Party under Franklin Roosevelt become identified with all of this, the champion of interventionist liberalism and social progressivism. Viewed as an organization, however, it had in many respects not changed much at all. For American political parties are not the disciplined formations that are nurtured by the requirements of parliamentary government. They are best understood as political holding companies for a vast array of politically interested national, state, and local groups supporting the candidacy or incumbency of individuals for public offices, ranging from Senate seats and state governorships to city councilmen, sheriffs, and district attorneys. The extent to which they are united by common ideas, as opposed to party tradition and raw ambition, varies both in the local context and over time. But if there is a rule to party unity in the United States, it is, not surprisingly, that ideological unity becomes more fragile as the breadth and diversity of a party's electoral following grows.

So it was with the Democratic Party after the landmark victory of 1936. At the polls Democrats had profited mightily from Roosevelt's presidency, wresting both the Oval Office and the Congress from the grip of a Republican hegemony that had looked irreversible in the 1920s. But at its core the Democratic Party was an alliance of northern commercial and southern agricultural interests, to which its newly broadened electorate had added organized labor and capital-intensive business. Public works such as the TVA helped to keep the South solid, but a good many other aspects of the New Deal were anathema to conservative Democrats of the Old Confederacy who, after all, had their seat in Congress long before Franklin Roosevelt was sworn in as president. Roosevelt never moved on civil rights legislation for fear of alienating southern congressional leaders whose votes he badly needed, but the sympathy of the FDR White House for the plight of black Americans was well known and much despised in southern constituencies. Moreover, conservative Democrats more generally were a bigger problem for the administration after 1936 than the emaciated GOP. Roosevelt's failure to marshall two-thirds of the congressional vote for his court-stacking plan was in part a measure of his failings as a party leader. Bored by organizational matters, he had never attempted as president to rebuild the party around a solid mass base and a coherent platform. Instead, he had relied upon his enormous personal charm to get along with the party's regional barons—Walter George of Georgia, "Cotton" Ed Smith of South Carolina, Millard Tydings from Maryland, Alva Adams in Colorado, Pat McCarran in Nevada—up to the point where he considered them a threat to the legislative menu of the second New Deal, outlined in broad strokes in the inaugural address of 1937.[33] At that point he attempted not a reorganization but a purge.

The purge was launched in the spring of 1938 by a fireside chat in which Roosevelt attempted to bring presidential influence to bear on the primaries and elections for the Seventy-fifth Congress by stating his personal concern that those nominated and elected have the right general attitude to the practical national needs of the day. It was followed by sporadic appearances around the country in which Roosevelt looked to tilt congressional primary contests within the Democratic Party in favor of avid New Dealers and against conservatives in the party. The move was the result of discussion that had been under way for months within the administration, and it had the enthusiastic support of top administration appointees such as Harold Ickes, Tommy Cocoran, and Harry Hopkins. Not surprisingly, then, the purge involved the use of federal public works funding to help the more progressive candidates against old guard Democrats. The harvest of all these efforts was utter defeat. Local Democratic organizations nominated and elected whomever they liked; in South Carolina Ed Smith waged a white-supremacist campaign and won with it. Aided further by a recession in the fall of 1938, the Republicans compounded the failure by posting big gains in the November polls: 81 seats in the House, 8 in the Senate, 13 governorships. A subsequent probe of Hopkins' activities during the campaign ultimately produced the *Hatch Act* of 1939, prohibiting political activities by federal employees.[34]

At the root of the defeat of 1938 were forces pulling Roosevelt in opposing directions. On the one hand, New Dealers within the administration and progressives across the country thought the steam had gone out of Roosevelt's reform program; on the other, the much bigger but unreconstructed Democratic Party was home to some of the most conservative, even reactionary, sentiment in the nation. The president's somewhat cavalier delegation of authority, combined with his reluctance to reveal his strategy even to some of his closest advisors, did little to calm either conflicts between rival personalities within the administration or the fear common to all of them that radical third-party forces in the country could do serious damage to the Democratic coalition. There was some justice to their worries. Across the country, the Depression and the New Deal had torn a good many political loyalties loose of their moorings, but it was far from certain that the Democratic Party could capture and keep them. Populists and demagogues such as Huey Long of Louisiana, Father Charles Coughlin, and Nevada's Pat McCarren intermittently showed enormous electoral potential, especially when they played hard to class resentment on a platform of social justice. There was also the worry that the more radical agendas typified by the LaFollettes in Wisconsin and Minnesota or by Upton Sinclair in California might yet turn the Democrats' left flank and bleed away enough votes to give the Republicans a fighting chance. Worries of this variety informed the attempted purge and the desire to remake the party. But in 1938 the administration's true believers were out of touch with the mood of the nation more generally. If anything, the electorate, while still under the Roosevelt spell, was in a conservative mood. Even in the run-up to the great victory of 1936, discontented Democrats such as Al Smith and Dean Acheson disapproved publicly of the 'socialist' direction Roosevelt had taken. The congressional ballot of 1938, with its sharp shunt toward the Republicans could be taken at face value.[35]

Although Roosevelt had clearly failed as a party manager on the terms attempted in 1937–38, his greatest triumphs as a national leader were yet to come. In fact, the project he cut out for himself as president, even conceding that he had progressed more by intuition than design, was so huge that it is hard to see how he could have won three successive elections, redefined popular expectations of government, and revamped the Democratic Party at the same time. Roosevelt's redefinition of presidential leadership, after all, was of profound import to a whole national body politic of which the Democratic Party was just a part.

Because in the 1930s the political shift in power between branches of the federal government was overwhelmingly to the benefit of the executive, the character and skills residing at the apex of the executive branch acquired a new and profound importance to the popular view of government. Clearly, this would have been so even if a personality other than Franklin Roosevelt had occupied the White House for twelve years. Roosevelt's status as a great president, however, is much more than an accident of circumstance. Roosevelt once compared the qualities of his "Uncle Ted" (actually a cousin) to those of the schoolmaster Wilson:

> Theodore Roosevelt lacked Woodrow Wilson's appeal to the fundamental and failed to stir, as Wilson did, the truly profound moral and social convictions. Wilson, on the other hand, failed where Theodore Roosevelt succeeded in stirring people to enthusiasm over specific individual events.[36]

If as president Roosevelt set out consciously to combine the vitality and energy of the one leader with the public philosophy of the other, who would dare to doubt the conclusion that he in large part succeeded? Franklin Roosevelt was among the greatest of politicians of any time, both gifted and studied, whose impact on the office of the presidency was to lift it in the eyes of the American people head and shoulders above the other branches of the remodeled federal government, an electoral monarchy whose occupant embodied the might and collective wisdom of an imperial republic. When scholars say that Roosevelt invented the modern Presidency, they mean that Roosevelt "was eminently successful in making of the Presidency the chief source of political leadership and of legislative ideas"; for the modern president Congress was no longer a deliberative assembly to be regarded with awe, but "a branch of the federal system to be brought into immediate contact with the Executive and into substantial concurrence with the legislative needs of the country, as identified and defined by the Executive."[37]

The modern presidency was the product of national emergency, both of the Great Depression and the governmental response to it, and the world war that followed, in the government-orchestrated popular mobilization for it. The fact that Roosevelt's unprecedented term in office very nearly encompassed this era meant that the modern presidency bears the stamp of his personality, above all in the popular expectations of presidential leadership nurtured by his definition of the nation's peril, the sacrifices required to meet it, and the ways he chose to communicate both.

Not the least of these vehicles was the technology of radio. The fireside chats offered Roosevelt two important assets in political leadership, one that might be most appropriately deemed "psychological" and another that was forthrightly political. In a time of economic distress and deep insecurity, Roosevelt made himself father-to-the-nation. What began in his inaugural address as an injunction against "fear itself," was continued in countless reassuring radio addresses to the nation over the following decade, at their peak reaching in excess of sixty million listeners. But radio also permitted Roosevelt to seize the political initiative by appealing to public opinion and cultivating popular support before submitting plans for specific legislative action to Congress. Obviously, Roosevelt's personal traits brought the two dimensions together with a special potency. He personalized government. So comfortable with the new medium was Roosevelt that a critic once complained that when he sat down before a microphone he seemed to be "talking and roasting marshmallows at the same time."[38]

The shifting balance of authority between the executive and legislature in the 1930s might have turned out otherwise were it not for the fact of the national Democratic tide that accompanied Roosevelt's election and reelection. For Democrats of the early 1930s in particular, whose partisan advantage over the GOP before 1936 remained tentative, had a vested interest in the president's success that trumped their loyalty to the principle of separated powers. In the 1934 congressional ballot the Democrats were able to enhance their hold on Congress in part because Roosevelt appealed to the electorate on their behalf in a fireside chat that asked the people "are you better off than you were last year?" [39] This appeal to the people was a more direct form of political communication than any previous chief executive had been able to employ, and it was doubtless of advantage to congressional Democrats that the new weapon of radio was at the disposal of *their* president. But every radio wave salvo of this variety was fired over the heads of Congress and the party leaders; as it pushed the executive branch to the center of national affairs in the public, so it pushed the party to the periphery and diminished the role of Congress as a deliberative assembly that hitherto had been the center-of-gravity of national politics.[40]

Before Roosevelt, the president of the United States was for most Americans a man in distant Washington. Only a tiny minority of the populace had occasion to see him or hear him in person. Since Roosevelt, the presidential voice has been an integral part of the ambient racket of daily public affairs. The introduction of this mode of political communication combined with Roosevelt's pioneering of it, by virtue of its very nature gave the executive a powerful tool in the cultivation of mass opinion. Those who at the time worried about the full potential of the tool had good cause. The other great radio politician of the 1930s, after all, was Adolf Hitler, whose rasping delivery held out to the German public an altogether different vision of economic salvation and national destiny. If by 1938 the New Deal had lost much of its momentum and possibly all of its focus, the problem of party unity and of national direction was now to be influenced decisively by the rapidly deteriorating diplomatic situation in Europe and the overwrought ambitions of the Empire of Japan in the Pacific.

From National to International Crisis

Franklin Roosevelt's electoral setbacks of 1938 and *Kristallnacht*, a first instalment in the darkest chapter of European history, occurred within days of each other. During the night of November 9th to 10th, 1938, the German Gestapo arrested thousands of Jews while Nazi brownshirts seized and/or destroyed Jewish property, at the same time putting to the torch synagogues from Vienna to Kiel. At a November 15 press conference Roosevelt denounced this latest tribute to barbarism, and the State Department promptly recalled its ambassador to Berlin. Officially at least, the United States and Germany were no longer on speaking terms. Observers at home and abroad were divided in their attitude to the Nazi regime generally, but domestic public opinion preponderantly favored at least a temporary suspension of diplomatic ties as appropriate in this particular instance. Moral outrage was good politics.[41]

But it was much more. In Roosevelt's case it was genuine personal conviction. More substantively, it was also a small but symbolic gesture in U.S. diplomacy, leading up to American involvement in World War II, and an important episode in Roosevelt's efforts to make the world hospitable to the American way of life by making the United States the arbiter of global peace. Before 1938 there was very little he could do to further this end. Congress passed the *Neutrality Act* of 1935, which imposed an impartial embargo of arms to belligerents in a foreign war. Roosevelt had wanted discretionary power for the President to embargo arms sales to an aggressor state while reserving the freedom to supply the victims of aggression, but the Senate would have none of it. Another *Neutrality Act* in 1936 further restricted executive prerogative by prohibiting loans to belligerents, to which the Senators added prohibitions on the export of war materials to the republican government fighting for survival in the Spanish Civil War. While

Roosevelt was ambivalent about supporting the Spanish government in any event, the act was a serious defeat for the presidential conduct of foreign relations.[42] American willingness to follow weak British and French policies on Spain also encouraged Berlin to ponder prospects for bloodless conquest elsewhere in Europe.

Roosevelt himself had a bit part in this development. Just prior to the outbreak of the Spanish conflict, after all, German troops marched into the Rhineland in open violation of the Treaty of Versailles, opposed only by a flurry of diplomatic squeaks from Paris. The move was a serious strategic threat to France and a huge gamble on Berlin's part, given that the German army was as yet in no condition to fight a war. But Paris was told that it would have no help from Britain in the event of a Franco-German clash, while Roosevelt himself refused even a formal condemnation of Germany's action. Appeasement was in its high season.

In Western Europe peace-at-any-price foreign policy was partly a product of the awful memory of World War I, a conflict so stupidly prosecuted, so horrific in its human cost, and yet so inconclusive in its outcome that it had destroyed the Old Continent's very concept of itself as a civilization. American hesitancy was founded on the historic Europhobia that is so often passed off as "isolationism," overlaid with a wholly understandable disappointment with the collapse of the Versailles settlement, and a now outdated but resilient notion of absolute hemispheric security. The latter in particular was underpinned in the 1930s by a wide spread nativist fear of the destruction of a way of life merely through contact with Europe's problems. Anyone in doubt about the strength of this sentiment learned a valuable lesson in the domestic politics of foreign policy through the ferocious opposition to American membership in the toothless World Court cultivated by the radio priest, Father Coughlin. As Senator Homer T. Bone of Washington state explained it, Americans should remain aloof of any direct challenge to Hitler, not in spite of their democratic values but *because* of them. "I am a believer in democracy and will have nothing to do with the poisonous European mess," he declared, "I believe in being kind to people who have the smallpox such as Mussolini and Hitler, but not in going inside their houses."[43]

Roosevelt regarded Germany both as the greater and more immediate threat to American interests in the 1930s, yet, because isolationism was a particularly Europhobic tradition, declaring the United States for the European democracies was especially problematic. In the early and mid-1930s, obviously, Roosevelt sought to protect the fragile domestic consensus on the New Deal from any of the fissures that an openly internationalist foreign policy would surely create. After 1937 things had changed. The New Deal consensus was breaking up, so there was less to preserve by diplomatic circumspection, and the deterioration of international affairs accelerated. While Hitler acquired a new interest in Czechoslovakia, a virtual creation of the Versailles treaty, Japan escalated an incident with China over the Marco Polo Bridge into a full-scale war. In the last two years of his second term, in other words, Roosevelt had a chance to build a base of political support in which foreign affairs played a more prominent role than hitherto, but he could lose everything to the vengeance of volatile public opinion if he mismanaged America's insinuation into the global power equation.

He had something of a base to work with, at least, in the corporate interests that had rallied to the New Deal in 1936. Many of them were managed by old family Protestants who felt the United States and Britain in particular shared a common political heritage. In this they were unquestionably right, but even where sentiment played no role, many of the rising multinationals of the interwar years wanted nothing quite so much as an open world market and low tariffs. Roosevelt's longest serving Secretary of State, Cordell Hull, took a personal hand in the establishment of a series of bilateral trade agreements designed to rectify some of the damage done by the *Smoot-Hawley Tariff Act.* He won thereby the approval and support of some of the most powerful, traditionally Republican, business leaders on Wall Street. The Council on Foreign Relations, lastly, sought and found evidence of Hitler's ill intentions first of all in Nazi Germany's autarkic economy and predatory trade practices.[44] A critical debate between foreign policy isolationists and the corporate internationalists supporting Roosevelt centered on the future of U.S. trade and the question as to whether in theory the American economy could continue to thrive if the practices in force in Germany succeeded in dividing global commerce into protectionist regional blocks. This question had huge implications, for if one decided that the answer to it was negative, the United States could in principle not abide the very existence of Nazi Germany or any approximation of it. Even given the hypothesis of a Nazi regime at peace with the United States, the European balance of power could no longer be a matter of indifference to Washington. American military thinking was increasingly concerned that German hegemony in Europe would facilitate only a transitory peace, during which Berlin would attempt to undermine the U.S. position in the Western Hemisphere. In the late 1930s the Export-Import Bank, a creation of Roosevelt's first term, was already attempting to help American companies cope with German penetration of South American economies with exclusive commercial policies.[45] While it is true that Roosevelt was not an ideologue of free trade, but was concerned above all with reestablishing American prosperity with any means available, his moral revulsion at Hitler's regime reinforced an internationalist outlook on trade matters whenever the State Department warned of lost American export markets. In the campaign of 1936 Roosevelt was already linking the restoration of global trade to the goal of mass prosperity, while warning that there was no place for dictatorship in any major state of a thriving global economy.[46]

The trade issue offered Roosevelt an influential corporate constituency to cultivate for a more extrovert foreign policy, but it was small considering the strength of the isolationists in Congress. Even some of Roosevelt's traditional supporters in domestic affairs simply didn't take the gathering signs of war seriously. When in 1937 and 1938 the administration attempted to balance the budget and reaped only a recession as reward, Roosevelt's efforts to stimulate the economy with a spending increase, part of it committed to larger defense appropriations, were commonly taken to be the real reason for his warnings about the threat of war. The House of Representatives only barely failed to pass the *Ludlow Resolution*, which would have required that only a national plebiscite could commit the United States to any war except when American territory itself came under attack. In 1938 Roosevelt was in a weak position domestically to make more than gestures of protest against Nazi aggression. His "Quarantine" speech of September 1937, in which he spoke about the threat to the Western Hemisphere posed by unchecked aggressor nations, was one such gesture. So too was his attempt to revise the Neutrality Act in the wake of Germany's occupation of Czechoslovakia six months after France and Britain had attempted, with FDR's support, to buy off Hitler at the Munich conference of September 1938 by awarding him the Sudetenland. Only the twin shocks of the German-Soviet invasion of Poland and the appalling collapse of France prompted public opinion and Congress to take military readiness seriously with a drastic increase in defense expenditures. Though most Americans still wanted to stay out of the war, a strong majority wanted beleaguered Britain to survive and were happy that the United States should provide aid. From that point onward Roosevelt's policy was directed toward determining the conditions under which the United States would enter the war, even as he assured his countrymen that his every effort strove in the opposite direction. Acts of Congress notwithstanding, the Roosevelt administration's neutrality had been a fiction since 1937; that of the United States would follow soon enough, but Roosevelt was in no position to concede this publicly.[47]

American relations with Japan exercised a powerful influence on the administration's European diplomacy. Many isolationists subscribed to the idea that the United States was a Pacific power that gave far too much attention to European affairs. And they had a certain case. The most significant consequence of the Spanish-American War, after all, had been the projection of American power westward to the Philippines. The U.S. bases there were well-fortified and had good reason to be. In 1931 Japan exploited the chaos of nationalist struggle in China and invaded Manchuria to establish the puppet state of Manchukuo on the Asian mainland, justifying the action under the banner of the right to "national self-determination" of the local populace in much the same way Hitler approached the Czech Sudetenland. In 1932 parliamentary government in Japan was suspended indefinitely with the murder of the prime minister, his finance minister, and a number of leading industrialists. Two years later Japan denounced the limits on naval power to which its government had agreed at the London Conference of 1930. These events themselves were manifestations of an internal power struggle within Japan itself, its civilian and military leaders equally divided on the future direction of the country to the point of administrative anarchy. But the situation shifted decisively in 1935 and 1936 to the advantage of the advocates of the expansionist foreign policy that led to the outbreak of Sino-Japanese hostilities on the Marco Polo Bridge in June 1937. Although Japan in the 1930s was clearly not in a league with Germany industrially and wildly out of its depth in even considering war with the United States, the fact of the Sino-Japanese War was a measure of the danger a militarized Japan posed: an industrializing nation cognizant of its legitimate vital interests in Asia, yet utterly wanting in any sense of proportion in the effort to secure them. Against this, Washington had the *Stimson Doctrine*,[48] not a declaration of foreign policy principles so much as a checklist, dating to the Hoover administration, of possible developments the United States would not tolerate in Asia. As president and politician, however, Roosevelt appreciated that a great many of his most influential countrymen, who would oppose any move to bring the United States into conflict with Germany, had a wholly different attitude toward Japan. So Japan figured prominently along with Germany in the Quarantine speech. After 1937 Roosevelt escalated his verbal attacks on Berlin and combined this with a cautious insensitivity to the interests of Japan in the western Pacific.

His goal was not to maneuver Japan into war. He sought, rather, to force that country to in effect show its diplomatic cards and thereby disabuse the American people of their attachment to the myth of hemispheric security. Initially he announced the termination of the Japanese-American Trade Agreement of 1911 and embargoed the sale of aircraft to Japan while loaning $25 million to China. When in 1940 Japanese troops moved into French Indochina, he imposed an embargo on steel and scrap metal, omitting oil due to the warning of Secretary of State Hull that its inclusion would bring war. Roosevelt was careful about risking the possible chances of moderates within the Japanese leadership to steer their country toward restraint, but he would not go so far as to sacrifice punitive diplomacy for that reason. He sought peace over war, but also clarity over fudge. Within a day of the steel embargo

Tokyo signed a Tripartite Pact with Berlin and Rome, and a wartime combination better known as the Axis became a reality. In terms of the massive and unqualified public support Roosevelt would need to take the United States into a world war, should it come, the world was sorting itself out nicely. But no president had walked this sort of tightrope since Abraham Lincoln waited patiently for the Confederacy to decide whether or not there was to be a civil war.[49]

In the European theater, meanwhile, German submarines attacked British shipping and bombed British cities. By the fall of 1940 a majority of public opinion in the United States had come around to the view that Britain's cause merited more than moral support. Still, 59 percent thought that top priority should be given to keeping the United States itself out of the hostilities. In such circumstances the presidential election of that year was bound to be one of the select few in which foreign policy issues were pivotal to the outcome. The course of the campaign, coming as it did when German air raids against Britain generally strengthened the argument of the interventionists, was to some degree influenced by the course of the war itself. Yet it was more decisively influenced by Roosevelt's reelection tactics, which combined initiatives to influence public sentiments that were turning more bellicose with bolder actions to test the resonance of the same.

His Republican opponent, Wendell Willkie, was the survivor of a four-way race for the GOP nomination. Although going into the Republican convention both Thomas Dewey, Robert Taft, and Arthur Vandenburg had stronger organizational assets, a delegate rebellion on the convention floor carried the day for Willkie. A comparative political amateur, Willkie waged a surprisingly skillful presidential challenge, yet found himself in fundamental agreement with most of Roosevelt's foreign policy goals. He therefore refuted isolationism and expressed support for the policy of aid to victims of aggression short of U.S. involvement, calculating that if he could neutralize foreign policy as an election issue, he could pull ahead of Roosevelt on domestic issues where the incumbent was vulnerable.

It was the wrong year to even try. Keeping a presidential distance from the early phase of the campaign, Roosevelt asked Secretary of the Interior, Harold Ickes, to respond to Willkie's opening gambit. Ickes thanked Willkie graciously for his support for the administration's policy and then put in the boot. In substance he said that, like it or not, Willkie was the candidate of bitter anti-Roosevelt isolationists, and that the Republican Party of 1940 could and should be likened to the French and British appeasers of Munich in 1938. Henry Wallace, Roosevelt's recently nominated Vice presidential running mate, then chimed in that to millions the president had become the symbol of besieged democracy, and that nobody wanted Roosevelt defeated more than Adolf Hitler. Denying that he meant to imply that Republicans were consciously giving aid to Hitler, Wallace then proceeded to imply precisely that.

Meanwhile, Roosevelt concluded secret negotiations to deliver destroyers to Britain in return for British bases. In this there was surely a quantum of personal fulfilment. Since serving as Assistant Secretary of the Navy under Wilson, he had never let go of the conviction that naval power was the nation's best bulwark of security, and now the United States was acquiring bases from the most famed navy of modern history. Although congressional Republicans attacked the deal as a dictatorial act of war, the public generally thought it a shrewd bargain. And they were right. Both Churchill and King George VI appealed personally to Roosevelt, describing Britain's situation as one of life and death. Consequently, Britain was prepared to shore up its naval assets with overage destroyers from the United States in exchange for the sale or lease of naval and air bases in seven United Kingdom possessions in Western Hemisphere. The United States thus acquired bases of enormous strategic advantage at a bargain, and Roosevelt projected American presence into the Atlantic as McKinley had done in the Pacific in the 1890s. There is a cliché to the effect that European statesmen are infinitely more cool and calculating than their plain and homespun American cousins, but if there was a Machiavellian hand in the destroyers-for-bases diplomacy of 1940 it was surely Roosevelt's. Of course, Roosevelt sincerely did want to help Britain; he just wanted the United States to profit from the helping. Help and self-help, the two were perfectly compatible.[50]

When Willkie's fortunes improved, Roosevelt's personal involvement in the campaign helped to take the edge off the

Republicans' revival in the polls by assuring voters that its was not his intention to send American boys to foreign wars. Very strictly speaking, this was true, but in confidential talks with foreign leaders Roosevelt had already revealed that he did not consider the European war a "foreign" conflict all, since it touched upon so many American vital interests. In September 1940 the *Selective Service Act* slid through Congress with little publicity and hardly a word from the president. Were he to tell the people the awful truth in one dose, he reasoned, they would vote him from office and turn policy over to an administration less willing to prepare the nation for the advent of the inevitable.[51] And the people trusted his instincts if not his promises. He had brought them through the Depression and would bring them through this. Franklin Roosevelt was on his way to an unprecedented third term, and the war in Europe was a good part of the reason. By the last week of the campaign the momentum was with him again. Somewhat out of step with the self-proclaimed sympathy of the press for the underdog, Dorothy Thompson announced for CBS News three days before the election that "a vote for Wendell Willkie is a vote for fascism."[52] In the end Roosevelt scored 449 electoral votes to Willkie's 82, winning with a margin of more than five million votes. It wasn't 1936 again, but Franklin Roosevelt now had a mandate that no other president had known.

The United States was now neutral only in words. With the problem of reelection behind him Roosevelt now deepened Washington's commitment to British victory in Europe. He initiated the *Lend-Lease* program, which avoided the prohibitions imposed by the neutrality acts by loaning war materials to Britain that London was to return (so went the story) after the war. When Britain could not pay, its overseas assets liquidated and its treasury bare, Roosevelt deferred payment for all American equipment and munitions. In a 1940 year-end radio address to the nation he then prepared the people for what turned out to be the most fateful year of the war. He told them that American civilization and American independence were now in greater danger than at any time and challenged them to transform the United States into "the great arsenal of democracy." Lend-Lease established the ligatures of an Anglo-American alliance. Roosevelt defended it publicly with the

claim that supplying Britain represented the best way to keep
the United States out of the conflict, but in objective terms it
increased the odds that German U-boats would soon torpedo
American shipping in the Atlantic. Other developments, certainly, meant that the U.S. presence there was about to increase
significantly. For aid to Great Britain was tempered by the conviction—a conviction not exclusive to Roosevelt and certainly
common to Wall Street—that at midcentury the United Kingdom was in many respects a sample of what was wrong with
the world: imperial preference in trade and closed colonial
systems that had nurtured the rivalries that triggered World
War I. When Denmark fell to Germany and its former possession, Iceland, offered to host British troops, Roosevelt was
prepared to view the arrangement as a European affair. However, when Canada proposed to establish a base on Greenland,
Roosevelt objected. As a Western Hemispheric nation at war
alongside Britain against Germany, Canada's position in
Greenland could draw the United States into the conflict;
equally, a Canadian presence in Greenland could simply be
the back door for a British base there too. Roosevelt expanded
the definition of the Monroe Doctrine and built a U.S. base
on Greenland.[53]

The year 1941 was the turning point in Europe and the Pacific. On June 22, Germany attacked the Soviet Union with
over three million men, the largest single offensive in history.
The assault, *Operation Barbarossa*, automatically put the massive Soviet population and terrain on the Allied side and influenced American policy on Europe decisively. Roosevelt's
response to the turn of events can only be called intuitive pragmatism. Although he had as yet no full appreciation of how
the world of great power politics was turning, the decline of
Britain and the rise of the Soviet Union, he diverted supplies
that London had expected to receive to Moscow's war effort.
He did so because he calculated that the Red Army was possibly the only force capable of prevailing against Germany in a
land war. At the very least, it could not hurt that the preponderance of Germany's war-making capacity was now being directed eastward, so Russia's ability to fight had to be maintained. American support for Russia worried Churchill and
flew in the face of popular distrust of the Soviet Union in the
United States. Churchill gave Roosevelt pessimistic assessments

of Russia's chances of survival, because he feared that American aid to Moscow would come at the expense of London. Americans who endorsed Lend-Lease because of a sense of cultural or ideological kinship with Britain, moreover, could never feel the same warmth toward Stalin's regime or the Russian people. But shoring up the Soviet war effort fit Roosevelt's feel for the unfolding of events so well that he was prepared to ignore both British sensibilities and the very public opinion he had hitherto so assiduously cultivated in order to achieve that most pragmatic of all goals: the victory of the Allied cause at the lowest material and human cost to the United States.

Of this policy it has been said that Roosevelt's assessment of geopolitics "temporarily overshadowed his commitment to American ideals and institutions and his belief that they could work for the world—his Americanism."[54] Perhaps. But the why-and-how of American arms in previous wars had been at least as pragmatic as it was idealistic, so Roosevelt was breaking with no tradition save that of Europhobia. And how could it be a setback for the prospects of Americanism in the world that two such totalitarian giants as the Third Reich and the Soviet Union were now locked in a death struggle that might last long enough to destroy both of them? Support for the Soviet Union was neither a popular policy nor a guaranteed success—far from it. According to the imperfect laws of international probabilities and the imperative of national security, however, Roosevelt rightly guessed that it was the responsible card to play. While Washington and London repeatedly delayed the invasion of the European mainland as the war in Russia ground on, Roosevelt had a capable emissary in Wall Street's Averell Harriman to convey with regrets the bad news to Stalin and to return with observations on the nature and ambitions of Stalin's Russia. By 1943 the German army had exhausted its capacity to prevail in the west through the conduct and outcome of its savage campaign in the east. The Americans sent in June 1944 to liberate Western Europe from that much-depleted German army would no doubt have happily forgiven Roosevelt for his lapsed Americanism, if indeed that's what it was, of 1941.

At approximately the same time as Germany shifted the war in Europe massively to the east, Japanese-American relations entered their final phase toward total collapse. Roosevelt did not want to see the Soviet effort against Germany compromised in any way, especially by a Japanese attack on Russia via Manchuria or Mongolia. He need not have worried. By the summer of 1941 Japanese thinking had already shifted in favor of a "southern strategy" of expansion, starting with a move into Indochina with its tin and rubber resources and its strategic purchase on China. Roosevelt's response was to freeze all Japanese assets in the United States. While he, with characteristic Roosevelt discretion, released sufficient funds to allow Japan to purchase oil, the State Department delayed the issuing of the export licenses necessary for the purchases. When Britain and The Netherlands also embargoed oil to Japan, that country's meager oil reserves set a new schedule for the achievement of Japanese strategic goals. Roosevelt, by contrast, wanted nothing so much as to slow the progress of events in Asia while holding firm to the U.S. commitment to China. Well into 1941 Roosevelt worked seriously for some sort of accommodation with Tokyo.

The most common account of the roots of the Pacific war tend to highlight the differing schedules of the two countries and the confusing diplomatic signals they gave each other. There is something to this depiction of events, especially in the Japanese case where in 1941 military planning and diplomatic efforts were competitive and disjointed, with the diplomats essentially "trapped by a military schedule"; Roosevelt's schedule, by contrast, was set by the progress of his communion with the American people and the fact that he would take his policy no farther than he could carry the great bulk of public support.[55]

At the most fundamental level, however, Japan and the United States understood each other very well. They simply had diametrically opposed interests: as much as Washington was determined that Japan abandon its campaign in China and accept the legitimacy of U.S. Open Door goals in Asia, Tokyo was not about to surrender the territory gained in ten years of war. Washington even had decoded diplomatic intercepts pointing to the probability of a Japanese attack on a U.S. Pacific base in late November or early December. Only the target remained uncertain, and Pearl Harbor seemed the most doubtful of all. Roosevelt, at least, had the assurances of the esteemed

Army General George Marshall that the Hawaiian base was too strong for Japan to dare a strike there.[56] Roosevelt in 1941 was prepared to make no significant concessions for peace with Japan, but he clearly had no interest in provoking the Japanese finally to toss the dice. On the very eve of the Japanese attack, Harry Hopkins mused that it would be better if the United States could be done with it and strike the first blow. Roosevelt responded that this was not an option, "we are a democracy and a peaceful people".[57] With this he summed up the logic of his whole approach to the imminent conflict, namely that he could take only a people fully confident of the rectitude of its cause into the kind of war the United States was about to wage.

Even after the attack of December 7 and Roosevelt's ringing request for a war message from Congress, there remained the awkward technical fact that nothing had been said about the state of affairs between Washington and Berlin. No matter, Hitler himself saved Roosevelt from this dilemma by declaring war on the United States. Because Roosevelt was at the time in possession of intercepted and decoded messages between Berlin and Tokyo, in which Germany assured Japan alliance in any war with America, the declaration came as no surprise.[58] In the Pacific the tide turned against Japan surprisingly quickly, in part because so many of the US ships "sunk" in the shallow water of Pearl Harbor were raised and salvaged; early American naval successes in the Coral Sea and at Midway enabled the United States to maintain the offensive initiative from 1942 onward.[59] And even Germany's greater weight among the Axis forces could not change the fact that the combined industrial strength of the Allies was twice that of the Axis powers and the combined war-making capacity three times as large. One aspect of hemispheric security, after all, was as yet not altogether fiction. The distance of the United States from the main theaters of conflict gave the Allies a massive long-term advantage: by the end of the war the United States had helped to supply both Britain's and Russia's war needs and had supplied itself in 1943–44 with 1200 major warships, and 2,000 heavy bombers, all the while unmolested by enemy bombing. The war was fought above all with a mind to bringing a massive Allied counteroffensive back on Germany and Japan. Air attacks on their cities were eventually conducted with almost complete air superiority and with the goal of the comprehensive destruction of their capacity to make war at all. The bombing visited terrible retribution on the German and Japanese populations, with a mind to dictating the terms of peace upon cessation of hostilities and subjecting both countries to a period of military occupation. At the end of World War II the United States was the only country with its industry completely intact. Although Germany's defeat in Europe occasioned the rise of the Soviet Union, Russia had suffered enormous losses, and in 1945 its GNP was only half that of the United States. Lastly, of all the major belligerents the United States emerged in 1945 with far and away the lightest casualty rate. If the reader will tolerate a cold cost-benefit calculus of American involvement in World War II, it is worth noting that few nations have redeemed such massive strategic advantages from a timely intervention in military conflict. Roosevelt's diplomacy and his skilled dismantling of the isolationist tradition deserve a good part of the credit for this. There was a good deal of deception involved, but it would be difficult to argue that deception, and not the force of events alone, eventually enlisted a united American people in the Allied cause. What remained, in the molding of public opinion in countless public addresses and fireside chats, is called statecraft.[60]

Welfare, Warfare, and World Order

This outcome was in large part the result of the determination of Roosevelt's diplomacy to enter the war in optimum circumstances. The national mobilization the war occasioned was itself, moreover, a consolidation of liberalism's victories in the New Deal. That this was true in the president's mind is evident in his address to Congress of January 7, 1941, just twelve months before the American welfare state became the warfare state. "There is nothing mysterious about the foundations of a healthy and strong democracy," he warned, so long as an elected government was mindful of "equality of opportunity" and "the enjoyment of the fruits of scientific progress in a wider and constantly rising standard of living"; in another State of the Union Address three years later he underscored the significance of the transformation the republic had undergone by observing that "We have accepted, so to speak, a second Bill of Rights under which a new basis of security and prosperity can be established for all, regardless of station, race or creed." The New Deal's reconstitution of American government had been relentlessly advanced in a thousand increments, but its champion had made no secret about the intentions of his handiwork.

Nor did he limit himself to the domestic sphere. In August 1941, before American participation in either theater of the war, Roosevelt met with Churchill off the coast of Newfoundland and signed the Atlantic Charter, shot through with Wilsonian principles and calling for a new international order pending defeat of Nazi Germany. The charter affirmed the Anglo-American commitment to the sovereign rights and self-government of all peoples, the right of victor and vanquished to "access, on equal terms, to the trade and raw materials of the world," and open seas. It also reiterated the third of the Four Freedoms, freedom from want, cited by the president in his address to Congress of January 7, 1941. Thus, where the charter advocated collaboration between nations in the promotion of improved labor standards, economic advancement, and social security so that "men in all lands may live out their lives in freedom from fear and want," it grafted British wartime collectivism and American New Deal liberalism onto the principles of the postwar foreign policies of the Anglo-American alliance. Regardless of what they chose to call it, Churchill and Roosevelt had committed their countries and the postwar international economy to a social democratic vision of the future of free enterprize and elected government. Within days of the historic meeting the charter's words were lost in the heavy traffic of preparation for war, but over the longer term its grand principles would not go away. They were to find substance in future American diplomacy, toward the British in the insistence that imperial preference could not stand, toward the Soviets in Roosevelt's admission that his special envoy Averell Harriman was right about Stalin's utter lack of integrity.[61]

With the Atlantic Charter internationalism had a symbolic victory. With American dominance in the victorious Allied war effort, that victory became substantive, even if Roosevelt himself initially attempted to play down the new significance of the principles enunciated off Newfoundland.[62] But having committed the United States to the Allied cause, he was equally concerned that the postwar settlement reflect American ideals of international order rather than fall back on European traditions of diplomacy. His concept of "Four Policemen"— the United States, Great Britain, the Soviet Union, and China— as enforcers of international peace was a mixture of Wilsonian ideals and balance-of-power logic. Through the United Nations (UN) he sought, too, to revive the League, but also to give to the great powers a vested interest in its success.[63] In securing domestic approval for the United Nations his administration proceeded with due attention to stealth. Secretary of State Hull studiously avoided any premature publicization of the UN. Even though public opinion polls conducted in 1942 concluded that only 10 to 15 percent of populace remained isolationist, in the congressional elections in November of the same year the Republican Party picked up a total of fifty-three seats in the House and Senate. In June 1943 Roosevelt informed the congressional leadership that he intended to commit the US to participation in the United Nations Relief and Rehabilitation Administration (UNRRA) by way of *executive agreement*. He faced the prospect of a Senate revolt when minority leader Arthur Vandenburg rallied the Foreign Relations Committee around the concern that executive agreements were now to be the routine for the conduct of foreign relations. Roosevelt and Hull quickly patched together a truce, but the episode served to remind them that in politics procedure can be as important as policy and that Wilson's tactlessness with the Senate in 1919 had cost him his postwar diplomatic agenda. More usually Roosevelt attempted to influence public opinion on the issue indirectly, as in sending his former presidential rival Wendell Willkie on a world tour to dramatize the United Nations concept of the People's Peace, while proceeding quietly with the blueprints for the postwar international organization. Press inquiries usually encountered official reticence, and "the American people had no idea of the intensive effort their government was making to prepare for the future peace".[4]

In the United States many of the enthusiasts of an internationalist diplomacy in 1932 had thought they had no particular reason for celebration at the election of Franklin Roosevelt. In 1944 those who believed that the Peace of Versailles had been lost not at Munich but in the U.S. Senate some twenty years earlier, now had occasion to fear that the dividend of military victory would be squandered again. They were mistaken. The presidential election of that year returned Roosevelt to office for a fourth term. It also deprived a good many traditional isolationists of their congressional seats. And the implications of the result for foreign policy, though it gave the Democratic Party its largest majority since the highpoint of the New Deal, could not be understood in terms of partisan loyalty alone. Republican leaders such as Vandenburg were personally encouraged by the apparent victory of internationalism in the court of public opinion and were now concerned to establish a bipartisan foundation for future diplomacy. John Foster Dulles, a close friend and advisor to the GOP nominee Thomas Dewey, had thought the Atlantic Charter in fact too modest in its approach to postwar international organization. Now he pledged his support to the reelected president "without regard to party" for the creation of the United Nations. The composition of the Senate Foreign Relations Committee shifted as the new Congress convened; five isolationists had been defeated at the polls, and only three of the committee's twenty-two members could be considered unredeemably opposed to the new internationalism.[65] If one interpreted the election of 1944 as a plebiscite on foreign policy, then it was impossible to avoid the conclusion that the citizens of the world's great democracy had learned something from the experience of the interwar years. The electoral landscape of American foreign relations had changed fundamentally since Woodrow Wilson's Senate defeat of 1920. Isolationism had been reduced to a cottage industry of the Republican right.

The American public had endorsed this national change of direction, but had not fully comprehended the full dimensions of its implications. At his last meeting with Stalin and Churchill, at Yalta in February 1945, Roosevelt's health was failing fast. Not long after his death many were to wonder whether his judgment in the last year of his presidency had not also been seriously impaired. The Soviet Union had claimed a place in his foreign policy even before the United States had entered the war in 1941, but it had been based on the hope that some form of American understanding with Stalin might conjure the image of a U.S.-Soviet alliance in the minds of the Axis leaders and actually deter them from aggression. During the war, of course, the shear size and depth of the Soviet Union became critical in grinding down the Nazi war machine and setting the stage for a counterattack on Germany from the East and West. But at Yalta Roosevelt still seemed to place some hope in Soviet cooperation in underwriting international peace after 1945, so much so that he accepted Stalin's assurances on Soviet intentions in Eastern Europe and was bitterly disappointed when Stalin betrayed them. Roosevelt's recognition of Soviet territorial claims in Asia, moreover, later contributed to the argument that the United States had lost the first diplomatic skirmish of the Cold War.[66] With regard to Poland in particular, Roosevelt, and to a lesser extent Churchill, treated the postwar settlement as if it were still negotiable. In reality, the Soviet leader was humoring them even as the presence of his armies on Polish soil facilitated a series of brutal political *faits accomplis* designed to incorporate Poland, and eventually much of Eastern Europe with it, into the Soviet system.[67] The roots of the Cold War and of a whole new dynamic to domestic politics are to be found at Yalta, and at Potsdam, and in the American public's discovery of the burdens of a superpower in an altogether new power struggle over the constitution of world order.

Notes

1 Robert A. Divine, *Roosevelt and World War II* (Baltimore, Md.: The Johns Hopkins University Press, 1969), p. 97.

2 Quoted in Arthur Schlesinger Jr., *The Coming of the New Deal* (Cambridge, Mass.: Houghton Mifflin, 1958), p. 1.

3 James MacGregor Burns, *Roosevelt, The Lion and the Fox* (New York: Harcourt, Brace & World, 1956), p. 20.

4 Frank Freidel, *Franklin D. Roosevelt: A Rendevous with Destiny* (Boston: Little, Brown, 1990) pp. 80–81; Richard Hofstadter, *The American Political Tradition* (New York: Vintage, 1954) pp. 316–317.

5 Albert U. Romasco, *The Poverty of Abundance: Hoover, the Nation, the Depression* (New York: Oxford University Press, 1965), pp. 169–170 and 230–234; Paul Conkin, *The New Deal* (New York: Crowell, 1967).

6 Freidel, *Rendezvous with Destiny*, pp. 162–163.

7 William Leuchtenburg, *Franklin Roosevelt and the New Deal* (New York: Harper and Row, 1963), p. 35; James MacGregor Burns, *The Crosswinds of Freedom* (New York: Alfred A. Knopf, 1989), p. 25.

8 Harris G. Warren, *Herbert Hoover and the Great Depression* (New York: Oxford University Press, 1959), pp. 142–147 and p. 194.

9 Arthur Schlesinger Jr., The *Politics of Upheaval* (Boston: Houghton Mifflin, 1960) pp. 263–264.

10 Herbert Stein, *The Fiscal Revolution in America: Policy in Pursuit of Reality* (Washington, DC.: AEI Press, 1996), p. 54.

11 Carl Cavanagh Hodge, *The Trammels of Tradition: Social Democracy in Britain, France, and Germany* (Westport: Greenwood, 1994), pp. 51–94.

12 Thomas Ferguson "Industrial Conflict and the Coming of the New Deal: The Triumph of Multinational Liberalism in America", in Steve Fraser and Gary Gerstle Eds., *The Rise and Fall of the New Deal Order, 1930–1980* (Princeton, N.J.: Princeton University Press, 1989), pp. 3–31.

13 Burns, *The Lion and the Fox*, pp. 202–205.

14 Scheslinger, *The Politics of Upheaval*, p. 488.

15 "Annual Message to Congress", *The Public Papers and Addresses of Franklin D. Roosevelt*, 5 vols. (New York: Random House, 1938) Vol. 5,

p. 14. On the anti-elitist spirit of Jackson in particular, and Roosevelt's interpretation of it, see Philip Abbott, *The Exemplary Presidency: Franklin D. Roosevelt and the American Political Tradition* (Amherst: University of Massachusetts Press, 1990), pp. 18–19 and 110–131.

16   William E, Leuchtenburg "The Election of 1936," in Arthur M. Schlesinger Jr. et.al. Eds., *The History of American Presidential Elections, 1789–1968*, 4 vols. (New York: McGraw-Hill, 1971), Vol. 4, pp. 2818–2843.

17   Burns, *Roosevelt, The Lion and the Fox*, pp. 291–303; also David J. Danelski and Joseph S. Tulchin, Eds., *The Autobiographical Notes of Charles Evans Hughes* (Cambridge, Mass.: Harvard University Press, 1973), pp. 304–307; John W. Chambers II, "The Big Switch: Justice Roberts and the Minimum Wage Cases," *Labor History*, Vol. 10, No. 1, 1969, pp. 44–73.

18   *Helvering et.al. v. Davis, 301 US 619 1937.*

19   Stein, *The Fiscal Revolution in America*, pp. 91–130 and 454–468; Walter S. Salant, "The Spread of Keynesian Doctrines and Practices in the United States," in Peter A. Hall, Ed., *The Political Power of Economic Ideas: Keynesianism Across Nations* (Princeton, N.J.: Princeton University Press, 1989), pp. 36–51.

20   Quoted in Freidel, *Rendezvous with Destiny*, pp. 240–241; Abbott, *Exemplary Presidency*, p. 112.

21   Thomas Ferguson, "From Normalcy to New Deal: Industrial Structure, Party Competition, and American Public Policy in the Great Depression," *International Organization*, Vol. 38, No. 1, 1984, pp. 85–94.

22   Ferguson, "From Normalcy to New Deal," p. 92; Ellis W. Hawley, *The New Deal and the Problem of Monopoly: A Study in Economic Ambivalence* (Princeton, N.J.: Princeton University Press, 1966), pp. 472–494.

23   Hawley, *The New Deal*, pp. 475–476.

24   Theodore Lowi, *The Personal President: Power Invested, Promise Unfulfilled* (Ithaca, N.Y.: Cornell University Press, 1985), p. 46.

25   Richard E. Neustadt, *Presidential Power* (New York: Wiley, 1960), pp. 5–6, p. 64, p.104 and 160; Lowi, *The Personal President, pp. 44–66.*

26   Leon Epstein, *Political Parties in the American Mold* (Madison: University of Wisconsin Press, 1986), pp. 141–142.

27   Quoted in David McCullough, *Truman* (New York: Simon & Schuster, 1992), pp. 155–156 and p. 213.

28 Robert Dallek, *Lone Star Rising: Lyndon Johnson and His Times, 1908–1960* (New York: Oxford University Press, 1991), pp. 107–108; Clyde Weed, *The Nemisis of Reform: The Republican Party During the New Deal* (New York: Columbia University Press, 1994), pp. 46–47; Barry Goldwater, *The Conscience of a Conservative* (New York: Hillman, 1960), pp. 16–24; Rudy Abramson, *Spanning the Century: The Life of W. Averell Harriman, 1891–1986* (New York: William Morrow & Company, 1992), pp. 239–240.

29 Quoted in Weed, *Nemisis of Reform*, pp. 47–48.

30 James T. Patterson, *Congressional Conservatism and the New Deal: The Growth of the Conservative Coalition in Congress, 1933–1939* (Lexington: University of Kentucky Press, 1967), p. 104.

31 V.O. Key, *Politics, Parties and Pressure Groups* (New York: Thomas Crowell, 1964), p. 192; Albert U. Romasco, *The Politics of Recovery: Roosevelt's New Deal* (New York: Oxford University Press, 1983), pp. 240–247.

32 Mario Einaudi, *The Roosevelt Revolution* (New York: Harcourt, Brace, 1959), p. 77; Freidel, *Franklin D. Roosevelt*, pp. 16–32.

33 Burns, *The Lion and the Fox*, pp. 358–366.

34 Leuchtenburg, *Franklin Roosevelt*, pp. 265–271.

35 James T. Patterson, "The Failure of Party Realignment in the South, 1937–1939," *Journal of Politics*, Vol. 27, 1965, p. 612.

36 Quoted in Freidel, *Franklin Roosevelt*, p. 23.

37 Einaudi, *The Roosevelt Revolution*, p. 122. See also Fred I. Greenstein Ed., *Leadership in the Modern Presidency* (Cambridge, Mass.: Harvard University Press, 1988), pp. 1–6; Stephen Skowronek, *The Politics Presidents Make: Leadership from John Adams to George Bush* (Cambridge, Mass.: Belknap, 1993), pp. 288–324.

38 Einaudi, *The Roosevelt Revolution*, p.123; Also William E. Leuchtenburg, "Franklin D. Roosevelt: The First Modern President," in Greenstein, *Leadership in the Modern Presidency*, p. 19.

39 Burns, *The Crosswinds of Freedom*, p. 37.

40 Lowi, *The Personal President*, p. 65.

41 Robert E. Herzstein, *Roosevelt and Hitler: Prelude to War* (New York: Paragon, 1989), pp. 232–234.

42 Richard A. Harrison, "A Presidential Démarche: FDR's Personal Diplomacy and Great Britain," *Diplomatic History*, Vol. 5, 1981, p. 249.

43   Quoted by Robert Dallek, *The American Style of Foreign Policy: Cultural Politics in Foreign Affairs* (New York: Oxford University Press, 1983), p. 115; also Douglas Little, *Malevolent Neutrality: The United States, Great Britain and the Origins of the Spanish Civil War* (Ithaca, N.Y.: Cornell University Press, 1985).

44   Robert A. Divine, *Second Chance: The Triumph of Internationalism in America During World War II* (New York: Atheneum, 1967), pp. 21–23; Ferguson, "From Normalcy to New Deal," pp. 90–91; Richardson Dougall, "The US Department of State From Hull to Acheson," in Gordon A. Craig and Francis L. Loewenheim Eds., *The Diplomats, 1939–1979* (Princeton, N.J.: Princeton University Press, 1994), p. 40.

45   Known as the Exim Bank, the Export-Import Bank was created in 1934 for the purpose of fostering trade with, and developing markets in, Latin America and the Soviet Union. Lloyd Gardner, *Economic Aspects of New Deal Diplomacy* (Madison: University of Wisconsin Press, 1964), pp. 123–132; Robert E. Sherwood, *Roosevelt and Hopkins, An Intimate History* (New York: Harper Brothers, 1948) p. 411.

46   John A. Garraty, "The New Deal, National Socialism, and the Great Depression," *American Historical Review*, Vol.78, No.4, 1973, pp. 907–944; Detlef Junker, *Der unteilbare Weltmarkt: Das ökonomische Interesse in der Aussenpolitik der USA, 1933–1941* (Stuttgart: Klett, 1975), pp. 279–284; "Campaign Address at St. Paul, Minnesota," *Public Papers and Addresses of Franklin D. Roosevelt*, Vol.5, pp. 418–423.

47   Robert A. Divine, *The Illusion of Neutrality* (Chicago: University of Chicago Press, 1962) pp. 162–285.

48   The Stimson Doctrine declared that the United States would not recognize any change that violated American rights, Open Door policy, China's territorial sovereignty, or the terms of the Kellogg-Briand Pact.

49   Robert E. Herzstein, Roosevelt and Hitler, p. 409; Robert Divine, *The Reluctant Belligerent: The American Entry into World War II* (New York: John Wiley and Sons, 1979) pp. 158–164.

50   Robert A. Divine, *Foreign Policy and US Presidential Elections, 1940–1948* (New York: New Viewpoints, 1974), pp. 46–54; Robert Dallek, *Franklin D. Roosevelt and American Foreign Policy, 1932–1945* (New York: Oxford University Press, 1979), pp. 243–245; Sherwood, *Roosevelt and Hopkins*, p. 364.

51   Cathal J. Nolan, "Bodyguard of Lies: Franklin D. Roosevelt and Defensible Deceit in World War II," in Cathal J. Nolan Ed., *Ethics and Statecraft: The Moral Dimension of International Affairs* (Westport, Conn.: Praeger, 1995), pp. 57–74.

52   Divine, *Foreign Policy*, p. 73.

53 Warren Kimball, *The Juggler: Franklin Roosevelt as Wartime Statesman* (Princeton, N.J.: Princeton University Press, 1991), pp. 60–61 and 112–114. Idem, *The Most Unsordid Act: Lend-Lease, 1939–1941* (Baltimore, Md.: The Johns Hopkins University Press, 1969).

54 Kimball, *The Juggler*, p. 40.

55 James MacGregor Burns, *Roosevelt, The Soldier of Freedom, 1940–1945* (New York: Harcourt Brace Jovanovich, 1970), pp. 133 and 144.

56 Burns, *Soldier of Freedom*, pp. 155–157; Jonathan G. Utley, *Going to War with Japan, 1937–1941* (Knoxville: University of Tennessee Press, 1985), pp. 178–181; Gordon W. Prange, *At Dawn We Slept: The Untold Story of Pearl Harbor* (New York: McGraw-Hill, 1981), p. 122.

57 Burns, *Soldier of Freedom*, p. 161.

58 Sherwood, *Roosevelt and Hopkins*, p. 441.

59 In the case of Midway Japanese troops were ultimately able to occupy the Aleutian islands of Attu and Kiska, but the Japanese Navy suffered a decisive defeat, involving the loss of 4 aircraft carriers, a heavy cruiser, over 200 aircraft and over 2,000 sailers. The Battle of the Coral Sea, by contrast, was a closer contest. In tonnage American losses were worse than those of the Japanese, and they included the loss of the carrier Lexington along with extensive damage to the carrier Yorktown. However, the battle also thwarted Japan's attempt to advance southward in an effort to dominate the Coral Sea and the approaches to Austrialia. It was thus a pyschological defeat and a strategic setback to Japanese war plans.

60 Gerhard Weinberg, *A World at Arms: A Global History of World War II* (New York: Cambridge University Press, 1994), pp. 894–920; Peter Calvocoressi and Guy Wint, *Total War: The Causes and Courses of the Second World War* (London: Allen Lane, 1972), p. 195.

61 Burns, *Soldier of Freedom*, pp. 125–133, 564–580, and 592.

62 Divine, *Second Chance*, pp. 44, 49, and 259–260.

63 Henry Kissinger, *Diplomacy* (New York: Touchstone, 1994), pp. 395–397.

64 Divine, *Second Chance*, pp. 52–53, 68–69, 71–73, and 117–119.

65 Divine, *Second Chance*, pp. 44–45, 242, and 260.

66 Edward M. Bennett, *Franklin Roosevelt and the Search for Security: American-Soviet Relations, 1933–1939* (Wilmington, Del.: Scholarly Resources, 1985), pp. 189–195; Herbert Feis, *Churchill, Roosevelt, Stalin: The War They Waged and the Peace They Sought* (Princeton, N.J.: Princeton University Press, 1957), pp. 489–530 and 638–648.

67 R.C. Raack, *Stalin's Drive to the West, 1938–1945* (Stanford, Calf.: Stanford University Press, 1995), pp. 11–36 and 87–98; Anne Armstrong, *Unconditional Surrender* (New Brunswick, N.J.: Rutgers University Press, 1962).

PART II

SUPERPOWER AMERICA

Chapter Four

The Permanent Crisis

Moderation is the silken string running through the pearl-chain of all virtues. –Thomas Fuller, *Holy and Profane States*

The surrender of Japan after the detonations of Hiroshima and Nagasaki marked not only the dawn of the nuclear age but also an entirely new era in American foreign relations and domestic politics. Consider the following facts: when the war started in Europe there were fewer than 190,000 men in the U.S. Army, and the air force "was too small even to provide the Germans with target practice"; on September 2, 1945 the United States emerged from the century's second global conflict triumphant in Europe and the Pacific, the world's first *superpower*[1] in charge at home of the only intact industrial economy and abroad of the shipping lanes of global trade. If ever a single state can be said to have enjoyed the status of hegemon, then surely it was the United States between 1945 and 1960.

In a nation historically insulated from the calamities of Asia and the geopolitics of Europe and understandably attached to the advantages that geography afforded it, this newly-acquired status of superpower was not wholly welcome. If anything, the popular impulse was to return America to normality as quickly as possible, even though since the Black Tuesday of 1929 normality had been hard to define. Washington responded accordingly. By the summer of 1946 the defense budget had been cut by 50 percent to about $11 billion, and not a single unit of the army or air force was at full combat-readiness. At home, an anticipated postwar slump in the economy never materialized. Instead, the Truman administration was faced with the problem of fighting inflation while maintaining employment at a level capable of absorbing the millions of returning servicemen. The passage of the *Employment Act* of 1946, with its formal recognition of Washington's responsibility to use its fiscal and monetary powers to prevent high unemployment, represented both a response to the immediate problem and a consolidation of the breakthrough made by Keynesian economics under New Deal social democracy.[2]

While the fundamentals of the economy were sound, the country was also beset by a combination of problems, including a rise in the cost of living, plus shortages of housing, automobiles, refrigerators, sugar, coffee, and meat, for which Truman apparently had no coherent response. His popularity plunged, and Republicans swept the congressional ballot of 1946, their first such victory since the Depression and their last until 1994. The new Congress featured fresh talents, among them Representatives Richard Nixon from California and John Kennedy from Massachusetts. But the talent that mattered in 1946 was with the GOP leadership; from their strengthened position, prominent Republicans such as Robert Taft, Arthur Vandenburg, and Joe Martin were determined to restore to the Congress the prestige and initiative it had lost to the presidency during the Roosevelt era of depression and war. Many of them, Taft in the lead, were also resolved both to reverse the reforms of the New Deal and to return the United States to a neoisolationist foreign policy.

The weather of international affairs and domestic politics was clearly not with them. Even when they succeeded, they failed. They passed, for example, the *Taft-Hartley Bill* of 1947, which represented a rollback of labor rights established under the Wagner Act,[3] yet Truman succeeded in portraying the Republican Congress as a conservative reaction to the New Deal in such a way as to form the domestic basis for his reelection bid in 1948 under the theme of the Fair Deal, a consolidation of the Roosevelt reforms. The establishment of the Council of Economic Advisors (CEA) gave the executive office the capacity to assess the economy from the perspective of public welfare and to formulate a variety of policy initiatives.[4] International developments meanwhile strengthened the hand of an extrovert foreign policy. In February of 1946 George Kennan,

Director of the State Department's Policy Planning staff in Moscow, transmitted the "long telegram," citing Soviet foreign policy as the greatest challenge American diplomacy had ever faced, a position he reiterrated publicly in a 1947 edition of *Foreign Affairs*, now rightly considered to be the Article One of the Cold War. Kennan's words expressed with eloquent drama the dire implications of Soviet expansion for the vital interests of the United States, and it bequeathed to U.S. foreign policy the guiding principle of the next forty years. In sharp contrast to the conditions of 1920, nothing in 1946–47 spoke for a return to normalcy, save perhaps the overactive imagination of isolationist Republicans.

The Test of National Character

In a sense the formal Cold War diplomacy of the United States began at the Potsdam Conference of July 1945, where Truman tussled with Stalin over the terms of Germany's occupation and accepted the East-West division of the country in order to contain Moscow's presence to only one zone of occupation. Attached since the early 1930s to the first official American delegation to Soviet Russia, George Kennan had by the end of World War II arrived at definitively more damning conclusions on the nature of America's wartime ally, and its threat to the kind of world in which the United States could prosper, than anything Truman had expressed at Potsdam or Roosevelt at Yalta. The sources of Soviet conduct in the world, he argued, were rooted in a traditional Russian sense of insecurity and inferiority, strengthened since 1917 by the ideological fervor of Marxism-Leninism, that exerted a constant pressure on Moscow's leadership to extend the limits of Soviet power and influence. He insisted in conclusion that "the main element of any United States policy toward the Soviet Union must be that of a long-term, patient but firm and vigilant *containment* of Russian expansionist tendencies."[5] Indeed, the very existence of the Soviet state was in a sense of greater significance to the American Century than the great military conflict only recently concluded:

> Surely, there was never a fairer test of national quality than this. In light of these circumstances, the thoughtful observer of Russian-Ameri-

can relations will find no cause for complaint in the Kremlin's challenge to American society. He will rather experience a certain gratitude to providence, which, by providing the American people with
this implacable challenge, has made their entire security as a nation
dependent on their pulling themselves together and accepting the
responsibility of moral political leadership that history plainly intended then to bear.[6]

Over the intervening years a good deal has been written to
the effect that Kennan's message was misunderstood, and that
Washington's application of containment was excessively military in nature. Still, Kennan's words were anything but equivocal, and it is hard to see how the practitioners of containment
were to interpret prudently his recommendation that the
United States "confront the Russians with *unalterable counterforce
at every point* where they show signs of encroaching upon the
interests of a peaceful and stable world"[7] without the commitment, among other things, of massive military resources.
Kennan's message was like a whisper in the ear of an administration whose postwar diplomacy had hitherto lacked not so
much conviction as direction, and it confirmed the suspicion
of many that in the last months of the Roosevelt administration the ailing president had not applied the best of his brain
to looming problems of Soviet-American relations.

It also featured the welcome tonic of clarity. There is no
doubt that Truman's acceptance of Kennan's analysis was influenced by the disastrous experience of appeasement of Germany in the 1930s and a Western willingness to read only the
more conciliatory signals from among the many mixed messages emanating from Berlin. But it is questionable that a less
simplistic interpretation would or should have altered the fundamentals of American policy. As it applied to Europe especially, containment was motivated above all by elementary prudence. Vital geopolitical terrain recently liberated by American
forces was on the very doorstep of the Soviet empire. Since
the same terrain was so distant from the United States, would
it have been at all wise to a adopt anything but a worst-case-
scenario interpretation of Soviet intentions in deciding American priorities for the future of Western Europe? The scale and
prosecution of World War II had taught the US military, not
surprisingly, to think in terms of correlations of power; from

the Joint Chiefs of Staff such thinking produced the extraordinary warning to the administration that the potential military strength of the Old World (in which they included Europe, Asia, and Africa) was greater than the Western Hemisphere. Based on the available evidence of the present and the experience of the past, any realistic assessment of U.S. interests in Europe could not favor an ambiguous commitment. Truman was saying as much when he told Congress that it was "far wiser to act than to hesitate."[8]

Containment represented the leitmotiv of an array of diplomatic, economic, and security initiatives, ranging from the creation of the North Atlantic Treaty Organization (NATO) in 1949 to the elaboration of the European Recovery Program (ERP), better known as the Marshall Plan, for the recovery of Western Europe's market economies. The changes were revolutionary both for Americans and Western Europeans, for the former because NATO was the "entangling alliance" *par excellance*, the existence of which symbolized America's permanent status as an Atlantic and European power, and for the latter because the Marshall Plan attempted to recast Western Europe in the American New Deal image, using public and private initiatives to bring about an integrated market and the kind of productive abundance that would transcend class divisions.[9] In Washington, congressional approval of the National Security Act established the National Security Council (NSC) and the Central Intelligence Agency (CIA), the former tasked with advising the president on the domestic and international dimensions of national security and to coordinate the activities of political and military leadership, the latter supplementing the information capacity of the Defense and State Departments in particular. To these was added the mandate of Bretton Woods institutions such as the General Agreement on Tariffs and Trade (GATT), the International Monetary Fund (IMF) and the World Bank in stabilizing a system of open multilateral trade among the key centers of industrial power outside the Soviet orbit: North America, Western Europe, and Japan. The lending powers of the Export-Import (Exim) Bank were enhanced in accordance with the appetite for American capital of developing countries. For both domestic and international reasons, the economic component of containment was no less vital than the diplomatic and military. Full-employment at home required reconstructed and growing overseas markets, open trade, and convertible currencies.

It all fell under the rubric of the *Truman Doctrine*, announced to Congress on March 12 1947, in an effort to secure legislative support for Washington's efforts in stabilizing the governments of Greece and Turkey against the political opportunity created for their enemies by domestic and international pressures. The president conjured for his audience a world set to choose *between two alternative ways of life* and stated that *it must be the policy of the United States to support free peoples who are resisting subjugation by armed minorities or by outside pressures.*

It was this policy that one of the most important papers in the history of American foreign relations attempted to implement. In January 1950 Secretary of State Acheson appointed Paul Nitze to head State's Policy Planning Staff with the specific task of drafting a report on the implications of Soviet nuclear weapons for Washington's international objectives. The resulting document, NSC-68, predicted that by 1954 the Soviet Union would have a nuclear capacity sufficient to destroy the United States and recommended that in the meantime the United States and its allies commit themselves to a massive military buildup capable of thwarting any and all Soviet designs for expansion, thus minimizing the likelihood that Russia and the United States would ever find themselves in a direct military confrontation. NSC-68's interpretation of Soviet intentions employed language every bit as ominous as Kennan's, but went further than any paper produced hitherto on the specifics of substance that would be required to back up US policy, most importantly defense expenditures of $35 billion annually over the next four years at least.

It is worth noting that Nitze proposed to cover the additional federal outlays in part through higher taxes rather than deficit spending but was advised against such a politically unpopular course.[10] Because NSC-68 did not create new objectives, but rather "operationalized" the Truman Doctrine, it was crafted to cultivate the requisite political support. Such support was all the more forthcoming with the advent of communist revolution in China and the outbreak of the Korean War. At the same time, however, something of a precedent was established with the decision to help finance an American commitment to the defense of South Korea by way of government borrowing. The Truman administration was prepared to, as Kennan had put it, "undertake this test of the national quality", yet balked at the prospect of letting the electorate feel the real weight of the test in its annual taxes. At the time nobody was in a position to say that America's struggle against communism would last for forty years, nor to predict that domestic partisanship over foreign relations over that period would influence the nature of U.S. Cold War diplomacy profoundly.

Practically from the outset, containment, as a foreign policy principle inaugurated by a Democratic administration, was denounced by a good many Republicans as inherently defensive in nature. The charge was fallacious, as many who made it privately conceded. With the acceptance of NSC-68, in fact, "U.S. diplomacy was imbued with an offensive spirit" that left "no room for neutrality."[11] It was by definition a strategy for the long game, but a game nonetheless in which thwarting the expansion of Soviet socialism was to be the precondition of its atrophy and defeat by the American vision of global liberal-democratic peace. The very wording of the Truman Doctrine implied an open-ended commitment, yet the calculated simplicity of its approach appealed to the appetite for clarity just as the mission of aiding free peoples resonated with the most fundamental American values. The Senate approved the original aid package for Greece and Turkey by 67 to 23, the House by 287 to 107. What's more, the issue enhanced the salience of foreign policy in the presidential election of 1948 and aided the hapless Truman's apparently hopeless battle against the Republican nominee, Thomas Dewey.

Foreign policy alone could never have carried the day for Truman, although the fact that the 1948 presidential election preceded both the communist triumph in China and the Korean conflict probably saved him from defeat. As the incumbent candidate he brought formidable assets to bear. Truman, so went the legend, had never sought the presidency, and yet he had managed to be in the right place at the right time. While he lacked the larger-than-life grandeur of Roosevelt, he was also among the most professional of politicians of his time and in some respects displayed "a better mix of political traits than his predecessor."[12] If the voters liked to see him as a home-spun article, that was all to the good. Because he understood that reelection depended on holding together the massive yet unwieldy New Deal electoral coalition by conjuring the specter of an unreconstructed Republican Party overturning the Roosevelt reforms, he threw his energy into attacking the GOP in a campaign that cut both ways. In one speech he would label the 80th Congress an obstructionist do-nothing legislature; in the next he would play upon the fear that a do-something Congress dominated by Republicans would be even worse. Better to just fire the GOP altogether.

But the situation in 1948 was complicated by the third-party campaign of Henry Wallace, erstwhile VP to Roosevelt and former Secretary of Commerce for Truman, who resigned from the cabinet in 1946 in protest of the hard line against the Soviet Union. The Wallace factor elicited a campaign of nuanced extremes from the Truman Democratic Party in which foreign policy had a critical role. On social issues it pitched leftward by stressing the Republican threat to the New Deal inheritance and cutting into liberal-Democratic support for Wallace's Progressive Party of America (PPA); in international affairs Truman used foreign policy announcements to enhance the leadership of the executive against the claims of a Republican Congress, while Democrats denounced communist infiltration of Wallace's Progressive movement. As is often the case in politics, where strategy alone did not secure the victory, luck made up the difference. American public opinion recoiled when a Soviet-sponsored communist coup toppled the government of Czechoslovakia and killed Czech Foreign Minister Jan Masaryk, making somewhat doubtful Henry Wallace's claim that communists were the closest thing to Christian martyrs. Seldom does electoral good fortune come in such heaping dollops. On election day the Democratic ticket established an early lead, even in GOP territory such as Wisconsin, Iowa, and Colorado. In the end, Truman votes translated into an electoral college victory of 304 to 189; on the same evening the electorate returned a Democratic majority in Congress.[13]

Now consider the Republican perspective on the election. A party that had not held the Oval Office since 1932 and that only two years earlier had regained Congress was now shut out of both. The party that since Lincoln had defined the essence of Americaness now discovered that America had been redefined. The popular resonance of New Deal liberalism and internationalism had not passed away with their creator, and to oppose either openly was to be hit by an electoral freight train. In 1948 the Democrats had it both ways. Whereas Roosevelt's party had combined social welfare with internationalist foreign policy, Truman's party owned both the New Deal and the Cold War. For Republicans the electoral depth and breadth of the welfare-warfare Democrats seemed to blot out the very sun.

In retrospect the 1948 election was a defining event, both for political partisanship in the United States and the new relationship between domestic politics and international affairs. Republicans were so badly shaken by their defeat that a new urgency, even panic, informed their efforts to somehow reinsert themselves into the nation's agenda in meaningful way. The nature of Truman's victory, and the GOP's response to it, together ensured that the partisan heat created by the 1948 campaign never really dissipated. If anything, the victory of the Chinese Communists and the flight of Nationalist forces to Taiwan in December 1949 increased it by a few degrees. In the wake of the presidential debacle, some Republicans—Alfred Landon, former presidential hopeful, at their fore—had already undertaken to redirect the party by denouncing the bipartisan approach to foreign policy with particular stress on what they saw as an impending diplomatic disaster in Asia. Isolationists had to recognize that their defeat in the 1940s had not been simply innovated in some devil's pact between Franklin Roosevelt and the Empire of Japan; instead, their assumptions about America's place in the world had been refuted by the bleak reality of global politics at midcentury.

But in crisis there was also opportunity. Once the Cold War had been introduced to the arena of American politics, anyone was free to redraw its dimensions internationally and its implications domestically. In the case of Chinese revolution in 1949 it was possible to charge that Truman had poured American resources into containing communism in Europe, only to let it seize power in the world's most populated nation. Where partisan advantage was at stake, it mattered little that Europe represented the original and principal fault-line of U.S.-Soviet rivalry. For a good many GOP isolationists the Chinese revolution was an irresistible opportunity "to freshen their stale program by passing it off as unilateralism"[14] while outbidding the administration's Cold War militancy. While Truman entangled America in multilateral commitments to Europe, Asia was sliding toward communist control. The influence of a China Lobby, dating to the efforts of Chinese Nationalists in the 1940s to get more American aid for their war with Japan and allying American and Chinese champions of the Nationalist cause to isolationist Republicans and anti-Fair Deal Democrats, increased exponentially.

That influence was based in part on the charge that the Truman had somehow "lost" China, implying a depth of American influence on the Asian mainland that had never really existed. The lobby came to focus much of its attention on the great edifice of U.S. diplomacy, the State Department, with an attack ranging from the legitimate criticism that Secretary of State Dean Acheson had been negligent of American interests in Asia[15] to the accusation that State had been comprehensively infiltrated by communists. With the outbreak of the Korean War, a particularly hysterical variety of the new Republican Cold War pugnacity gained the upper hand.

At its most visceral this pugnacity was personified in Senator Joseph McCarthy of Wisconsin, whose first public allegation that over two hundred communists were in the employ of the State Department was made four months before North Korea's invasion of South Korea on June 24, 1950. Because Truman's reelection campaign of 1948 had already raised the domestic political exchange rate of anticommunism with its rough treatment of the Wallace camp, McCarthy's charges were dropped in a doubly explosive environment. And although McCarthy's sundry investigative activities were a direct product of the new politics of Cold War in the United States, they drew much of their appeal from a deeper conservative backlash to New Deal liberalism, and reopened conflicts adjourned by the partisan truce of the World War II. McCarthy and his supporters were also driven by the need to further their congressional careers with visibility offered by any issue that offered itself. McCarthy, after all, had been preponderantly a

Roosevelt supporter in the 1930s, but recognized that in a traditionally Republican state such as Wisconsin, where he ran for the Senate, he would have to refashion his platform in line with local tastes.[16] In the new reality of Cold War the communist/security issue was important to ambitious Republicans who had lacked McCarthy's appetite for scandal. The fusty isolationism of the old GOP represented by Ohio Senator Robert Taft had little to offer them. By 1952 they looked to General Eisenhower to rescue the GOP from electoral oblivion, but they looked to McCarthy as well. Eisenhower offered the national prestige required of a presidential candidate; McCarthy offered the kind of dynamism, that, however unpredictable, captured headlines and gave Democrats sleepless nights.

Korea emboldened the Wisconsin Senator to make increasingly spectacular, reckless and unsubstantiated charges over the following four years, until, by the time of his repudiation, he had done untold damage to the lives of hundreds of loyal public servants and left a permanent poison of mutual suspicion between conservative Republicans and liberal Democrats regarding almost every controversy of American public life. Not that concerns about the security of government were invalid. In August 1949 the Soviet Union exploded its first nuclear device. Then in February 1950 Klaus Fuchs, a scientist who had worked on the Manhattan Project, was convicted of passing information to Moscow. In September 1949 the Soviet Union conducted the first successful atomic test of a research program that benefitted directly from information provided by Fuchs.[17] Representative Richard Nixon led an investigation of Alger Hiss, who had perjured himself about giving classified material to a communist agent. Still, a good many other junior politicians cut their congressional teeth on McCarthyite scandalmongering, while too many senior Senators allowed an otherwise unsubstantial figure to set the general tone of American politics. Long after McCarthy's death, McCarthyism's method of character assassination by association had a home in American public life.

There was nothing altogether new or uniquely American in the phenomenon, but the vicious quality it gave to the normal rough-and-tumble of congressional politics coarsened public affairs. The onset of the Cold War had subjected the American public to a series of shocks that were in some ways as jarring as Pearl Harbor. In place of the anticipated return to normality after VE and VJ Days the sense of national emergency endured and even intensified due to McCarthy's inquisition against the enemy within. The Soviet Union, wartime ally, had been exposed as threat every bit as sinister as the Third Reich with aspirations reaching from Berlin to Seoul. To some it seemed that the victory gained by the material and human sacrifice of the war was being frittered away by a negligent diplomacy. To others it now appeared that America's greatest contest of arms was after all only the overture to a longer, more thankless struggle. The little republic of 1787, its free institutions and what de Tocqueville once described as its "natural democratic peacefulness" had never been built for this. George Kennan was undeniably right about one thing: a test of national quality like no other was now upon the American people.

The test recalibrated the relationship between domestic politics and foreign affairs and brought up new questions about the relationship between the national executive and legislature. Since its inclusion in the founding document, the *Supremacy Clause* had attracted little attention, much less controversy. But in superpower America a constitutional article providing that treaties made under the authority of the United States "shall be the supreme Law of the land; and the Judges of every State shall be bound thereby" took on a new light. Accordingly, Senator John Bricker of Ohio set out to amend the constitution with a proposal that henceforth all executive agreements and treaties be subject to congressional approval. The idea had broad appeal among Congressmen, mainly Republicans but also Democrats, concerned that in the post-World War II international environment a president had the authority to commit the United States and its people, through treaties with foreign governments or membership in international organizations such as the UN, to undertakings over which they had no control. Without the imperial traditions of the great European powers, traditions established prior to the age of democratic reform, there existed little sympathy in the United States with the idea that a government's activities abroad should be somehow insulated from unpredictable changes in public sentiment at home. Because many of the amendment's enthusiasts had open sympathies with the McCarthy hearings, Bricker had the support of those who imagined the country to be in the grip of a massive conspiracy to subvert its sovereignty.

Amendments to the constitution, moreover, had become something of vogue among conservatives of the Eighty-third Congress. Bricker's was the most important of some 107 proposals referred to committees. But in a republic based like no other on the principle of democratic self-government through Congress, sympathy for the Bricker amendment could not be dismissed simply as a case of the vapors. A president's capacity in an international crisis to invoke the imperative of vital national interest in a way that implied changes to domestic priorities was of legitimate concern. Even accounting for the emotional atmosphere into which it was introduced, the amendment was bound to arouse the interest of the sober as well as the hysterical, those who wanted to restrict executive prerogative in the conduct of foreign relations and those who imagined "that the ratification of proposed United Nations covenants on human rights, labor, and genocide could force upon American society socialized medicine, mandatory unionization and racial desegregation".[18] At the time of its introduction, the amendment's cosponsors in Congress included two future presidents, Lyndon Johnson and Richard Nixon, both of whom in time adopted a wholly different perspective on executive powers.[19]

Still, in 1950 it looked to the electorate that in the case of Korea, especially, the executive branch possibly didn't know what it was doing. At the time of the North Korean invasion an intelligence report on North Korean objectives offered that "there is no possibility that the North Koreans acted without prior instruction from Moscow. The June 25 move against South Korea must therefore be considered a Soviet move."[20] And yet the invasion caught Washington by surprise. At the time many critics of the administration charged that it need not have, given that Secretary of State Acheson had made a speech in January in which he appeared to exclude Korea, along with Taiwan and Indochina, from the list of vital American security interests. Dean Rusk, who as Acheson's Deputy Undersecretary of State was the first in the capital to receive the news of North Korea's aggression, had only four days earlier told a congressional committee that the probability of invasion was remote.[21]

The impact on Rusk and others was powerful. Korea woke the ghost of Munich, of Western civilization again unprepared for or unequal to threats to its survival and security, and transformed the policy of containment, a policy inspired by the Soviet challenge specifically to Western Europe, into a global commitment. There were disturbing superficial parallels to Germany, and, in the emotional mix of present crisis and past failures, the effort to think clearly about American security interests was hardly furthered by the declaration of General MacArthur, in one of many hyperbolic moments, that Europe would be won on the battlefields of Asia. What began as a diplomatic confrontation between Washington and Moscow over the postwar settlement in Germany, was now acquiring a certain abstract quality, derived in part by the very concept of containment itself. Henceforth, there was in Washington little patience for the argument that there were some crises, even some communist-inspired crises, to which the United States did not necessarily have to respond.

Korea was a formative experience in other respects as well. One of Washington's principal diplomatic goals was to demonstrate the merits of collective security through UN action in which ultimately fifteen other countries were involved, but the passage of the *Uniting for Peace* resolution in the General Assembly and the subsequent use of UN forces north of the thirty-eighth parallel drew Communist China into the war. At the same time, President Truman increased the power of the executive branch enormously by dispatching U.S. troops to fight in what he described as a "police action" without a declaration of war from Congress, while the reintroduction of the draft helped to increase the total of American ground forces from 630,000 to 1 million. Even after the stabilization of the military situation, cease-fire talks lasted for two years, and the conflict ended with over 34,000 American dead and Korea's partition apparently permanent, by any calculation a fantastically expensive police action. Thus, containment was a logically coherent strategic concept for America's assets and limitations at the outset of the Cold War, but its application in Korea was satisfying to nobody. Congressional opinion of the UN's authority and the use of American forces formally under the auspices of an international organization ranged from ambivalent to hostile, reflecting in part the public sentiment that the limited diplomatic and military dividends of the war's outcome amounted to an illogical or even immoral compromise of the national policy of defeating global communism.

It was into this context that Dwight Eisenhower was elected as the 34th President of the United States. Eisenhower was a Republican by conviction as well as affiliation, but his nomination for the presidency in 1952 was never the foregone conclusion that many have since assumed. Notwithstanding his status as national war hero, he did not have the party credentials held by his rival Robert Taft. Neither was his brand of Republicanism, in so far as it was known, as representative of the party. Far more typical of prevailing opinion within the GOP were such major speakers at the 1952 convention as General Douglas MacArthur, Herbert Hoover, Joseph McCarthy, and Representative Joe Martin. Eisenhower's supporters had to fight a very determined campaign in order to make the nomination contest competitive in the first place, by wresting control of the nomination away from the Taft organization. Eisenhower could easily have lost had his organization not fought so effectively, led largely by Henry Cabot Lodge and the Citizens for Eisenhower Committee. Eisenhower's emergence was not a triumph for the process of nomination-by-primary that has dominated American politics since the 1960s, but it did underscore the effectiveness of candidate-centered organization in a way that had similar implications for the decline of political parties in the United States.[22]

Compared to the Republican nomination struggle, the presidential election of 1952 was anti-climactic. After all, the Democrats had held the White House since 1932. Eisenhower had a very rare combination of popular appeal and expert credentials, the plain-spoken Man from Abilene, yet a soldier-statesman with first-hand experience in the stakes of international issues. Churchill, De Gaulle, Adenauer . . . Ike knew them all. As a presidential party, the Democrats were in a weak position. The foreign policy of the Truman administration was in tatters and national politics had been dominated by foreign policy, due above all to the direction of events in Asia, the

Chinese revolution and the frustrations of the Korean war. The fact that Truman did not seek reelection gave Democrats the chance to unify behind the candidacy of Adlai Stevenson. The nomination of the urbane Stevenson, a well-born graduate of Princeton, former congressman and the governor of Illinois, was the product of two things: President Truman's misplaced faith in the power of Stevenson's political pedigree and intellectual credentials, combined with a nomination system in which the party convention itself could still make a difference to the outcome.[23] Although Estes Kefauver won most of the Democratic primaries in 1952, Truman and the party leadership engineered a third-ballot rally for Stevenson. While the Democratic nomination was essentially a choice of who was to lose to Eisenhower, the episode is significant for another reason. Stevenson offered above all knowledge and reflectiveness, decent qualities but also qualities with which the Democratic Party of 1952 was too impressed for its own good. To the massive social coalition that under Roosevelt and Truman had made the Democrats the nation's dominant partisan force was added a rather persistent vanity that the Democratic Party held something of a monopoly on intelligence as well. In retrospect, those who later defended Stevenson as simply the best Democratic candidate available in a lost electoral cause had a legitimate point. But equally, it was not to be the last time that Democrats mistook intelligence and eloquence as evidence of, or a substitute for, political skill. From the outset Stevenson was a reluctant candidate, never convinced that he had a chance against a national hero. And because Eisenhower had the internationalist perspective that could save the GOP and the United States from isolationism, Stevenson considered his opponent an altogether respectable candidate to end twenty years of electoral dominance that in Stevenson's view had made the Democrats sloppy.[24] The electorate agreed. Eisenhower defeated him 442 electoral votes to 89.

Domesticating the Cold War

During the campaign of 1952 Eisenhower promised to "go to Korea", an implicit pledge to end the war one way or another. The commitment reflected two things: that if elected he wanted to start a new administration with as clear a desk as possible and was prepared to consolidate and retrench in Asia in order to do it; that additionally he was not especially interested in Asian affairs and was about to return the Cold War diplomacy to its primary theater, Europe. But he did not want John Bricker's help and hated his amendment. Eisenhower knew that many of the amendment's backers had never read its text, yet assumed its provisions could have prevented agreements such as Potsdam and Yalta. While the amendment in fact had no relevance to either, because they were international political accords not treaties, its impact on real treaties of the future and possibly the past, would in Eisenhower's view, subject them "to ceaseless challenge of any of the states" and thereby introduce chaos to the foreign affairs of the United States; even in the best light the amendment would, in his view, seriously qualify the president's clear responsibility to conduct foreign policy by notifying friend and foe alike that Washington was not serious about American leadership in the world.[25] Ultimately, Eisenhower was able, with hard lobbying, to mobilize a sufficient number of GOP votes to deprive Bricker of the two-thirds majority he needed to prevail. At base, Bricker's initiative was isolationism of a particularly juvenile kind, but it also touched nerves among conservative anti-New Dealers and states' rights advocates whenever its backers charged that Washington could use international treaties to impose social reform on Americans. After the amendment's defeat, its political constituency went into hibernation.

Eisenhower's eight-year presidency was a good part of the reason. His greatest contribution to his country was to reestablish a measure of civility in public affairs. Even an avid Stevenson supporter such as Hubert Humphrey conceded in his memoirs that "it is a simple fact that the election of Dwight Eisenhower permitted substantial diffusing of the explosive nature of American politics."[26] Eisenhower attempted to domesticate the Cold War by reducing its human and material costs, while settling U.S. foreign policy into the kind of patient diplomacy that containment necessarily implied. In the process, he tried to return the country to realistic expectations of presidential leadership in a great democracy governed by a constitution based not on imperial virility but on the preservation of human freedom. Since the early 1930s American public affairs seemed to have been in a more-or-less constant state of agitation. Even if crisis-weary Americans had no realistic picture concerning what constituted political normality prior to the Great Depression and World War II—they might have been appalled to find out—Humphrey's tribute was essentially an appreciation of the fact that the Eisenhower years seemed somehow to invent a kind of normality all their own. Half of the reason for the relative calm of the period was its sustained prosperity; the other half was the administration's success in making the national commitment to the Cold War sustainable by making its burden tolerable to the electorate.

Eisenhower also recovered the Oval Office for the bewildered Republican Party for the first time in twenty years and thereby restored a measure of the party's confidence. Over the eight years of his presidency the fact alone that the Republicans competed on a more equal footing with Democrats, who remained in control of Congress, did a good deal to tone down shrillness within the GOP's ranks. Republicans no longer had to shout in order feel that they counted for something, for they had the nation's highest office. This reconciled the party's mainstream with New Deal liberalism and established a broad bipartisan consensus on the new fundamentals of American foreign policy. The electoral utility of bashing containment was hard for Republicans to resist in the electoral atmosphere of 1952, so when John Foster Dulles, Eisenhower's appointee-designate for Secretary of State, coined the concept of *liberation* as an alternative to the Democrats' alleged abandonment of the peoples of Eastern Europe to Soviet oppression, it found its way onto the GOP platform.[27] In the short term, the word was most useful in establishing unity within the GOP concerning the inadequacies of containment, but after Eisenhower's election and Dulles' appointment as Secretary of State it enjoyed almost no substantive application to U.S. policy in Soviet Eastern Europe beyond the broadcasts of the Voice of America. Bipartisanship in foreign policy after the election was possible partly because Eisenhower and Dulles reconciled internationalist Republicans to containment by indulging their hatred of it during the election.

Eisenhower came to office with rather well-developed theories about the defense of American interests abroad and on the appropriate conduct of pubic affairs more generally. Partly derived from the explicit procedural norms of a military background, his approach to the office was somewhat reactive and self-consciously constitutional. He believed in a staff system of clearly delineated responsibilities in which all executive appointees could assume that they had Eisenhower's fullest confidence. He also believed that government should at all times emanate dignity, and the president's role was less to seek public visibility than to ration it, to appear to be above politics while remaining steadfastly, and even covertly, results-oriented. During his eights years in office, critics thought Eisenhower's White House excessively rigid and bureaucratized; his low-key leadership was routinely censured as muddled and indirect, even irresponsible.[28] This was especially true in the case of the McCarthy hearings and the Bricker amendment, in which Eisenhower avoided public condemnation of the activities of a senator whose actions he considered not only unwise but immoral. In McCarthy's case Eisenhower defended his restraint by virtue of the Senate's constitutional right to conduct what enquiries its membership deemed necessary and on the basis of his personal desire to deprive a political lowlife of the publicity of a presidential condemnation. His approach to the Bricker amendment, a provision with the potential to hamstring any coherent conduct of American foreign relations, was to buy time by announcing White House support for refinements to the original draft until Senate majority support for Bricker unravelled. In neither episode did Eisenhower take an overtly principled stand.[29]

But it is debatable whether he was therefore guilty of indifferent presidential leadership, especially since in a good many other instances his native caution was salutary in its effect. Eisenhower was no crusader for civil rights. While the *Civil Rights Act of 1957* was a breakthrough for federal powers to seek injunctions against any deprivation of voting rights, its passage was more a product of Lyndon Johnson's bipartisan Senate leadership than of presidential vision. And yet Eisenhower applied the letter of the Constitution and the authority given him by the Supreme Court's landmark 1954 decision, *Brown v. Board of Education of Topeka* with the force of the federal government, when in 1957 the issue of segregated schools came to a crisis in Little Rock, Arkansas. The Court's decision in the *Brown* case that segregated education deprived black school children of their rights of equal protection guaranteed them by the *Fourteenth Amendment,* overturned at a stroke the constitutional legitimacy of the doctrine of "separate but equal" established by *Plessy v. Ferguson* in 1896 and set the stage for the civil rights revolution of the late 1950s and 1960s.[30] Given that the Court was now demanding that the United States live up to the principles of its constitution with specific regard to the countless injustices suffered by its black citizens based not only·illiberal laws but also on the ingrained prejudice of successive generations, *Brown* made the civil rights movement of the next two decades well-nigh inevitable. When in September 1957 Governor Orvil Faubus of Arkansas mobilized the state's national guard to prevent black students from attending high school, Eisenhower communicated to the Governor the obligation and the intent of federal government to uphold the law. In deference to the tradition of states rights, he then gave the Governor time and opportunity to apply the law himself from the statehouse. But when Faubus allowed mobs of white protestors to prevent the attendance of nine black students, Eisenhower federalized the Arkansas guard and reinforced their numbers with troops from the 101st Airborne to uphold the Constitution with fixed bayonets. He cited federal precedent going back to 1792 when Congress gave the president the "authority to use the state militia and the armed forces of the United States to put down an insurrection."[31] The leaders of the civil rights movement and a majority of public opinion outside the South agreed that he had done the right thing. A decade later, when the civil rights movement was in full swing, Eisenhower's action was scarcely remembered, and his administration was viewed as a period of conservative timidity. In 1957, however, he was often criticized for the "excess" of his action by people who should have known better. Even such a future presidential champion of civil rights legislation as Lyndon Johnson deplored the use of troops as imprudent and provocative.[32]

Although the incident cost the GOP any immediate hope of wooing southern votes away from the Democrats, there is no evidence that Eisenhower lost sleep over the possible electoral damage done by an action he considered an elementary obligation of his office. Perhaps it was the personal confidence of a public figure whose place in history was secure before he came to the White House. But equally, Eisenhower's actions were decisive, though limited, and informed by a concern to turn the nation away from the growing tendency to see the correction of all injustices as necessarily the responsibility of the federal government. Washington could and must uphold the law, but no action of government could itself eradicate racial discrimination.[33]

Whatever their origins, the instincts evident in Eisenhower's handling of the Little Rock crisis were also present in his conduct of foreign affairs. When rioting broke out in East Berlin in June 1953 and Soviet troops crushed the uprising with customary brutality, he declined to abide by the liberation plank of the GOP platform and remained comparatively silent about the Soviet action. The Yalta and Potsdam agreements, no matter how one felt about them personally, were diplomatic realities, the substance of which the United States was in no position to overturn in any quixotic gesture to the miserable millions of Eastern Europe. If containment was the first article in the constitution of post-1945 American foreign relations, Eisenhower was determined to abide by it. Where American vital interests were at stake, he was prepared to act with economy of purpose and with a premium on discretion.

This is where the CIA fit rather conveniently into his logic for conduct of foreign policy. At the high end of superpower relations the Eisenhower years witnessed a greater emphasis on nuclear weapons—rather, the open threat of their use—as a deterrent against challenges to American interests and allies. But equally, Eisenhower committed himself to a reduced reliance on military assets generally. His New Look foreign policy cut defense expenditure overall and reduced the projected 1954 budget from $41 billion to $36 billion, while stressing *massive retaliation*,[34] alliance maintenance, and covert activities as more cost-effective instruments than conventional land forces. It drew directly from the Korean experience, and it told Congress and the people that under Eisenhower fewer American soldiers would be shipped to overseas crises. So for a president with Eisenhower's appetite for results with discretion, the CIA offered alternatives to the conduct of Cold War that implied few of the human and political costs involved in military commitments such as Korea.

This was aptly demonstrated by the agency's involvement in the overthrow of the nationalist prime minister of Iran, Mohammed Mossadeq, and his replacement by Mohammed Reza Shah Pelavi in 1953. In 1952 Mossadeq had moved to nationalize British oil interests operating in his country when London refused to offer profit-sharing schemes similar to those offered by U.S. companies in Saudi Arabia. Even with a mind to British self-interest in the affair, the Eisenhower White House agreed with British concern that Mosaddeq might become dangerously dependent on support from communists. In an NSC meeting of March 4, 1953 Secretary of State Dulles played hard on this fear, conjuring for the council a scenario in which Iran "succumbed" and some 60 percent of the world's oil reserves in the region fell under communist control; by contrast, Eisenhower worried aloud about saving face for London while taking action that needed no congressional mandate yet would not result in charges of administrative failure from the legislature if the measures proved inadequate. A CIA-aided coup fit these requirements nicely. After the Shah's fall in 1979, when the fundamentalist regime of the Ayatollah Khomeini swore undying hatred for the United States, the 1953 operation was criticized as the most short-sighted interventionism.[35] But in terms of the stated requirements of containment, consider the facts about the Iranian experience in 1953 relative to the recent ordeal of Korea: for the price of some careful planning and day's mischief on the streets of Teheran, the United States acquired for some twenty-five years a client-state and increasingly well-armed ally with one border on the soft underbelly of the Soviet Union and another on the Persian Gulf. American oil companies also got a share of Iran's oil production.[36] Small wonder that Eisenhower found more work for the CIA.

The next covert action was the overthrow of the Arbenz government of Guatemala in 1954. In a purely geopolitical sense it probably helped to protect U.S. control of the approaches to the Panama Canal. But the case against Arbenz as a closet communist and probable puppet of Soviet interests was weak. The intervention seems to have been a product of the Dulles brothers' desire to protect the interests of the United Fruit Company in Guatemala, combined with a particularly crude application of Cold War anticommunism. The political dividends were also limited. The success of the operation encouraged the CIA to view much of Latin America as something of a playground, yet it did not prevent the establishment of a Soviet presence in the hemisphere. That came with the Cuban revolution in 1959. The Guatemalan episode is worth noting, because it was typical of the kind of intervention that could have been politically damaging to the President, especially since Arbenz had been democratically elected. Covert operations had the merit of low-cost effectiveness, yet involved an administration in activities that flew in the face of popular American democratic values in the pursuit of geopolitical expedience. So Eisenhower undertook to protect the dignity of the presidency with a series of administrative innovations, starting with the establishment of the Operations Coordinating Board, designed to protect the president from congressional attack and public embarrassment with bureaucratic circuit breaking crafted to achieve what came to be known as *plausible deniability*. Over the long-term it didn't work. In fact, on the very day that the U.S. Ambassador to the UN, Henry Cabot Lodge, denied to the Security Council any American role in the affair, the *New York Times* published a column "With the Dulles Brothers in Darkest Guatemala." Still, it was a more-or-less inevitable product of the contradictory demands on the Cold War presidential office of superpower America, namely that the actual and imagined ambitions of global communism be thwarted at every turn with no offence whatever to the Constitution.[37] Under the circumstances Eisenhower became understandibly protective of the CIA. When a freshman senator from Montana, Mike Mansfield, introduced a proposal for congressional oversight of the CIA that he considered a sober alternative to McCarthyite excesses, Eisenhower hardly bothered to distinguish between responsible legislative behavior and the rogue senator from Wisconsin, fuming that only over his own dead body would McCarthy get a foothold on the agency.[38]

Allowing for the obvious differences in methods and means, Eisenhower preferred to view his foreign policy as applying the same principles abroad as at home. "What Little Rock was to law in the United States," he wrote in self-congratulatory moment, "Suez was to law among the nations: an example of the United States government's staking its majesty and its power on a principle of justice."[39] When in 1956 Britain and France responded to the nationalization of the Suez Canal by Egyptian President Gamal Abdel Nasser by conspiring with Israel to seize control of the canal zone militarily, Eisenhower's determination to place the United States firmly on the side of anticolonialism led the administration to condemn the invasion in the UN Security Council and to exert enormous economic pressure on America's allies in order to secure their withdrawal from the canal zone. Controversy about the prudence of Eisenhower's actions has never died away, especially because they occurred at the same time as the brutal Soviet repression of the Hungarian uprising. While there was never a serious chance that the United States would intervene on behalf of the Hungarian revolt, what percentage was there in allowing the Suez crisis to eclipse the news of Hungary on the front page of the world press? Implicit in Eisenhower's thinking at the time, and consistent with the logic of containment, was that the entire Warsaw Pact represented, for the time being, lost terrain, while the Middle East remained center board in the great chess match with Moscow.

If, in other words, one ignored adverse publicity in the short term and kept an eye on these essentials, the United States would emerge from 1956 on the right side of principle. It is doubtful that Eisenhower was guilty of cynicism on this issue. At one point he told the NSC staff that if American public opinion found in favor of Britain and France, he was willing to lose the upcoming 1956 presidential election to Governor Stevenson. Resentment at being deceived by his European allies, whom he had tried to warn against using force, was also a factor.

Had either Eisenhower or Dulles spelled out precisely what would be the full consequences of military action, admittedly, they might have avoided the need to humiliate them in the United Nations.[40], but at base London and Paris had been the victims of their own imprudence and arrogant impulse to teach Nasser a lesson. Certainly, American reaction to the Anglo-French invasion had a defensible logic and an historical legitimacy reaching back to Wilson. If America's allies viewed Washington as only a junior partner at Versailles in 1919, in 1956 they needed reminding that roles had reversed; they had violated the Tripartite Declaration of 1950 (according to which the United States, Britain, and France had pledged to maintain the status quo in the Middle East by not supplying either Israel or the Arab states with major shipments of arms) and they had deliberately deceived Washington in the process. Now they were in effect openly challenging the United States to stand by them or to uphold the principle of rule-of-law that Washington had professed to be at the very core of an American-led postwar global order. When the United States chose the latter, insisting before the United Nations on the primacy of law and treaty obligations, Eisenhower won the praise of a good many Third World states, although applause from the Middle East was scattered at best.

    If Eisenhower's actions over Suez were prompted by "hearts and minds" considerations over the image in the Arab world of the United States as a champion of anticolonialism, he might have reminded himself of what he had told Dulles in 1954 when discussing Iran, namely that American support for the state of Israel meant that in many Middle Eastern quarters the United States was already more hated than Britain. Morover, because Washington had withdrawn U.S. financial support for Nasser's ambition to build the Aswan High Dam months prior to the crisis, due to the accurate perception that Nasser was playing one superpower against the other, the United States had already cut its options. As of March 1956 Washington and Cairo were already, in a sense, antagonists.[41]

    In a region as politically volatile as the Middle East Suez was bound to have an immediate ripple effect. Nasser's moral victory moved admirers among nationalist army officers in Iraq to launch a successful coup in July 1958. By August Eisenhower had found it necessary to land 14,000 U.S. troops on the beaches of Beirut to ensure that Lebanon would not be next. Aside from Little Rock, it was the only use of U.S. military force during his presidency. An important biproduct of America's Middle-Eastern travails was the presidential pursuit of congressional approval for the *Eisenhower Doctrine,* a draft resolution authorizing the president to use the armed forces of the United States on behalf of the sovereignty of any Middle Eastern state requesting aid against external aggression from "international communism." In the face of congressional questioning, both Eisenhower and Dulles had to concede that there was no immanent Soviet threat in the region, but the resolution's utility to the White House was hardly isolated to U.S. policy in the Middle East alone. Suez had underscored the importance of strategically located developing states to U.S. interests, and Eisenhower was looking for advance congressional approval to intervene with an array of diplomatic assets ranging from military force to economic aid, because international crises could not be expected to fit into a congressional timetable for debating and at last deciding the depth of American interest. Because fighting international communism had been the mission of US policy since Truman, citing its presence in the Middle East was designed to convince Congress that the President needed the authority and resources to respond quickly to crises there, with obvious implications for other theaters of the Cold War. The doctrine, in other words, represented as much an attempt to free the Oval Office from some of the constraints of the Constitution, and to diversify the tools at the executive's disposal, as a policy specific to its Middle Eastern diplomacy.[42]

Certainly, a case could be made for a similar approach to presidential prerogative in other corners of the global arena. In the case of American support for Chinese Nationalist forces, headquartered since the revolution of 1949 on the island of Tawain, they found application in Eisenhower's policy on the offshore islands of Quemoy and Matsu. In the *Mutual Defense Treaty,* signed by Washington and the Republic of China in 1954, the United States pledged itself to oppose an armed attack not only on Taiwan and the adjacent Pescadores but also on other territories according to mutual agreement. "Other territories" was a veiled reference to the possibility that communist China might attack the islands of Quemoy and Matsu as a prelude to the invasion of Taiwan. Eisenhower then asked Congress for a resolution to "establish the authority of the President as Commander-in-Chief to employ the armed forces of this nation promptly and effectively for the purposes indicated if in his judgement it became necessary".[43] The wording was deliberately silent on Quemoy and Matsu. While the House passed the resolution 410 to 3, the Senate entertained an amendment designed to clear up the ambiguity by explicitly excluding the two islands from the realm of U.S. commitment. Eisenhower and Dulles spared no effort to defeat the amendment, and eventually secured Senate approval of the original resolution 83 to 3.

In so doing, they accomplished two things. The *Formosa Doctrine* "authorized the President in advance to engage in a war at a time and under circumstances of his own choosing".[44] Simultaneously, it cast the shadow of *massive retaliation* over Peking's interpretation of Washington's intentions; if, as Dulles had counselled, the objective was to "keep the Reds guessing,"[45] the Formosa Doctrine accomplished this in more ways than one.

In mid-1956 repeated threats by Peking that Chinese communist forces would soon take Formosa influenced American policy elsewhere in the region, especially in French Indochina. Between 1945 and 1949 the policy of the United States had been to oppose the postwar reestablishment of French colonialism in Indochina, but the Korean conflict shifted emphasis toward helping France fight communist insurgency until in 1953 the Eisenhower administration finally assumed responsibility for the management of Vietnam's deepening crisis. Years later, when the Vietnamese war consumed American foreign policy and domestic politics, it became a standard observation among American allies that Washington had never appreciated the essentially nationalist spirit of North Vietnamese aggression. In fact, Washington understood earlier than Paris the likely fate of France's decadent colonial regime, but in light of the Korean experience far greater significance was given to the fact that in 1950 Chinese troops were massed on the borders of Tonkin while Moscow and Peking recognized Ho Chi Minh, the leader of North Vietnam, as the legitimate head of a unified Vietnamese state. It didn't help matters that in France the most vocal critics of colonial policy in Indochina were members of the French Communist Party, among West European communist parties the most calcified Stalinists available, or that Washington rightly feared for the very stability of the beleaguered French Fourth Republic itself. The rhetoric of European leaders themselves, such as the remark by West German chancellor Konrad Adenauer that he did not want to be-

come Europe's "Chiang-Kaishek," tended to blur distinctions
between the European and Asian theaters of the Cold War
in terms both of the interests at stake and the tactics of
diplomacy.[46] Eisenhower had been advised that even the supply of military training and logistical support to South Vietnam against
insurgency from the communist north would affect American
military capacity in Japan, Korea, Okinawa, and Formosa.[47]
Immediately after the defeat of the French garrison at Dien
Bien Phu, a nine-nation conference on the future of Vietnam
convened in the old League of Nations building (unfortunate
symbolism) in Geneva in May 1954. Partly because relations
between Washington and Peking were currently so tense, the
American delegation was given no mandate to negotiate seriously, even though Peking's preference was for the permanent
partition of Vietnam. But there was an important subtext to
the administration's attitude. To the most powerful nation in
the world, the institutionalized stalemate of Korea represented
an outcome not to be duplicated elsewhere. So a fleeting but
possibly significant chance to involve other national interests
in stabilizing the Vietnamese situation, in a way that might in
time have mitigated North Vietnam's appetite for aggression,
was passed over.[48] Eisenhower was concerned above all to avoid
unilateral American military commitments to South Vietnam.
And yet he and Dulles threw the diplomatic prestige of the
United States behind support for the shaky regime of Ngo Dinh
Diem, whose government declined to hold free and fair elections to confront democratically the issue of the country's unity
or partition. In 1957 the Vietcong launched a fresh series of
military operations in the south. By that point the Eisenhower
administration had unwittingly made its own contribution to
America's greatest foreign policy disaster, at the time a minor
skirmish of the Cold War.[49]

Beyond his native caution, one obvious reason for
Eisenhower's restraint in Vietnam was the Eurocentrism characteristic of his worldview generally, a disposition derived from
his command of Allied forces during World War II and his
subsequent tenure as Supreme Allied Commander (SACEUR)
from 1950 to 1952. American policy during the Suez crisis
and the toppling of Mossadeq were both the product of a policy

in which European interests and nationalism in the Middle East were thought to be linked.[50] Eisenhower and Dulles never lost sight of the fact that the Cold War had begun in Europe and would probably end there. Their diplomacy in the region realized a good deal of sober continuity with the priorities established by the Truman administration, above all in the creation of a credible conventional deterrent to Soviet aggression with the incorporation of West Germany into the NATO alliance. When in 1954 discussions for the creation of a European Defense Community (EDC) came to an impasse because of the proposal's rejection by the French parliament, Dulles threatened an "agonizing reappraisal" of the American commitment to Western Europe yet switched very smoothly to the NATO vehicle for Germany's contribution to Western security.[51]

Eisenhower-Dulles Cold War diplomacy was orthodox above all in its aggressive anticommunist rhetoric. Eisenhower never lived up to the rhetoric, and there is no evidence he ever intended to. The theme of liberation had been useful in the partisan electoral struggle with the Democrats, in planting in the minds of a sufficient number of voters the idea that the Democrats were somehow less resolute that the goal of American policy was the ultimate *defeat* of communism. At its core, the administraion's official vernacular was about popular consent. As Secretary of State, Dulles' pronouncements on America's place in the world were designed to give the people "a foreign policy that they thought they understood and could support," a task for which he employed "the language of American Protestantism" in the cause of spreading American righteousness against communist evil.[52] Certainly, it was wholly compatible with Kennan's language of 1947 in word, and it was a good deal more compatible in deed than Dulles would have cared to admit publicly. Once one moved from explaining U.S. actions at home to implementing policy abroad, the theme of liberation exhausted its practical utility rather quickly. In Hungary as elsewhere Eisenhower's foreign policy essentially recognized the Soviet sphere of influence and declined to interfere in it.[53] Eisenhower's fundamental goal, to which his actions and the public explanation thereof were committed, was the domestication of the Cold War. The Eisenhower administration sought to stabilize the conduct of American foreign relations at a lower level of material and human cost than the Korean conflict, and to do so in a fashion that was both intelligible and respectable to the American public. Only under these conditions would it be domestically sustainable over the long haul that containment required.

The fact that until the late 1950s at least the administration for the most part succeeded was no small accomplishment. Eisenhower exhibited commendable restraint in the application of military force in situations of questionable utility to national and Western security and in keeping the nation's commitments in line with its capacity. It should also be noted that he did so during the period when the superpower potential of the Soviet rival was actually realized. Eisenhower thus steered U.S. foreign policy through the transition from a situation of strategic invulnerability to one in which the Soviet nuclear threat was actual rather than theoretical and did so without crisis in national confidence.[54]

At least it should have been so, but by late 1958 there was a blemish. In October 1957 the Soviet Union launched the world's first artificial satellite. Critics saw Eisenhower's collected response to *Sputnik* as evidence of complacency or even senility. Quite suddenly, his understanding of the national interest and a president's responsibility to it were wholly out of step with the changing sentiment of his mercurial people. Eisenhower was confident that the United States enjoyed a commanding lead in any meaningful measure of strategic capacity, and, because he could not identify with the popular sense of panic over *Sputnik,* he never committed his energies toward convincing his countrymen that the sky was not falling. Only very reluctantly did he break with fiscal orthodoxy and finally approve defense appropriations he considered unnecessary and possibly a distortion of the economy.[55] Such is the fate of Eisenhower's brand of conservatism in a political system as deeply democratic as that of the United States in the second half of the twentieth century. He had to speak to popular perceptions of vulnerability created by *Sputnik*, a situation in which reference to the facts availed him remarkably little. After reelection in 1956, moreover, he was no longer in a position to direct public debate on foreign policy in the spirit of a leader who could be around beyond 1960. It is one of the disadvantages of term limits that often the people most qualified to lead debate of a critical issue are sidelined by the brutal political fact that as of a definite date in the not so distant future their views will count for nothing electorally. To an activist and visionary president with the right allies in Congress, the term limit can have the liberating effect of removing any inhibitions imposed by pending electoral concerns, but for a second-term incumbent who is suddenly perceived to be not ahead of events it is debilitating.

Because of the attention he gave to international affairs, Eisenhower clearly was not ahead of events on the domestic front, so *Sputnik* gave ambitious Democrats an angle of attack on Eisenhower precisely in the realm where he was assumed to be invulnerable. In the congressional elections of 1958 they claimed a commanding 75 to 34 majority in the Senate and a 282 to 154 lead in the House. With this leverage and the fact of Eisenhower's looming retirement in two years, they were in a position to set the agenda for the 1960 presidential year. In the period between 1957 and 1960 a new vocabulary, replete with "missile gaps" and "fallout shelters" established itself in the public discussion of international affairs. As the presidential year approached, Democratic hopefuls such as John Kennedy and Lyndon Johnson pulled a reversal of the Republican fear-mongering of the early 1950s by charging in ever-shriller language that the United States was in danger of falling behind in military preparedness. For Eisenhower, lame duck status meant watching the field of presidential candidates define the election of 1960 partly around an issue that he knew to be fallacious. Moreover, Johnson's congressional initiatives to make the United States the world leader in space, including the creation of the National Aeronautics and Space Agency (NASA), added an entirely new dimension to the rivalry with Moscow. In the 1947 the Cold War was about security; by 1957 it was also about prestige.[56]

Events themselves also contrived to create an atmosphere of crisis in superpower relations and a sense of failure in the Eisenhower White House. In 1959 the Cuban revolution installed a communist regime, friendly to Moscow and overtly hostile to Washington, on the Caribbean doorstep of United States. In May 1960 a summit conference with Soviet Premier

Nikita Khrushchev broke up in the wake of the U-2 affair and negotiations on a nuclear test-ban treaty in Geneva ground to a halt. One of the most successful stewards of American foreign policy who had strived and largely succeeded in bringing stability to Cold War diplomacy left office muttering to himself about failure. In his parting address to the American people, however, Eisenhower borrowed from George Washington and ended fifty years of public service with a warning that the crusade the United States had taken upon itself might damage the very fiber of its society unless the nation matched ends with means. More specifically, he noted the prospect of extravagant defense expenditures "due to the acquisition of unwarranted influence, whether sought or unsought, by the military industrial complex", and predicted that "we cannot mortgage the material assets of our grandchildren without risking the loss also of their political and spiritual heritage."[57] In its own way, it was as appropriate to its time as Washington's farewell.

Let Us March

By his own admission, one of Eisenhower's greatest disappointments was the defeat of his vice president, Richard Nixon, by the Massachusetts Senator John Kennedy in the 1960 presidential election. The election itself marked a seachange in the mood of American politics in the 1960s, for if Eisenhower's talent had been to assure, Kennedy's was to enliven. Adlai Stevenson appreciated this at the time of Kennedy's triumph in securing the Democratic nomination. "Do you remember that in classical times when Cicero had finished speaking, the people said. 'How well he spoke'", Stevenson asked an audience in California, "but when Demosthenes had finished speaking they, said 'Let us March'?"[58] This skill alone was in large part responsible for getting him to inauguration day. Kennedy's ability to think on his feet had been critical to important primary victories on the way to the Democratic nomination. Ambivalent audiences in West Virginia and Texas had listened as Kennedy's eloquence turned the issue of his Catholicism into an issue of their tolerance without so much as whiff of patrician arrogance. The same skill parried Harry Truman's bitter attack on his youth and inexperience; when, at the Los Angeles convention that nominated Kennedy on the first ballot, Lyndon Johnson brought up the matter of Kennedy's record of poor congressional attendance, the young senator's unperturbable humor made the question look petty.[59] Finally, Kennedy's victory in a televised debate against Nixon is widely regarded as that moment in modern American politics when style most emphatically trumped substance, if not for the first time then certainly before a mass audience of unprecedented size. [60] Kennedy's talents, admittedly, would probably not have sufficed on election night had not the Democratic Party machine of Mayor Richard Daley in Chicago helped him win the pivotal state of Illinois. But therein lies the irony. Himself an indirect beneficiary of machine politics, Kennedy succeeded making in his adversaries look like the creatures of corruption and himself as the prototype New Democrat immune to vested interest. A considerable coup.

The presidential race of 1960 was decided in Kennedy's favor by a sliver of some 113,000 votes. Kennedy was at least partly successful in reconstructing the Democratic New Deal coalition that Eisenhower had taken apart in 1952 and 1956. His choice of Lyndon Johnson, a Texan, as a running mate enabled him to make a strong showing in the South, while he captured the northeast and bigger midwestern states such as Michigan and Illinois. Yet although his margin in the electoral college was 303 to 219, Kennedy actually a carried fewer states than Nixon. Election analyses concluded that the president-elect had profitted by the vague sense of crisis in foreign affairs, yet conceded that Nixon was consistently stronger when attention turned to specifics.[61]

From the perspective of the 1990s the notion that Kennedy was a major president is in many respects hard to defend. The fact of his election, and of the violent and premature end of his term in office, are the most significant features of his truncated presidency. He certainly a offered a style of presidential leadership that few have been able to imitate successfully, but was otherwise a transitional figure in the general trajectory of American politics in the 1960s—a tribute on the one hand to the new power of the visual media in conveying and shaping political leadership, yet a politician far less representative of

his party than Lyndon Johnson who succeeded him and governed much longer with greater consequence. Possibly more
than anyone else, Kennedy appreciated how assets peculiar to
him had overcome a spotty résumé. And so he cultivated them.
He maintained and improved his campaign organization even
after assuming office, building it into an electoral machine
that was in some respects superior to that of the Democratic
Party. Ever mindful of his narrow victory over Nixon, he also
came to view governing itself as part of a constant campaign
that ran between elections, and he came to rely on speech-
making as a primary mode not only of presidential communication but of presidential governance.[62] Like no other president since Roosevelt, Kennedy invested heavily in the theory
that reelection would depend more upon what he seemed to
do rather than what he actually did.

   During his term in office this differential was most evident,
though not always obvious, in the realm of civil rights. In the
months running up to the 1960 election the leaders of the
civil rights movement, taking their cue partly from the *Brown*
decision of 1954 and the use of federal force against segregated schools in Arkansas in 1957 but mostly from the mani-
fold injustices imposed on black citizens ever since Reconstruction, had established a good deal of momentum in campaigns
designed to break the back of racial segregation for good. The
movement was divided on which political party's candidate to
endorse for the presidential contest, just as the parties themselves were divided on whether to exploit or duck the civil
rights issue. The history of their party in the Old Confederacy
being what it was, the Democrats were more divided than the
Republicans, and Kennedy had been among those senators who
voted for an amendment to the 1957 Civil Rights Act that weakened the legal strength of the final legislation.[63] While prominent civil rights leaders such as Martin Luther King Jr. tilted
toward Nixon at the outset of the 1960 campaign, Kennedy
held out the promise that, if elected, he would sign an executive order that would eliminate racial discrimination in housing at the stroke of a pen. Once in office, however, Kennedy
moved with a caution uncharacteristic of a civil rights crusader,
delaying action on the executive order until after the congressional elections of 1962. When the freedom rides of the spring

1961 encountered violent reaction from the white populace, both the president and Attorney General Robert Kennedy called for a "cooling off" period in such a way as to imply the federal government was the neutral arbiter in a childish shoving match while placing worried phone calls to state and municipal officials who clearly had no intention of guaranteeing the physical safety of the freedom riders.

Clearly, Kennedy wanted the mantle of progressivism in civil rights, but not at the price of offending the Dixiecrat tradition in his party. Strictly speaking, there was some constitutional merit to the attorney general's argument that general law enforcement was the responsibility of the states, as well as to the observation that government alone could never deliver meaningful equality to black Americans. But when the law had clearly broken down in Little Rock in 1957, Eisenhower, a president with less progressivist vanity than either of the Kennedys, had not held himself to such a prudish interpretation of federalism.[64] Not until the civil rights movement had achieved sufficient momentum and attention to be called "The Negro Revolution"—that is to say the status of a sociopolitical watershed that would neither go away nor adapt itself to the presidential calendar—were Kennedy's energies committed to integrating black citizens into the national democracy, most notably in drafting the *Civil Rights Act of 1964*. Still, for years after their untimely deaths civil rights activists thought of both the Kennedy brothers as heros of their cause, and court historians assiduously recorded the tributes of civil rights leaders who at the time were perhaps too grateful for what support they got to admit to themselves that the real heros of civil rights were entirely within the ranks of their own movement.[65]

In domestic affairs more generally Kennedy combined a vision of vigorous liberalism, typified by his first State of the Union address, with fairly cautious stopgap measures to promote economic growth. He was instinctively a conservative in economic matters, but was elected in the midst of a recession and came to accept the advice of chief economic advisor Walter Heller that the commitment to balancing the budget should be downplayed, and that what was to be avoided at all costs was a sluggish economy combined with high unemployment and a deflationary policy. This was a significant shift. Until

Kennedy, balancing the budget was viewed as a moral imperative as much as any technical requirement of the economy.
Under Heller's influence, Kennedy essentially discredited the
symbolic connection between the balanced budget and morality, deficit spending and profligacy. He also racheted up
Washington's responsibility a significant notch or two; the new
standard was now balancing the budget at full employment.
Kennedy's antirecession initiatives themselves actually had little
effect on the business slump of 1961, but then their intention
was largely to create the impression of dynamism rather than
its fact. The president's advisors boasted about the
administration's First Hundred Days, evoking memories of
FDR's initial skirmishes with the Great Depression. The implicit comparison was ridiculous, of course, but it was not to
be a decade in which any sense of proportion was especially
valued.[66]

For in 1960 something intangible but powerful was also at
work. It had been presaged by the often personal and vitriolic
attacks on Truman in 1946, and it symbolized nothing so much
as the exalted status of the presidency at the end of the
Roosevelt era. Under Roosevelt the office had acquired not
only new powers but also an imperial aura and the function of
a depository of popular hopes and anxieties. In 1946 criticisms
of the president were often more personal than political. More
tellingly, they invoked the memory of FDR with a cruel twist.
In 1946 it was popular in Texas to wonder aloud what Roosevelt
would do were he still in office and then to ask what Truman
would do if he were still alive.[67] Between 1933 and 1945 a standard had been set in the Oval Office that no subsequent occupant could attain. Eisenhower had moved in the opposing direction and attempted to reduce popular expectations of
government generally, and of the chief executive specifically,
but among the other factors that elected John Kennedy in 1960
was a vague sense that the nation was in a malaise and that the
election of a new and young president could itself initiate something of a national renaissance.

In reality neither the economy nor civil rights really had
the president's genuine interest. "Kennedy's heart", notes one
of most astute analysts of the civil rights cause, "was in the
great struggle with the Soviet Union, and he didn't conceive
of race relations in the United States as a problem of similar

magnitude and complexity."[68] For many scholars even today Kennedy's inaugural lives in memory as an inspirational masterpiece, and it is not unusual to witness them carried away by their own accounts of how in this and other instances Kennedy seemed to speak in public "as Byzantine emperors appeared on states occasions: Sheathed in gold, suspended between heaven and earth."[69] The theme of New Frontier, first coined by Kennedy in his acceptance of the Democratic nomination, was underscored in a speech that conjured the passing of the torch of national mission *to a new generation of Americans*, while noting to friend and foe that *we shall pay any price, bear any burden, support any friend, oppose any foe to assure the survival and success of liberty.*

The message of Kennedy's inaugural may well have been influenced by the advice of more experienced, but not necessarily more seasoned, students of foreign policy. A look, for example, at an article published in April 1960 by Dean Rusk, Kennedy's and later Johnson's Secretary of State, reveals an acceptance of truly enormous responsibilities for U.S. foreign relations. After observing that the presidency "has become an office of almost unbearable responsibilities," Rusk directed a stern warning to the officeholder on which the fulfillment of all those responsibilities are alleged to depend:

> . . . the modern Presidency cannot limit itself to a national interest narrowly defined. Recorded in solemn treaties and rooted in common interest and circumstance, we are a partner in great coalitions which now include more than 40 nations. Our power has reduced our sovereignty and our decisions must take into account the needs and hopes of those whose fates are linked with ours. If the President fails to meet the demands of leadership of a nation-in-coalition, a reluctant or resistant United States cannot be dragged along by others and coalitions as now constituted would rapidly disintegrate.[70]

An extraordinary statement. But not altogether logically consistent, and tantamount to saying that the President cannot define a *national* interest at all. Rusk's reminder on the burdens of multilateralism notes simultaneously that the alliances for which the economic and military power of the United States represents the keystone are rooted in *common interest and circumstance*, yet warns that a crisis of American credibility arising from the president's policy would lead to the disintegration of those same alliances. At home the president must communicate to his people the essence of the nation's mission in the world and justify the burden that they will bear, and yet he dare not put a rhetorical foot wrong for fear of alienating America's allies. Kennedy therefore can be forgiven for not living up to his rhetoric and not altogether heeding Rusk's nightmare of collapsing alliances.

As it turned out Kennedy's foreign policy was notable above all for inconsistency and mediocre results, and was always a good deal less sophisticated than its spokesmen believed. Behind the brave new world international relations jargon that was *de rigueur* in the Kennedy White House was a Cold War orthodoxy alloyed only by the president's impatience with patience, the very essence of containment as first prescribed by George Kennan. When Fidel Castro transformed the Cuban revolution into a communist dictatorship, Kennedy dusted off a blueprint for his overthrow—a CIA plan concocted in the last weeks of the Eisenhower administration and based on the assumption that an invading army of 12,000 Cuban exiles would excite an irresistible popular uprising. When the Bay of Pigs operation went awry, Kennedy refused air support to the invasion force with the argument that he didn't want American fingerprints on the fiasco. He seems to have been the only one who imagined that some form of denial was plausible, forgetting perhaps that in the Caribbean the United States had long ago surrendered its innocence and that it had been surrendered in Cuba first of all. Instead, the Bay of Pigs set something of a pattern of half measures for the rest of Kennedy's administration. If one took at face value Castro's boast that he would export his revolution all over the Caribbean, after all, the case could easily have been made for a full-blown American invasion. From the outset Kennedy thought the plan was flawed. Yet he opted for cleverness over courage and reaped the appropriate reward of moral cowardice.[71]

In the Berlin crisis of 1961 the Kennedy administration anticipated drastic action from the Soviet side to counter the slow death of the East German state through the flight of its citizens. The charge against Kennedy is not that he was taken by surprise by the erection of the Berlin Wall (for he was not) but that he might have prevented the action by taking a firmer line on Western rights of access to all of Berlin under the

Potsdam Agreement. Kennedy fully understood the reasons for the erection of the Berlin Wall, namely that for the Soviets stopping the flow of refugees from East Germany was possibly necessary to the maintenance of the entire Warsaw Pact. On July 25 Kennedy delivered a speech over television in which he professed his determination to make good on the American commitment to Berlin, yet referred only to West Berlin, thus possibly encouraging Moscow to understand that the United States would not act to defend Western rights of access to all of the city. Kennedy was aware that the United States was in no military position to threaten truly punative action save that of nuclear war against the Soviet Union over Berlin, due to the comparative weakness of U.S. conventional forces in the Berlin area.[72]

There were two equally legitimate ways to view Berlin. One could argue that, since the Cold War had really started over the division of Europe, there was in principle no more appropriate place for the Kennedy administration to live up to the bold rhetoric of the inaugural. Certainly, Kennedy had advice at his disposal that told him so, while public opinion endorsed to the tune of 80 percent a policy of keeping American forces in Berlin "even at the risk of war." The Wall stemmed the hemorrhage of refugees and permitted the East German economy to recover, so that for thirty years it became an asset rather than a liability to the Soviet Bloc. This perspective involved risk, to be sure, but at the time the American nuclear advantage was enormous.[73] If, on the other hand, one believed that the inherent superiority of liberal democratic government and capitalism would eventually deliver victory to the United States if it stuck with containment, then the flight of Germans from East Berlin, and the desperate Soviet response to it, were evidence that the Cold War was being won. Within the context of containment Kennedy's policy was defensible if not emotionally satisfying.

The worsening situation in Berlin certainly influenced Kennedy's disastrous summit meeting with Premier Khrushchev in Vienna in June 1961. Still, the best evidence is not that Moscow thought Kennedy weak over the Berlin crisis, and consequently tested him with the stationing of Soviet missiles in Cuba, but rather that during the Khrushchev years the Soviet

Union had a cowboy in the Kremlin whose "hairbrained schemes," as the Soviet Presidium later put it, brought the world as close as it has ever come to nuclear war largely on the strength of his own blustering stupidity.[74] Kennedy handled both the confrontation with Moscow itself and the public relations of the Cuban crisis very responsibly. He awarded too much to Khrushchev, however, as consolation prizes for a Soviet climb-down. His agreement to the withdrawal of obsolete U.S. Jupiter missiles from Turkey was trivial; more serious was his promise, as part of the trade-off with Moscow, never to invade Cuba and hence to accept a communist regime in military alliance with Moscow and avowedly aggressive intentions for the whole of the Caribbean. Dean Acheson thought that, on the face of the evidence, an air strike and overthrow of Castro were perfectly defensible initiatives and that the administration was in too much of a hurry to put the crisis behind it rather than wring concessions from Khrushchev in his moment of humiliation.[75]

In Cuba and elsewhere, assessments of Kennedy's term in office will always be especially speculative in nature due to the fact of his assassination. "The heart of the Kennedy legend," wrote James Reston, "is what might have been."[76] This is probably nowhere more evident than in the recurring and often juvenile debate as to whether Kennedy, had he lived, would have extracted the nation from Vietnam, whether a bullet alone prevented a change in the unfortunate course of U.S. policy in Southeast Asia. In fact, there is no clear evidence that Kennedy intended either to withdraw from Vietnam or to increase radically the American commitment there. Instead, two facts stand out: between his inauguration and death Kennedy increased the American contribution to South Vietnam's security to the level of 16,000 military advisors, while his public statements on U.S. goals in Indochina tended toward the militant. At a press conferences he compared Vietnam to World War I, World War II, and Korea, and only weeks before his assassination stressed that the United States was not in Vietnam to see it lost.[77]

Some scholars have given Kennedy primary responsibility for the fiasco that Vietnam became, and there is some evidence that he conceded a U.S. policy of neutralization for Laos in return for a much tougher stand in Vietnam. "Despite the rhetoric of bold, new thinking," goes the verdict, "Kennedy and his advisors never fundamentally reassessed American foreign policy assumptions," but instead "endowed them with more vigor and less patience."[78] Unfortunately, Vietnam was a poor candidate for impatience. Even more unfortunate for Vietnam and the whole course of American foreign relations, Kennedy changed American policy there to an Asian variation on the Alliance for Progress and development programs he applied to Latin America. He continued support for the regime of Ngo Dinh Diem without imposing stiff conditions for such support as might have, in the most optimistic scenario, made Diem's government more efficient, democratic, and popular. He then applied the *strategic hamlet* policy to South Vietnam, according to which key villages got both military security and development aid, for the purpose of actually transforming the socioeconomic reality of the villages and with it their political orientation. In essence Americans were to create a democratic political culture while defending South Vietnamese sovereignty. Add water and stir.

Any illusions about the viability of this policy should have been abandoned when Diem's troops fired on a Buddhist religious gathering in May 1963, thus setting off a series of Buddhist self-immolations in protest. The raw material of a democratic South Vietnam was in little evidence and Diem was making enemies of the most benign elements in his society. The strategic hamlet program was a disaster in social engineering, turning thousands of Vietnamese into dedicated enemies of the government.[79] So Kennedy then authorized American support for the coup that toppled and murdered Diem only three short weeks before his own death in Dallas.

Additionally, Kennedy cut his options in Southeast Asia in the diplomatic sense in much the same way as Eisenhower had done before before him. Because he rejected any agreement based on neutral status while negotiating neutrality for neighboring Laos, he focused the foreign policy and prestige of the United States in Indochina more narrowly than ever on the survival of the South Vietnamese regime, yet complicated the defense of the same. Communists in Laos flouted the agreement and North Vietnam used Laotian territory to penetrate deep into South Vietnam, to which the United States could respond only with covert operations. Hanoi's failure to abide by the neutrality accord was a bitter disappointment for Kennedy, but why he ever hoped that North Vietnam would stand by its commitments is unclear.[80] Generally he had better instincts on Vietnam than many of his senior advisors. He appreciated that in Asia the travail of containment had been especially problematic for both Truman and Eisenhower. He also understood that the American people expected the United States to thwart any advance by communism in principle, but were in fact unlikely to bear *any* burden to do so.[81] It was the president's job. When in doubt about this and the whole history of American involvement in Indochina—an involvement stretching in one form or another all the way back to FDR— Kennedy had Secretary of State Dean Rusk assuring him that just about everything would be lost if he did not stay the course. By the time of Kennedy's death, all sense of proportion in Vietnam was gone, and Kennedy's successor, Lyndon Johnson, despite his gargantuan political skills, was less likely than anyone to restore it.

Notes

1   Gerhard L. Weinberg, *A World at Arms: A Global History of World War II* (New York: Cambridge University Press, 1994) p. 87. No precise definition of *superpower* ever evolved. The term was used for the duration of the Cold War to distinguish global reach of the United States and the Soviet Union from that of the *Great Powers* of the nineteenth century more generally, and a group that between 1945 and 1990 came to include not only the superpowers but also Britain, China, France, Germany, and Japan. Superpower status incorporated not only the capacity to wage all-out nuclear war and to absorb a less than all-out nuclear attack but also industrial self-sufficiency and the technological capacity to stay abreast of other nations. Nations in alliance with a superpower were often dependent on it for the supply of advanced weapons and the advantages of the most modern communications and transportation. See Hans J. Morgenthau, *Politics Among Nations: The Struggle for Power and Peace* (New York: Alfred E. Knopf, 1985) p. 138.

2   James D. Savage, *Balanced Budgets and American Politics* (Ithaca, N.Y.: Cornell University Press, 1988), p. 174.

3   Officially called the *Labor-Management Relations Act*, the legislation placed limitation on labor union activities, regulated internal arrangements of unions, and strengthened the position of individual workers. It also outlawed the closed shop, jurisdictional strikes, secondary boycotts and political activities, while making it legal for both unions and employers to sue each other for contract violations.

4   Created by the *Employment Act* of 1946, the CEA became a staff agency of the Executive Office of the President (EOP). It made recommendations to the President on the "maintenance of employment, production and purchasing power," that were subsequently included in the President's economic report to Congress.

5   George Kennan, "The Sources of Soviet Conduct," *Foreign Affairs*, Vol.25, No.4 July, 1947, pp. 566–582, p. 575; David Mayers, *George Kennan and the Dilemmas of U.S. Foreign Policy* (New York: Oxford University Press, 1988), pp. 28–47 and 89–131; Wilson D. Miscamble, *George F. Kennan and the Making of American Foreign Policy* (Prinecton, N.J.: Princeton University Press, 1992), pp. 20–33.

6   Kennan, "Sources of Soviet Conduct," p. 582.

7   Ibid. On Kennan's ambivalent pronouncements on the application of containment See: Thomas G. Paterson, *Meeting the Communist Threat, Truman to Reagan* (New York: Oxford University Press, 1988), pp. 132–134.

8   Quoted in David McCullough, *Truman* (New York: Simon and Schuster, 1992), p. 608; Melvyn Leffler, *A Preponderance of Power* (Stanford, Calif.: Stanford University Press, 1992), p. 11; Les K. Adler and Thomas G. Paterson, "Red Fascism: The Merger of Nazi Germany and Soviet Russia in the American Image of Totalitarianism, 1930s-1950s," *American Historical Review*, Vol.75, No.4, 1970, pp. 1046-1064.

9   Michael Hogan, *The Marshall Plan: America, Britain, and the Reconstruction of Europe, 1947-1952* (New York: Cambridge University Press, 1987) pp. 22-23; Charles S. Maier, *In Search of Stability: Explorations in Historical Political Economy* (New York: Cambridge University Press, 1987), pp. 121-184.

10   Leffler, *Preponderance of Power*, pp. 355-360; Paul H. Nitze, *From Hiroshima to Glasnost: At the Center of Decision* (New York: Grove Weidenfeld, 1989) pp. 96-97; Ernest R. May Ed., *American Cold War Strategy: Interpreting NSC 68* (Boston: Bedford Books, 1993).

11   Leffler, *Preponderance of Power*, p. 357.

12   Robert H. Ferrell, *Choosing Truman: The Democratic Convention of 1944* (Columbia: University of Missouri Press, 1994), p. 90; McCullough, *Truman*, pp. 193-342.

13   Robert Divine, "The Cold War and the Election of 1948," *Journal of American History*, Vol.59, No.1, 1972-73, pp. 90-110.

14   Selig Adler, *The Isolationist Impulse: Its Twentieth Century Reaction*, (New York: Collier, 1957), p. 374.

15   In January, 1950 Acheson had sketched out, rather too briefly, the American perimeter of security in the Pacific. The fact that neither Korea nor Taiwan were mentioned in the briefing later became the basis of charges that he had unwittingly encouraged the North Korean invasion. In his memoirs Acheson is unrepentant. See Dean Acheson, *Present at the Creation: My Years at the State Department* (New York: W. W.Norton, 1969), p. 358. On romantic images of China based to a large extent on the writings of American foreign correspondents in the 1930s and 1940s see Steven W. Mosher, *China Misperceived: American Illusions and Chinese Reality* (New York: Harper-Collins, 1990) pp. 49-69; also Ellen Schrecker, *The Age of McCarthy* (Boston: Bedford Books, 1994), pp. 66-69.

16   Paterson, *Meeting the Communist Threat*, p. 103; Robert Griffith, *The Politics of Fear: Joseph R. McCarthy and the Senate* (Amherst: University of Massachusetts Press, 1987) p. xvii and pp. 6-11.

17   John Lewis Gaddis, *The United States and the End of the Cold War: Implications, Reconsiderations, Provocations* (New York: Oxford University Press, 1992), p. 98; *New York Times*, January 14, 1993, p. A12.

18   Richard O. Davies, *Defender of the Old Guard: John Bricker and American Politics* (Columbus: Ohio State University Press, 1993), p. 154; also Duane Tannanbaum, *The Bricker Amendment Controversy: A Test of Eisenhower's Political Leadership* (Ithaca, N.Y.: Cornell University Press, 1988).

19   Robert Dallek notes that Johnson's reluctance was based on a desire to avoid the political costs of openly opposing a measure that was initially popular, but that he was in the end a critical ally for Eisenhower in engineering its defeat. Robert Dallek, *Lone Star Rising: Lyndon Johnson and his Times, 1908–1960* (New York: Oxford University Press, 1991), pp. 435–437. Nixon, as a Senator, had maintained close ties and parallel viewpoints with Bricker. As Eisenhower's vice-president, his ability to support the amendment evaporated.

20   Quoted in Thomas J. Schoenbaum, *Waging Peace and War: Dean Rusk in the Truman, Kennedy, and Johnson Years* (New York: Simon and Schuster, 1988), pp. 211–212.

21   Ibid., pp. 209–210.

22   Herbert S. Parmet, *Eisenhower and the American Crusades* (New York: Macmillan, 1972) pp. 73–101; Leon Epstein, *Political Parties in the American Mold* (Madison: University of Wisconsin Press, 1986), p. 109.

23   McCullough, *Truman*, pp. 889–905; Nelson Polsby and Aaron Wildavsky, *Presidential Elections: Strategies of American Electoral Politics* (New York: Scribner, 1980) p. 225.

24   Porter McKeever, *Adlai Stevenson, His Life and Legacy* (New York: William Morrow, 1989), pp. 173–198.

25   Dwight D. Eisenhower, *The White House Years, 1953–1956: Mandate for Change* (Garden City, N.Y.: Doubleday, 1963), p. 281.

26   Quoted in McKeever, p. 264.

27   Cathal J. Nolan, *Principled Diplomacy: Security and Rights in US Foreign Policy* (Westport, Conn.: Greenwood, 1993), pp. 107–106.

28   Fred I. Greenstein, "Leadership Theorist in the White House," in Fred I. Greenstein Ed., *Leadership in the Modern Presidency* (Cambridge, Mass.: Harvard University Press, 1988), pp. 76–107.

29   Eisenhower, *Mandate for Change*, pp. 279–285; Davies, *Defender of the Old Guard*, pp. 153–183.

30   Henry J. Abraham, *Freedom and the Court: Civil Rights and Liberties in the United States* (New York: Oxford University Press, 1988), pp. 425–426; Donald W. Jackson and James W. Riddlesperger, "The Eisenhower Administration and the 1957 Civil Rights Act," in S.A. Warshaw and

Galambos, *Reexamining the Eisenhower Presidency* (Westport, Conn.: Greenwood, 1993), pp. 85–101.

31   Quoted in Dwight D. Eisenhower, *The White House Years, Waging Peace, 1956-61*, (Garden City, N.Y.: Doubleday, 1965), p. 169, n.10.

32   Parmet, *Eisenhower*, pp. 503–513; Dallek, *Lone Star Rising*, p. 528.

33   Eisenhower, *Mandate for Change*, p. 8.

34   The concept of *massive retaliation*, posing the hypothesis of the use of nuclear weapons against the Soviet Union or Soviet client states, was thought to provide the United States with greater insurance against the possibility that American interests or allies would ever be endangered. In essence it sacrificed a degree of flexibility in U.S. military options for the supposed psychological edge derived from the fear among potential American adversaries that nuclear annihilation might be the cost of reckless behavior.

35   *Foreign Relations of the United States* (hereafter *FRUS*), *1952-54*, vol. 10, pp. 692–701; Mark Hamilton Lytle, *The Origins of the American-Iranian Alliance, 1941-1953* (New York: Holmes and Meier, 1987), pp. 192–203 and 205–218.

36   A good deal of the planning for the coup, even the involvement of American agents, was completed by Great Britain, so that it was difficult to trace Mosaddeq's overthrow to Washington.

37   Rhodri Jeffreys-Jones, *The CIA and American Democracy* (New Haven, Conn.: Yale University Press, 1989) pp. 91–93: Richard Immerman, *The CIA in Guatemala: The Foreign Policy of Intervention* (Austin: University of Texas Press, 1982). The administration also needed British cooperation in covering its tracks in Guatemala, a favor made somewhat more problematic by the fact that among the CIA's activities had been the accidental sinking of a British freighter. Sharon I. Meers, "The British Connection: How the United States Covered its Tracks in the 1945 Coup in Guatemala," *Diplomatic History*, Vol.16, No.3 1992, pp. 409–428.

38   Jeffreys-Jones, *The CIA*, p. 78.

39   Eisenhower, *Waging Peace*, p. 175.

40   Diane B. Kunz, *The Economic Diplomacy of the Suez Crisis* (Chapel Hill: University of North Carolina Press, 1991) p. 93.

41   Compare *FRUS 1952-1954*, vol.10, pp. 692–701 with *FRUS 1955-1957*, pp. 902–916; Kunz, *Economic Diplomacy*, pp. 65–72; William Stivers "Eisenhower and the Middle East," in Richard A. Melanson and David

Mayers Eds., *Reevaluating Eisenhower: American Foreign Policy in the Fifties* (Urbana: University of Illinois Press, 1987), p. 213.

42   Paterson, *Meeting the Communist Threat*, pp. 159-190; Stephen E. Ambrose, *Eisenhower, The President* (New York: Simon and Schuster, 1984), pp. 376-388.

43   Quoted in Ambrose, *Eisenhower, The President*, p. 233

44   Ambrose, *Eisenhower, The President*, p. 235.

45   John Lewis Gaddis, *The Long Peace: Inquiries into the History of the Cold War* (New York: Oxford University Press, 1987), p. 135.

46   Irwin M. Wall, *The United States and the Making of Postwar France, 1945-1954* (New York: Cambridge University Press, 1991), pp. 233-262; Alexander Werth, *France, 1940-1955* (London: Robert Hale, 1956), p. 539; Thomas Alan Schwartz, *America's Germany: John J. McCloy and the Federal Republic of Germany* (Cambridge: Harvard University Press, 1991), p. 118.

47   At a meeting of the NSC in June 1956, Eisenhower noted Peking's threat to invade Formosa and observed that no similar danger existed in Vietnam. At the same meeting Admiral Arthur Radford, Chairman of the Joint Chiefs of Staff, outlined the options for US contributions to military participation in the event of North Vietnamese aggression. *FRUS, 1955-1957*, Vol.1, pp. 695-709.

48   Stanley Karnow, *Vietnam, A History* (New York: Penguin, 1983), pp. 197-205; Arthur Combs, "The Path Not Taken: The British Alternative to U.S. Policy in Vietnam," *Diplomatic History*, Vol.19, No.1 1995, pp. 33-57; Raymond Aron, *On War* (Garden City, N.Y.: Doubleday, 1959), p. 27.

49   George C. Herring, *America's Longest War: The United States in Vietnam, 1950-1975* (New York: Wiley, 1976), p. 46.

50   Stivers, "Eisenhower and the Middle East," pp. 194-206.

51   Rolf Steininger, "John Foster Dulles, the European Defense Community, and the German Question," in Richard H. Immerman Ed., *John Foster Dulles and the Diplomacy of the Cold War* (Princeton, N.J.: Princeton University Press, 1990) pp. 79-108.

52   Richard D. Challener, "The Moralist as Pragmatist: John Foster Dulles as Cold War Strategist," in Gordon A. Craig and Francis L. Lowenheim Eds., *The Diplomats, 1939-1979*, (Princeton, N.J.: Princeton University Press, 1994) p. 160.

53   Challener, "Moralist as Pragmatist," pp. 135–160; Ambrose, *Eisenhower, The President,* p. 355.

54   Raymond Garthoff, *Assessing the Adversary: Estimates by the Eisenhower Administration of Soviet Intentions and Capabilities* (Washington, D.C.: Brookings, 1991), p. 52.

55   Robert A. Divine, *The Sputnik Challenge* (New York: Oxford University Press, 1993), pp.vii–viii; Savage, *Balanced Budgets*; Walter LeFeber, *America, Russia and the Cold War, 1945–1990* (New York: McGraw-Hill, 1991) pp. 196–199; Rowland Evans and Robert Novak, *Lyndon B. Johnson: The Exercise of Power* (New York: Signet, 1966) pp. 204–209.

56   Dallek, *Lone Star Rising,* pp. 529–533.

57   Quoted in Parmet, *Eisenhower,* pp. 570–572.

58   Quoted by Mary McGrory, "The Perfectionist and the Press," in Edward P. Doyle Ed., *As We Knew Adlai* (New York: Harper & Row, 1966) p. 177. See also Robert Fairlie quoted in Kathleen Hall Jamieson, *Eloquence in the Electronic Age* (New York: Oxford University Press, 1988), p. 177.

59   See Theodore C. Sorenson, *Kennedy* (New York: Harper & Row, 1965) p. 165. See also Dan B. Fleming, *Kennedy vs. Humphrey, West Virginia, 1960* (Jefferson, N.C.: McFarland, 1992); Kathleen Hall Jamieson, *Packaging the Presidency: A History and Criticism of Presidential Campaign Advertising* (New York: Oxford University Press, 1984) pp. 122–168.

60   Jamieson, *Packaging the Presidency,* pp. 158–161; Angus Campbell et. al. *Elections and the Political Order* (New York: Wiley, 1966), p. 124; Theodore White, *The Making of the President, 1960* (New York: Athenaeum, 1961).

61   Robert A. Divine, *Foreign Policy and US Presidential Elections, 1940–1948* (New York: New Viewpoints, 1974), pp. 282–287.

62   Epstein, *Political Parties,* pp. 109–110; Roderick P. Hart, *The Sound of Leadership* (Chicago: University of Chicago Press, 1987), p. 30.

63   The amendment included a provision for trial by jury for state officials charged with violating court orders on voting rights. Taylor Branch, *Parting the Waters: America in the King Years, 1954–63* (New York: Simon & Schuster, 1988), pp. 220–221.

64   Branch, *Parting the Waters,* pp. 426–429; Donald Nieman, *Promises to Keep: African Americans and the Constitutional Order, 1776 to the Present* (New York: Oxford University Press, 1991) pp. 164–165.

65   Arthur M. Schlesinger Jr., *A Thousand Days: John F. Kennedy in the White House* (Boston: Houghton Mifflin, 1965), pp. 950–977.

66 Savage, *Balanced Budgets*, pp. 176–178; J.F. Heath, *Decade of Disillusionment: The Kennedy-Johnson Years* (Bloomington: Indiana University Press, 1975), pp. 62–67.

67 McCullough, *Truman*, p. 520.

68 Nicholas Lemann, *The Promised Land: The Great Black Migration and How it Changed America* (New York: Vintage, 1991), p. 115.

69 Henry Fairlie, *The Kennedy Promise* (New York: Dell, 1972), pp. 72–73.

70 Dean Rusk, "The President," *Foreign Affairs*, Vol.38, No.3, April 1960, p. 359.

71 Michael R. Beschloss, *The Crisis Years: Kennedy and Khrushchev, 1960–1963* (New York: Edward Burlingame, 1991), pp. 118–125.

72 Beschloss, *The Crisis Years*, pp. 266–283.

73 Thomas Allen Schwartz, "Victories and Defeats in the Long Twilight Struggle: The United States and Western Europe in the 1960s," in Diane B. Kunz Ed., *The Diplomacy of the Crucial Decade: American Foreign Relations in the 1960s* (New York: Columbia, 1994), pp. 120–123.

74 James G. Blight and David A. Welch, *On the Brink: Americans and Soviets Reexamine the Cuban Missile Crisis* (New York: Hill & Wang, 1989) p. 284.

75 Beschloss, *The Crisis Years*, p. 521. See also Raymond L. Garthoff, *Reflections on the Cuban Missile Crisis* (Washington, D.C.: Brookings, 1989) pp. 154–192. It has subsequently been revealed that Kennedy never officially finalized the agreement not to invade, because he was rightly troubled that the U.S. would thereby tie its own hands against robust action in response to any future arms build-up in Cuba. Acheson's proposal for more aggressive action during the crisis might well have been disastrous as well, given that the Soviets had deployed tactical nuclear weapons on Cuban soil and had given middle-ranking officers authority to use them.

76 Quoted in William E. Leuchtenburg, *In the Shadow of FDR* (Ithaca, N.Y.: Cornell University Press, 1993), p. 119.

77 Tom Wicker "Committed to a Quagmire," *Diplomatic History*, Vol.19, No.1, 1995, pp. 167–171.

78 For example Lawrence J. Basset and Stephen E. Pelz, "The Failed Search for Victory: Vietnam and the Politics of War," in Thomas G. Paterson Ed., *Kennedy's Quest for Victory: American Foreign Policy, 1961–1963* (New York: Oxford University Press, 1989), pp. 223–252; James N. Giglio, *The Presidency of John F. Kennedy* (Lawrence: University of Kansas Press, 1991), pp. 240–241.

79 Bassett and Pelz, "The Failed Search for Victory," p. 239–244.

80   Karnow, *Vietnam*, p. 248; Bassett and Pelz, "The Failed Search for Victory" pp. 228–231; Dean Rusk, *As I Saw It*, (New York: W.W. Norton, 1990) p. 429.

81   David Kaiser, "Men and Policies: 1961–69," in Kunz, *Diplomacy of the Crucial Decade*, p. 19.

Chapter 5

One War, Two Presidents

In the opinion of all men he would have been regarded as capable of
governing, if he had never governed. –Tacitus, *Annales*

Between 1964 and 1974 the American presidency became the
impossible job. Two of the ablest politicians the country ever
produced, Lyndon Johnson and Richard Nixon, were destroyed
by their responses to the demands of the office. Anyone appreciative of the capacity of these men at the time would have
thought the chances of such an outcome remote.

Johnson was elected to represent the tenth congressional
district of Texas in 1937 and graduated in 1948 to a Senate
seat after a decade's apprenticeship in the House. He became
Democratic whip in 1951, party leader in 1953. Thereafter his
art of compromise, tactical agility, powers of persuasion, and
ability to make the Democratic majority work with a Republican administration made him a figure of legend in Congress.
When in 1960 he lost the Democratic nomination to John
Kennedy and subsequently served as vice president, Johnson
was a president-in-waiting; when he assumed presidential duties after Kennedy's slaying, the nation acquired a chief executive who understood the workings of the federal government
better than possibly anyone.

Nixon was first elected to the House in 1946 and the Senate
in 1950. He made a national name for himself as the principal
congressional investigator of the activities of State Department
official Alger Hiss, and as a political survivor when he saved
his place on the Eisenhower presidential ticket with the "Check-
ers" speech of 1952. After serving two terms as an especially

active vice-president, Nixon lost the presidential election of 1960 to Kennedy by the narrowest of margins. Even after a failed gubernatorial bid in California in 1962, Nixon stayed in the swim of GOP politics until he had by 1968 built the personal political organization that brushed aside all other candidates for the Republican nomination in that year. Nixon's narrow defeat of Humphrey finally put him in the White House at the very peak of his formidable abilities.

Neither, then, was undone by inexperience or a failure of stamina. On the contrary, each was in his own way so extraordinarily effective in the application of acquired political skills that their combined efforts took the imperial presidency to its high-water mark. Yet despite the considerable rehabilitation that time and sober historiography have facilitated, the Johnson-Nixon decade constitutes a single melancholy chapter in American political history. The names of the late presidents carry with them the stigma of failed administrations, the memory of which provokes intemperate generalizations connecting the trauma of an entire nation to the personalities of two men. Notwithstanding significant differences in temperament, political pedigree, and legislative priorities, there were unmistakable similarities in their respective approaches to the use and abuse of presidential prerogative. Their expansive definition of executive authority provoked congressional initiatives to reestablish the constitutional balance, in which the Senate Watergate hearings and impeachment proceedings against Nixon represent only the most spectacular episodes. Such initiatives were often so mismanaged or deflected from their purpose by the multiple stresses of domestic and foreign policy issues that they constituted abuses in themselves. In a multitude of ways they compounded rather than reduced obstacles to the governability of the United States in the 1970s.

The relationship between domestic and foreign affairs during the Johnson and Nixon administrations was in some respects more intense and problematic than at any time since the Great Depression. Johnson's simultaneous prosecution of the Vietnam war and passage of the Great Society legislation extended the fiscal and political capacity of the New Deal consensus to the breaking point. Nixon's crisis-management of the American commitment in Southeast Asia reversed the policy

established 1964–68 with a process of negotiation and graduated withdrawal, yet deepened the conflict between the executive and legislative branches inherited from Johnson. The
superpower *détente* crafted by Nixon was as much a product of
the mounting burden of the Cold War foreign policy as of diplomatic philosophy itself. Yet conservative critics of Nixon set
the agenda for Reaganism with their attack on *détente* as an
amoral accommodation with Moscow. They also attacked the
rising cost of the American welfare state under Great Society
liberalism, which Nixon attempted to reform yet never subjected to frontal assault. Viewed from this perspective, Barry
Goldwater's failed presidential bid of 1964 and Ronald
Reagan's election to the Oval Office in 1980 are merely different episodes in the glacial emergence of a new conservatism
to the fore of American public affairs. At the same time, the
crisis of New Deal liberalism occasioned by Johnson's excesses
at home and abroad destroyed the Democratic Party as the
dominant electoral force in American politics; reduced to
Congress, Democrats then used legislative authority to thwart
Nixon's efforts to rationalize Johnson's welfare legacy while
measuring his foreign policy with their own standards in moral
absolutes. Democrats have ever since seemed incapable of any
realistic calculation of American national interest in global
affairs.

So the Johnson-Nixon years have a lot to answer for. If a
reexamination of the period is to extract useful lessons concerning the governance of the United States, then perhaps the
most meaningful questions that can be applied are these:
whether other presidents would have acted in a fundamentally
different fashion, or whether between 1964 and 1974 the demands on presidential leadership in fact departed from what
can reasonably be expected of mere mortals. If these two presidents could not meet those demands, could anyone?

Welfare and Warfare in the Age of Excess

Lyndon Johnson inherited the Oval Office from an assassi-
nated President. Thus deprived of his own electoral mandate
until November 1964, he sought legitimacy for his actions by
emphasizing continuity in his first presidential address to Con-

gress. "I was the trustee and custodian of the Kennedy administration," he later wrote, "I considered myself the caretaker of both his people and his policies."[1] Above all, this meant furthering the cause of black civil rights at home and staying the course of established policy abroad. The essential difference between Johnson and his martyred predecessor in 1963 was not policy but authenticity and capacity. Johnson's long service in the U.S. Congress and emergence as one of the greatest majority leaders in the legislature's history had endowed him with an infinitely broader array of political assets, personal contacts, and legislative savvy than Kennedy. Johnson was equipped to achieve much more from the Oval Office than Kennedy had been likely to accomplish had he lived. This Johnson knew when he competed with Kennedy for the Democratic nomination in 1960. And while he appreciated that the want of a personal electoral mandate on the day of his improvised swearing-in deprived his authority of full popular legitimacy, Johnson also knew that the peculiarity of his circumstance offered certain opportunities.

It is worthwhile noting that from the start Johnson did not simply adopt Kennedy policies. Rather, in the first year of his presidency he appropriated Kennedy's name on behalf of his own interpretation of Kennedy initiatives. Johnson's own ideological pedigree was full-blooded New Deal liberalism. As a Texan, he combined a mixed set of attitudes on civil rights with the legislative leverage sufficient to pass the Civil Rights Bill of 1957 and a desire to stay in the mainstream of national politics by dissociating himself with southern segregationism. When he became president, admittedly, the country was formally committed to a set of political goals in Southeast Asia, but Johnson himself had helped to establish those goals. Dispatched to Vietnam by Kennedy on a fact-finding tour in early 1961, Johnson returned to remind the president about the disastrous French experience in Vietnam, yet concluded that U.S. policy should be vigorous and informed by a sense of urgency, because "the basic decision in South East Asia is here."[2] As president, Johnson brought sense of urgency both to American policy in Vietnam and the cause of reform at home sufficient to transform Washington's political landscape by 1965.

The civil rights issue was critical to Johnson both personally and politically. In the short term it made good his claim on continuity with the Kennedy administration; over the long term it was the point of departure for his ambition to be the greatest liberal reformer ever. And in no realm is there stronger testimony to the fact that the only measure of success Johnson truly respected was the legislative record. He secured passage of the *Civil Rights Act* of 1964, the most important civil rights legislation of the century, and added to it the *Voting Rights Act* of 1965. Even these were only part of what became a massive executive agenda of education and social reform, antipoverty initiatives, and affirmative action programs that Johnson organized under the rubric of *The Great Society*. Between late 1963 and 1966 there were points at which a combination of national political circumstance and the president's determination brought about a de facto suspension of the separation of powers.

The classic case in point is the Civil Rights Act of 1964. Back in 1954 the Supreme Court's decision on *Brown v. the Board of Education* had given the signal that federal initiatives to end racial segregation had the unqualified blessing of the United States Constitution. The climate of national emergency following upon the Kennedy assassination and intensified by the explosion of the civil rights movement, on the streets of southern cities and on the screens of suburban televisions, gave Johnson the opportunity to rally both public opinion and congressional votes behind his initiatives. His own political courage and tireless drive did the rest. Johnson's contribution was not the fact of the bill's passage, for Kennedy had been in a position just prior to the assassination to pass important civil rights legislation, but in the preservation of its comprehensiveness in the face of the Democratic Party's tawdry legacy in civil rights in the South. Johnson refused any compromise of the bill's content. Once the legislation had cleared the House in February 1964, he made it plain that he was prepared to break a Senate filibuster by holding all other congressional business ransom to the success of the civil rights package. Dealing directly and unsubtly with Senators Richard Russell, the aged leader of the southern Democrats, and Everett Dirksen, Senate Republican leader, he then marshalled the two-thirds majority necessary to invoke cloture and end debate, both on the civil rights issue and on a critical tax cut, with a crushing executive branch victory. Obviously, Johnson was able to draw on Republican support in both chambers, but in facing civil rights reform head-on he was asking the Democratic Party to face possibly massive electoral costs in the South.[3]

The tax reduction was as historic as the civil rights bill and was also linked to it politically. It involved "the first major stimulative measure adopted in the postwar era at a time when the economy was neither in, nor threatened imminently by recession"; moreover, it passed in July 1964 at a juncture where "the federal budget was in deficit and federal expenditures were rising."[4] It represented in part a breakthrough for Keynesian economics in peacetime, an event in incubation ever since Walter Heller first lectured President Kennedy on the possibilities of full-employment budgeting in 1961. As vice-president Johnson had been doubtful about such a departure from fiscal orthodoxy, but now he reversed positions. After convincing sceptics on the Council of Economic Advisors (CEA) that a pledge to trim appropriations commensurate with the reduction in revenues would turn the flank of opposition in Congress, it could hardly be a bad thing that the passage of his civil rights initiative was accompanied by a commitment to leave more money in the pockets of the American middle class. Nor could it harm the cause of the presidential 1964 election, only four months away. Advising an aide on the rhythm of the political seasons and legislative sessions, Johnson once noted that the fourth year of a presidential mandate was "all politics."[5]

Johnson's civil rights reforms were the most sweeping of their kind since Reconstruction. As an instrument of public policy, the legislation built upon the foundations of New Deal liberalism by giving Washington, in Title IV of the final bill, authority to cut off federal funds to state or local governments practicing discrimination. Because such authority involved hundreds of grant-in-aid programs amounting to some 15 percent of state revenues, the Civil Rights Act proved very effective in forcing compliance with the administration's goals for ending the segregation of schools and public accommodations. It also established the Equal Employment Opportunity Commission (EEOC) to investigate and conciliate allegations of discrimination by employers or employment agencies based on race, religion, gender, or national origin. The key to the president's success was his political depth. Himself a creature of the legislative process, Johnson had "established relationships with leading congressmen and their families that broke down the wall of reserve characteristic of their contacts with Kennedy."[6] For liberal activists in the Democratic Party and the civil rights movement Johnson's actions were something of a revelation, especially when it "became clear that the substance of Johnson's aspirations was more often than not identical to theirs."[7] It turned out to be a short-lived lesson. During the 1960 Democratic primary season the same activists had cared little for the substance of the candidates when under the spell of the new politics; by 1967–68 they would again reactivate the stock caricature of Johnson, the vulgar Texan all too comfortable with the established relationships and backroom dealing of the old politics. Calling the civil rights legislation of 1964, "a proud triumph," Johnson was actually understating the dimensions of his achievement, but within months he was astounded at the apparent lack of gratitude for his actions among politically active black Americans. That too was in part a product of the difference between the tradition of New Deal liberalism in which Johnson was steeped and the politics of mass activism of the 1960s, a change which in the civil rights movement was perhaps most vividly reflected in the mounting prestige of leaders such as Malcolm X relative to Martin Luther King Jr., who was clearly the moral force of the movement in the first half of the decade. But equally it was an appreciation by civil rights activists generally of the critical role played by their own tenacious dedication during the 1950s.

In the meantime, Johnson took himself and the Democratic Party to a sweeping victory in the presidential election of 1964. Undeniably, he was helped by his recent success with civil rights legislation, for which there had been broad public support, as well as by his reassurance during the campaign that he was not about to increase precipitously the American commitment in Vietnam. But his reelection bid probably got its strongest single boost from the Republican Party, which nominated Senator Barry Goldwater for the Oval Office. Admittedly, in 1964 it was unlikely that any Republican could have turned Johnson out of office. He had handled the transition phase following upon the Kennedy assassination by pushing civil rights, a Kennedy initiative, to the top of the national agenda and then drawn upon his own legislative assets to make it the first business of the federal government; in effect, the Republican nominee had to take on the popular memory of Kennedy and the energies of Johnson combined into one force. In the Goldwater nomination, however, conservative control of the Republican Party's national organization trumped the more moderate position of the GOP rank-and-file and nominated a candidate from the far right of the both the party and the nation. Goldwater's platform was built on such extreme positions on civil rights, welfare, and foreign policy, that it was hardly necessary for the Johnson campaign to do more than stress the enormous responsibilities that the incumbent was currently handling so well, while enhancing Goldwater's image as dangerous, doctrinaire, out of touch with his time, and singularly unsuited for presidential authority.

That being the case, Johnson's campaign was extraordinarily aggressive. He ignored the well-oiled organizational machinery that Kennedy workers had constructed for the 1964 presidential year and made himself the captain of a secretive but highly effective anti-campaign, based on devastating attacks on Goldwater's ideas and personality. Some features of the Johnson campaign were clearly excessive, especially in light of the fact that Goldwater had no reasonable chance of election. When the Goldwater people produced a campaign button saying "In Your Heart You Know He's Right", Johnson's countered with a duplicate design scoffing "In Your Guts You Know He's Nuts." A television spot showed a little girl pulling petals from a daisy while the voice of Armageddon counted down to the launch of a nuclear missile. In sum, the Johnson propaganda prophesied the abolition of social security and nuclear holocaust under a Goldwater presidency.[8]

It was as if Johnson wanted the Republican Party to vanish from the electoral map. On November 3 1964 it very nearly did. Johnson took 61.05 percent of the popular vote against Goldwater's 38.47 percent, for a plurality of nearly 16 million votes and a distribution that in the electoral college translated to a 486 to 52 landslide. In a band of five southern states stretching from Louisiana in the west to South Carolina in the east, the vote swung strongly toward the GOP in a fashion that presaged things to come in future elections. But outside of the these states, where the Civil Rights Act legislation accounted for the administration's losses, Goldwater beat Johnson only in his home state of Arizona.

From the perspective of the 1990s, both the farcical campaign and the lopsided result were a disservice to American government. In 1964 the United States was at a crossroads of domestic and foreign policy. Yet only on the issue of civil rights was there any popular appreciation of the actual and potential stakes of the Johnson-Goldwater mismatch. Goldwater seemed to personify by turns the virulent anticommunism of the John Birch Society and the encrusted Taft Republicanism of 1952. The Johnson anticampaign portrayed him as such, and Goldwater's own speeches tended to embellish the caricature. Of course, there was more to Goldwater Republicanism than rasping reaction. At the high-water mark of New Deal Democratic liberalism, Goldwater represented no less than the first blip of the conservatism that became the dynamic force of American politics in the late 1970s and elected Ronald Reagan to the presidency in 1980. Four years prior to the 1964 election, Goldwater protested the bipartisan acceptance of New Deal liberalism as "an unqualified repudiation of the principle of limited government," and, recalling De Toqueville, warned of the decay awaiting any society that "put more emphasis on its democracy than on its republicanism"[9]—in Goldwater's view a philosophical error in that it prized equality over liberty. While Goldwater applauded the principle upheld by the Supreme Court in the *Brown* decision, he opposed as a violation of states' rights any new powers given to Washington to force compliance to the decision. He likewise attacked welfare, agricultural regulation, and trade union collective bargaining rights as federally mandated violations of individual liberty and self-government wholly incompatible with the intention of the Founders in 1787. Equally pernicious in Goldwater's view, were the higher levels of taxation required to finance the array of programs now on offer from Washington. "The root evil," he maintained, "is that the government is engaged in activities in which it has no legitimate business," meaning that "as long as the government acknowledges responsibility in a given social or economic field, its spending in that field cannot be sub-

stantially reduced."[10] Goldwater was not alone with these views
in the 1960s. William F. Buckley Jr., editor of the *National Review*, was only the best-known of a clutch of highly articulate
conservative critics of the received orthodoxy of New Deal liberalism, among them James Burnham, Whittaker Chambers,
John Chamberlain, and Willmore Kendall. Over the next decade of changing circumstance Buckley's criticisms in particular gathered sufficient appeal to make the Goldwater of 1964
seem something altogether different from the role of crank
assigned to him by Lyndon Johnson. But to the electorate of
1964 he seemed pinched, uptight, and not altogether rational.
So Johnson's massive victory in the presidential ballot translated into an equally impressive showing for Democrats in
Congress. They picked up two seats in the Senate and swept
up thirty-seven in the House, thus giving Johnson in the Eighty-
ninth Congress a Democratic majority so large that some commentators spoke of a one-and-a-half party system.[11]

The repudiation of Goldwater Republicanism, a blow from
which some thought the GOP might never recover, left Johnson
free to go beyond civil rights to the host of antipoverty programs and welfare reforms he christened the *Great Society* in
an address to the University of Michigan graduation class of
May 22, 1964. Johnson held out to his audience a vision of
abundance and liberty for all. At its core were the *Voting Rights
Act* of 1965[12] and the *War on Poverty*, but it also encompassed
education reform, jobs training, *Medicaire* and *Medicaide*, urban development, pollution regulation, as well as programs in
the arts and humanities. Voting rights and antipoverty initiatives were logical responses to the political pressures of the
civil rights movement. The civil rights legislation of 1964 and
the Voting Rights Bill of 1965 moved to protect for black
Americans the exercise of fundamental liberties guaranteed
to all citizens of the United States by the Constitution; the
War on Poverty was qualitatively different, but it was also attuned to the civil rights agenda to the extend that disproportionate numbers of black Americans lived below the poverty
line. It claimed a high priority with Johnson even before the
1964 election, partly by virtue of this linkage, but also because
so much of it was Johnson's own inspiration rather than
Kennedy's. After the election victory, Johnson imposed a tight

timetable for legislative action on the Great Society. Until 1966 he had sufficient strength in both chambers of Congress to break the alliance of conservative Democrats and Republicans that otherwise could block his programs or gut them of their substance. A decision by the House leadership to apply a twenty-one day rule helped with the imperative of expediency,[13] but Johnson's approach had its costs. The shear volume and complexity of the legislation, crammed through the window of opportunity available, meant that political haste too often trumped legislative content with the result that the coherence of many bills suffered. This alone does not change the fact that the Great Society attacked some of the nation's domestic ills quite effectively.[14] Twenty years later black voters were going to the polls at approximately the same rate as whites; the opportunity of higher education had opened to people from a broader diversity of social backgrounds; health care had been improved; environmental pollution entered the vocabulary and conscience of the nation.

For many of the enthusiasts of the Johnson reforms, Medicare represented the crowning achievement. Franklin Roosevelt had intended to include national health insurance in the *Social Security Act* of 1934, but in the end declined an all-out fight with the American Medical Association over the issue. Because President Kennedy had initiated studies on a health plan shortly after his election in 1960, there was already a certain administrative momentum behind it at the time of his assassination that Johnson wanted to exploit. Ever conscious of the political calendar, Johnson pulled out all the stops to pass health insurance legislation within the life of the Eighty-eighth Congress and before the election of 1964. But the Senate version of the bill was stalled in conference in October, primarily because of the reservations of the House Ways and Means Committee, thus eliminating any chance of passage before the election. The Democratic landslide settled the issue with its induction of lopsided majorities in both chambers and a proportional shift in the composition of Ways and Means Committee. The legislation passed and was signed into law in July 1965. In retrospect Johnson might have been well-advised to use the massive mandate he received in 1964 to spend more time with Medicare, given that its considerable long-term cost to the nation's fiscal resources turned out to be buried in the structure of its financing.[15] Still, it is difficult to second guess a president with Johnson's experience in legislative leadership. Political capital is not the same as money in the bank or even a promising stock. Left alone, its value evaporates.

The Johnson reforms in general crossed a critical divide, not surprising really considering the convergence of factors in the mid-1960s: a liberal Democratic administration working with a majority Congress and backed by a liberal Supreme Court in a decade of growing prosperity and a consumer culture committed to nothing quite so much as excess. It linked the constitutional imperative of the civil rights movement, equality before the law, with the goal of greater socioeconomic equality across racial lines. It blurred the border between the political and the economic to the point that the welfare provisions elaborated by the Johnson administration were interpreted by many not as a political good, the content of which could and should be revised with changes in the priority of public policy, but as fundamental rights on a par with access to the ballot box. Indeed, those provisions that have the status of *entitlements* are in principle immune from debate, because they are legal obligations of the federal government, an unfortunate fact if and when Washington finds that the resources it can bring to discretionary spending are thereby diminished. The quality of the Great Society's long-term contribution to domestic reform, moreover, was probably compromised both by the haste of its passage, the attendant problems of its administration, and its unhappy fate in sharing the attentions of the administration with the Vietnam conflict.[16]

And there was more than a touch of irony in this, for the priority that Johnson gave to the Great Society informed his choice of policies in Vietnam. Firm in the belief that the credibility of the United States was on trial with allies and foes alike, he nonetheless avoided any open declaration that in Southeast Asia the nation was involved in a struggle of major dimensions. This stemmed in part from the very nature of the original U.S. commitment to Vietnam under Eisenhower and Kennedy. American military might was not applied in the pursuit of a victory in traditional terms, but rather as a means to end North Vietnamese aggression and extract an acceptable diplomatic settlement from Hanoi. Years later, Robert MacNamara, Secretary of Defense for Kennedy and Johnson and a major contributor to the Vietnam policy of both administrations, speculated that Kennedy, had he lived, would probably have withdrawn from Vietnam, yet conceded simultaneously that by the time of his arrival in the Oval Office Johnson faced a situation "eminently more dangerous than the one Kennedy had inherited from Eisenhower."[17] Johnson was above all determined to insulate the domestic political environment from any external shocks that might endanger the Great Society's project of reform. Consequently, he did not so much wage as manage the war. Since there was no policy to win the war, with Johnson or before him, success meant doing whatever it took not to lose the war. As long as he had not visibly failed in Vietnam, Johnson reasoned, the domestic consensus he needed for the Great Society was safe. He was asking his countrymen to extend a portion of the unprecedented prosperity of their time to less fortunate citizens, a project that could not be furthered by the creeping consciousness that the nation was already fighting an enemy almost as implacable as poverty on the other side of the world and would need many, many more soldiers in order to prevail.

In the summer of 1964 Johnson was himself fighting a rearguard action against Republican foreign policy. In foreign affairs traditional Republican isolationism had clearly passed away. But if America's goals in the Cold War were worthy, in Republican eyes almost all of the methods employed by Democrats in their pursuit were not. Goldwater advocated repudiation of all disarmament agreements with Moscow, suspension of diplomatic relations with the Soviet Union, and U.S. withdrawal from the United Nations. He also echoed Republican "Asia First" critics of the Truman administration at the time of the Korean War with the charge that America's system of anticommunist alliances was wholly defensive in nature. Goldwater understood the logic of containment as it was first applied to Western Europe, namely that under conditions of strategic stalemate the United States and its allies could bring to bear the trump of a superior economic system in order to undercut the political viability of the Warsaw Pact over the long haul. But in any election year the incumbent administration can count on nothing so much as a caricatured misrepresentation of its policy. In 1964 this is what Johnson got from Goldwater. No matter, the incumbent was perfectly capable of defending himself. Johnson combined a measured presidential rhetoric on foreign affairs with blistering campaign attacks that questioned Goldwater's very sanity. To this he added vigorous action in the Gulf of Tonkin crisis of the kind that permits presidents to change the whole complexion of an election campaign with one bold stroke. In some respects Johnson's comparatively restrained statements on Vietnam were reminiscent of Franklin Roosevelt's campaign pledge of 1940 to keep the United States out of the war in Europe; equally, however, his concern to erase all credibility from the Republican charge that he was administering a soft or defensive policy in Southeast Asia made the Tonkin crisis a political opportunity of the first order.

On August 2 and 3 U.S. warships off the coast of North Vietnam experienced both real and imagined attacks from North Vietnamese torpedo boats. Johnson ordered retaliatory air strikes and submitted to Congress a resolution asking for the authority to *take all necessary steps to repel any armed attack against the forces of the United States and to prevent further aggression,* and declaring that the United States was *prepared, as the President determines, to take all necessary steps, including the use of armed force, to assist any member or protocol state of the Southeast Asia Collective Defence Treaty requesting assistance in defence of its freedom.* "Part of being ready," Johnson later wrote, "was having the advance support of Congress for anything that might prove to me necessary."[18] In substance, the *Southeast Asia Resolution* was much more than this. It gave to the executive the power to interpret for itself what was appropriate in virtually any situation and extended to Johnson a congressional line of credit for the application of military force. Even in the Tonkin incident itself, it cannot be said that Johnson's action subsequently proved to be either necessary or all that effective.

Johnson actions are a lesson in the importance of opportunity and timing to the seasoned politician. Because he submitted the resolution to Congress after the passage of his civil rights package, it could not run interference on his legislative agenda. Yet it had the immediate electoral benefit of putting the lie to Goldwater's foreign policy criticisms just prior to

the presidential ballot in November. Moreover, and its geographic point of impact, Asia, was precisely where the Republicans had been claiming for a over a decade that Democrats
were weak. It simultaneously gave Johnson the power to define for the nation the nature and scope of US interests in the
western Pacific. At time of the 1964 election Johnson had in
hand a strategy, formulated by the Pentagon, gradually to increase the American military pressure in Vietnam north of
the seventeenth parallel, at the core of which were proposed
bombing attacks against North Vietnamese targets for the purpose of forcing Hanoi to cut back its support of communist
insurgency in the south. In February 1965 Johnson imple-
mented *Operation Rolling Thunder*, and in March two battal-
ions of U.S. Marines landed at Da Nang, thus introducing an
American combat presence to Vietnam for the first time.[19]
Johnson had crossed a qualitative and quantitative divide. Both
Eisenhower and Kennedy before him made their own contributions, by allowing U.S. policy in Southeast Asia to continue
on an ambivalent course of qualified commitment. But Johnson
was a politician temperamentally hostile to patient caution.
As the greatest liberal activist president since Franklin
Roosevelt, he was possibly more ill-suited than any of his generation to deal with Vietnam with a prudent mixture of action
and restraint.

And the nation approved. Johnson wanted to be tough in
Vietnam. The best evidence is that Congress and the people
wanted to be tough too. The House of Representatives passed
the *Southeast Asia Resolution* 416 to 0, the Senate 88 to 2. A
Lou Harris Poll published on August 10 revealed that no less
than 85 percent of the respondents endorsed the air strikes.
Public approval of the President's general policy in Vietnam,
meanwhile, increased from 58 percent to 72 percent. When it
later became apparent that the administration had misled Congress and the public concerning the North Vietnamese attack
on U.S. naval vessels that had provoked the Tonkin incident,
criticism of Johnson tended to focus on the fact of this deception rather than on the propriety of any resolution as comprehensive as the one Johnson secured and course he was setting
for American policy. Thereafter a myth grew around Vietnam
to the effect that Johnson had been singularly deceitful in the

conduct of a war that might have been avoided altogether had the administration simply told the truth from the start. Johnson *was* guilty of deception at the time of Tonkin, but the hardest truth of all was that his actions reflected the mood of a nation, Congress, and the press, all of whom "did not want to fight a major war in Asia but also did not want to be forced out of Vietnam."[20] The electoral mandate given Johnson in 1964 was widely interpreted as an endorsement of his civil rights legislation and a determined stand in Vietnam.

Ultimately, Johnson deepened the U.S. military engagement to the point that by 1967–68 the disastrous course of events there eclipsed all other issues in American foreign affairs and domestic politics. Because Vietnam became the most traumatic experience of American foreign policy of the late twentieth century, the question looms large as to why he proceeded as he did. The influences on Johnson's Vietnam policy were multiple, but they all tended to push in the same direction: the application of greater increments of pressure on North Vietnam in pursuit of an acceptable diplomatic settlement. Until November 1967, the stated preference of a majority of Americans was for an escalation of the nation's military effort.[21] Over the preceding months and years popular militancy on Vietnam had a good deal of coaching—from Johnson, to be sure, but also from Kennedy before him. As in civil rights, the circumstance of Johnson's ascension to the presidency in 1963 moved him to strike the chord of continuity. If it can be said that Kennedy's intentions on civil rights tended toward the progressive but were unclear, the rhetorical legacy of the late president on Southeast Asia was certainly less equivocal. Kennedy's statements on the struggle against communism in the Third World—before, during, and after his campaign for the Oval Office—were so numerous and so hyperbolic as to lend personal sincerity to his inaugural pledge that the United States would indeed bear *any* burden and fight *any* foe. Leaving aside for a moment the fact that the Cold War had begun in Europe and eventually would end there, their cumulative effect was to raise exponentially the costs of withdrawal for his successor.

Johnson also retained the principal Kennedy foreign affairs advisors, most notably Dean Rusk, Robert McNamara, and

General Maxwell Taylor, not only upon assuming presidential office in the wake of Kennedy's death, but also after receiving his own electoral mandate. As a group they were married to a certain set of assumptions and goals in Vietnam, and they joined the Johnson and Kennedy administrations together in a seamless web of ad hoc policymaking.[22] The man who was for Johnson the most trusted of all, Dean Rusk, had thrown down the gauntlet to President Kennedy in 1960. Thereafter his views on Southeast Asia generally and Vietnam specifically provided a plodding *basso continuo* for American policy for all of the Kennedy and Johnson years. Rusk had never fully recovered from the awful surprise of Korea and had since convinced himself that the U.S. must contain Chinese expansionism in Southeast Asia by thwarting Hanoi's bid to unify Vietnam. Whenever Johnson had occasion to doubt, Rusk shored up his resolve with same superlatives he had directed toward Kennedy. Should the integrity of US commitments even appear to be compromised, he warned, "the communist world would draw conclusions that would lead to our ruin and almost certainly to world war."[23] Haunted by such fantastic pessimism, Rusk explained to Congress the military and diplomatic substance of the administration's policy in Vietnam with half-truths and lies of omission.

A critical feature of Lyndon Johnson's conduct of the war in Vietnam was that, as a war, it amounted to a gargantuan half-measure. While North Vietnam never wavered in its intention to unify the country by force, Johnson never responded to the aggression by occupying the north. The bombing, moreover, was throughout subject to political restrictions because of a genuine worry about the scale of civilian casualties and a concern not to widen the conflict, a concern which at its extreme led to the extraordinary decision not to bomb Soviet defensive missile bases in North Vietnam while they were under construction. Instead, Johnson's step-by-step transformation of counterinsurgency into a land war involving 523,000 U.S. troops, but in which his military was denied the luxury of a genuine military strategy, bore the stamp of the president's New Deal pedigree. For the leader and the philosophy there existed no problem, foreign or domestic, that would not yield to the requisite resources administered by the right program.

But if Johnson believed in his own capacity to manage a war in Asia and simultaneously carry out major reforms at home, he clearly also thought that national political circumstance left him little chance to ever choose between priorities. Had he decided to tell Congress and the nation that the Vietnamese domino was not so strategically vital after all, he would have inaugurated the very politics of limitations that became the lot of his successor, Nixon, and "sparked national debate about just what could be done and what forgone."[24] There was no reason to suppose that the goals of his Great Society would survive a contest with categorical imperatives of an international struggle to which the nation had been committed for nearly two decades.

By the time Johnson had become president gone was any sympathy for the argument that there were some battles the United States did *not* have to wage in order to prevail against communism. Yet the fact that South Vietnam did fall to communism had virtually no discernible impact whatever on the length of the Cold War or the comprehensiveness of the American victory after 1989. In the 1960s, however, the original logic of containment had become so abstract that Washington was prepared to believe in principle that the defence of Saigon was as vital as that of West Berlin. Johnson contributed more to the debacle than any other single president, but there is something wrongheaded and mischievous in searching among the presidents for blame, or to say in effect that the government simply deceived its people with its foreign policy. The question as to what other presidents might have done is itself a game based more often on wishful thinking than a determination to live with the facts. We know, for example, that, as Vietnam turned into a ground war, even a former president as cautious as Eisenhower became furious with Johnson for his policy, but above all because of its restraint.[25] There were presidential exercises in deception, but in Johnson's case they where no more frequent and spectacular than those of previous administrations. If the actions of the Johnson administration fooled the Congress and the people into thinking that they could wage war in Asia and build the Great Society at home without either a major increase in their taxes or other unpleasant shocks to the decade of consumption, both Congress and the people had colluded in the effort. A great democracy had made a great mistake.

With the Tet Offensive of early 1968, great swaths of the American middle class began to see it as such. Although North Vietnam was roundly trounced by American forces militarily, the evidence that Hanoi's ability and willingness to fight was apparently as robust as ever wore away popular patience with the president's policy. The war's political management had long since become more complicated, in any event, once middle-class college students had begun to receive draft notices. And the circle was squared when civil rights leader Martin Luther King Jr. publicly opposed the war, in part because black Americans accounted for a disproportionate number of draftees. To contemplate the urban race riots and the college antiwar protests of the mid and late 1960s together is to be amazed at the speed with which Johnson seemed to lose all influence over the events he had set in motion. Vietnam, of course, was easily the biggest factor in the erosion of public trust in his presidency. On the campuses the groundwork had been laid by the growing popularity of New Left critiques of American democracy and culture based on pop-Marxism and the writings of C. Wright Mills, Michael Harrington, and William Appleman Williams; in 1965 "teach-ins" questioning both the logic and morality of American foreign policy were held at universities across the country and were popular, not surprisingly, among the many thousands of students eligible for induction. By the time of the Tet Offensive the anti-war movement had a mass base[26] that in 1968 broadened its appeal, helped by print and television journalism that often misrepresented the implications of events such as Tet, and intensified its activities. One of the too-frequent tragedies of democratic politics is that otherwise sound citizens, having come to realize that their government has lied to them in any significant degree, will promptly imbibe any and all nonesense about that government circulated by the government's less scrupulous critics.

The sense of general disarray in the nation's domestic and foreign policy was profound and mostly legitimate. "Leadership was fraying at the very center," remembered Clark Clifford who was unlucky enough to become Secretary of Defense after Robert McNamara's resignation, "something very rare in a nation with so stable a government structure."[27] Johnson's decision not to run for reelection in 1968 then plunged the Democratic Party into an orgy of fratricide over the nomination of his successor and the awful electoral implications of eight years of foreign policy failure. Johnson himself had played the biggest single role in creating these conditions. His attempt to reaffirm New Deal liberalism in a time of plenty and to administer the Vietnam conflict like a New Deal program had subjected the Democratic Party's coalition to more strain than it could bear and damaged the very authority of the office he occupied.[28]

The costs of the Johnson administration to the nation more generally were both short and long term. Even considered alone, the fiscal outlays of the Great Society were very considerable, but they increased in political controversy as its programs had to compete with the Vietnam conflict for the revenue resources of the nation. Spending by the federal government, both on the Great Society and the Vietnam war, helped to fuel the consumer boom of the 1960s, but less than a decade later conservative critiques of the Great Society were to blame Johnson's policy for the inflation of the 1970s and the spiraling federal budget deficits of the 1980s. In point of fact Johnson's last budget produced a modest surplus for the Fiscal Year 1969, but only after a pitched battle with Congress to hike individual and corporate tax liabilities by 6 percent. And the Johnson administration clearly did change popular perceptions concerning the responsibility of government for counteracting with its budget formula the ebb and flow of economic activity and underwriting middle-class prosperity. Keynesian economics had earned only the guarded acceptance of the Roosevelt administration as one of a variety of ways that the nation could end the worst *depression* of its history. Johnson's spending on domestic and foreign policy, during a period not of extreme economic distress but of unprecedented mass prosperity, implied that Washington was now somehow accountable for the business failures and broken personal dreams that accompanied major and minor recessions as well. Was it not, however, intrinisic to the very logic of Keynesianism that one aimed for budget surpluses in times of growth in order to build the resources for periods of adversity? In January

1967 Johnson finally went to Congress looking for increased taxes, but was refused. If he had been prepared to call Vietnam a war and confess that he needed funds to fight it, the congressional leadership commented, he might not have been turned away. But Johnson had never considered that admission acceptable when extending the scope and reach of New Deal liberalism beyond anything Roosevelt had contemplated and under circumstances entirely different. For Johnson the Great Society was characterized by abundance and liberty, but a generation later conservatives were to argue that liberty was the prerequisite of abundance, that only a free market unfettered by excessive regulation and protected from the ravages of inflation caused by excessive government spending could produce wealth for the rich and the poor alike. In the meantime, the architect of the Great Society "was the instigator of the Great Inflation".[29]

The Great Heretic

Richard Nixon was elected in 1968 to manage this crisis. Six years later he was driven from office in disgrace, leaving the country with a legacy that was in many ways more troubling than the one Lyndon Johnson had passed off to him. During his term in the White House, Nixon became the most controversial and the most widely disliked of the modern Presidents. Defeated by Kennedy in 1960, Nixon lost a bid to be governor of California and announced his retirement from politics in 1962. But in 1968 he was a study in political rehabilitation, whose reemergence and performance in the GOP primaries of 1968 reminded influential Republicans at the state and local level why he had been first among them in 1960: Nixon had a strong political constituency in the country and that a center-right Republican with internationalist credentials might well have a majority constituency in the conditions created by Vietnam and the internal crisis of Democratic Party. Though prominent Republicans were predisposed to Nixon at the outset, it was his impressive performance in the primaries of New Hampshire, Wisconsin, Pennsylvania, Indiana, Nebraska, and Oregon that convinced a majority of them that he had a respectable crack at winning.[30]

On the face of it at least, the Democratic nomination was much more competitive. After the assassination of Robert Kennedy, it centered on the challenge posed by Senator Eugene McCarthy to the front-running Vice President Hubert Humphrey, whom McCarthy supporters dubbed a stand-in for Johnson, a favorite of the Democratic party machines, and apologist for the Vietnam war. Although this image of Humphrey was largely caricature, given that old urban machines of the Democratic Party were now a pale shadow of their former selves and Humphrey's support at Chicago was no more manipulated than that of any one else, it was a caricature that played well to political innocents, the leftward activists calling for an 'open' Democratic convention in Chicago, and those who ultimately turned the convention into a brawl with the Chicago police while the nation looked on. Humphrey later opined that the catastrophe of Chicago alone, rather than Nixon, had deprived him of the presidency. The election was close enough that he might have been right. Nixon's plurality on election night was a half-million votes. He took all the western and midwestern states he had captured in his 1960 loss to Kennedy and added others. The electoral college gave him a healthy margin of 301 to 191, however, partly because the third-party candidacy of the segregationist Alabama governor George Wallace captured five states in the south. Southern Democrats who resented Johnson's civil right legislation and had voted for Goldwater in 1964 now parked their votes with Wallace's American Independent Party, a symbol of the crumbling of the Democrats' one-time electoral bedrock in the Old Confederacy and of a growing national backlash against liberalism. Both Nixon and Humphrey attempted, with little success, to peal off parts of the Wallace vote. During his presidency Nixon appealed to it indirectly with his-law-and-order platform, but also with economic nationalism. Inside the Nixon White House the kind of sensibilities that supported Wallace in 1968 had a spokesman in speechwriter Pat Buchanan, whose overtly populist nationalism was of intermittent use to Nixon but which in 1992 and 1996 was a much larger force in the Republican Party.[31]

Nixon's electoral mandate of 1968 was tenuous. The outgoing Johnson himself appreciated the president-elect's situation:

He was a minority president, faced with a Democratic Congress and elected by only 43.4 percent of the vote. But if he was a minority president, he was not a president of the minorities. Less than 10 percent of the black voters and a small percentage of the Spanish-speaking voters cast their ballots for him. Nor was he a president of the so-called doves. This meant that the most vocal and volatile segments of our society were most alienated from the new President.[32]

None of this meant he was less than president. One great virtue of the electoral college is that its arithmetic conveys the message that the candidate who wins the states wins the presidency, all of it. But it did mean that Nixon needed bipartisan cooperation from Democrats in order to find any positive resonance for his initiatives in Congress and to attempt to build an electoral coalition, from the middle of the political spectrum outward, for reelection in 1972. He would have to govern from the center.

Nixon was still attempting to define a political center in the last months of his second administration, and it was the inherent dilemma of being a centrist, isolation, that contributed most to his downfall. For a centrist has to talk with both extremes of the political spectrum and in times of polarized politics often finds that he has few reliable allies in either camp. "Too much of what has been written about his efforts to meet the requirements of presidential initiative," wrote Theodore Lowi a decade after Nixon's resignation, "has aimed to show him as a pathological personality when in fact a more dispassionate look will show that he was a rational person dealing very rationally with the requirements of the job."[33] Another president with an altogether different personality, in other words, would likely have thought it necessary to do many if not all of the things that earned Nixon such ignomy.

More to the point, Lyndon Johnson had done many of those things. Immersed in the same national crisis as Johnson and therefore subject to similar, often conflicting, pressures, the 37th president reached for many of the same levers as the 36th. Too many of the studies of the period conclude that Nixon left the presidency under siege and play thematically on the darkness of his administration, willfully overlooking the fact that the Oval Office was an embattled and somber place on the day of his arrival. And it was clearly not the conjuring of an overactive imagination that many members of Congress, the press, and the public of 1968 looked to a new administration to assume responsibility for the greatest national crisis since World War II, yet sought simultaneously to limit executive prerogative above all in the realm of foreign relations. The debt of congressional mistrust following upon Johnson's escalation of the Vietnam conflict armed with the authority of the Southeast Asia resolution was now Nixon's to pay. During his briefings of the president-elect, Johnson advised the outmost secrecy in the determination of executive policy. "The leaks can kill you," Johnson warned with more accuracy than he could have guessed, "even with all the precautions I take, things still leak."[34]

Nixon might well have listened with a measure of scepticism to the advice of an outgoing executive so visibly broken as Johnson. Yet if he had any doubt about the variety and determination of the forces arrayed against presidential governance, a member of one of the most hostile constituencies, the press, felt obliged to disabuse him of it. Political columnist David Broder wrote in the *Washington Post* in October 1969 that the student peace movement and Congress above all planned to make a rational management of foreign policy quite impossible, all with a mind to destroying Nixon's presidency in much the same fashion as they had destroyed Johnson's. This they would do, Broder went on, by framing all discussion of American policy, especially Vietnam, in terms of moral imperatives; "a war that is unpopular, expensive and very probably unwise is labelled as immoral, indecent and intolerable."[35] Thus, it followed that any president who allowed the war to continue was himself indecent, immoral, and intolerable. Broder never mentioned the role of the news media in all this, but then Nixon had the more fundamental warning, as it were, from the horse's mouth.

Nixon dealt with this problem in his first term by adopting a plebiscitarian approach to national leadership, in effect speaking to the nation over the heads of Congress and the press. It is an approach to which all presidents resort at different points of their term, but it favors more charismatic personalities than Nixon's. Roosevelt had perfected it, and Reagan was to use it very effectively during the 1980s. For a centrist like Nixon it involved splitting the differences between the policy preferences of rival political constituencies in an effort to draw at least probational political support from each.

Political consultants today can command an enormous salary for recommending this strategy and pretending without a blush that it is an original idea, especially when their advice is accompanied by statistics. The first explicit indication of it from Nixon came on November 3, 1969 in a television address to the nation in which the president called upon "the great silent majority of my fellow Americans" to support him in the kind of negotiated settlement in Vietnam that would permit a dignified withdrawal. Betting that the majority of the American people were attuned to, or were at least willing to suspend their judgment of, his policy on Vietnam, Nixon was in essence saying that the more vocal and negative commentary from Congress and the press did not speak for national sentiment and could therefore not be permitted to dictate national policy. This reasoning was fine and well, so long as the president had some indication that the silent majority, when no longer silent, was indeed with him. Public opinion polling on Vietnam provided sufficient, if imperfect, evidence that it was so. At the height of the peace demonstrations in 1969 and 1970 the pro-Nixon enthusiasm of blue-collar labor poured out into the streets of New York in the form of counterdemonstrations in support of the administration's policy that degenerated into a pitched battles with peace activists.

But did the silent majority speech indeed reflect Nixon's philosophy on presidential leadership in foreign policy? Could it? A survey of Nixon's policy on Vietnam specifically and foreign affairs more generally indicates that it provided the defense for executive prerogative, not because the American people agreed with the president's policy, but because it could not be demonstrated that a majority of them disagreed. Moreover, it was not only Nixon's right but also his responsibility as chief executive to interpret for himself what was in the national interest of the United States and its citizens. Although Nixon had received only 43 percent of the vote in 1969, neither the Constitution nor the people would be willing to say that he bore only 43 percent of the liability for any errors in foreign policy.

The most articulate defense of this philosophy came from the English Tory Edmund Burke in his *Speech to the Electors of*

Bristol, but it had been reiterated by Nixon's nemesis of 1960, John F. Kennedy, who practiced it hardly all:

> The voters selected us, in short, because they had confidence in our judgment and our ability to exercise that judgement from a position where we could determine what were their own best interests, as a part of the nation's interests. This may mean that we must on occasion lead, inform, correct, and sometimes even ignore constituent opinion, if we are to exercise fully that judgement for which we were elected. But acting without selfish motive or private bias, those who follow the dictates of an intelligent conscience are not aristocrats, demagogues, eccentrics or callous politicians insensitive to the feelings of the public. They expect—and not without considerable trepidation—their constituents to be the final judges of the wisdom of their course; but they have the faith that those constituents—today, tomorrow or even in another generation—will at least respect the principles that motivated their independent stand.[36]

The Nixon administration wanted to be judged on its eligibility for reelection according to its concrete achievements rather than the perceived nobility, or lack thereof, of its purposes. The White House devoted considerable effort toward publicizing the goals of the executive's initiatives as well as the progress toward their completion. Simultaneously, the administration proceeded from the assumption that the silent majority represented a vast middle ground of American public opinion where hearts and minds could be won either by Nixon or by those who would thwart his efforts. And the evidence is overwhelming that the Nixon White House began where the Johnson administration had left off: from the assumption that an alliance of vocal and articulate critics in Congress, the print and electronic media, the academic community, and the antiwar and civil rights movements was out to destroy their presidency no matter what its intentions or accomplishments.

Nixon sensed that the silent majority consisted of Americans who felt that as the debate on the national direction increased in volume, it also became more distant from their personal concerns, that the most vocal and articulate coteries of the Democrats and Republicans were dominated by upper-middle-class activists who fought political battles with moral fervor and a moralistic vision. The self-image of these activists was reinforced by the argument of social science of the late

1960s and early 1970s to the effect that "post-materialist values"—in retrospect, a concept of breathtaking arrogance—were of increasing importance to the content of public discourse in America.[37] The sentiments of the silent majority were the ground for a battle between "them and us." Vietnam in particular was now no longer just the hottest theater of the Cold War, it was at the principal faultline of an increasingly polarized domestic political spectrum.

Nixon and his advisors came to exaggerate the stakes of the contest, along with the requirements for a victory that was deemed imperative if Nixon's prescriptions for the nation were to succeed. It goes along way toward explaining the adversarial posture the administration adopted in its relations with Congress and the Washington press corps in particular. The posture was stiffened when in June 1971 the *New York Times* published classified documents on American policy on Vietnam, later known as the Pentagon Papers, leaked to its editors by former Defense Department official, Daniel Ellsberg. The documents themselves were a record of policy development in the Eisenhower, Kennedy, and Johnson years and represented no special threat to Nixon's administration. He felt, however, that "we've got to get Ellsberg nailed hard on the basis of being guilty of stealing the papers," because decisions to release documents made by individuals without the responsibility "ruins an orderly government."[38] Nixon was right of course, but he overreacted. In the legitimate interest of stopping leaks that could endanger the confidentiality of the current conduct of foreign policy he wanted security tightened further. In the political interest of discrediting Ellsberg personally, he gave, in effect, his White House staff license to undertake whatever the FBI would not, and involved his administration in a sequence criminal activities beginning with a burglary in the office of Ellsberg's psychiatrist and leading to Watergate.[39] Basing its decision in the First Amendment, the Supreme Court upheld in *New York Times v. the United States, 403 US 713* the right of the press to print the Pentagon Papers over the administration's efforts to prevent publication. In the end, Nixon's efforts to stop all leaks at their source were more damaging to himself and the presidential office than were the papers themselves. As much as a year before Watergate even broke as a news item, he ordered members of the White House "plumbers" to undertake covert activities against the Democratic Party and liberal organizations of an order that amounted to impeachable offenses.

Had Nixon's foreign policy been driven by this kind of brawling, it would have stood no chance of success. What is clearly remarkable about the administration was its substantive achievements abroad in foreign policy in spite of the often visceral spirit of the debate about foreign policy at home. Superpower *détente* and step-by-step withdrawal from Vietnam, responded to the popular conviction that the burden of overseas commitments had become intolerable. In an address to Congress in February of 1970, Nixon formally enunciated his foreign policy doctrine with the pledge that *the United States will participate in the defense and development of its allies and friends,* yet cautioned that *America cannot–and will not–conceive all the plans, design all the programs, execute all the decisions, and undertake all the defence of the free nations of the world. We will help where it makes a real difference and is in our interest.* In the Vietnam experience, in other words, a turning point had been reached for all of American foreign relations. Since the enunciation of the *Truman Doctrine,* the dilemma of American foreign policy had been to bridge the gap between commitments the United States had taken on and the resources necessary to sustain them. Nixon, in effect, decided to stop trying with the the methods that Kennedy and Johnson had employed. The *Nixon Doctrine* represented no less than a renunciation of the Kennedy inaugural commitment to bear *any* burden and fight *any* foe to ensure the survival and success of liberty. Neither the Cold War nor the fundamental foreign policy goals of the United States, as set forth by Truman, were abandoned. Nixon sought, however, to proceed with a much greater emphasis on the diplomatic over the military tools of statecraft. Whether one saw it as the overdue victory of realism over idealism or simply a grudging acknowledgment of relative decline, Nixon's diplomacy was a radical departure.[40]

Rapprochement with China was clearly the most radical component of all, given that it redefined the Sino-American relationship fundamentally, and thus had critical implications for Washington's relationship with Moscow. In essence Nixon decided to a approach formal American relations with the world's two leading communist powers from a national rather than an ideological perspective. When he flew to Peking in February 1972 it was as if American diplomacy had switched quite abruptly to three-dimensional chess. In fact, Nixon's National Security Advisor, Henry Kissinger, had secretly done much of the groundwork over the preceding year, but the sense a dramatic change created by the visit appealed to Nixon's taste for bold *faits accomplis*. Nixon and Kissinger shaped *détente* diplomacy alone, cutting out the State Department altogether; Secretary of State, William Rogers, was consulted little more than the White House wallpaper. The drama of the China visit also suited the requirements of a foreign policy which was essentially retrenchment without disengagement. Starting with Khrushchev, Moscow had so mismanaged its relations with Peking during the 1960s as to give Washington ample space for wedge diplomacy. One did not have to abandon the cause of anti-communism in order to focus more forthrightly on the goal of containing the influence of Soviet Russia. After all, Franklin Roosevelt had found it convenient to support the Soviet Union against the more immediate peril of Nazi Germany. Why should Richard Nixon now balk at the chance to tease the age-old Russian fear of encirclement with his China diplomacy in order extract a spirit of greater cooperation from Moscow on arms limitations, European security, and the Middle East?[41]

The China diplomacy also had the genius of common sense in it that Nixon must have savored. Because he believed that the Soviet Union and China were no longer revolutionary forces in international relations, the United States could and should engage their foreign policies in a project for global stability based on American recognition of their status as great powers. With the trauma of having "lost" China now some twenty-three years in the past, a Republican president with Nixon's Cold war credentials could now engage in the kind of "Asia first" diplomacy that would complicate the diplomatic landscape for the Soviet Union in a much more immediate sense than for the United States. His visit had the effect of breaking the taboo on a country the United States had excluded from the United Nations for two decades, thus "promoting the readmission of Peking to the great game of inter-state relations and giving the men in the Kremlin an additional reason for an understanding with Washington."[42]

Yet not all Republicans thought it cause for celebration. For the influential conservative columnist William F. Buckley Jr., the China diplomacy was a "staggering capitulation" of the American commitment to Taiwan, all the more galling because it came from a Republican administration in the face of the GOP's Asia First tradition. Nixon, Buckley charged, was guilty of heresy:

> We have lost—irretrievably—any remaining sense of moral mission in the world. Mr. Nixon's appetite for a summit conference in Peking transformed the affair from a meeting of diplomatic technicians concerned to examine and illuminate areas of common interest into a pageant of moral togetherness at which Mr. Nixon managed to give the impression that he was consorting with Marian Anderson, Billy Graham and Albert Schweitzer. [. . .] Mr. Nixon is so much the moral enthusiast that he alchemizes the requirements of diplomacy into the coin of ethics; that is why when he toasted the bloodiest, most merciless chief of state in the world, he did so in accents most of us would reserve for Florence Nightingale. [43]

Generally, however, journalists and academics joined in a chorus of approval. In order to square this radical shift in US diplomacy with the priggish moralism they too often applied to the messy world of international relations, they rhapsodized the achievements of the Chinese revolution with accounts of their own experiences in the People's Republic that fell little short of fiction.[44] Buckley's reaction was actually the critical exception. In retrospect it was also more important, because it symbolized the rejection by articulate conservative opinion of Nixon's revisions to Cold War strategy and presaged things to come.

The goal of Nixon's foreign policy was to bring the nation's overseas commitments back into line with its capacities. This involved above all a recognition that global politics had changed very considerably since Kennedy's extraordinary inaugural challenge to American global leadership. Tension between the Soviet Union and the People's Republic of China had increased to the point of military confrontation across the Ussuri River; a new government in West Germany sought more normal relations with Moscow, undaunted by Soviet repression of the "Prague Spring" in Czechoslovakia; the European Community and Japan had become major forces in the global economy; and many governments of the Third World were motivated by national aspirations that fit only uncomfortably into the crude categories with which American Cold War diplomacy had become too comfortable. At the foundations of Nixon's foreign policy was an authentic conservatism. It was concerned with the pragmatic use of American power and sensitive to both the possibilities and limitations of the United States.

In what remained the most problematic theater of the Cold War Nixon's procedure dealt with demonstrated limitations. It was sensitive not only to the prevailing winds of public opinion but also to its nuances. In May 1971 68 percent of the respondents to a public-opinion poll said that the U.S. should get out of Vietnam, yet only 29 percent endorsed withdrawal if it were to lead to a communist victory, while as few as 11 percent agreed to a disengagement that could endanger American lives. It was Nixon's view that the Vietnam conflict had seriously weakened the United States and had destroyed domestic unity on which successful diplomacy ultimately depended. The key to recovering a quantum of domestic consensus therefore was to end the war and to bring to foreign policy a cost-effectiveness that seemed to have been lost altogether during the Johnson administration. The goal of "peace with honor," coupling gradual withdrawal and negotiations with Hanoi, answered the public's desire to be rid of the Vietnam millstone without forthright acknowledgment that the misadventure of the past decade had ended in a comprehensive diplomatic and military defeat. For his American audience the essence of Nixon's message was that fewer of their sons would be called to arms in pursuit of U.S. goals abroad. As he initiated the withdrawal of troops from Vietnam, he also abolished the draft system of *selective service* that dated to the Roosevelt administration.

In its relations with major allies in Europe the administration's corollary to withdrawal in Vietnam was a combination of carrot-and stick-stimulants. With the suspension of the gold convertibility of the dollar in August 1971 and the imposition of a 10 percent surcharge on goods entering the

American market from Western Europe, Nixon put his European trading partners above all on notice regarding the leadership burdens of the global economy. The wealthy nations of the European Community should no longer view the United States both as the guarantor of their security and an open market for their subsidized export industries. But at the same time Nixon and Kissinger quietly underwrote the *Ostpolitik* of the center-left Brandt-Scheel coalition in West Germany, in so far as its establishment of a new German dialogue with Moscow and other Warsaw Pact capitals supplemented superpower *détente*.

There were always significant limitations to *détente* from the American side. In the Middle East the United States would have compromised the principles of the *Eisenhower Doctrine* had Nixon accepted Moscow as a partner in peace diplomacy. When the Soviet Union called for a superpower-sponsored cease-fire during the 1973 Yom Kippur War between Israel and the Arab states of Egypt and Syria, Nixon rejected the proposal outright and underscored his point by putting U.S. forces on alert for the first time since the Cuban Missile Crisis. Kissinger thereupon achieved a American-brokered agreement in which Israel surrendered strategic terrain in the Sinai in return for Cairo's formal recognition of the Jewish State's right to exist. The episode has been cited as an achievement of superpower cooperation, but in substance it was evidence of Nixon's fundamental view that, though the Kremlin's appetite for prestige could be stroked, the Soviet Union's very nature disqualified it from real equality with the United States.[45]

Although this was readily apparent to anyone at the time who took the trouble to follow the Nixon-Kissinger diplomacy, there was in Congress an alternative interpretation of the plus-and-minus of *détente*. When the administration attempted to bring to bear the assets the United States had as an economic power by proposing to grant Most Favored Nation (MFN) status to the Soviet Union as a positive incentive for reasonableness, Congress moved to impede the proposal, though it passed the Export Administration Act liberalizing export controls in 1969. In 1972 Senator Henry Jackson (D-Washington) at first threatened to delay Nixon's arms agreements with Moscow and then led a coalition of congressmen in insisting that the administration tie increased trade to improved Soviet standards on improved human rights. Ultimately, it subjected Nixon's *Trade Act of 1974* to the *Jackson-Vanik Amendment* linking MFN privileges with freer Jewish emigration from the Soviet Union. Both conservative Republicans and liberal Democrats united behind Jackson-Vanik. Some were motivated by hostility to *détente* in principle; others sought to assert the moral imperative Buckley claimed had disappeared from American foreign policy. For a broad coalition of congressmen, the amendment at least had the apparent virtue of checking executive prerogative in foreign affairs. Yet it also set the logic of Nixon's economic diplomacy on its head, by turning positive incentives for more civilized Soviet behavior in the global arena into a critique of Moscow's domestic affairs.[46] Under the cloud of Watergate, the conflict dragged on into the Ford administration. Congress got the better of it when Ford signed the Trade Reform Bill with amendments in January 1975.

Thus, while Nixon and Kissinger established the best bilateral relationship Washington had enjoyed with Moscow since the onset of the Cold War, Congress undermined its domestic foundations. The Strategic Arms Limitations Talks (SALT I) and Anti-Ballistic Missile (ABM) treaties of May 1972 are two cases in point. For all their shortcomings, the agreements initiated both frank discussion of strategic arms and agreement to limit deployment of certain nuclear weapons. Initially Congress approved both. But soon some congressional critics denounced the idea of accepting nuclear parity with Moscow, while others observed, correctly, that SALT I was not a sufficient check to the arms race. For others the as yet unended Vietnam conflict was simply more important. And since for them *détente* diplomacy in Moscow and Peking had no obvious direct bearing on a Vietnam settlement, its value was questionable.[47] For Nixon and Kissinger such an attitude was an example of the tail wagging the dog. Vietnam was a wasteful war inherited from a previous administration, and disengagement from it was integral to the administration's foreign policy; but superpower *détente*, continuing the Cold War with more pragmatism and less idealism, was the very essence of that policy, the keystone of the Nixon Doctrine. Nixon regarded operations such as the bombing and subsequent U.S. invasion of Vietcong sanctuaries in Cambodia as essentially rearguard actions to buy time for a graduated American withdrawal from Vietnam, rather than wholesale flight. His critics, on the campuses and in Congress, saw the action as an escalation of the conflict from a president ostensibly committed to do just the opposite. Nixon expected protest against the Cambodian operation, but the depth of the outrage and the shooting of protesting students at Kent State University shook him badly.[48] To the extent that the two sides of the argument differed fundamentally concerning just what was the most important issue of the entire foreign policy agenda of the 1970s—an end to the Vietnam nightmare or superpower *détente*—there was never sufficient ground for understanding between them. Congress passed legislation to cut off funds for the Cambodian operation. Nixon vetoed, thus leaving himself theoretically in the position of being able to conduct foreign policy in Southeast Asia only as long as Congress fell short of the two-thirds vote required to still his poisoned pen.

Nixon's struggle with Congress over foreign policy was multidimensional. The partisanship influencing the relationship between any Republican president dealing with a Democratic majority in the legislature was only the most obvious. There was the added fact that Congress was determined to reverse the trend toward executive dominance that reached its post-1945 apex when Johnson came away with a blank check to deal with the Tonkin crisis. Finally faced in Vietnam with the apparent limits of American power, Congress attempted, by passing the *War Powers Resolution* over Nixon's veto in 1973, not only to blot out the memory of the Tonkin Resolution but to recover the terrain of foreign affairs it had surrendered to successive Cold War presidents. The fact that the Johnson administration had misled Congress over policy in Indochina had fostered a willful self-delusion among its members that they had not been coauthors of that policy. So an initiative that had been unthinkable for thirty years "looked to be unstoppable in 1973," above all "because the growing unpopularity of the conflict had finally made it safe and even advantageous for Congress to insist on shared responsibility with the president in national commitments."[49] Yet despite its strong language the resolution left the president with the initiative in deploying American forces for up to ninety days without consulting Congress. From an historical perspective, it was similar in spirit to the neutrality acts of the 1930s, and it recapitulated the congressional inclination to swaddle American foreign policy in the majesty of principle. The resolution was a highly symbolic affair, motivated above all by a will to dissociate Congress from the outcome of decisionmaking on Vietnam and from the president now responsible for the mopping up.[50]

Henry Kissinger was the sole member of the administration, or for that matter of the federal government, whose relationship with the president approximated a partnership. And without discounting Kissinger's major contribution to the triumphs of *détente* diplomacy, the evidence is that Nixon was himself the principal architect of the changes wrought between 1968 and 1974 and Kissinger the engineer of its implementation. As early as 1967, while Kissinger still insisted that the United States must not accept defeat in Vietnam, Nixon seems to have done just that and was contemplating a post-Vietnam order in Asia with the observation that "we simply cannot afford to leave China forever outside the family of nations," concluding that American diplomacy should begin to "fashion the sinews of a Pacific community." [51] But this is not the point. Rather, the talents of the president and his national security advisor were both compatible and complementary enough to constitute what was in Nixon's view a self-sufficient arrangement. A senior State Department official once described both Nixon and Kissinger as "incurably covert,"[52] but from the perspective of the Oval Office in the late 1960s, the most obvious response for an embattled executive's difficulty with foreign policy management was, logically, to be covert. On Nixon's orders Kissinger and his staff developed procedures that centralized foreign policy authority as never before, permitting the Oval Office and the NSC to bypass altogether senior authority in the State Department and the chiefs of federal intelligence agencies.[53] An arrangement that the president deemed imperative to the conduct of foreign relations in a phase of simultaneous crisis-management in Vietnam and new departures with Moscow and Peking, also served to isolate the Oval Office as never before. In time it aroused suspicions, some ridiculous, others justified, about the intentions and integrity of the occupant. Lyndon Johnson had dealt with the most sensitive matters of his foreign policy through the ad hoc consultations of his Tuesday lunch sessions. But ultimately even these had not sufficed to give him either the discretion he sought or, in the worst instances, the elementary confidentiality required for national security. Nixon moved to fix the flaws in Johnson's system by drawing the radius of its inner circle smaller still.

The imperative of tight executive control over the announcement and progress of presidential initiatives might have become less of a lightning rod for critics of the administration had it been confined to the realm of foreign policy. This was, of course, not the case. Like no other president before him Nixon depended on his White House Chief of Staff, H.R. Haldeman, to police day-to-day access to the Oval Office as well as to carry out directives emanating from it. The counsel of collective deliberation suffered in proportion to Haldeman's success at the job. Nixon believed that over the long term he could deal effectively with foreign policy and domestic issues only if he could be protected from the routine intrusion of political and administrative minutiae into his understanding of the larger picture of increasingly complex national and international issues. Above all, the Oval Office could show no tolerance for breaches of confidentiality. Newly aroused to this issue by the Ellsberg case, Nixon briefed his cabinet in June 1971 on the realities of his philosophy, warning "Haldeman is my prat boy—he'll be down the throat of anyone here regarding leaks if they affect the national interest. When he talks, it's me talking, and don't think it'll do any good to come and talk to me, because I'll be tougher than he is. That's the way it's going to be."[54] Thus, the enormous responsibility given to Haldeman, a man who routinely deprecated his authority as purely administrative, in fact left him and the White House staff in a position to make and carry out decisions in the vast grey terrain between the secretarial and the political. It was on this terrain that the administration's criminal activities grew.

The most infamous of them, the burglary by Nixon's staff of the offices of the Democratic National Committee (DNC) in the Watergate apartment complex, took place in a year when Democrats posed no electoral threat whatever to the prospects of a second Nixon term. Their primary season was a near chaos, troubled on the right by George Wallace's enormously popular independent campaign against busing for the desegregation of schools; weakly represented down the middle by Hubert Humphrey; and driven on the left by the wholly unelectable George McGovern. After their Chicago debacle in 1968, the Democrats had undertaken to open up the party, so much so that by 1972 it was itself something of a laboratory rat for the new politics of participation. Gone was the great party of the Roosevelt-Johnson decades with its sprawling electoral coalitions, the pro-Nixon labor demonstrations in New York having represented nothing so much as a growing disenchantment of the blue-collar vote with its traditional political ally. McGovern's nomination to the Democratic presidential ticket represented the culmination of deep-seated changes within the party,[55] which in 1972 saw young activists helping him campaign on a platform of progressive taxation, guaranteed income, busing, defense cuts, environmentalism, and amnesty for draft evaders. Their triumph placed the party well to the left of public opinion, and to onlookers the moral fervor they brought to the McGovern cause looked adolescent, amateurish, and even antipolitical. When guidelines for the Democratic convention stipulated that specified percentages of delegates had to be young, black, or female, their suspicions were confirmed. When George Wallace decided against running and removed the danger of a loss of potential Republican votes on the right, the stage was set for Nixon to demolish McGovern.

The election of 1972 was a mirror image of Johnson's landslide against Goldwater in 1964, Nixon capturing every state save Massachusetts. With over 60 percent of the popular vote, he was also the first Republican to take a majority of the Catholic and blue-collar vote. McGovern carried the black, Jewish, and youth vote, but there is no evidence that the campaign mischief of the Nixon campaign organization made the slightest difference to the outcome on either side of the equation.

One Nation Republicanism

The bad news in the ballot of 1972 was that Nixon had no coattails. Republicans fell well short of a majority in the House, and they actually lost two seats in the Senate. This did not

234 One War, Two Presidents

augur well for the president's self-assigned task of reuniting the country from the center of the political spectrum.

Perhaps in anticipation of this he had from the outset attempted to give his administration bipartisan credentials. The appointments of Kissinger to head the NSC and Democratic Senator Daniel Patrick Moynihan as an advisor in urban affairs were designed to give his administration bipartisan style and substance. In late 1970 the addition of John Connally, former governor of Texas and erstwhile protegé of Lyndon Johnson, as Secretary of the Treasury consolidated the picture of a president straining at the restrictions of traditional Republican conservatism. Connally's acceptance of the post reflected both a new flux in partisanship in the early 1970s and the self- destruction of the Democratic Party as a presidential election force. Connally had long been considered by many, not least of all himself, to be of presidential caliber. But in 1971 Connally's pragmatic conservatism and glib self-confidence were no longer welcome in the Democratic Party. His time on the Nixon cabinet was, it turns out, a way station on the road to oblivion.

In the meantime, Connally's abilities and approach to government had a home on the president's team. In August and September of 1972 Nixon effused to his advisors about a new version of the "one-nation" conservatism championed by British Prime Minister Benjamin Disraeli in the last century. He envisioned a "new philosophy and a new way," a "national coalition that shares common views regarding what the country ought to be, at home and abroad," a coalition based on "the old values" that recognized the need for pragmatic domestic reform and an assertive foreign policy. His observation that FDR's New Deal coalition was founded on common fears rather than common values was not altogether inaccurate.[56] But it overlooked the fact that a durable community-of-interest between business and labor gave Roosevelt's base a left-of-center gravity that Nixon's could not have. If Nixon did not explicitly locate his own political home to the right-of-center, he ran a long-term risk of having no home at all. In any democracy a centrist constituency is difficult to hold together, even in the best of times. In circumstances such those in America in the early 1970s it seemed to Nixon imperative to try, yet a policy

that is objectively responsible in looking to the long term often angers more key political constituencies with its costs than
it satisfies with its responsibility.

The elaborate balancing act attempted with the 'Nixon
Shock' of 1971 and the federal budget is a case in point. While
Congress considered the *Burke-Hartke* initiative for import restrictions to remedy a U.S. trade-deficit, Nixon combined his
surcharge on imports with wage-and-price controls to chill
domestic inflation. His suspension of the dollar's gold convertibility then brought down the entire Bretton Woods system of multilateral monetary management. Wage controls angered organized labor, so the import surcharge was designed
to compensate the discipline demanded from American workers with punitive measures against their foreign competition.
The unilateral cancellation of Bretton Woods, meanwhile, sent
a message to trade competitors that the United States would
act decisively to secure its national interest in trade against
real and alleged abuses of the system—in Connally's memo-
rable words, "screw them first."[57] At the root of the
administration's actions was a desire to hold down unemployment and inflation on the home front, while coupling the benefits of superpower *détente*, namely the reallotment of defense
expenditure to domestic priorities, with a restructuring of relations with America's more prosperous allies.

In January 1971 Nixon provided midterm reflections on his
performance for a television interview for all the major net-
works. After announcing to a surprised audience that he
thought himself a Keynesian in economics, he went on to cite
clean air, clean water, open spaces, and welfare and health reform as worthy goals for the future. Nixon was adamantly and
openly opposed to busing in the name of racial integration,
but appreciated that the Supreme Court in 1971 was not. His
Philadelphia Plan, designed to end the exclusion of black workers from the construction industry by requiring builders to set
target for minority manpower utilization was *affirmative action*
by any other name.[58] Conservative Republicans recoiled.
Among them was speechwriter Buchanan, who accused his boss
of adopting a liberal Democratic agenda. Like Buckley's salvo
against the China diplomacy, it was another episode in the
realization of conservative Republicans that Nixon was not one

of them. At the time the president's heresy had no immdediate consequence among rightward Republicans who still believed in Cold War orthodoxy, balanced budgets, and the creed of self-reliance. But at a deeper level Buckley's article and Buchanan's protest were minor seismic events in the transformation of conservative opinion and the Republican Party. It needs to be pointed out, moreover, that what capital Nixon lost among conservatives, he did not gain with liberals. Nixon's refusal to lobby Congress hard for the *Family Assistance Plan (FAP)* gave his welfare reform serious legislative problems from the start, but liberal Democrats never liked its rationalization of federal bureaucratic power in any event. Nor did they care for his want of integrationist enthusiasm in the face of a growing popular anti-busing revolt.[59] His administration's initial position on fiscal policy, meanwhile, was to caution Congress against spending that would further darken the deficit picture. The nation was living and warring beyond its fiscal means. But when expansionary forces in the economy appeared to flag, Nixon turned himself to fiscal and monetary stimulants. For 1971 he proposed to increase spending by 7.5 percent and to trim taxes by $2.7 billion. While this combination added to the deficit in 1971 and 1972, by 1974 the administration had wrestled the deficit down from $23 to $2.2 billion.[60] Critics have charged that over the long-term Nixon's international monetary initiatives and trade protectionism sacrificed coherence and vision for drama, but in the early 1970s the thicket of short-term exigencies was dense enough to keep the administration's energies fully engaged.[61]

When Nixon took the time to apply himself to a problem, his conclusions regarding the appropriate policy were often intellectually impressive. As president he wanted to be seen as a compassionate conservative on welfare issues. He never successfully projected this image, but his difficulties in welfare reform also stemmed from the very nature of the problem itself. His initiatives in New Federalism and family assistance are cases in point. Whereas New Federalism involved a reorganization of the now vast array of federally-administered programs with a mind to enhancing their cost-effectiveness, the Family Assistance Plan presented to Congress and the nation August 8, 1969 proposed to replace government services with a guaranteed income for the poor. Both sought to decentralize the administration of welfare in ways that would restructure Johnson's Great Society and cut across the grain of New Deal liberalism. But where New Federalism's revenue sharing opted for *block grants* to state and local government over *categorical grants* managed by Washington, it challenged congressional prerogative in the pursuit of national welfare objectives. More fundamentally, it threatened the vast array of federal *entitlement* programs put in place by the Johnson administration along with the mutually-supportive relationship between the government bureaucracies administering them and the more well-organized lobbies benefitting from them, neither of which had a vested interested in a final victory over poverty or any of the other social ills Lyndon Johnson had set out to eradicate. This, at least, was Nixon's view.[62] It was certainly democratic government, but in the hands of the U.S. Congress it had become corrupting and demoralizing and quite incapable of achieving the social justice liberals had claimed was the nation's most important mission. One could, in fact, debate even the democratic claim; another generation of conservative Republicans was already preparing to do so. Nixon, on the other hand, was saying that liberalism was failing on its own terms.

For its part, Family Assistance foundered in Congress on the political economy of welfare and self-conscious ideological posturing. Because it proposed to overturn the welfare *services* strategy of the Great Society in favor of an income strategy that would diminish the numbers and the influence of social workers, it provoked the hostility of welfare professionals associations. At the same time, lobbies for welfare recipients, such as the National Welfare Rights Organization (NWRO), threatened dire electoral consequences for congressmen from urban ghetto constituencies unless they voted against the Nixon plan. Congress "anti-fappers" formed an odd majority of convenience composed of liberal Democrats charging its guaranteed income was not enough (Senator Eugene McCarthy dubbed it the Family Annihilation Plan) and conservative Republicans opposed to a guaranteed income in principle but also pointing out the fact that the FAP would increase the nation's absolute number of welfare recipients. Reaction to it also scrambled the boundaries of partisanship. Among its Republican casualties was Representative George Bush from Texas, who later lost his bid for a Senate seat to a Democrat who accused him of wanting to put more Americans on the welfare roll. Miraculously, the House passed the bill 243-155 in April 1970, but the Senate subjected it to multiple revisions before killing it 52 to 34 in October 1972, three years after its introduction.[63] One-nation republicanism in welfare reform was a hard sell on the left and the right. The same was true of the Supreme Court. When lobbies such as the NRWO argued that welfare services were more than public policy to be amended to meet the changing fiscal and social circumstance of the nation, the Court thought they had a case. In a series of decisions handed down in the late 1960s and early 1970s, [64] the Warren Court defined a variety of welfare provisions as *entitlements* to which recipients had an enforceable right, thus adding legal inertia to political resistance on the issue of welfare reform by increasing the absolute number of government expenditures considered mandatory and immune from political debate.[65]

These were important episodes. Nixon had attempted to square what he saw as government's obligations in welfare with the traditional Republican philosophy of individual self-reliance and the country's fiscal resources. Congress defeated him. A generation later President Reagan rejoined the battle with much less subtlety. In the meantime, Nixon used executive powers of veto and *impoundment* to confound congressional appropriations he deemed likely to exceed the capacity of the federal budget. Congressional fury over his impoundment of extrabudgetary funds for water pollution control led to the *Budget and Impoundment Control Act of 1974* and the creation of the Congressional Budget Office (CBO). The act was an attempt to recover for Congress budgetary powers that had over the decades been delegated to the executive, in part by establishing in the CBO a capacity at the very least to analyze the complex figures behind the president's annual budget message.

But to members of Congress in both parties it also held out the additional promise that open budget formulation in the legislature would permit them to score political points. Republicans wanted to flush "spenders" out into the light of public scrutiny and ridicule their nefarious schemes. Democrats hoped to force the conservative priests of budget balance to admit that their doctrine of states' rights was a cover for malign parsimony and that the "waste" they lamented actually built highways, supported farmers, and helped the working poor. Both sides claimed to speak for the People, and both sides actually believed it.[66]

The act's passage, moreover, should not be considered separately from the larger controversy surrounding the presidency. Between reelection in 1972 and late 1973, Nixon had been largely successful with his veto of spending bills, but, as Watergate revelations eroded public support for his administration, the goal of wresting budgetary authority from him hands became politically viable and indeed profitable in light of the moral high-ground the Senate Watergate hearings gave to the congressional investigation of the imperial presidency. The act's great significance, then, was as a congressional victory in a political struggle with the White House over jurisdictional terrain. It did not establish new policy or set new priorities for the federal budget, but its implications for American politics over the following two decades easily exceeded in significance the scandal that engulfed the Nixon presidency in the year of its passage.

Over the intervening twenty years Nixon's name has lost none of its capacity to provoke rage. Contemplating some of the rather fawning eulogies that followed his death on April 1994, one journalist fumed that the nation had obviously forgotten the constitutional moral of his administration, yet dedicated the remainder of his copy to Nixon's character, "vindictive, foulmouthed, and determined to replace the rule of law with corporate despotism."[67] Both journalists and politicians are wont to claim that there is a constitutional lesson in virtually every issue on the public agenda, but the greater lesson of Nixon's presidency is more political than constitutional. It gets so little attention because its message is so unpleasant, especially when Nixon's term in office is considered together with Johnson's. In foreign policy Nixon generally undertook to bring the nation's commitments back into line with its capabilities after Johnson had taken the Vietnam conflict into the dimen-

sion of the surreal. To a nation reared on twenty years of hubris, he emphasized limitations. His one-nation Republicanism on the domestic front attempted essentially the same thing.
New Deal liberalism was born of the Great Depression, the
most profound economic and political crisis the nation had
ever faced. What power of interventionist government FDR
created to answer popular misery in the worst of times, Lyndon
Johnson extended in the best of times. His Great Society committed government to the elimination of poverty, without asking the American people to pay the cost.

By the time of Nixon's election the political economy of the
Great Society was so embedded in the constituency interests
of Congress, that any and all attempts to rationalize its vast
catalogue of programs were construed as a conservative attack on the very principle of welfare. In substance they
amounted to an effort to require Washington to retain only
those programs, in number and in nature, for which the body
politic would pay. In Nixon's entire foreign and domestic policy
agenda, in other words, was one message: the United States
was living not so much beyond its means as beyond its political will. Buried under the noise of the national Watergate tan-
trum were fundamental choices of national self-definition,
choices that American government and its electorate refused
to make. The Vietnam War was the natural destination less of
the Cold War itself than of welfare-warfare liberalism's interpretation of it. It is one thing to undertake military containment of communism and another to encourage client states to
undertake democratic reforms that would undermine the long
term appeal of communism. It is quite another again to treat a
war and a campaign of democratic reform as one and the same
thing. The best evidence is that the Johnson administration
could never decide where war ended and politics began. In his
defense, neither could Congress.

By 1974, however, it had decided how to apportion blame.
For its part, the Nixon administration unraveled over revelations concerning the president's knowledge of Watergate and
related activities. Because Nixon had, in fact, endorsed such
activities fairly early in his first term, his abuse of executive
authority was systematic and serious enough to justify impeachment. Two decades later, however, America's agonies over

Watergate seem quite out of proportion to the nature of the scandal. Nixon's actions against real and imagined political enemies were in part the product of a personality matured on the notion that politics is war by other means. Yet many of those same actions were also logical responses to the situation Nixon inherited from Lyndon Johnson, so much so that the Nixon presidency cannot be understood without an adequate appreciation of what preceded it. The nation attempted too much in the 1960s. It had been challenged to do so by Kennedy's inaugural, but it was Johnson who launched a full frontal assault on the whole notion of limited aspirations, doing serious damage to limited government in the process. Once he decided not to run in 1968, the presidency was an institution in crisis, itself the lightning rod for widespread anger over flawed domestic reforms and a humiliated foreign policy in which Congress and the public had, increment by increment, colluded. In substance, the Nixon administration was about retrenchment in domestic affairs and orderly retreat abroad. In deed rather than word his meassage to the nation was that it could not bear all burdens and fight all foes. The homage given to Nixon on the occasion of his death in 1994 was a symbolic admission by the People of the accuracy of the message and of the fact that he had, after all, got some things right. But in 1974 they wanted nothing so much as to shoot the messenger.

Notes

1   Lyndon Baines Johnson, *The Vantage Point:Perspectives on the Presidency, 1963–1969* (New York: Popular Library, 1971), p. 19.

2   Quoted in Stephen Ambrose, The *Rise to Globalism: American Foreign Policy Since 1938* (New York: Penguin, 1991), p. 206; Department of State, *Foreign Relations of the United States, 1961–1963: Vol. I, Vietnam 1961*, (hereafter FRUS), pp. 149–157; Robert Dallek, *Lone Star Rising: Lyndon Johnson and His Times, 1908–1960* (New York: Oxford University Press, 1991), p. 370, pp. 496–527 and pp. 548–552.

3   Irving Bernstein, *Guns or Butter: The Presidency of Lyndon Johnson* (New York: Oxford University Press, 1996), pp. 44–52.

4   Arthur Okun, *The Political Economy of Prosperity* (New York: W.W. Norton, 1970), p. 47; James D. Savage, *Balanced Budgets and American Politics* (Ithaca, N.Y.: Cornell University Press, 1988), pp. 177–178; G.L. Bach, *Making Monetary and Fiscal Policy* (Washington, D.C.: Brookings, 1971), p. 116.

5   Harry McPherson, *A Political Education* (Boston: Little, Brown, 1972), p. 268; Herbert Stein, *Presidential Economics: The Making of Economic Policy from Roosevelt to Reagan and Beyond* (New York: Simon & Schuster, 1984), p. 27.

6   Alonzo L. Hamby, *Liberalism and its Challengers, From F.D.R to Bush* (New York: Oxford University Press, 1992), p. 258.

7   Hamby, *Liberalism*, p. 257.

8   Rowland Evans and Robert Novak, *Lyndon Johnson: The Exercise of Power* (New York: Signet, 1968), pp. 488–495; Kathleen Hall Jamieson, *Packaging the Presidency: A History and Criticism of Presidential Campaign Advertising* (New York: Oxford University Press, 1964), pp. 169–220; Theodore White, *The Making of the President, 1964* (New York: Atheneum, 1965), pp. 324–326.

9   Barry Goldwater, *The Conscience of a Conservative* (New York: Hillman, 1960), p. 19 and 22.

10 Goldwater, *Conscience*, p. 68.

11 Bernstein, *Guns or Butter*, p. 155.

12 The *Voting Rights Act* of 1965 sought to remove restrictions on voting that had been employed to discriminate against black and other minority citizens. It made illegal the application of literacy tests as a qualification for voting and authorized the federal government to

register voters in any state where less than 50 percent of eligible voters appeared on voting lists. Its provisions were reiniforced and extended by the Voting Rights Acts of 1970, 1975, and 1982.

13 Under the action the House Rules Committee had twenty-one days to report its recommendations on a bill, after which the chairman of the legislative committee involved could ask the Speaker of the House on behalf of his committee to allow the bill to be called up without a ruling.

14 It has been estimated, for example, that the Great Society generated some 2 million new government jobs, a disproportionate number of them going to black applicants. Michael K. Brown and Steven P. Erie, "Blacks and the Legacy of the Great Society," *Public Policy*, Vol.29, No.3, 1981, pp. 299–330; see also John E. Schwartz, *America's Hidden Success: A Reassessment of Public Policy From Kennedy to Reagan* (New York: W.W. Norton, 1988), pp. 17–70.

15 James L. Sundquist, *Politics and Policy: The Eisenhower, Kennedy and Johnson Years* (Washington, D.C.: Brookings, 1968), pp. 287–321; Dennis S. Ippolito, *Uncertain Legacies: Federal Budget Policy from Roosevelt through Reagan* (Charlottesville: University of Virginia Press, 1990) pp. 165–169.

16 V.D. Bornet, *The Presidency of Lyndon B. Johnson* (Lawrence: University Press of Kansas, 1983), pp. 219–375; Ippolito, *Uncertain Legacies*, pp. 209–213.

17 Robert S. McNamara, *In Retrospect* (New York: Times Books, 1995) pp. 96–101.

18 Johnson, *Vantage Point*, p. 116.

19 Bernstein, *Guns or Butter*, pp. 336–338; Walter LaFeber, "Johnson, Vietnam, and Tocqueville," in Warren I. Cohen and Nancy Bernkopf Tucker Eds., *Lyndon Johnson Confronts the World: American Foreign Policy, 1963–1968* (New York: Cambridge University Press, 1994) p. 61.; Brian Vandemark, *Into the Quagmire: Lyndon Johnson and the Escalation of the Vietnam War* (New York: Oxford University Press, 1991), pp. 23–38.

20 Lesley Gelb and Richard Betts, *The Irony of Vietnam: The System Worked* (Washington, D.C.: Brookings, 1979), pp. 292–293; Ian Maitland, "Only the Best and the Brightest?," *Asian Affairs*, Vol.3, 1976, pp. 263–272; George C. Herring, "The War in Vietnam," in R.A. Divine Ed., *Exploring the Johnson Years* (Austin: University of Texas Press, 1981), pp. 39–40.

21 William L. Lunch and Peter W. Sperlich, "American Public Opinion and the Vietnam War," *Western Political Quarterly*, Vol.32, 1979, pp. 21–30.

22 James N Giglio, *The Presidency of John F. Kennedy* (Lawrence: University of Kansas Press, 1991), pp. 240–241; Lawrence J. Basset and Stephen E. Pelz, "The Failed Search for Victory: Vietnam and the Politics of War," in Thomas G. Paterson Ed., *Kennedy's Quest for Victory: American Foreign Policy, 1961–1963* (New York: Oxford University Press, 1989), pp. 223–252; Idem, *Meeting the Communist Threat* (New York: Oxford University Press, 1988), pp. 191–210; Paul H. Nitze, *From Hiroshima to Glasnost: At the Center of Decision* (New York: Grove Weidenfeld, 1989), pp. 250–261.

23 Larry Berman, *Planning a Tragedy: The Americanization of the War in Vietnam* (New York: W.W.Norton, 1982), p. 92; Thomas J. Schoenbaum, *Waging Peace and War: Dean Rusk in the Truman, Kennedy, and Johnson Years* (New York: Simon & Schuster, 1988), pp. 214–215, p. 224, 230–234, and 441–453.

24 Doris Kearns, *Lyndon Johnson and the American Dream* (New York: Mentor, 1976), pp. 282–285; Stephen Skowronek, *The Politics Presidents Make: Leadership from John Adams to George Bush* (Cambridge, Mass.: Belknap, 1993), p.344.

25 As early as July, 1965 Eisenhower advised Johnson to "go all out" and told the President that success now depended on the willingness to do what was militarily necessary rather than subordinating military necessity to diplomatic and political considerations. Stephen Ambrose, *Eisenhower, Soldier and President* (New York: Simon & Schuster, 1984), pp. 559–560.

26 Charles DeBenedetti, *An American Ordeal: The Antiwar Movement of the Vietnam Era* (Syracuse, N.Y.: Syracuse University Press, 1990), pp. 107–109; Melvin Small, *Johnson, Nixon, and the Doves* (New Brunswick, N.J.: Rutgers University Press, 1988).

27 Quoted in Bernstein, *Guns or Butter*, p. 478.

28 John Morton Blum, *The Progressive Presidents: Roosevelt, Wilson, Roosevelt, Johnson* (New York: W.W. Norton, 1980), pp. 163–203; Skowronek, *The Politics Presidents Make*, pp. 325–360.

29 Bernstein, *Guns or Butter, p. 378.*

30 Theodore White, *The Making of the President, 1968* (New York: Atheneum, 1969), pp. 128–137.

31 Michael Kazin, *The Populist Persuasion: An American History* (New York: Harper-Collins, 1995), pp. 221–242.

32 Johnson, *Vantage Point*, pp. 553–554.

33 Theodore J. Lowi, *The Personal President: Power Invested, Promise Unfulfilled* (Ithaca, N.Y.: Cornell University Press, 1985) p. 143.

34   Quoted in Stephen Ambrose, *Nixon: The Triumph of a Politician,* 1962–72 (New York: Simon & Schuster, 1989), p. 242.

35   David S. Broder, "A Risky New American Sport: The Breaking of the President," *Washington Post,* October 7, 1969, p. A19. The article was taken very seriously in the Nixon White House. See William Safire, *Before the Fall: An Inside View of the Pre-Watergate White House* (New York: Doubleday, 1975), pp. 171–180.

36   John F. Kennedy, *Profiles in Courage* (New York: Harper & Brothers, 1956), pp. 16–17. For the key passage from Burke, see Ross J.S. Hoffman and Paul Levack, *Burke's Politics: Selected Writings and Speeches of Edmund Burke on Reform, Revolution and War* (New York: Alfred Knopf, 1959), p. 115.

37   E.J. Dionne Jr., *Why Americans Hate Politics* (New York: Simon & Schuster, 1991), p. 13.

38   H.R. Haldeman, *The Haldeman Diaries: Inside the Nixon White House* (New York: Putnam, 1994), p. 303 and 311; Ambrose, *Nixon: The Triumph of a Politician,* p. 446.

39   Ambrose, *Nixon: The Triumph of a Politician,* pp. 449–451; Joan Hoff, *Nixon Reconsidered* (New York: Basic Books, 1994), pp. 294–300.

40   Robert S. Litwak, *Détente and the Nixon Doctrine* (New York: Cambridge University Press, 1984); W. David Clinton, *The Two Faces of National Interest* (Baton Rouge: Louisiana State University Press, 1994), pp. 183–214; Michael Mandelbaum, *The Fate of Nations* (Cambridge: Cambridge University Press, 1988), pp. 169–170; Paul Kennedy, *The Rise and Fall of the Great Powers* (London: Fontana, 1989), pp. 525–527.

41   Herbert S. Dinerstein, "The Soviet Outlook: America, Europe, and China," in Robert E. Osgood Ed., *Retreat From Empire? The First Nixon Administration* (Baltimore, Md.: The Johns Hopkins University Press, 1973), pp. 124–128.

42   Raymond Aron, *The Imperial Republic: The United States and the World, 1945–1973* Trans: Frank Jellinek (Cambridge, England: Winthrop, 1974), p. 131.

43   William F. Buckley Jr., "Veni, Vidi, Victus," *National Review,* March 17, 1972, p. 258. On the extraordinary diversity and inconsistency of American attitudes toward China, see Steven W. Mosher, *China Misperceived: American Illusions and Chinese Reality* (New York: Harper-Collins, 1990).

44   See for, example Mosher, *China Misperceived,* pp. 139–160.

45   Keith L. Nelson, *The Making of Détente: Soviet-America Relations in the Shadow of Vietnam* (Baltimore, Md.: The Johns Hopkins University Press,

1995), pp. 77–79; Richard W. Stevenson, *The Rise and Fall of Détente: Relaxations of Tension in U.S.-Soviet Relations, 1953–84* (Urbana: University of Illinois Press, 1985), p. 165.

46   Ambrose, *Nixon, The Triumph of a Politician*, pp. 614–617; Raymond Garthoff, *Détente and Confrontation: American-Soviet Relations from Nixon to Reagan* (Washington, D.C.: Brookings, 1994), pp. 104–106; Marshall I. Goldman, *Détente and Dollars: Doing Business with the Soviets* (New York: Basic Books, 1975). The most favored nation principle is integral to the General Agreement on Tariffs and Trade (GATT) system of global trade, under which the United States sought a leveling-up of trade liberalization by insisting that all participants of a multilateral trading system should enjoy the same "most-favored" status and be thus free from bilateral discriminatory practices. The United States withdrew MFN status from the Soviet Union during the Korean War.
     The amendment was proposed by Henry Jackson (D-Washington) and Charles Vanik (R-Ohio), backed by seventy-three cosponsors in the Senate. It required specifically that Moscow ease its restrictions on Jewish emigration and that the U.S. withhold sales of grain, access to technology, and credits pending Soviet concessions on the demand. Beyond the grain sale, the U.S. Exim Bank had approved a loan of $202 million for the Soviet purchase of American industrial equipment, while some three-hundred US firms were interested in business with the Soviet Union.

47   Thomas G. Paterson, *Meeting the Communist Threat, Truman to Reagan*, (New York: Oxford University Press, 1988), p. 232.

48   As a military operation the Cambodian incursion had mixed results at best. It set back Hanoi's ability to run offensive operations in South Vietnam, but was not at all the crippling blow Nixon and Kissinger claimed. Given the ferocity of domestic protest, moreover, it did not convey a message of American resolve sufficient to bring advantages in peace negotiations. Ambrose, *Nixon: The Triumph of a Politician*, pp. 360–361.

49   Congressional movement toward the resolution began immediately in the wake of the Cambodian operation. The *Cooper-Church Amendment* to military appropriations from the Senate Foreign Relations Committee required American troops to leave Cambodia by June 30. A parallel motion, the *Hatfield-McGovern Amendment* required further that all American forces leave Vietnam by June 30, 1971. Stephen Ambrose, *Nixon: Ruin and Recovery* (New York: Simon & Schuster, 1991), p. 61. Sotirios A. Barber, *On What the Constitution Means* (Baltimore, Md.: The Johns Hopkins University Press, 1984), p. 174.

50   Barbara Hinckley, *Less than Meets the Eye: Foreign Policy Making and the Myth of the Assertive Congress* (Chicago: University of Chicago Press, 1994).

51 Richard M. Nixon, "Asia After Viet Nam," *Foreign Affairs*, Vol.46, No.1, 1967, p. 121 and 124; Walter Isaacson, *Kissinger, A Biography* (New York: Simon & Shuster, 1992), pp. 139-146.

52 Thomas Hughes, quoted in Isaacson, *Kissinger*, p. 141.

53 Quoted by Joan Hoff-Wilson The Corporate Presidency", in F.I. Greenstein Ed., *Leadership in the Modern Presidency* (Cambridge, Mass.: Harvard University Press, 1988) p. 185; Nelson, *The Making of Détente*, pp. 76-77.

54 Haldeman, *Haldeman Diaries*, p. 311.

55 James Q. Wilson, *The Amateur Democrat: Club Politics in Three Cities* (Chicago: University of Chicago Press, 1966) pp. 1-31.

56 Haldeman, *Haldeman Diaries*, p. 493, 505, and 506.

57 John S. Odell, *U.S. International Monetary Policy: Markets, Power and Ideas as Sources of Change* (Princeton, N.J.: Princeton University Press, 1982), p. 263.

58 The Court's decision in *Swann v. Charlotte-Mecklenburg Board of Education, 402 U.S.1 (1971)* held that all remnants of state-imposed racial segregation of schools must be eliminated and stated further than federal district courts had wide authority to achieve this goal, including busing and racial quotas. For Nixon's thinking on the Philadelphia Plan, see Herbert S. Parmet, *Richard Nixon and his America* (Boston: Little, Brown, 1990) pp. 598-601.

59 Ambrose, *Nixon: The Triumph of a Politician*, pp. 404-407.

60 Savage, *Balanced Budgets and American Politics*, pp. 182-183.

61 Robert Solomon, *The International Monetary System, 1945-1981* (New York: Harper & Row, 1982), p. 191.

62 In the interpretation of Theodore Lowi's *End of Liberalism*, published in 1969, the view was entirely legitimate. Theodore Lowi, *The End of Liberalism: Ideology, Policy, and the Crisis of Public Authority* (New York: W.W. Norton, 1969). *Block* grants involve the transfer of federal funds to states and municipalities for broad policy goals, discretion on the implementation of specific programs remaining with state and local governments. Responsibility for *categorical* aid, by contrast, remains with the federal bureaucracy.

63 Hoff, *Nixon Reconsidered*, pp. 115-137; Daniel Patrick Moynihan, *The Politics of a Guaranteed Annual Income* (New York: Random House, 1973), esp. pp. 302-345; Vincent J. Burke and Vee Burke, *Nixon's Good Deed, Welfare Reform* (New York: Columbia University Press, 1974), esp. pp. 129-220 Theodore R. Marmor and Martin Rein, "Reforming the Welfare Mess: The Fate of the Family Assistance Plan, 1969-1972," in

Allan P. Sindler Ed., *Policy and Politics in America: Six Case Studies* (Boston: Little, Brown, 1973).

64 For example *Shapiro v. Thompson, 394 US 618* (1969); *Sniadach v. Family Finance Corp.,395 US 337* (1969); *Thorpe v. Housing Authority, 393 US 268* (1969); *Goldberg v. Kelly, 397 US 254* (1970). The latter decision held that welfare benefits could not be withdrawn without due process, and in effect defined economic and social benefits as rights rather then privileges.

65 Whereas in fiscal year (FY) 1967 entitlements claimed 37 percent of total outlays and 60 percent of all uncontrollable spending, by FY 1980 entitlement spending accounted for 60 percent of total outlays and close to 80 percent of uncontrollable spending. Dennis S. Ippolito, *Congressional Spending* (Ithaca, N.Y.: Cornell University Press, 1981), pp. 213-214.

66 Ippolito, *Uncertain Legacies,* pp. 18-19; Joseph White and Aaron Wildavsky, *The Deficit and the Public Interest: The Search for Responsible Budgeting in the 1980s* (Berkeley: University of California Press, 1989) p. 13.

67 Lewis Lapham, "Morte de Nixon," *Harper's,* July 1994, p. 6.

Chapter Six

All of the People, All of the Time

"And having looked to government for bread, on the first scarcity
they will turn and bite the hand that fed them." -Edmund Burke,
Thoughts and Details on Scarcity

The presidential ballot of 1976 was a reaction to the overlap-
ping traumas of Vietnam and Watergate, now fused in the
public subconscious into one nightmarish episode in national
humiliation, rather than a vote to make James Earl Carter President of the United States. Little else explains Carter's sudden
rise from obscurity to the nation's highest office.

Even after the election the American people had very little
measure of who or what Jimmy Carter was. His own answer to
that question during his campaign was essentially to say that
he was nothing like the criminals of Watergate. Carter ran less
against Gerald Ford than against the memory of Nixon, a strategy that was aided to some degree by Ford's presidential pardon of his predecessor and retention of his secretary of state.
Carter sought consciously to be unlike Richard Nixon in all
things, especially in the realm of foreign affairs. As candidate
and president-elect he often cast Henry Kissinger as Nixon II,
a secretive operator who "only permitted Congress to become
involved in the decision-making process when it was politically
expedient for him to do so"; in interviews before and after the
election, Carter promised a bipartisan approach to foreign
policy and to "let the American people be involved as deeply
as possible."[1] Carter's genuine zeal for open government ran
parallel to internal reforms undertaken by Congress. Also partly
a response to the national appetite for atonement that followed

the Watergate scandal, these reforms were designed to check the powers of committee chairs and to afford junior congressmen greater opportunity to influence public policy. Their overall effect was to multiply, through a proliferation of committees, the number of decision-making centers in the legislative branch, with little positive impact on the coherence and hence quality of public policy. Within two years of their election, moreover, both Carter and the Ninety-fourth Congress experienced a powerful backlash to their policies and the priorities they had set for the nation. The administration's inability to deal effectively with economic stagnation, high inflation, and geopolitical crises facilitated a Republican offensive that in 1980 elected Ronald Reagan to the White House on a platform of Cold War orthodoxy, low taxes, and a balanced budget.

Reagan's election is widely viewed as a watershed in modern American politics. Faced with the diminished economic security of the 1970s, the middle class is thought to have turned away from the New Deal legacy and rejected explicitly the notion that expansive governmental authority could contribute to economic recovery. For many who rallied to Reagan's platform, however, "small government" meant little more than lower taxes, and the new conservatism of the Reagan years turned out to be highly selective in terms of challenging popular expectations of government in more general terms. Reagan-era conservatism never had an electoral impact on Congress proportional to its presidential success. Continuing Democratic dominance of Congress in the 1980s and into the 1990s meant that a reduction in the entitlement commitments of the federal government consistent with the conservative promise of Reaganism never occurred. Instead, a pattern, which is today the root cause of the crisis of governance in the United States, established itself and remains in force today: American voters elect one branch of the federal government pledged to roll back the national budget deficit, yet return another to protect their entitlements and ensure that the sacrifices involved in such any deficit-reduction effort will not be booked to the taxpayers of their district. That this is so is particularly evident since the end of the Cold War and the emergence of new international circumstances that permit a more lucid discussion of the domestic priorities of public policy in the United States, free of the forty-year burden of institutionalized international emergency. During the Bush and Clinton administrations, both the executive and legislative branches grappled only very marginally with the symptoms rather than the causes of the federal deficit, above all because of a preference for following rather than informing public opinion.

Democratic Redemption

In one important respect the election of Jimmy Carter was a testimony to the decline of his party and the rise of the new conservatism. Carter ran as independently of the Democratic Party as any candidate in living memory. His nomination represented the complete triumph of Carter's personal campaign organization; a primary system that permitted a little-known politician suddenly to become a household word; and above all the luck of momentum gained in early primary victories to generate the kind of sustained funding that could turn a candidacy that merely looked serious into a serious candidacy.[2] If the primary season can in some respects be likened to a horse race in which gamblers are permitted to change their bets during the race, then the 1976 Democratic nomination represented an altogether new version of the dark horse victory.

Carter's aloofness from ideological battles wracking the Democrats also helped. He offered himself as a unifier, both of party and nation, and, as the 1976 primary season progressed, it dawned on more and more Democrats that an unknown quantity such as Carter just might succeed with the mission, above all because he was unknown. He had never been a factor in national politics before, and very few Democrats active at the national level had scores to settle with Jimmy Carter. Carter's book, *Why Not the Best?*, a campaign pitch dressed as an autobiography, itself made a virtue of the fact that nobody knew him. It quoted everyone from Reinhold Niebuhr to Dylan Thomas, while lauding the music of Richard Wagner and Bob Dylan. It had praise for all and offense for none.[3]

With one notable exception, the government of the United States in Washington. The centerpiece of Carter's strategy was to convince the Democratic Party that he could return the South, in 1976 anything but solid after the divisions caused by Lyndon Johnson's civil rights legislation and the bridgehead on southern electoral sentiment gained by Nixon Republicans, to the Democratic fold. The basis of party unity for a Carter nomination, and thereafter for a united Democratic run at the presidency, was to be an attack on federal arrogance and bureaucratic incompetence, a theme with perennial appeal in the states of the Old Confederacy but now even more potent after George Wallace's maverick campaign of 1968. After stunning victories in the Iowa caucuses and the New Hampshire primary, Carter was crushed in the Massachusetts primary. But then his victory in the Florida primary, beating Wallace 34.3 percent to 30.6 percent, demonstrated the potential of Carter's particular brand of anti-Washington strategy in the south. By June 1976 Carter had with subsequent primary victories all but tied up the Democratic nomination and had made national redemption led by honest and answerable government the theme of his campaign against the beleaguered incumbency of Gerald Ford.

When one remembers that Ford was only officially Carter's opponent, the real demons of the politics of redemption being the abuse of executive power by Presidents Johnson and Nixon, it was remarkable not that Ford went down to defeat but rather that the 1976 election was as close as 297 to 241 electoral college votes. Even more remarkable was the fact that Carter took southern states such as Alabama, Arkansas, the Carolinas, Florida, Georgia, Kentucky, Louisiana, Mississippi, Oklahoma, Tennessee, Texas, and West Virginia by combining over 80 percent of the black vote with a strong showing among rural lower-income whites. In a region where the party had for decades relied on the local appeal of troglodyte segregationists, Carter was a New Democrat whose triumph reflected both the emergence of a New South and Carter's ability to attract the votes of Richard Nixon's silent majority in the not-so-new South. It was as close as any candidate had come to realizing the dream of the Populist Thomas Watson in the 1880s.[4]

Having profited from the divisions between more established Democrats to emerge the winner, Carter needed as president a project to reunite them and focus their energies. He found it in the theme of international respect for human rights and committed his administration to close coordination with Congress in the development of human rights diplomacy. After eight years of bitter confrontation between the executive and legislative branches, Carter could in 1977 count on nothing so much as a loud voice from a resurgent Congress in every realm of public affairs. Carter had no expertise nor a history of interest in foreign policy. Nonetheless, foreign relations offered a certain utility in finding his footing with the legislature; sound Wilsonian principles on human rights represented one of the few things on which Democrats could establish a cozy consensus in 1977, so Carter possibly reasoned that human rights diplomacy could form the basis of Democratic unity in dealing with some of the more contentious domestic issues. This was all the more important because Carter had no sense of the folkways of Congress that had been such an asset to Lyndon Johnson, and neither was he able to assume any executive autonomy of Congress in the conduct of foreign affairs like Nixon. Congress had signaled its intention, with the *War Powers Resolution of 1973* and the *Congressional Budget and Impoundment Control Act of 1974*, to reverse in both the domestic and foreign policy realms the thirty year-trend of accumulated executive prerogative.

The Congress of the 1970s encountered serious difficulty in accomplishing the task in any coherent fashion. Gone were the benefits of strong legislative leadership, not only that typified by the legendary House Speaker Joe Cannon before World War I but also the subtle arts applied by Sam Rayburn and Lyndon Johnson in the 1940s and 1950s. Reforms designed to end the abuse of power by committee chairmen were supplemented by still more to discard the principle of seniority in appointment of key committee and subcommittee posts. Especially zealous in the implementation of the new rules were the seventy-five new "Watergate" Democrats elected to Congress in 1974 to deal with the corrupt Washington establishment. They ousted incumbent committee chairmen, mostly southern conservative Democrats, and replaced them by secret ballot with younger colleagues, mostly northern liberal Democrats. Thus, the electoral backlash to Watergate had its greatest long-term impact on the legislative rather than the executive branch:

the Carter administration, as it turned out, lasted only four years, but the freshmen of 1974 were around for much longer. And their impact was profound. Whereas the challenge for Lyndon Johnson and Sam Rayburn had been "to wheedle and plead with committee chairmen who held the keys to legislative action, the problem of Robert Byrd and Tip O'Neill, in the 1970s, was to organize the new individualism—or new fragmentation—into some kind of working whole."[5] The new Democrats had set out to make the place more democratic, and to the extent that they had obliterated the vestiges of bossism and established their right to be led only on their own terms, they had succeeded. For his own part, Carter needed to establish a productive liaison with an institution he hardly knew, yet deciding where to begin was a challenge in itself.

Still other reforms changed the relationship between legislators and their constituents in significant ways. New campaign finance rules contained in the *Federal Election Campaign Act* of 1974, again a reaction to Watergate and revelations of corruption in Nixon's reelection committee, sharply reduced the financial contributions individuals could make to a federal campaign; sanctioned the use of federal revenues in financing presidential though not congressional campaigns; and permitted both companies and unions holding government contracts to establish permanent organizations to lobby Congress. The reforms were intended to diminish the influence in campaign financing of individual, wealthy donors and encourage the practice of seeking campaign finance from a large number of small donors. Their effect was twofold: they made political action committees (PACs) the natural vehicle for financial contributions to electoral campaigns at the federal level, and they focused PAC financing on congressional campaigns by dedicating federal finance guarantees to presidential campaigns.[6] After 1974 the number of PACs, along with the diversity of the PAC constellation and the number and variety of their fundraising/campaigning activities, exploded. They have ever since been an object of enormous controversy, but are neither the vehicles of open government their advocates promised nor the bacteria of corruption their detractors insist. Participatory democracy, the invention of the self-important New Left of the 1960s, had to assume some practical form in order to have any substantive meaning. Inside the parties it took the form of the amateur democrat; outside it took the form of the PAC.

The real victim of both PAC proliferation and the demise of old-style congressional leadership was, and is, political brokerage. PAC funding became ever more important to success in congressional races, and the PACs' technique in extracting the legislative *quid pro quo* from successful candidates became progressively refined. Lawmakers were now more closely and routinely in touch with organized, articulate, and vocal constituency interests than ever. In the lawmakers' day-to-day reality, the People were redefined: no longer the voters back home in the district, but rather the jacket-and-tie of a public-interest law firm knocking on their office door. The result was to make the ligatures connecting individual legislators to the specific views of the best organized PACs more meaningful than those connecting them to other legislators through party, committee, or caucus. With the coalition-building powers of congressional leadership already broken, Congress in he 1970s came to resemble nothing so much as a legislative fleamarket. "Those who want to represent the broad public interest," observed Senator Kent Conrad of North Dakota, "find themselves in a terrible dilemma."[7]

Carter was, in other words, dealing with a Congress in which the freshmen Democrats of 1974 interpreted their individual electoral mandates in a fashion that in no fashion deferred to more senior legislators, much less to Carter himself as first-among-Democrats, first because they were not tempermentally inclined to, but more so because electorally they could ill afford to. One of the commonest criticisms of Carter was that he never understood Congress. In fact, incomprehension resided at both ends of Pennsylvania Avenue. If in the wake of Watergate the American people had in 1974 and 1976 sought an alternative to the professional politics exemplified in the presidencies of Johnson and Nixon, they had certainly found it. Amateurs were everywhere.[8]

Carter's human rights diplomacy did not give him the congressional leverage and support he had hoped for. The application of the human rights imperative via initiatives such as the Jackson-Vanik Amendment, which predated Carter's election, "let members of Congress curry constituent favor; use the power of the purse to participate in key decisions about foreign policy; and hold the executive branch increasingly accountable to the 'sense of Congress',"[9] even when Congress displayed little sense itself about the substance of American foreign relations. By the end of Carter's first year in office both Republicans and Democrats in Congress were openly critical of Carter's foreign policy, and it is not going too far to say that in many instances the criticism itself was the point. For the Democrats in particular this was more than a little unfair, given that Carter simply adopted wholesale the human rights diplomacy they had promoted in Jackson-Vanik. Though emphasizing his intention to preserve superpower *détente,* Carter publicly cited Moscow's routine violations of human rights standards and sent a letter of support to Soviet dissident Andrei Sakharov. When Moscow responded angrily to his break with the etiquette of *détente* by threatening to hold the negotiation of SALT II hostage to Carter's silence on human rights, a fairly elementary lesson in reciprocal linkage, most of Carter's principal advisors on foreign policy were genuinely surprised.[10]

The tension between Carter's desire to carry on with *détente* yet imbue U.S. foreign policy more explicitly with moral purpose was reflected in his cabinet itself. His Secretary of State, Cyrus Vance, preferred to advance the cause of human rights with unassuming discretion. This approach clashed with that of Zbigniew Brzezinski, who as National Security Advisor saw the human rights issue as a means to inject the administration's diplomacy with the essence of American values while throwing Moscow on the defensive ideologically.[11] On coming to office a confrontation with the Soviet Union was in many respects the last thing that Jimmy Carter wanted. Yet his policy, and a good deal of the advice he was getting, led him inevitably in that direction. So as it turned out, Carter's first year was dominated by relations with Moscow, and by the end of it relations were soured.[12]

In one respect this was an appropriate manifestation of change in the political weather. Whereas in 1969 the American people wanted nothing so much as an exit from Vietnam, a demand that resonated nicely with Nixon's plan to align the fundamental goal of containment with an overall redirection of the military burden abroad by way of new emphasis on balance-of-power diplomacy, by 1977 the national mood on foreign affairs was one of fatigue and bitterness, fatigue after three decades of the Cold War burden, bitterness at the horrific price paid for a lost cause in Southeast Asia while Moscow looked on. Each in its own way, the executive and legislative branches of the late 1970s reflected conflicting popular sentiments on foreign policy. Neither the electorate nor its government consciously sought acrimony with the Soviet Union, but equally neither was receptive to the argument that since the rhetoric of human rights caused offense in Moscow it should be struck from the lexicon of foreign affairs. The national challenge taken up in 1947 originated with the Soviet Union after all, and human rights diplomacy could be legitimately viewed as a return to first principles. *Détente* had served its purpose, but it was just possible that its possibilities had been exhausted.

So, despite the complications it created for relations with Moscow, the human rights principle was authentic and legitimate. The problem lay with Carter's declaration of it as an absolute, which in application it could never be. He criticized past American support for repressive military dictatorships and pressured several of them to undertake democratic reforms. While he managed some successes, his failures captured the headlines. The governing junta of tiny El Salvador murdered domestic opposition with aplomb and ignored Carter's punitive suspension of military aid; when the regime hurtled toward defeat by leftist guerillas and actually stepped up its repression, Carter restored aid.[13] The episode claimed more attention in the United States than the importance of El Salvador ever justified, and it polarized articulate opinion on foreign policy in Central America. Conservatives demanded American support for the junta in the name of anti-communism; liberals assumed that since the Salvadorean regime was demonstrably evil, its enemies must be champions of tolerance. Both sides despised Carter. In China, where Nixon had mixed *détente* with containment to underscore the anti-Soviet fundamentals of the Cold War, Carter's human rights diplomacy was never applied. Thus, the avowed policies of *détente*, open diplomacy, and human rights found him talking ceaselessly about the goals of his foreign policy in terms that often complicated their achievement. If a foreign policy is going to be ridiculed as hypocritical, as it inevitably will, its spokesmen should have something to show for their hypocrisy.

Carter did score two outright diplomatic achievements, one in Central America, the more important in the Middle East, but human rights diplomacy played no significant role in either case. The Panama Canal treaties of 1978, the product of negotiations going back far beyond Carter's arrival in office, ceded to Panama control of the canal in the year 2000 and outlined the terms on which the Panamanian government was to assume authority over the waterway. The debate over the treaties was among the most acrimonious in the nation's history, not least of all because they came under hysterical verbal assault from conservatives, the most prominent of which was California governor and presidential aspirant Ronald Reagan. The canal was a symbol of American might. The debate about it was a catalyst for the New Right's assault on Carter's administration and a test of the conservative movement's ability to win the higher ground in public opinion, even as it lost the struggle over ratification itself. At points it became so bitter that Carter later wondered whether in retrospect it had been worth the trouble. If in politics "doing the right thing" is its own reward, it was the only reward Jimmy Carter could savor.[14]

Carter's brokerage of the Camp David Accords between Israel and Egypt built upon the achievements of the Nixon administration in the region, above all by formalizing with the help of massive U.S. economic and military aid the tentative peace accomplished by Henry Kissinger's shuttle diplomacy. At the time nobody would have given Carter much chance of success. Although originally a piece in crisis management when a disingenuous attempt to involve the Soviet Union in a Middle Eastern agreement broke down, Carter's hosting of direct talks between Israeli Prime Minister Menachem Begin and Egyptian President Anwar Sadat required both courage and skill, and Carter came up short on neither.[15] Under enormous pressure, he personally guided the talks through setbacks and secured an agreement that, however vague and imperfect, established a foundation for more comprehensive stability in the world's most volatile region. In a sense American successes in

Middle Eastern diplomacy took place at the expense of *détente*, but the reason for this originated with the Soviet Union and was probably unavoidable in any case. Moscow resented its exclusion from the project of Middle East peace, rightly concluding that in American eyes the Soviet Union had never really overcome the mark of inferiority Kennedy had given it over its reckless commitment to Cuba. Nixon had made that plain at the time of the Yom Kippur War and Carter was now underscoring it.[16]

If one were forced to account for Jimmy Carter's election defeat at the hands of Ronald Reagan by virtue of one or two factors alone, then those would surely be the Iranian revolution of 1979 and the loss of a major American client state to a rabidly anti-American theocracy under the Ayatollah Khomeini, followed by the Soviet invasion of Afghanistan. Carter would have faced a significant challenge to his reelection prospects by virtue of the poor economy alone, but Iran and Afghanistan together sealed the administration's fate.

In Iran the United States had invested enormous trust in the ability of the Shah to keep Iran a more or less uncritical ally. Politics and geography together made Iran "much more clearly an American vital interest than Vietnam or South Korea had ever been,"[17] for the Soviet Union a nuisance similar to that posed by Cuba to the United States with the difference that Iran was much more potent in its own right. Yet by the late 1970s there was such enormous popular disgust with the Shah's westernization of Iran that its stability was being assiduously undermined by domestic opposition and exiled political enemies such as Khomeini. Given the poor quality of American intelligence on Iran at the time, the Carter administration was taken off guard by the terminal crisis of the Shah's regime and its remarkably easy overthrow. When an Iranian mob stormed the US embassy and took its occupants hostage, the administration entered its darkest hour. The crisis became a fourteen-month media vigil, daily agitating the rage of the American public at the nation's humiliation and Carter's inability to end it; in fact, he may well have worsened his position by stating publicly in the midst of the crisis that his first and last thoughts were for the welfare of the hostages. After negotiations for the hostages' release broke down, Carter's failed rescue operation resulted in the immediate resignation of Secretary of State Vance and a terminal slide in public opinion polls. The Iranian revolution was deeply disturbing to the Soviet Union as well, especially given the fundamentalist nature of the Khomeini regime and its potential influence on the Islamic populace of the southern Soviet republics. So when the Shah fell, Moscow acted. After attempting initially to curry favor with the new Khomeini regime, it moved to consolidate its influence in neighboring Afghanistan by invasion, pushing Hafizullah Amin from power and installing in his place Babrak Karmal, if not to secure an outright Soviet puppet at least to prevent the emergence of an anti-Soviet regime in Kabul.[18] Thus, within a few short months a huge shift of power had taken place in the Middle East. The United States had lost a vital ally in Iran; Soviet power seemed to be moving southward toward the Persian Gulf; and the entirely new force of Islamic fundamentalism entered the power equation of the region.

The fatally wounded administration responded with the *Carter Doctrine*, a declaration that the United States would regard as a threat to its vital interests any Soviet aggression directed at the Persian Gulf. It thus underscored the Truman Doctrine and the Eisenhower Doctrine, but at the time it seemed like a shot fired over the shoulder by a cavalry in headlong retreat. Carter's "on-the-job training," noted James Fallows in June 1979, "has been costly for all of us."[19] This was nowhere more true than in foreign policy.

Republican Restoration

And yet Carter's problems were by no means limited to foreign policy. For reasons ranging from inflation to Arab oil power and gas rationing, from the Iranian hostage crisis to the Soviet invasion of Afghanistan, his was considered a failed administration. Carter's final resort to a more combative way with the world didn't look authentic. Ronald Reagan's did. In 1976 the nation thought it wanted an honest leader in the White House, but by 1978 at the latest found it that it much preferred an effective one.[20]

While the dynamics of Carter's defeat were simple enough, they are only part of the story of 1980, and not the more inter-

esting part at that. Reagan's nomination and landslide victory
of 1980 were jointly interpreted as a "conservative revolution"
in America, a dramatic end to the era of New Deal liberalism
and the electoral dominance of the Democratic Party. The rise
of conservative sentiment in the country, certainly, was very
real, but it was also composed of a variety of middle-class concerns, many of which bore no clear positive relationship to
each other. In the context of the Carter presidency, it was a
national revolt against the burden of state and federal taxes in
a decade of high inflation and the eroded purchasing power
of the dollar, foreshadowed by the passage of Proposition 13
in California in 1978.[21] For public policy analysts and wage
earners alike it also challenged the efficacy of the social welfare and antipoverty initiatives of Lyndon Johnson's Great
Society along with the very legitimacy of affirmative action
programs spawned by the civil rights movement. Social conservatives meanwhile cited the decline of the American family
as the fundamental economic and social unit, connecting its
apparent demise to the sexual revolution, the women's movement, abortion rights, and the public subsidy of single-parent
families by the welfare rolls. Wall Street questioned both the
wisdom of long-standing regulatory norms and their impact
on the dynamic of profit and reinvestment, while citing the
budget deficit and corrosive effects of inflation as the sources
of falling confidence in American international leadership. The
politically attentive public bemoaned the sense of national
decline, the listless conduct of the Cold War, and the
unreliability of allies whose security the United States had
underwritten for over three decades. Virtually everyone
deemed the country to be under siege from violent crime and
drug abuse, with or without the requisite evidence at their disposal. In the age of PACs every one of these and countless
other related and unrelated issues begat a variety of conservative public-interest lobbies, some of them extremely influential and innovative in the development of direct-mail campaign
fundraising by way of computer-generated contributor lists.

Direct mail fundraising, of course, was not an exclusive terrain of conservative PACs. Many liberal PACs were as good or
better at generating campaign finance. It was the coincidental
perfecting of direct-mail techniques and the ripening of conservative political grievances that made the new conservatism

especially dynamic. While the direct-mail approach enjoyed a low response rate relative to more traditional forms of fundraising, computer-generated mailing lists tapped into the resources of thousands of small contributors and thus opened up whole new frontiers in political financing. Not surprisingly, some of the most successful fundraisers, such as the NCPAC's (National Conservative) Terry Dolan and Richard Viguerie, became spokesmen in the cause to discredit the liberal inheritance and conceded not a second of deference to more established supporters of the Republican Party and its electoral cause. Resort to *independent expenditure*[22] also facilitated the use of emotionally-charged, highly ideological political advertising, either on behalf of a Republican candidate or against his opponent, which in many cases amounted to little more than political thuggery. Again, liberal PACs were no more restrained in this regard than their conservative counterparts, but political circumstance from the late 1970s onward favored the conservative pitch. At times the very vitality that fueled right-of-center politics was also the source of partisan fractiousness. When Ronald Reagan named Richard Schweiker his preference for vice-presidential running mate in 1976, Richard Viguerie denounced Schweiker as a closet-liberal. William F. Buckley Jr. spoke out in defence of Schweiker, noting that his presence on a Republican ticket could facilitate the construction of a conservative majority coalition. The episode momentarily exposed tensions between neoconservative intellectuals such as Buckley, George Will and Daniel Patrick Moynihan and New Right political organizers such as Viguerie, Howard Phillips, and Paul Weyrich; a similar cleavage ran between conservative journalists such as the whiggish William Safire and the populist Pat Buchanan, both of whom had once written speeches for Richard Nixon.[23]

In 1980 Reagan benefitted from both the in-your-face zeal of New Right populists at countless GOP fundraisers and primaries, along with the new intellectual prestige of neo-conservative commentators and research foundations setting the tone of national debate on economics issues. Neither elected him, though, the voters' assessment of Jimmy Carter did. Members of the broad social coalition that had formed the base of the Democratic Party for four decades deserted the incumbent in multitudes, dispelling the notion that the Carter presidency could be the vehicle for Democratic recovery from the great unraveling of the Johnson-McGovern years. In a very real sense the desertion was reciprocal. Between 1968 and 1972, after all, McGovernite Democrats, attempted to cleanse the party of the less fashionable aspects of its welfare-warfare heritage. The "underappreciated legions" of white, blue-collar voters, who thought the United States had made a mistake in Vietnam but had not committed a crime, voted for Nixon's honorable peace. In 1980 they could not recognize in the Democratic Party anything but a shadow of the party of Franklin Roosevelt, and they voted for Reagan in much larger numbers than they ever had for Nixon. [24]

Compounding the impact of the swing in the blue-collar vote was a significantly lower turnout generally from groups with an historical predisposition toward the Democrats: black voters, Catholics, Jews, urban dwellers. Even female voters primarily interested in the furtherance of women's rights were of little help to Carter, despite the fact that the Republican platform opposed both the *Equal Rights Amendment* (ERA) and advocated a constitutional ban on abortion. The evidence is that the GOP has ever since paid an increasing electoral cost among female voters over both issues, but in 1980 Reagan was spared major damage. The New Right had pushed hard for the constitutional ban on abortion and against the ERA, so Reagan profited mightily from the support of social conservatives on election day; meanwhile, the independent candidacy of John Anderson did well among ERA supporters and probably deprived Carter of more potential votes than it did Reagan.[25] In any event, both the economy, especially inflation, and foreign policy were much more potent issues. Last, it is worth remembering that in 1980 reelection was considered by many to be well within Carter's reach, and that this was so until the closing round of the campaign. Indeed Carter's organizers and much of the national press thought that Reagan's reputed personal meanness made him the least likely GOP nominee to prevail against the incumbent. When Reagan's performance in the October 28 debate dissolved this image, the election became a plebiscite on the state of the nation (what Carter had wanted to avoid) and a contest of personalities (what

Carter had wanted). He lost both resoundingly. The debate, televised to over sixty million viewers, was probably the most decisive since the Kennedy-Nixon match of 1960. Even analysts who welcomed Reagan's victory with wringing hands, conceded that it amounted to "a landslide of no confidence in the incumbent administration."[26]

Reagan's supporters called it a revolution. What prompted that interpretation was the across-the-board rejection of the Democratic Party reflected in Reagan's victory in forty-four states, accompanied by thirty new seats in the House and a gain of twelve in the Senate, where the GOP was in control for the first time in twenty-eight years. Reagan's strongest gains were in the mountain states and western farming states, plus in the South where Carter's populist appeal of 1976 simply evaporated. Additionally, electoral demographics such as the long-term economic decline of the traditionally liberal industrial northeast, set against the rise of postindustrial entrepreneuralism in the predominantly conservative south and west, were thought to give the Republicans a critical advantage in the electoral college of the future. Reagan had also come to the election with a fairly straightforward political philosophy of limited government and lower taxes, strong defense and balanced budget. Although there were predictable problems with this platform's definition of conservatism, it was reasonable to conclude that the consensus sustaining New Deal liberalism was at last broken beyond repair. Having failed to predict the dimensions of Reagan's triumph, academics and leading members of the national press corps now tripped over one another to emphasize the profundity of what had occurred. The people had reacted not only to inflation, recession and a 12 percent unemployment rate, they explained, they had also been moved by a deep sense of national insecurity and American decline recorded in both the federal balance-of-payments and massive trade deficits. Beyond Carter's inability to project American strength and resolve abroad, his party's historic formula of regulatory government, Keynesian demand-management, and social welfare had been rejected.

The numbers of the election seemed to confirm it, and yet the claim that the result signaled a revolution in the way Americans wanted to be governed was overwrought. What occurred in 1980 was not a partisan realignment of the caliber of 1896, or 1932 to 1936, but a dealignment that is still underway. The 1970s' economy-of-scarcity and the limits of *détente* had set Carter up for the fall. His performance in the Oval Office had, especially during the Iranian crisis, brought the national frustrations of a decade to critical mass . When Americans went to the polls in 1980, many of them simply opted for the challenger over the incumbent; many others unquestionably voted to overturn the regulatory and legislative record of the Johnson years, when liberalism had puffed itself up from a successful economic renovation of industrial capitalism into a social and cultural philosophy—and they took a tireiron to the Democratic Party in the process.[27] The Republican Party, by contrast, seemed a more dynamic and united force than it had been at any time since the 1890s, armed with a compelling message of limited government that resonated in the historic subconscience of the American people. So the shift of presidential preference and partisanship was easy and sweeping. That of public philosophy was more difficult and qualified.

This was obvious fairly early in the Reagan presidency. Reagan was hardly sworn-in when in 1981 he took congressional Republicans into battle over the nation's budget priorities and recorded early victories with which Republicans and conservative Democrats could identify. By moving with speed and focus, the administration turned the direction of public policy and altered the terms of the debate about the American past and future. Reagan's ideologically pitched defense of his policies, especially those of tight money supply, sharp tax reductions, cuts in government expenditures, and high interest rates, accomplished at least a probationary acceptance from the electorate and its Congress. It is fair to say, in fact, that Reagan motivated Congress with the power and obvious appeal of his persuasion of the public. That persuasion was based on the argument that free enterprize, prosperity, and American democracy itself were under threat unless and until the size of government and the breadth of its regulatory ambit were reduced. Far and away the most effective White House rhetorician since FDR, Reagan's message spoke to a philosophy of limited government that preceded the New Deal and harkened back to Lincoln. It had its Jeffersonian moments as a well, such as Reagan's insistence that Washington would return regulatory powers to the states, but the essence of the message was that New Deal and Great Society liberalism had led the Republic astray. A restoration was at hand.

The new president himself was less a prisoner of ideology than many of his supporters. Among the many true believers he brought to the White House was a corps of solid pragmatic advisors who ultimately appealed to Reagan's appetite for results. During his first week in the White House Reagan made social conservatives ecstatic by making the antiabortion March for Life the first nongovernmental group to receive a presidential audience, yet he agreed with his Chief of Staff, James Baker III, that substantive presidential initiatives on abortion would amount to mischiefs best avoided. Instead, he poured his energies into the passage of the *Economic Recovery Tax Act*, involving projected accumulated savings of $750B; a budget reconciliation resolution to reduce domestic spending by $35B; cuts in aid to families with dependent children, food stamps, minor welfare and antipoverty benefits; plus savings on Medicare and Medicaide.[28] The administration's Legislative Strategy Group (LSG), coordinated by Baker, sought to draw public attention to the budget deficit—the gap between big government services Americans consumed and the small government taxes they were willing to pay—and to score early legislative successes that Congressmen could defend back in their districts before public attention inevitably waned and resistance set in. Reagan himself was at the fore of the administration's congressional liaison in 1981, talking personally with individual legislators in much the same relentless way that Lyndon Johnson worked Congress over his civil rights agenda. In the end Reagan got most of what he wanted in terms of early legislative victories, turning the flank of the Democratic leadership in Congress in a way they never thought possible.

Officially, Reagan's first year in office made fiscal discipline, monetary rigor, and supply-side economics into the new yardsticks of sound economic governance and paid at most lipservice to many other conservative causes whose enthusiasts thought his election a watershed in the political culture. Reagan further appreciated that winning public acceptance of even his economic priorities would be far easier in principle than in practice, however encouraging the experience of 1981. The administration balked at multiyear reductions in Social Security expenditure for fear of the political cost of revising such a centerpiece of the New Deal legacy, a fear enhanced by Democrats who publicly envisaged a savaging of retirement and welfare benefits and made Republicans in Congress worry over their reelection chances in 1982. David Stockman, who as Reagan's budget director was the author of the planned cuts, felt so betrayed by the reversal that he precipitated a crisis in the administration by allowing William Greider to publish his complaints about wrongheadedness in the White House in *The Atlantic*. Later, Stockman wrote a kiss-and-tell book in which he accused himself of naiveté in not having realized that "our Madisonian government of checks-and-balances" was inherently conservative and compelled contemporary public policy to cling to the history that preceded it; he concluded that "the American electorate wants a moderate social democracy to shield it from capitalism's rougher edges."[29] He was right about both, the original intentions of the Founders and the contemporary preferences of the people.

Thus, even in the early phase of President Reagan's first term it was obvious that candidate Reagan's platform of lower taxes accompanied by a balanced budget was untenable. This is no criticism of Reagan. All election platforms are invitations to credulity, and Reagan's of 1980 had been no more brazen than those of many of his predecessors. However, the administration's plans for massive increases in defense appropriations really did take its economics into the voodoo realm Reagan's Vice President, George Bush, had once prophesied.[30] If Reagan's first priority was to lower taxes, his second was surely to refocus foreign policy on a Cold War orthodoxy firmly rooted in his own militant anticommunism. In fact, not since John Foster Dulles had such an apparently crusading spirit governed American diplomacy. The key difference between the Cold War diplomacy of the Eisenhower and Reagan administrations is that the former attempted to keep defense costs within the parameters of fiscal responsibility and suffered for it, while the latter took the national deficit to a new high with lavish defense appropriations and was rewarded. By the mid-1980s the politics of fiscal rectitude had been taken over by

Congress in the form of the Gramm-Rudman-Hollings budget balancing initiatives, which in the end made their own compromises on a politically defensible deficit-reduction formula. Even setting aside ideological differences between Democrats and Republicans in the legislative branch over fiscal priorities, honest congressional efforts in budget discipline had to contend with Reagan's absolute opposition to tax increases set against his radical increase in defense appropriations. Indeed, the White House only reluctantly supported the Gramm-Rudman-Hollings bill of 1985 because of the threat of future transfers to domestic programs of funding for the administration's defense policy.[31]

Allegations of Reagan's trigger-happy attitude toward superpower relations, evidenced for his critics in his words and weapons, were unfounded. To an unprecedented extent, in fact, Reagan's defense and foreign policies were tailored to every nuance and contradiction of public opinion,[32] at the core of which was an expressed desire to defeat communism where it threatened, combined with a post-Vietnam aversion to military interventions in pursuit of that end. So the administration mixed strong words with defense readiness and a willingness to fight wars by proxy. Carter's foreign policy moralism itself had not been the bone of contention for conservative attacks on his diplomacy. Jeane Kirkpatrick, a Reagan Democrat and the administration's ambassador to the United Nations, charged rather that Carter foolishly applied the same standard to right-wing authoritarian regimes friendly to the United States as he did to the Soviet Bloc.[33] Initially, candidate Reagan wanted to steer well clear of human rights advocacy, but it simply offered too much ideological coherence to be ignored. His administration's approach to human rights diplomacy argued in effect that right-wing dictatorships were incidentally brutal, while Soviet-style socialist states were inherently brutal. Yet another conservative Democratic, Senator Daniel Patrick Moynihan, actually put it best in citing Marxism as a state ideology with totalitarian ambitions, given its expressed intention to change the very nature of human kind. "Authoritarian regimes of the Right," he noted, "commit abominations in practice; communist countries commit abominations on principle."[34] The groundwork for a strategic remilitarization of the Cold War, meanwhile, was an aggressive assertion of American perceptions of the world in the 1980s. This is where Carter's moralism found its Reaganite counterpart, in the attack on the Soviet Union as not just a superpower rival to the United States, but a cancer on the prospects of all humanity. The Reagan administration was particularly well-endowed with speech writers, but among the most influential of them over the long term was Tony Dolan, who wrote the now legendary "Evil Empire" speech the president delivered to the National Association of Evangelicals at a GOP fundraiser in March 1983. For Dolan one of the principal functions of the presidency of the United States was by definition to "instruct a confused world in why liberal democracy was morally superior to totalitarianism."[35] The strongest words stopped little short of blaming Moscow for all the troubles of the world, including bad weather. After the national funk of the 1970s, however, this approach was emotionally satisfying to the American public. A simple man conveyed a simple message that resonated powerfully with its audience above all because of its simple truth.

For the administration it rested on the sincere conviction that the Soviet arms buildup, especially the deployment in Eastern Europe of medium-range, multiple warhead SS-20 missiles, would have to be answered by a demonstrated American willingness to increase nuclear tensions. Some of Reagan's defense commitments were inherited from the Carter administration, the development and deployment of Pershing II and Cruise missiles in Western Europe for example, but Reagan approved an increase of defense spending of $32.6B, over and above the $200.3B requested by Carter, for an across-the board enhancement of American military power. Reagan's Secretary of Defense, Caspar Weinberger, not only defended the additional spending with reference to the scale of growing Soviet strategic capacity but also cited the readiness of the administration to oppose the military adventures of Moscow and its allies in secondary theaters of the Cold War.[36]

The latter policy was pounced upon by Reagan's critics as evidence that the administration would take the country into another Vietnam, especially in the case of Nicaragua where the leftist Sandinista regime became a favored whipping boy of its most ostentatious anticommunists, a charge that the Iran-

Contra scandal eventually revealed to be only half fantasy. For their part the Soviets worried that the new defense spending would be employed for political intimidation, and they too were half right. Reagan was restrained in his application of direct military force in the Third World, but in Europe he was more than happy to dabble in a new version of the Eisenhower-Dulles concept of "roll-back." In the summer of 1982 the president authorized covert operations to support the Solidarity trade union movement in its open challenge to the government of Poland. In consultation with the Vatican, Washington gave the CIA a major role in sustaining Solidarity in its darkest days and ultimately in eroding Moscow's hold on a major Warsaw Pact state.

Both initiatives, the defense buildup and covert intervention, took place at a critical phase in the history of the Soviet state, because with the death of Leonid Brezhnev in 1982 the era of its most stable development came to an end. Brezhnev was followed by Yuri Andropov and Konstantin Chernenko, neither of whom offered any new vitality to an now ossified regime: whereas U.S. policy had appeared rudderless to Moscow during the Carter years especially, it now appeared to have at least recovered its convictions just the as Soviet Union was in geriatric arrest. Almost immediately, as well, the Soviet adventure in Afghanistan became a national burden that contributed in significant measure to radical changes that eventually took place under Mikhail Gorbachev. In other words, just at the point where it became obvious to the Kremlin leadership that their country was badly overextended, Washington was cranking up pressure on the Soviet bloc in Europe. Moscow thought it saw potential for exploiting American-West European differences. The Europeans were annoyed by the U.S. boycott of the 1980 Moscow Olympic games over Afghanistan, and they resented more substantively American attempts at economic sanctions, including the attempt to stop completion of the Siberian gas pipeline and other arrangements that brought profitable contracts to West European corporations. Although European governments, especially that of West German Chancellor Helmut Schmidt, had originally insisted on an upgrading of NATO's nuclear defenses in Europe, Green movements and "peace" activists organized massive protests against the deployment of the Pershing and Cruise weapons. Schmidt's government fell partly over the political heat of the missiles issue, but governmental power in Bonn promptly switched from a center-left to a center-right coalition headed by Helmut Kohl, who lived up to Schmidt's commitment. The support of Britain's prime minister, Margaret Thatcher, was never in doubt, despite aggravations arising from the American invasion the Commonwealth nation of Grenada to topple a Marxist junta in the autumn of 1983. When the European missile deployments went ahead, Moscow withdrew from arms talks in Geneva.

The Soviet leadership was disturbed even at the replacement of Alexander Haig as Secretary of State, whom they saw as a pragmatist, with George Schultz. In fact, Haig was dropped because his mercurial personality fit badly into a cabinet in which Reagan liked to delegate authority in exchange for discretion. In Schultz the United States acquired one of most quietly effective Secretaries in the history of the office and a steadying influence on the entire administration, a man of high personal integrity and immense stamina, who placed emphasis on painstaking negotiation on limited agreements with Moscow, especially on arms, all the way through the critical final years of the Cold War. [37] Schultz was initially skeptical of the controversial Strategic Defense Initiative (SDI), Reagan's concept of a space-based ballistic-missile defense system, but moved to support the president once he realized how deeply committed Reagan was to it; he became an SDI enthusiast, once he appreciated the worry SDI caused in Moscow.[38] If Moscow did not find Schultz to its liking, it had only to look at Caspar Weinberger, Secretary of Defense, and Richard Perle, Assistant Secretary for International Policy, to see that there were no soft spots on the Reagan team. In the conduct of foreign policy generally Reagan essentially reestablished an imperial approach to the presidency. He ignored the War Powers Resolution of 1973, using both a highly military definition of Cold War rivalry, which underscored his own position as commander-in-chief, and his abilities as a popular communicator to intimidate Congress into bowing to the central assumptions of his diplomacy. It helped, of course, that the massive increases in defense spending offered to compensate key congressional districts for the social welfare cuts that Reagan pursued domestically.

It was not until 1986 that Congress decided to really assert itself, on that occasion over the Iran-Contra revelations that administration officials had conducted a freelance foreign policy by aiding anti-government guerillas in Nicaragua in circumvention of express congressional prohibitions. If Schultz represented the high road of American diplomacy in the Reagan years, Iran-Contra represented the low end, and it was one of the most remarkable features of the administration that it managed to keep a clear head in the fundamentals of its diplomacy while squalor reined at the periphery. Ultimately, Senate investigations of the administration's efforts to topple the government of Nicaragua uncovered a rabbit warren of foreign policy misconduct involving Reagan officials in extralegal activities, the full implications of which far exceeded those of the Watergate affair. The fact that the investigations never had consequences comparable to those suffered by Nixon revealed not only that the Reagan administration was possibly more diligent in covering its tracks but also that Congress declined to attack directly an enormously popular presidency.

Between 1981 and 1983, Reagan did not accomplish much internationally. West European allies had ambivalent feelings about vocal American support of the Solidarity movement in Poland; when martial law was declared there and West Europeans heaved a collective sigh of relief, Americans concluded that their West European allies lacked any fiber at all, that they would happily ignore any repression in Eastern Europe and even balk at the small duty of periodic lipservice to democratic ideals, just to hang on to the comforts of *détente*. At the same time, a whole new rich variety of appalling possibilities was looming in the Middle East. The Palestinian Liberation Organization (PLO), now firmly ensconced in Lebanon, was involved in border skirmishing with Israel. When it became nuisance enough to prompt an Israeli invasion of Lebanon in June 1982, Reagan sent U.S. troops to help enforce a ceasefire. The American embassy in Beirut was bombed, killing 46 people, and in October 1983 a U.S. Marine barrack too was bombed at the cost of 241 men. American Middle East diplomacy was a shambles. These setbacks might have cost the administration dearly but for two important factors. The American public responded positively to Reagan's return to Cold War orthodoxy, on the one hand, and his unapologetic defense of American interests in the Third World, on the other. There was at the time a palpable public willingness to wait through mistakes and humiliations for the results Americans expected this administration capable of delivering. Above all, Reagan and his foreign policy advisors maintained their initial focus on the primacy of American-Soviet relations. Both the tough talk and the increases in defense spending signaled that the retrenchment of the Nixon years and the self-doubt of the Carter years were at an end.

By 1984 Reagan was prepared to turn a corner in bilateral relations with Moscow. While continuing to lambaste the Soviet Union for its violations of the ABM Treaty, his speech on January 16 of that year claimed credit for having restored American confidence and pledged the administration to "engage the Soviets in a dialogue as serious and constructive as possible."[39] The year, as it turned out, was not especially kind to improved relations, but this was due as much to the passage of Kremlin leadership from Andropov to Chernenko as to the minor international irritants that punctuated the year.

The presidential election 1984, nevertheless, was a walkover for Reagan. Whereas in 1980 Minnesota, Georgia, Hawaii, West Virginia, and Maryland resisted the Reagan tide, in 1984 only Minnesota spoke up for Walter Mondale. Behind the ease of reelection was, at this point at least, the confidence Reagan had returned to the nation. Both informed critics and disgruntled ill-wishers dubbed him the "Teflon President" for his ability to survive gaffs and scandals, and there emerged as well a cottage industry for pundits offering blue-smoke-and-mirrors explanations for his success. But in fact Reagan's approach to presidential office was a throwback to Franklin Roosevelt, and the enormous line of political credit extended to him in the face of limited achievements is testimony to special assets of inspirational optimism. After a succession of failed presidencies, Johnson through Carter, Reagan was a walking refutation of the idea that there was something fundamentally wrong with United States. After only four years his performance had become "a confirmation of older beliefs that the system is sound and that the problem is simply getting the right person into the office."⁴⁰ The sea change this brought about could not be adequately recorded in statistics of public opinion, and those social scientists who tried to do so still look back on the Reagan years bewildered and somewhat annoyed, almost as if they had just seen a unicorn.

Reagan's mandate of 1984 gave him the signal to continue with the policies he had put in place and the freedom to deliver on the promise of his presidency. The United States of 1984, unlike 1974, was well-positioned to pursue a diplomacy of superpower supremacy. If Reagan's American critics could not appreciate this, the leadership of the Soviet Union—in March 1985 changing yet again, this time from Chernenko to Mikhail Gorbachev—could. The Soviet Union of 1985 was bogged down in Afghanistan, and Reagan was in possession of intelligence information that the Soviet economy was under possibly terminal pressures even excluding the costs of maintaining its vast empire. The first meeting between Reagan and Gorbachev took place at Geneva in November 1985, after the Soviet leader had proposed ambitious cuts to intermediate nuclear forces (INF) in Europe. They struck an INF agreement in principle, which at the time represented a significant step on arms reductions. The next summit, that held in Reykjavik in October, did not equal it in terms of results but was nevertheless more important. Between the two meetings, the Chernobyl nuclear power plant disaster occurred and "revealed fresh flaws in the Soviet fabric," both in the fact of the accident itself and in Moscow's pathetic attempts to enforce a news blackout after the fact. Wondering whether the the Soviet system was ripe for a fall, Secretary of State Schultz in particular pressed the matter of aggressive U.S. demands for reductions in the Soviet ballistic missile inventory. Public statements from Gorbachev to the effect that a radical reordering of Kremlin priorities was in the offing further indicated that the time could hardly be better to encourage precisely that sentiment with a hard line at the negotiating table.⁴¹

This is what Gorbachev encountered at Reykjavik. Although the summit there had been planned as an interim working session, the size and quality of the Soviet delegation, including the Chief of the General Staff and Deputy Defense Minister

Akhromeyev, reflected the hopes that Gorbachev had set on the meeting. In response to a set of impressive Soviet proposals, the much more modest American delegation initially brought nothing very new to the table, yet at Schultz's behest finally set forth a plan to eliminate virtually all ballistic missiles in a phased process of reductions. Gorbachev dropped a demand that British and French nuclear forces be frozen at existing levels, but then focused more narrowly on limiting American research on SDI. It was over Reagan's refusal to negotiate away any aspect of SDI that the summit broke up under the cloud of having failed to go the final yards toward an historic agreement. Certainly, in the aftermath of the summit Gorbachev publicly stressed his profound disappointment again and again, each time leaving no doubt where the onus for failure resided. In the end he protested too much, at one point convening an international Forum for a Nuclear-Free World in Moscow in the name of the survival of all humanity, and gave away his near panic to reach an agreement. Finally, in February 1987 he proposed the elimination of all superpower INF forces in Europe without appended conditions, on strategic arms, Anglo-French forces, or SDI.[42] From that point onward, the Cold War was in the endgame.

It was an extraordinary turn of events, not least of all because it seemed to have turned so much on SDI, a nonexistent space weapons system that had been a preoccupation for Reagan since 1983 and seemed to have become the same for his Soviet counterpart, even though the Soviets came to the conclusion that SDI was unlikely to produce a deployable ballistic missile defense system. After Reykjavik, both Reagan and Gorbachev came under domestic pressures for their conduct of foreign policy, Reagan in the investigation of the Iran-Contra affair, Gorbachev from the charges of reformer Boris Yeltsin that change in the Soviet Union was not proceeding quickly enough and was, in fact, endangered by reactionaries in the Politburo. Gorbachev's problems were more serious, given the evidence that he was losing control of the reform agenda he had set in motion. It was during this phase that the Soviet leader assiduously courted the favor of Western public opinion with countless testimonies to Soviet good intentions and finally his signature on the historic INF Treaty signed in Washington in December 1987. In the treaty the Soviet Union made asymmetrical concessions to arms reductions that experts had long assured were quite impossible. Reagan's persistence and the sound advice he received, particularly from Schultz, were a key factor in the dimensions of what was by early 1988 widely regarded as an American victory in the forty-year struggle over the final meaning of the twentieth century. To his credit Reagan never lost sight of the core meaning of that struggle. He accepted arms reductions as significant yet turned to the fundamental, political dimension of the Cold War in a speech at the Berlin Wall in June 1987. If reforms in the Soviet Union and changes in Soviet foreign policy were indeed as well-intentioned as Gorbachev claimed, he protested, then the Wall and its barrier to human freedom should be reduced to rubble. Even analyses that are loath to credit Reagan's tough stance for the fact that even this too came to pass, concede that as Gorbachev yielded one American demand, Reagan did not reciprocate in kind but rather piled on another . . . all the way to the demand at the Wall. Reagan's message was that the Soviet state could not buy the good will of the United States with arms reductions alone; its leadership would have to make the changes that removed both the political source as well as the military fact of its security threat to the United States and its allies.[43]

This Gorbachev ultimately did, but not without the aid of the astute diplomacy of Reagan's successor, George Bush. Bush was both qualified professionally and as suited temperamentally to the transition of superpower relations as possibly any president could have been. Given the facts in 1988 of peace internationally and prosperity at home, Reagan's Vice-President entered the campaign against the Democratic nominee Michael Dukakis with significant advantages. His victory also conformed to the general pattern of GOP presidential successes of the previous twenty years in its sweep of the South, the mountain states, and much of the farm belt; the Dukakis vote was scattered over the northeast, the midwest, and the northwest, managing to capture only New York from among the big prizes of the electoral college.[44] Bush's campaign was often surprisingly predatory considering the circumstance of 1988 and the comfort of his win. It featured attacks on the character of Dukakis and portrayals of his term as Governor of Massa-

chusetts designed to caricature him an unreconstructed liberal now anathema to the mainstream of political sentiment;
television ads slamming prison furlough programs in Dukakis'
state played hard on law-and-order issues in a way that some
critics thought obliquely racist. The strategy was based on the
concern of Bush's campaign organization that he establish a
position on the right of the spectrum and a rapport with the
populist, social conservatives to whom Bush appeared altogether too moderate and patrician. The determination, "to
allow no one to get between Bush and the conservative movement" was especially important in the South, and the GOP
campaign manager, Lee Atwater, a native of South Carolina,
spared no effort to establish Bush's credentials with the far-
right of the party in the southern states in order to consolidate the Republican majority of 1980 and 1988.[45] This feature
of Bush's triumph of 1988 was critical, by virtue of its absence,
to his defeat in 1992. So, too, were Bush's priorities as president and the priority he gave to international affairs over domestic politics.

This was dictated not only by Bush's personal preferences
but also by the force of events themselves. Furthermore, Bush
will be remembered as more than the caboose of the Reagan
train by virtue of his management of the all-important final
phase of Cold War diplomacy and the first post-Cold War challenge to American interests in the Persian Gulf. The first of
these great events was obviously the more important. Beginning in the summer of 1989, the Cold War ended where it
began, Germany. That it ended in Soviet capitulation on entirely Western terms was a product of enormous miscalcula-
tions of Soviet diplomacy and American and German agility
in capitalizing on every Soviet error.

Though Bush came to the White House as an apostle of continuity with the foreign policy of his predecessor, together with
his secretary of state, James Baker III, he adopted a cautious
attitude toward the changing relationship with Moscow, so
much so that he was accused of being nostalgic for the certain-
ties of the Cold War. He took the trouble, however, to cultivate
a personal relationship with Mikhail Gorbachev in anticipation of the understanding he would need of Soviet motives in
the project to move bilateral relations between the two coun-

tries "beyond containment," as he put it. A case can be made for saying that the Cold War began to end when Hungary opened its border with Austria and citizens of the German Democratic Republic took the opportunity to visit the West with no intention of returning. But it is beyond debate that the critical line was crossed when Gorbachev declined to support the East Berlin government of Eric Honneker in its desire to meet popular protest in the streets of East Germany with firmness and, if necessary, force; instead, Gorbachev calculated that East German communism could be renovated along much the same lines as the *glasnost* and *perstroika* reforms he had personally initiated in the Soviet Union. More important still, Gorbachev assumed that there existed a reservoir of popular legitimacy for the East German regime upon which the Honneker government could draw in a project of reform. In the test of that hypothesis East Germans citizens committed themselves to the irreversible destruction of the GDR as soon as the Honneker government showed any sign of compromising with their demands for democratization. Once it became apparent that events were headed toward some form of new relationship between the two German states, Bush decided that in 1989 boldness was the better part of caution, and he accelerated the agenda of change toward the absorption of the former Soviet puppet by West Germany whose security the United States had underwritten for forty years.

British Prime Minister Margaret Thatcher and French President Francois Mitterrand both betrayed a preference for delaying, if not confounding entirely, progress toward that goal. But when Chancellor Kohl asked Bush for some public tribute to Western solidarity with a mind to encouraging further change in the East, the president gave German unity its biggest single push. In an interview with the *New York Times* on October 24, 1989, a full sixteen days before the breach of the Berlin Wall, he declared that "I don't share the concern that some European countries have about a reunified Germany,"[46] and erased at a stroke any notion that the United States harbored misgivings about the full legitimacy of West German democracy or concern that a unified Germany would again threaten the security of its neighbors. As the negotiation process for German reunification got underway, Bush held out for the membership of reunified Germany in NATO. This was not an outcome anyone would have wagered likely in 1989, when the Soviet imperium was not yet in the advanced stages of implosion and America's allies in London and Paris were hardly bringing the best of their creative energies to the historic events unfolding almost daily. Yet Bush backed Chancellor Kohl with the appropriate mixture of firmness and face-saving assurances to Moscow. It is possible that Bush took the political measure of Gorbachev at a summit arranged in Malta in December of that year, where Gorbachev claimed that his domestic reforms were modeled on an emulation of Swedish socialism; his remarks revealed a breathtaking ignorance of market economics that indicated little appreciation of the forces he was unleashing inside his country.[47] Although Reagan's foreign policy and Gorbachev's reforms together set the stage for Germany's reunification and the dissolution of the Warsaw Pact, Bush's command of the intricacies of American-Soviet and German-Soviet relations at this juncture, and his choice for discretion in not crowing American victory to the world, contributed immeasurably to the sweeping nature of that victory. No country has ever done as much for another as the United States did for Cold War Germany and the bloodless end to its forty-year condition as the fault-line of superpower confrontation.[48]

America's Business

Bush's diplomatic achievements in Europe are all the more noteworthy when one remembers that they were not fully completed when the administration waged a war for the liberation of Kuwait after Iraq's invasion of that country in August 1990. In terms of the international juncture in which it was undertaken, Iraq's action was a monument to folly. With the Cold War over and the Soviet Union preoccupied with the momentous events taking place within its own border, the United States was clearly less constrained in its response to a Middle East crisis than at any point over the previous thirty years. The prominent role of the United Nations, first in condemning Iraq's aggression and finally in authorizing the use of force to drive the Iraqi army from Kuwait, would not have been possible without Soviet cooperation. And the cooperation was considerable. Of almost equal importance was the unqualified cooperation and aid of the United Kingdom, led at the time by Margaret Thatcher and then John Major, in maintaining a firm position on the imperative of Iraqi withdrawal and the willingness to use force. None of this takes anything away from Bush's success in pulling together a massive alliance of international opinion to oppose Iraq; extracting the appropriate formal resolutions from the United Nations; delivering promptly on the pledge to use military power against Iraq when the UN's demands were not met; and restraining Israel from responding militarily to Iraqi missile attacks on its population.

Bush also crafted his response to the Iraqi invasion to meet both his responsibilities as commander-in-chief and the sensibilities of the American people regarding military force in a post-Vietnam context. Iraq invaded Kuwait on August 2. Bush declared on August 5 that the United States would not recognize Iraqi sovereignty in Kuwait, and on August 7 dispatched the first American military units to Saudi Arabia in order to deter possible Iraqi incursion into Saudi territory from Kuwait. By mid-October a total of 200,000 U.S. troops had reached the Persian Gulf region, and Secretary of State Baker was refusing to promise that the administration would seek congressional approval before launching an attack on Iraq. A month later Bush stepped up pressure on Iraq with a decision to nearly double his troop commitment to the Gulf; with a number of armored units already in place, combined American and coalition forces were approaching a mass capable of sustaining a ground war. Politically, the rapid escalation the U.S. military presence in the Gulf had the merit of putting Congress in a difficult position. Its members could debate the issue of military force in principle, yet had to steer clear of any appearance that they did not fully support the American troops already sitting in harm's way. Bush prodded congressional sensibilities on the matter of unity by citing Iraqi newspaper reports of deeply divided sentiment among American lawmakers, implying in a less than subtle fashion that a cacophonous congressional debate of his policy would be dangerously close to providing "aid and comfort" to the enemy.[49] A group of forty-five Democrats then dragged the debate into the political sandbox by filing a lawsuit to force the White House to seek congressional approval prior to the launch of any offensive against Iraq. Federal Judge Harold Greene declined a ruling. When Secretary of State Baker reported to the Senate Foreign Relations Committee on December 5, 1990 that military force, should it prove necessary, would be used "suddenly, massively and decisively," he spoke to the assembled Senators of the memory of Vietnam, a war waged hesitantly, incrementally, and unsuccessfully.[50]

The administration also refuted the notion that the free flow of oil somehow represented a less than admirable motive for the application of military force. Derived from a sophomoric notion that principled diplomacy is conducted only for readily intelligible moral ends and that the moral and material are mutually exclusive motivational categories for the conduct of public affairs, it was perhaps inevitable that the argument would be raised as a reason why the United States should not live up to the responsibilities of the one remaining superpower. According to an analysis by the Overseas Development Council, Iraq's sudden occupation of Kuwait disrupted the global oil market to the extent that some 137 countries faced the serious prospect of watching their annual oil bills increase by $100 to $300 billion, with the serious possibility that many of the poorer developing states would ultimately face debt default. While the United States was by far the greatest consumer of oil, Energy Secretary James Watkins was thus speaking in global terms when he noted that "life as we know it today is not possible without oil."[51] Moreover, postcommunist and developing economies were significantly more vulnerable to an oil shock than the United States or its principal Western allies, the World Bank testified in September 1990, and the balance-of-payments of at least sixty countries had already been seriously hurt.[52]

Meanwhile, Bush received the blessing of the international community with the passage of UN Security Council Resolution 678 on November 29, authorizing "all necessary means" to eject Iraq from Kuwait if it failed to withdraw voluntarily by January 15, 1991. After refusing for months to acknowledge that Congress had a role to play in deciding the issue of force, Bush at last asked for a congressional resolution. When on January 12 the Congress voted to authorize Bush to go to war,[53] the president had his diplomacy and domestic politics into synchronization, 400,000 U.S. troops in place, and all his congressional ducks in row. Starting on January 16, Operation Desert Storm did the rest. It was Woodrow Wilson's revenge on a wretched century.

In view of a performance in international crisis management widely regarded as brilliant, few would have guessed in summer 1991 that George Bush would lose his presidency to a little-known governor of Arkansas whom many in his own Democratic Party derided as an overambitious frat-rat. Going into an election year with an economy in recession itself worsened Bush's reelection prospects, but other factors were at work as well. The president's role as commander-in-chief has a problematic and at times highly volatile relationship to his status as an elected officeholder: diplomatic setbacks are almost always politically costly, while foreign policy successes only occasionally bring marginal electoral rewards. In the early 1990s there was for Bush the additional and vastly more important fact that with the end of the Cold War one of the principal structural features of electoral competition of the past forty years, one that had since the late 1960s favored Republicans, was falling away. Even as the administration's energies were almost wholly committed to the Gulf crisis, in fact, there was evidence of the political ground shifting beneath Bush's feet in the actions of fellow Republicans who thought America's real business was at home. In the fall of 1990 Bush faced an open revolt of GOP legislators against the administration's proposed tax increases in the federal budget for the fiscal year 1991. The revolt was in part the result of congressional maneuvering by both Democrats and Republicans, but it was also a reaction to Bush's break with a commitment to never increase taxes he had made at the GOP convention that nominated him in 1988. It was led by the Republican House minority whip, Newt Gingrich, who threw down the gauntlet to the administration by proclaiming that he would rather let the sequestration mechanisms of the Gramm-Rudman budget law take effect than agree to a tax hike. Bush was so taken aback by the ferocity of reaction within his own party that he badly mismanaged the negotiation of a final settlement. The settlement was less significant than the fact of the crisis itself, for it is rightly regarded as the beginning of the end for the Bush presidency.[54]

From the heights of international diplomacy Bush's fall to earth in 1992 stands as one of the great reversals of political fortunes. The source of his misfortunes was with his party itself and the deep cleavage running through the ranks of those who called themselves conservative Republicans. Bush's budget deliberations were influenced preponderantly by a concern to do something responsible about a federal deficit that had grown exponentially during the Reagan administration and the first two years of his own tenure. He had thought that it was integral to a conservative philosophy of government to balance receipts with expenditures. His foil in Congress, Newt Gingrich, defended his own position in the debate by invoking the old-time religion of early Reaganism and claiming that the economy would grow into a balanced budget through the enhanced revenue derived of greater economic activity achieved by keeping taxes down. What was apparent by the resolution of the conflict, however, was that some conservatives care primarily about balancing the budget while others care mostly, or solely, about holding down taxes. This was the rock on which Republican unity shattered in 1992 and cost Bush the White House.

In retrospect Bush could possibly comfort himself with the thought that he had been put in an impossible position. For a Republican president deficit reduction was hard enough when faced with a Democratic Congress defending entitlements, but a rebellion by GOP House Minority Whip Newt Gingrich made any move in a responsible direction quite impossible. Not that Gingrich was not representative of a broader sentiment in the land. Bush's problem was the same as David Stockman's in the 1980s. The American public had expectations of government services that were social democratic, yet accorded low taxes a status akin to a birthright of citizenship.

The 1980s had deepened the the deficit and made national debt a major feature of the political landscape, partly as a result of Reagan's defense budgets, yet also because Republicans and Democrats could not agree, beyond the gimmickry of Gramm-Rudman, on how to control spending. With Cold War politics cleared from the agenda, there was no challenge to the national character more obvious than this one. Only in a negative sense, however, had any consensus emerged on what to do about it:

[But] probably what the parties agreed on was even more important than their disagreements. They agreed not to impose any large costs on the middle class. This ruled out a large part of the area in which significant debt reduction would have to be found. And presidents and members of Congress who took that position represented the wishes of the American people or, at least, thought they were doing so.[55]

And they were right. In March 1992 Senator Warren Rudman, co-author of the Gramm-Rudman initiatives, appeared on the McNeil-Lehrer Newshour to explain why he was resigning from the Senate. He asked himself whether it was worth it to stay, because the country was in serious decline and there existed no resolve to do something about it. When asked who was to blame, he said that Congress was at fault, the president was at fault, and the electorate was at fault. Rudman observed further that any man in the street will tell you that something must be done about the deficit, but that people actually resented real action because it cost them. He used the example of a means-tested health bill that was working through the House, and noted how a mob in Chicago swarmed Dan Rostenkowski's car, then Chairman of the House Ways and Means Committee, and rocked it. "They wanted to literally kill him," [. . .] because they might have to pay a few hundred dollars more."[56] In April of the same year Governor George Voinovich actually burst into tears before a crowd protesting the elimination of General Assistance in the state, undertaken in response to a $1.5B budget deficit. The alternative would been to raise taxes, but Voinovich was only too familiar with the political disasters that have befallen governors who tried while his own attempts to persuade the state legislature to agree to higher taxes on cigarettes and alcohol had failed.

It was into this context, worsened by the fact of an economy in recession, that George Bush took his reelection bid. Even before 1992 the Republican right had begun to doubt Bush's Reaganite credentials. To their question, "is he really one of us?," Patrick Buchanan's answer was a resounding "No." Bush's derelictions as a leader of the conservative movement in the country were cited as the source of his problems with a core political constituency; his signature on the 1991 *Civil Rights Act*, which contained certain affirmative action provisions, and his change of heart on taxes were cited by Buchanan as among the reasons for his decision to mount a primary challenge to Bush for the GOP nomination. George Bush, Buchanan told anyone who would listen, had betrayed "most successful political movement of the second half of the twentieth century."[57] Buchanan had no serious chance of prevailing against Bush for the GOP nomination over the long run, but his strong showing in the New Hampshire primary of 1992 highlighted issues of economic insecurity and mixed them with enough nativist demagoguery to set the stage for the more serious challenge mounted by the independent candidacy of Texas billionaire H. Ross Perot.

Ross Perot's "shapeless populism", observes one of the better analyses of the 1992 election, "tapped into a vein of history literally as old as the American Nation, the revolt of the burghers against a distant and unfeeling crown."[58] The fact that it was shapeless and of eccentric ideological content at a juncture of general economic unease meant that it had infinitely more potential than Buchanan's civil war with a sitting Republican president. Perot could strike in any direction, above all because the central theme of his campaign was a professed disgust with all professional politicians and the shallowness of the contemporary process that elected them. The fact that he struck most forcefully at Bush was a product both of personal animosity and the nature of the issues in 1992. Over the course of his off-again-on-again campaign Perot pounded away at the theme of national decline, symbolized by the deficit, and the *North American Free Trade Agreement* (NAFTA), an extension to Mexico of the Free Trade Agreement the Reagan administration had signed with Canada in the late 1980s. Once Buchanan's challenge to Bush had done its damage and the anti-NAFTA primary campaign of Democratic presidential aspirants had tapered off, Perot's campaign picked up the nativist sentiment aroused over the winter and spring of 1992. In retrospect it was imperative to Bush's fortunes that he make a principled stand in defense of NAFTA, connecting his New World Order governed by law and open markets to future domestic prosperity and the free market dynamism that had been central to Reaganite Republicanism. In 1992 this was critical to any re-election effort, but it was doubly important for a Republican president such as Bush to draw together the strands of his post-Cold War foreign and domestic policies through the trade issue in the effort to consolidate the electoral realignment Republicans had begun to celebrate with Reagan's election in 1980. The free trade issue was bound to cut against him among voters struggling with the pressures of an increasingly integrated global economy, but there is no evidence that Bush decided to make it cut for him with others.

Under these conditions, the Democratic nominee, Bill Clinton, had only to run a disciplined campaign in order to win with a plurality of votes. This he did, but his 43 percent was actually less than the 46 percent taken by the losing effort of Mike Dukakis in 1988. In 1992 the Republican electoral coalition fell apart, starting with the wedge Buchanan had inserted between Bush and populist conservatives, Lee Atwater's nightmare of four years earlier. Perot ran the most potent third-party campaign since Teddy Roosevelt's of 1912, and he cut up the center-right vote just as thoroughly; at 19 percent of the national poll his candidacy deprived Bush of crucial percentages in many of the states that figured prominently in the GOP victory of 1988. Clinton was thus able to make nonsense of the notion that the conservatism of southern and western states gave a "lock," to the Republican party in the electoral college.[59] It was a noteworthy achievement, yet not one based on any groundswell for the president-elect. Instead, Bush's inability to maintain the unity of the Republican presidential coalitions of the 1980s frittered away the advantage an increasingly conservative nation is thought to give to candidates of the center-right.

The most important question about contemporary politics is perhaps whether it is indeed possible to maintain that unity without the consensus the domestic politics of Cold War had given to the GOP. In 1992, after all, both Buchanan and Perot had thought Bush's Persian Gulf diplomacy a setpiece in self-serving cynicism altogether unrelated to the daily lives of average Americans. The evidence of the Clinton years, furthermore, is that an ascending Republican Party will have to face predominantly domestic issues more squarely with a concern first of all for divisions amongst themselves. Viewed as a drama in three acts, the electoral battles of 1992, 1994, and 1996 seem to convey this message.

The Clinton administration got off to a shaky start and had a spotty legislative record in its first two years. It is the particular mixture of the administration's successes and failures, however, that make its experience instructive as to the current context. The centerpiece of the Clinton program, comprehensive health care reform, went down to defeat because of the administration's clear inability to marshall legislative discipline even among Democrats; an extremely effective lobby against the legislation by health insurance companies; and the sheer Great Society girth of the reform package itself. Yet Clinton succeeded in securing congressional approval for the NAFTA trade agreement negotiated by the Bush administration and exhibited a good deal of both skill and determination in the process. In the first instance a Democratic majority was of little use to him; in the second he prevailed because he put together the votes of Democrats and Republicans, facing throughout the most determined opposition to NAFTA from protectionist congressmen in his own party. A Democratic president, in other words, could succeed only with a Republican agenda. This in itself helps to explain the distancing of the administration from Democrats in the legislative branch even before the electoral debacle the president's party suffered in 1994.

Clinton's emphasis on domestic issues over foreign policy clearly reflected both personal preferences and the mood of the nation. Public debate about foreign policy and security issues during Clinton's first term was not saddled with the extraordinary demands that characterized the Cold War decades. The administration was comparatively short on foreign policy expertise, but also fortunate with regard to the relative lack of serious international crises with direct implications for American interests. The conduct of its relations with China and post-Soviet Russia was hardly impressive or especially coherent, but its reactions to the Balkan conflict generally and Bosnia specifically were defensible in their logic and may yet yield positive results. At this writing there is no such thing as a *Clinton Doctrine*, and perhaps the closest thing to it was expressed in a speech the president made before the General Assembly of the United Nations in September 1993. In it Clinton expressed the intention of his administration to keep the United States fully engaged in global affairs, yet cautioned that it could not be expected to have an answer to every pressing global issue. He went on to observe that *throughout the world . . . there is an enormous yearning among people who wish to be masters of their own economic lives,* and echoed Nixon by stipulating that *where it matters the most and where we can make the greatest difference, we will, therefore, patiently and firmly align ourselves with that yearning.*[60] Thus, a president who by his own testimony, drew inspiration from John Kennedy for the spirit of his government seemed to have drawn from Richard Nixon for the logic of its approach to the broad foreign affairs. There remains, however, a lamentable poverty of conceptual development of foreign policy in the Clinton White House in the face of evidence that the administration will face challenges in the Middle East, from China, and in the incorporation of Eastern European states into NATO. What was fundamental for Presidents Roosevelt through Bush remains fundamental for Clinton. The articulation of any foreign policy must square international expectations of the United States with what can realistically be expected of the citizens of the world's one remaining superpower. Americans have in this century done more for civilized behavior between states and respect for human dignity than can legitimately be expected of any one nation. They have failed when they neglected to measure the real chances of democracy abroad against a sober assessment of the requirements of the continuing vitality and security of their own great republic. Much of what happens in the world in the next century will remain America's business, but not all of it . . . and not all of the time.

So, while the Clinton foreign policy exists in name rather fact, the administration's starting assumption that in the mid-1990s its first business must be at home is entirely appropriate. For that reason the clear lack of progress in domestic fence-mending between 1992 and 1996 is all the more damning, yet responsibility for it cannot be booked to Clinton alone. The Congress of 1992–1994 exhibited nothing quite so clearly as the continuing atrophy of the Democratic Party and an utter lack of direction for which the Democrats were roundly rewarded in the of autumn 1994, the autumn of their legislative majority having already lasted much longer. The Democrats got an idea of what was in store for them when they miscarried the passage of their crime legislation in August of 1994. A common congressional practice is to approach contentious legislation with an *omnibus* strategy, that is, ensuring the passage of a controversial item by including with it other items that are attractive in a bipartisan majority and wrapping the entire package with some spending incentives for an approving vote. The controversial items in the 1994 crime package were death penalties and gun control; the enticements included federal funding for more police officers, prison beds, and a $33B spending price tag. Under the tried-and-true tactics of the Democratic-dominated Congresses of the past three decades, Senate Majority Leader Dick Gephardt and House Speaker Tom Foley would normally have been able to marshall a majority. But on August 11 they failed by 210-225, and Republicans went immediately to the offensive. The crime bill that Congress eventually passed was a humiliation to the Democrats, and Republicans used the crime bill in the fall of 1994 as an example of typical congressional 'boondoggling' of crime legislation. The point here is not the bill but the fact that ineffective leadership and lack of discipline stopped the Democrats from passing a bill with the stealth it required. In order to save what they could they had to submit to an undressing in public in an episode symptomatic of the Democrats' decline as a congressional force. With congressional elections of November the axe fell. The Republicans elected 74 freshmen and increased their overall strength in the House by 53 seats. By defeating Thomas Foley of Washington they toppled the first sitting Speaker of the House since Galusha Grow of Pennsylvania lost the gavel in his reelection bid of 1862. The elevation of minority whip, Newt Gingrich, to the Speaker's Chair represented the first time a Republican from the South occupied that post. Any notion among Democrats that Clinton's electoral coup of 1992 had somehow signaled a resurgent party could now be abandoned as the most pathetic self-delusion.[61]

The Republican leadership, certainly, interpreted the result of November 1994 as a fundamental and conscious shift to the right, a conservative electoral upheaval on a par with Ronald Reagan's capture of the Presidency fourteen years earlier. Armed with that assumption the new Republican Congress vowed to translate its November platform, the Contract with America, directly into its legislative program for the 1995 session. The 104th Congress was about to make history. At the time the press was full of commentaries about the historical parallels, along with speculation on whether the Republicans would mismanage their new majority and suffer defeat two years down the road. Standard wisdom at the time was that the two situations were only superficially comparable, more specifically that the New Deal liberalism that the GOP majority of 1946–48 had been so foolish as to challenge had by 1994 lost its legitimacy.

The Republicans began 1995 with the assumption that New Deal liberalism had at least lost its vitality. On a broad front, they attacked middle class entitlements more aggressively than anything the Reagan administration ever anticipated, in some cases drawing a bead on programs important to majority-Republican constituencies—all with a mind to budget balance in seven years. They did so with the conviction that their mandate of 1994 reflected a national ideological shift in a clearly conservative direction, which, allowing for the indeterminate contours of the conservatism, it was. If they thought that the contours didn't matter, George Bush and David Stockman could have told them otherwise. The evidence of that was most vivid in Orange County, California, where in 1978 the conservative revolution had begun and American tax policy had "slipped its moorings."[62] In 1995, some nine months after the county announced to the world the dimensions of its fiscal crisis, a blue-ribbon panel issued a report identifying Orange County's own officials and citizens as the source of problem, principally in an antitax revolt that had pinched local resources to the point that the county owed $800 million to bondholders and other creditors. While voters had rejected a sales tax boost aimed at repaying their debts, they wanted to maintain growth in county services and prompted county officials to make risky bets on the bond market. One commentary noted that many people wanted to see Orange County's distress as a symptom of the general citizenry's outrage with big government, but pointed out that, given its background, the county's reluctance to meet its obligations resembled "a restaurant diner who declines to pay for a meal because he overate."[63] While Newt Gingrich obviously looked to the low-tax aspect of Orange County's political culture, Bill Clinton possibly appreciated its unsated appetite for government services.

In any event, it was on a defense of those services that Clinton based his reelection bid. In June 1995 he offered a ten-year plan to balance the federal budget and subsequently appeared to move in the GOP's direction by agreeing to engage in discussions on a seven-year plan. Clinton then went to the offensive on December 6 1995, by vetoing the Republican balanced-budget package. He singled out a defense of Medicare and Medicaid for particular attention, and in a clever piece of political theater rubbed salt in the GOP's wounds by signing the veto message with the very pen President Lyndon Johnson had used to sign Medicare and Medicaid into law in 1965. A key point of disagreement was the Republican effort to end the *entitlement* status of Medicaid by transforming it into a program of block grants for the states, thus removing another of the many structural blocks to revision of federal budget priorities. At its height, the stand-off between Clinton and Congress shut down the federal government, an outcome that both press and public thought preponderantly the result of Republican refusal to compromise with the president.

But after a year's work in turning the Contract with American into law, Republicans were understandably concerned that even a watered-down version of their plan at last become law. Consequently, in the budget negotiations of December 1995, they conceded considerable ground to the President in an attempt to get an agreement, yet in public opinion were cast in the role of the intransigents. By Christmas many were convinced that President Clinton had never intended to sign any budget-balancing package and had adroitly maneuvered them into a public relations rout.[64] The episode heralded the beginning of Clinton's remarkable recovery in public opinion over the course of the all-important 1996 presidential year. Armed with the veto pen, he edited the script of the conservative revolution and transformed it into a morality play on responsible executive authority correcting the excesses of a conservative Congress run wild.

There remained a good deal of confident talk among Republicans even after they admitted to themselves that the President had turned their flank, but they never recovered their composure. For fiscal year 1996 Clinton sent to Congress a budget with modest spending cuts and tax relief, in effect challenging Republicans to go further, and in the 1996 presidential year either to claim the glory or take the heat at the polls. His argument that Republicans would have a difficult time paying for steeper tax cuts, moreover, was made from a position of relative strength. Between 1992 and 1995, after all, a modest nominal reduction of the deficit was achieved after years of a generally steep increase under the GOP administrations of Reagan and Bush that peeked at $290.4 billion in 1992.[65] Clinton repeatedly enticed the Republican leadership with statements indicating room for compromise, then struck ostensibly principled postures over issues on which he would not give in. Together with the GOP's lack of legislative guile, they permitted the Clinton administration to begin its reelection bid early by highlighting outstanding differences between itself and the Republican Congress, Bill Clinton in effect running against Newt Gingrich before the GOP had even decided on a presidential nominee.

An increment at a time, Republicans began to back away from their hard spending positions of 1995. In the summer of that year Congress embraced a seven-year budget-balancing plan permitting $487.4 billion in federal spending for fiscal year 1997, but by October 1996—after the collapse of budget negotiations in autumn 1995, two government shutdowns, continuing resolutions, and more negotiations—the figure had inflated to $503 billion. The GOP retreat was in part a recognition that the protracted crisis had served to damage Republican presidential hopes in 1996, but was influenced more directly by the worry that the GOP had overplayed its legislative hand and would sustain serious losses in the congressional ballot of 1996. Underlying the Republicans' problems was the yawning differential between electoral politics and interest group politics. The lesson of the 104th Congress was that an electoral platform based on radical cuts in federal spending can succeed handsomely at the polls, but that when it is introduced to Congress as legislation, an altogether different political battle begins:

> One problem is that despite Republican criticism of government, there appear to be few programs that lack a vocal constituency. When cuts were suggested, grass-roots support quickly emerged for federal education aid, veterans hospital construction, libraries, zoos, the arts, public broadcasting, environmental programs, water projects, even noxious weed eradication program in inland waterways.[66]

The 104th Congress reflected the dynamics of the separation of powers in the age of PACs set against the backdrop of an eroded national consensus on the fundamentals of public policy. "Grass roots support" never simply "emerges," it is mobilized. In very short order the insurgent Republicans were required to deal with two publics: the People as a mass of individually expressed voter preferences and the People as a constellation of organizationally articulated interest lobbies, each with a material stake in Washington's taxing and spending priorities. To be reelected under these circumstances, meeting the imperative of a balanced budget yet maintaining services the public expected, requires something pretty close to fooling all of the people all of the time.

Republican doubts that an unpopular president could transform his defense of middle class entitlements into a winning reelection bid began to evaporate when Colin Powell announced his decision not to run for the Oval Office. Powell, former Chairman of the Joint Chiefs of Staff and military architect of victory in the Gulf War, had represented to many Republicans the hope of nominating the first black American to the presidency with a very plausible chance of election. This was based in part on the unspoken assumption that black Americans would automatically vote for Powell, thus transforming one aspect of the traditional formula of partisanship overnight and to Republican advantage, to which was added the additional assumption that a majority of voters generally would see Powell as a latter-day Eisenhower. Powell's explanation that he did not really have fire-in-the-belly to be president, set the conservative press to wondering "whether the current political system is sifting through possible candidates and, in Darwinian style, weeding out those who lack the toughness and stamina for the job—or whether it is turning away people who should be in the process."[67] Had Powell declined to run because he did not want to put himself and his family through the ordeal of a primary season that by the 1990s bore no resemblance to a process whatever?

It then answered its own question by observing that also among those who decided not to run for the GOP nomination were the likes of former Defense Secretary Dick Cheney, former

Education Secretary William Bennett, and former Housing Secretary Jack Kemp, all of whom would have been dependent on money from activists and extremist PACs along with endorsement from ideological godfathers such as Paul Weyrich. In 1996 none of this deterred Patrick Buchanan, who is his own ideological godfather. In 1996 he played much the same role against Senator Bob Dole, the GOP front-runner, as he brought to 1992 by attacking George Bush in the New Hampshire primary. Buchanan's forthright position against abortion had a powerful appeal to social conservatives and was combined with protectionist trade ideas, foreign policy isolationism, and an anti-Wall Street rhetoric that essentially accused corporate America of exporting jobs to cheap-labor economies. The popularity of Buchanan, as well as the strength of the campaign waged by billionaire Steve Forbes, represented nothing so much as a Republican Party nostalgic for Ronald Reagan and apparently at a loss in 1996 in building the kind of presidential coalition that with Reagan seemed effortless in 1980 and 1984.

Starting with the South Carolina primary they nevertheless tried. It was here that Dole took control of the nomination contest. In South Carolina the Christian Coalition, one of the most powerful voices of the kind of social conservatism that back in the 1970s gave an entirely new vitality to the Republican electoral cause, had possibly its best state organization. Under the leadership of Ralph Reed, the Coalition has sought to integrate the religious right into the GOP mainstream. South Carolina is also the home state of the late Lee Atwater, the former chairman of the Republican National Committee who during the Bush administration argued that the Republican Party should seek to cultivate a national electoral majority for moderate conservatism by being a "big tent" both ideologically and culturally, uniting blue-collar conservative white and minority voters, religious and economic conservatives, business, and suburbia. Moderate Republicans reasoned that if other state GOP organizations could be made to approximate the one in South Carolina, their party could probably realize in 1996 a critical realignment as historic as that of 1896. The South Carolina win triggered others in the primaries that followed, putting Dole in a commanding lead.[68]

Yet South Carolina was not a microcosm of the national conservative vote, much less the nation, and Dole never came within respectable reach of capturing the White House in public opinion over the duration of the 1996 campaign. Voter preferences favoring Clinton over Dole by a wide margin remained remarkably stable before and after the party conventions and into the last two months of the campaign. In the critical weeks of September and October Dole's support never reached 40 percent, while Clinton's rarely dipped below 50 percent. This stability of choice was doubtless a product of one of the poorest presidential campaigns in the history of the Republican Party, one in which Dole never gave the electorate a compelling reason for firing the incumbent in exchange for himself, yet it seemed increasingly plausible as election day approached that voters had made up their minds months earlier during the administration's struggle with the GOP Congress. This itself makes the outcome of the 1996 election all the more noteworthy because of what did not happen, for the presidential ballot of 1996 was in many respects a side-show next to the congressional contest. In the first post-Cold War election in which neither foreign policy nor trade pacts played any role in voter choice, the ballot of 1996 could be assumed to be determined by domestic issues more than any election since 1936. The fact that Clinton was reelected handily, and was at no point in serious danger of losing, would seem to justify the conclusion of liberal commentators like E.J. Dionne, taken a full month before the election day, that "we might consider admitting that while we do want better government, we also want about as much of it as we have now, and possibly more."[69]

Conclusion

To leave the discussion there, however, is to overlook what is arguably the more important aspect of the vote of 1996 and the tensions underlying it. The same electorate that returned Bill Clinton for a second term also returned the Congress it had elected in 1994, with little change in its majority position and almost none in the personnel of the majority. In effect, the election consolidated the positions of the Republican Congress, committed officially to reducing the absolute size and the functional ambit of the federal government, and of the Democratic president, committed to defending many of the entitlements on which the size and scope of that government depend. The situation is a reversal of the 1980s, when a Republican executive squared off with a Democratic legislature over many of the same issues.

It is qualitatively different for two reasons: the constitutional fact of a congressional legislative authority and the political fact of victory in the Cold War. Because it is in Congress that the hard decisions and votes are ultimately taken to decide which programs will survive and which will not, the survival of a conservative Republican legislature in 1996 says more about the desire of the people to restore the traditional ethos of limited government than did the election of Ronald Reagan in 1980. Because they nonetheless returned a president who would veto much of their handiwork, it may concluded that the federal government has been given a mandate to debate item-for-item the vast array of services that Washington administers against the available evidence that Americans will be willing to pay for them in taxes. There is no inherent value in a balanced budget itself, but a peoples' resolve to approximate it is a yardstick, more moral than economic, of their understanding of the day-to-day meaning of limited government. This is truer in 1996 than it was in 1980, because no balance will be struck between ends and means without targeting services to the middle class rather than simply zeroing-out programs for groups unable to defend themselves in the political arena.

The kind of legislative inertia that sets in when branches of the federal government oppose each other was in the 1980s given the name gridlock. The Founders called it the separation of powers, and it is a product of their determination that a body politic should not move decisively in any direction without a consensus on what that direction should be. So there would be no sense of urgency in the current situation, were it not for the fact that the New Deal's revisions to public policy in the United States have made government legally responsible for more things than the Founders ever conceived, while the People have since the 1980s reacquainted themselves with the doctrine of self-government and self-reliance on which the Constitution is founded. If the People's definition of self-government reaches no further than their tax bill, the entitlement state will by way of fiscal collapse eliminate their capacity to be self-governing at all.

The Republican majority in Congress, or whatever might replace it, will bear prime responsibility for focusing on this, the most fundamental aspect, of their conservatism and for leaving aside the social and cultural crusades that are the legitimate objects of society and culture, but not of government. At the end of the twentieth century there is more than enough work in determining how—program by program, entitlement by entitlement—the American body politic is to live within the fiscal parameters it has set for itself. To permit themselves to be diverted from this would almost certainly betray the cause of restoration they claim to represent and their chance of representing it any longer. The Democratic Party of 1997 is a husk of its former self, but will not remain so indefinitely. Clearly, the GOP is the party of ideas in contemporary America, but its leadership will have to concede, initially to themselves, that their party is shot through with contradictory impulses and that, in substantive terms, the nation is not nearly so conservative as Republicans like to imagine.

And it is with body politic, after all, that the more elementary soul-searching will have to begin. The American republic, founded on a philosophy of representative government, has over the past century been systematically and comprehensively made evermore democratic, to the point that it is now at its congressional core more thoroughly representative of the best and the worst of its citizenry than it has ever been. America's elected politicians are no more corrupt than those of any other democratic nation; and they usually apply no more cynicism to their duties than the competing imperatives reelection and truly responsible representation require of them. The end of the century presents the public and its government with a situation highly favorable to the ultimate success of this project in national redefinition. The economy is fundamentally strong and the United States has prevailed in the great international conflicts of the past fifty years, its values of liberty and democracy more radiant then ever. It is an hiatus that will doubtless pass quickly enough, and should be acknowledged as such. In the United States of today it is literally true that the People can only be fooled if they contrive to fool themselves.

Notes

1   *Time*, November 8, 1976, p. 11 and November 15, 1976, p. 12.

2   Leon Epstein, *Political Parties in the American Mold* (Madison: University of Wisconsin Press, 1986), p. 93 and pp. 102-103; Nelson Polsby, *The Consequences of Party Reform* (New York: Oxford University Press, 1983), p. 204.

3   Martin Schram, *Running for President, 1976: The Carter Campaign* (New York: Stein & Day, 1977), p. 69; Dan F. Hahn, "The Rhetoric of Jimmy Carter," *Presidential Studies Quarterly*, Vol.14, No.2, 1984, pp. 265-288.

4   Schram, *Running for President*, pp. 75-85 and 360-362; Kandy Stroud, *How Jimmy Won: The Victory Campaign From Plains to the White House* (New York: William Morrow, 1977) pp. 261-281 and 419-434.

5   James L. Sundquist, *The Decline and Resurgence of Congress* (Washington, DC.: Brookings, 1981), pp. 367-395.

6   Larry Sabato, *PAC Power: Inside the World of Political Action Committees* (New York: W.W. Norton, 1984), pp. 7-10. Political action committees are registered interest lobbies that collect money from their membership for contribution to the election campaign expenses of individuals and political parties. In the wake of the 1974 legislation two basic varieties of PAC emerged: those exclusive to an organization (company, union), drawing money from its membership and fully accountable to the membership, and independent PACs that solicit money from the general public to be spent on selected candidates. All PACs are non-party organizations in the sense that they are neither formed by nor directly connected to political parties. Their organizational independence notwithstanding, they can be and often are highly partisan.

7   Quoted by Philip H. Stern, *Still the Best Congress Money Can Buy* (Washington D.C.: Regnery Gateway, 1992), p. 141.

8   Charles O. Jones, *Trusteeship Presidency: Jimmy Carter and the United States Congress* (Baton Rouge: Louisiana State University Press, 1988), pp. 47-67.

9   Sandy Vogelgesang, *American Dream, Global Nightmare: The Dilemma of U.S. Rights Policy* (New York: W.W. Norton, 1980), pp. 120-124.

10 Burton Kaufmann, *The Presidency of James Earl Carter Jr.* (Lawrence: University of Kansas Press, 1993), pp. 37-42; Cathal J. Nolan, *Principled Diplomacy: Security and Rights in US Foreign Policy* (Westport: Greenwood, 1993), pp. 139-140.

11   Zbigniew Brzezinski, *Power and Principle: Memoirs of the National Security Advisor, 1977–1981* (New York: Farrar, Strauss & Giroux, 1983), pp. 148–149; Cyrus Vance, *Hard Choices: Critical Years in America's Foreign Policy* (New York: Simon & Schuster, 1983), p. 46

12   Raymond Garthoff, *Détente and Confrontation: American-Soviet Relations from Nixon to Reagan* (Washington, D.C.: Brookings, 1994), pp. 563–566.

13   Walter LaFeber, *Inevitable Revolutions: The United States in Central America* (New York: W.W. Norton, 1993), pp. 242–255.

14   Jones, *Trusteeship Presidency*, pp. 156–160. J. Michael Hogan, *The Panama Canal in American Politics: Domestic Advocacy and the Evolution of Policy* (Carbondale: Southern Illinois University Press, 1986), pp. 114–131; Alan Crawford, *Thunder on the Right: The 'New Right' and the Politics of Resentment* (New York: Pantheon, 1980), pp. 89–91 and 181–182; Walter LaFeber, *The Panama Canal: The Crisis in Historical Perspective* (New York: Oxford University Press, 1989), pp. 219–221.

15   William B. Quandt, *Camp David: Peacemaking and Politics* (Washington, D.C.: Brookings, 1986); Kaufman, *The Presidency of James Earle Carter Jr.*, pp. 117–121; Garthoff, *Détente and Confrontation*, pp. 580–582.

16   Harry Gelman, *The Brezhnev Politburo and the Decline of Détente* (Ithaca, N.Y.: Cornell University Press, 1984), pp. 155–156.

17   Stephen Ambrose, *Rise to Globalism: American Foreign Policy Since 1938* (New York: Penguin, 1991), p. 305.

18   Michael A. Ledeen and William H. Lewis, "Carter and the Fall of the Shah: The Inside Story," *Washington Quarterly*, Vol.3, No.1, 1980, pp. 3–40; Gelman, *The Brezhnev Politburo*, pp. 151–152 and 169–170.

19   James Fallows, "The Passionless Presidency II", *The Atlantic*, June 1979, p. 81.

20   Gaddis Smith, *Morality, Reason, and Power: American Diplomacy in the Carter Years* (New York: Hill Wang, 1986), pp. 246–247.

21   A California businessman, Howard Jarvis, collected a sufficient number of signatures for a petition to force a referendum on Proposition 13, cutting property taxes by $7 billion and placing limits on the ability of local government to raise the lost revenue by other means. On June 6, 1978, California voters approved the proposal by a 2–1 margin.

22   *Independent expenditure* can be defined as money spent by a group or individual in support of or in opposition to a candidate for public office, but which is made without the consultation or cooperation

from any candidate in the campaign. Independent finance was thus subject to no limit in terms of the amount that could be spent legally.

23   Crawford, *Thunder on the Right*, pp. 118–119 and 176–180.

24   Nelson W. Polsby, "The Democratic Nomination," in Austin Ranney Ed., *The American Elections of 1980* (Washington D.C.: American Enterprise Institute, 1981), pp. 37–60.

25   William Schneider, "The November 4 Vote for President: What Did It Mean?," in Ranney, *The American Elections of 1980*, pp. 212–262; Kaufman, *The Presidency of James Earle Carter Jr.*, pp. 197–214.

26   Walter Dean Burnham, "The 1980 Earthquake: Realignment, Reaction, or What?," in Thomas Ferguson and Joel Rogers Eds., *The Hidden Election: Politics and Economics in the 1980 Presidential Campaign* (New York: Pantheon, 1981) p. 127.

27   William G. Mayer, *The Changing American Mind: How and Why American Public Opinion Changed Between 1960 and 1988* (Ann Arbor: University of Michigan Press, 1992), pp. 315–317.

28   Lou Cannon, *Reagan* (New York: G.P. Putnam's, 1982) p. 316; Robert Dallek, *Ronald Reagan, The Politics of Symbolism* (Cambridge, Mass.: Harvard University Press, 1984), pp. 3–60; Charles O. Jones, "Ronald Reagan and the U.S. Congress: Visible-Hand Politics," in Charles O. Jones Ed., *The Reagan Legacy: Promise and Performance* (Chatham, England: Chatham House, 1988), pp. 38–39.

29   William Greider, "The Education of David Stockman," *The Atlantic*, December 1981, pp. 27–54; David Stockman, *The Triumph of Politics* (New York: Harper & Row, 1986), p. 9 and pp. 376–394; William Niskanen, *Reaganomics: An Insider's Account of the Policies and the People* (New York: Oxford University Press, 1988), pp. 36–40.

30   During the primary contest for the 1980 GOP nomination Bush had ridiculed the conflicting economic components of Reagan's platform as "voodoo economics."

31   Dennis Ippolito, *Uncertain Legacies: Federal Budget Policy from Roosevelt through Reagan* (Charlottesville: University Press of Virginia, 1990), pp. 78–79, 143–145 and 239–240.

32   William Schneider, "Rambo and Reality: Having it Both Ways," in Kenneth A. Oye, Robert J. Lieber, Donald Rothchild Eds., *Eagle Resurgent? The Reagan Era in American Foreign Policy* (Boston: Little, Brown, 1983) pp. 41–72.

33   In 1980 William F Buckley Jr. conceded the legitimacy of Carter's emphasis on human rights, while criticizing him for reducing the claims of human rights in US foreign policy "to an almost unparalleled state of confusion." See "Human Rights and Foreign Policy: A Proposal,"

Foreign Affairs, Vol.58, No.4, 1980, p. 792; Jeane Kirkpatrick, "Dictatorships and Double Standards," *Commentary*, Vol.68, No.5, November 1979, pp. 34-45; Joshua Muravchik, *The Uncertain Crusade: Jimmy Carter and the Dilemmas of Human Rights Policy* (Lanham: Hamilton Press, 1986).

34　Quoted in Muravchik, *Uncertain Crusade*, p. 62.

35　William Ker Muir Jr., *The Bully Pulpit: The Presidential Leadership of Ronald Reagan* (San Francisco: Institute for Contemporary Studies, 1992), pp. 73-78.

36　Raymond Garthoff, *The Great Transition: American-Soviet Relations and the End of the Cold War* (Washington, D.C.: Brookings, 1994), pp. 33-35.

37　Canon, *Reagan*, pp. 394-395. For Haig's side of the story see his *Caveat: Realism, Reagan, and Foreign Policy* (New York: Macmillan, 1984), especially pp. 56-58 and 73-94.

38　George Schultz, *Turmoil and Triumph: My Years as Secretary of State* (New York: Charles Scribner's Sons, 1993), pp. 246-264; Paul B. Stares, *Space and National Security* (Washington, D.C.: Brookings, 1987); Sidney D. Drell, *The Reagan Strategic Defense Initiative: A Technical, Political, and Arms Control Assessment* (Cambridge, England: Ballinger, 1985).

39　Quoted in Garthoff, *The Great Transition*, p. 143.

40　Stephen Skowronek, *The Politics Presidents Make: Leadership from John Adams to George Bush* (Cambridge, Mass.: Belknap, 1993) p. 411.

41　Schultz, *Turmoil and Triumph*, pp. 714-717.

42　Garthoff, *The Great Transition*, pp. 291-305; D. Oberdorfer, *The Turn: From the Cold War to a New Era* (New York: Touchstone, 1992), pp. 183-207.

43　Garthoff, *The Great Transition*, p. 315; Richard Crockatt, *The Fifty Years War: The United States and the Soviet Union in World Politics, 1941-1991* (New York: Routledge, 1995), pp. 356-368

44　*Congressional Quarterly Weekly Report*, November 12, 1988, pp. 3241-3245.

45　Elizabeth Drew, *Election Journal: Political Events of 1987-1988* (New York: William Morrow, 1989), p. 144; Kathleen Hall Jamieson, *Packaging the Presidency* (New York: Oxford University Press, 1992), pp. 459-492; Laurence W. Moreland Ed., *The 1988 Presidential Election in the South*, (Westport, Conn.: Praeger, 1991), pp. 255-276.

46　Philip Zelikow and Condoleezza Rice, *Germany Unified and Europe Transformed: A Study in Statecraft* (Cambridge, Mass.: Harvard University Press, 1995), pp. 93-94.

47   Zelikow and Rice, *Germany Unified,* pp. 125–131; Michael Beschloss
     and Strobe Talbot, *At the Highest Levels: The Inside Story of the End of
     the Cold War* (Boston: Little, Brown, 1993), p. 159; James A. Baker III,
     The Politics of Diplomacy: Revolution, War, and Peace, 1989–1992 (New
     York: G.P. Putnam's, 1995), pp. 168–171.

48   Manfred Görtemaker, *Unifying Germany, 1989–1990* (New York: St.
     Martin's, 1994), pp. 174–175, and 188-189; Gregory F. Treverton,
     America, Germany, and the Future of Europe (Princeton, N.J.: Princeton
     University Press, 1992) pp. 180–181; Konrad H. Jarausch, *The Rush to
     German Unity* (New York: Oxford University Press, 1994), p. 201.

49   *Congressional Quarterly Weekly Report,* December 1, 1990, p. 4004. Ar-
     ticle III, paragraph 3 of the Constitution defines a disloyal act as
     "levying war against [the United States] or adhering to their enemies,
     giving them aid and comfort." Senator Trent Lott, a Republican from
     Mississippi, also said that any debate that appeared to back away from
     the president's policy would amount to "aid and comfort to Saddam
     Hussein."

50   *Congressional Quarterly Weekly Report,* December 8, 1990, p. 4116

51   *Congressional Quarterly Weekly Report,* January 5, 1991, p. 21.

52   By the time war came, and possibly a good deal earlier, the Bush ad-
     ministration had decided that the opportunity to cut Iraq down to
     size militarily was possibly not such a bad thing. Lawrence Freedman
     and Efraim Karsh, *The Gulf Conflict: Diplomacy and War in the New
     World Order* (Princeton, N.J.: Princeton University Press, 1993) p. 186
     and 439.

53   Freedman and Karsh, *The Gulf Conflict,* pp. 228–260. The Senate voted
     52 to 47 for authorization, the House 250 to 183. *Congressional Quar-
     terly Weekly Report,* January 12, 1991, p. 65

54   David Mervin, *George Bush and the Guardianship Presidency* (New York:
     St. Martin's, 1996), pp. 127–157; *Congressional Quarterly Weekly Re-
     port,* September 8, 1990, pp. 2820–2822.

55   Herbert Stein, The *Fiscal Revolution in America: Policy in Pursuit of
     Reality* (Washington, D.C.: American Enterprize Institute Press, 1996)
     p. 592.

56   *McNeil-Lehrer News Hour,* Wednesday, March 25, 1992. WNET New
     York, Show no.4298.

57   Richard Brookhiser, "Gravedigger of the Revolution," *The Atlantic,*
     October 1992, pp. 70–78; Jack Germond and Jules Witcover, *Mad as
     Hell: Revolt at the Ballot Box, 1992* (New York: Warner Books, 1993),
     pp. 130–135; Peter Goldman et.al., *Quest for the Presidency, 1992* (Col-
     lege Station: Texas A&M University Press, 1994), p. 318.

58 Goldman, *Quest for the Presidency*, p. 424.

59 *Congressional Quarterly Weekly Report*, November 7, 1992, pp. 3548–3552.

60 *Congressional Quarterly Weekly Report*, October 2, 1993, p. 2680.

61 *Congressional Quarterly Weekly Report*, November 12, 1994, pp. 3207–3214 and 3232–3239 and December 23, 1995, pp. 3871–3973.

62 Ippolito, *Uncertian Legacies*, p. 27.

63 *Wall Street Journal*, September 7, 1995, p. C1.

64 *Congressional Quarterly Weekly Report*, December 9, 1995, pp. 3703–3708 and 3721–3725.

65 *Congressional Quarterly Weekly Report*, February 11, 1995, pp. 403–411.

66 *Washington Post*, October 2, 1996, p. A4.

67 *Wall Street Journal*, November 9, 1995, p. A5 and A24.

68 *Wall Street Journal*, February 29, 1996, p. A18; *New York Times*, March 2, 1996, p. 8; *Congressional Quarterly Weekly Report*, March 9, 1996, pp. 636–645.

69 *Washington Post*, October 4, 1996, p. A23.

Maps of Electoral College Votes

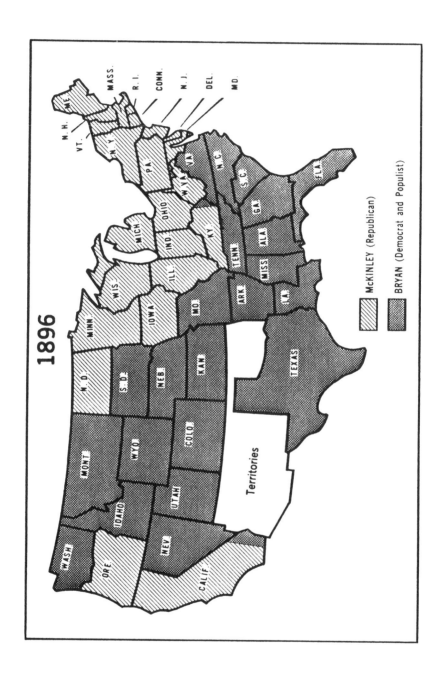

1896

McKINLEY (Republican)

BRYAN (Democrat and Populist)

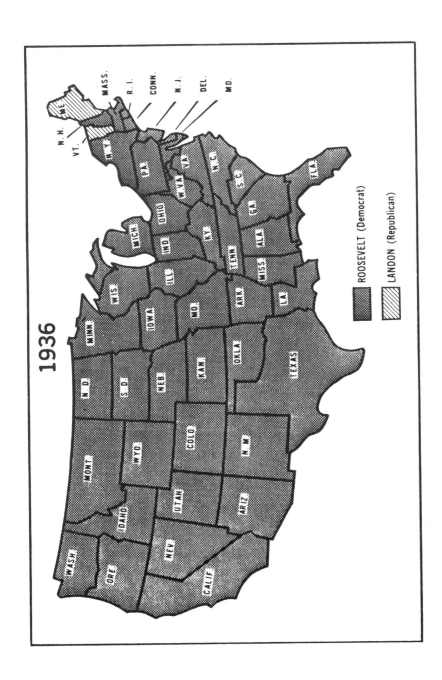

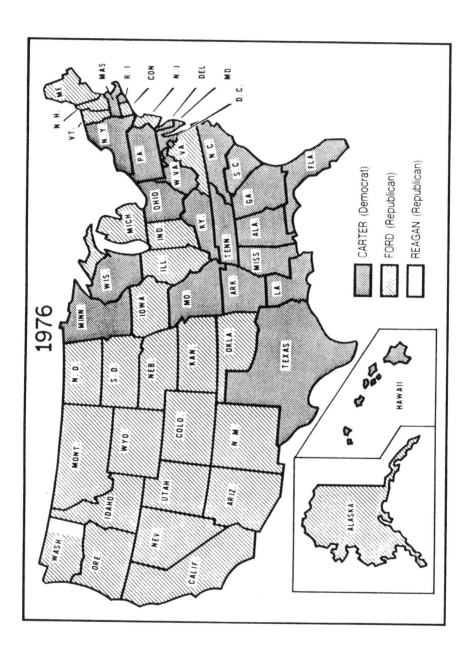

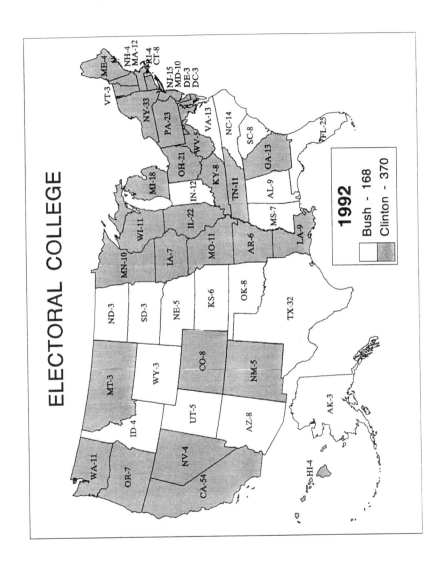

ELECTORAL COLLEGE

1992

Bush - 168
Clinton - 370

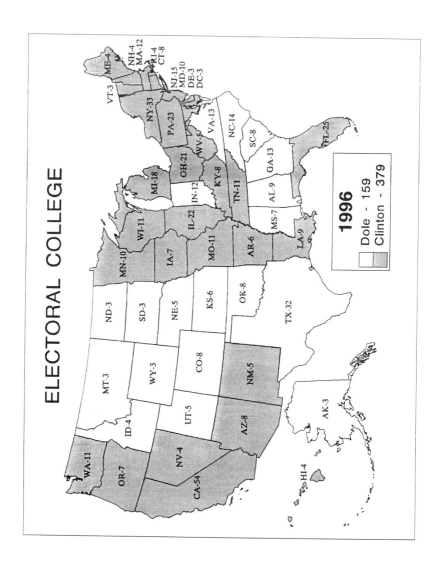

Select Bibliography

Abbott, Philip, *The Exemplary Presidency: Franklin D. Roosevelt and the American Political Tradition*. Amherst: University of Massachusetts Press, 1990.

Abraham, Henry J., *Freedom and the Court: Civil Rights and Liberties in the United States*. New York: Oxford University Press, 1988.

Abramson, Rudy, *Spanning the Century: The Life of W. Averell Harriman, 1891–1986*. New York: William Morrow & Company, 1992.

Acheson, Dean, *Present at the Creation: My Years at the State Department*. New York: W.W. Norton, 1969.

Adams, John, *The Works of John Adams*. Charles Francis Adams, Ed. Boston: Charles C. Little and James Brown, 1851.

Adler, Les K., and Paterson, Thomas G., "Red Fascism: The Merger of Nazi Germany and Soviet Russia in the American Image of Totalitarianism, 1930s–1950s," *American Historical Review*, Vol.75, No.4, pp. 1046–1064.

Adler, Selig, *The Isolationist Impulse*. New York: Collier, 1957.

Allen, Oliver E., *The Tiger: The Rise. and Fall of Tammany Hall*. New York: Addison-Wesley, 1993.

Ambrose, Stephen E., *Eisenhower, The President*. New York: Simon & Schuster, 1984.

———, *Eisenhower, Soldier and President*. New York: Simon & Schuster, 1984.

———, *Nixon: The Triumph of a Politician, 1962–1972*. New York: Simon & Schuster, 1989.

———, *Nixon: Ruin and Recovery, 1973–1990*. New York: Simon & Schuster, 1991.

———, *The Rise to Globalism: American Foreign Policy Since 1938*. New York: Penguin 1991.

Ammon, Harry, *The Genêt Mission*. New York: W.W. Norton 1973.

———, "The Genêt Mission and the Development of American Political Parties," *Journal of American History*, Vol.52, No.4, 1966, pp. 725–741.

Armstrong, Anne, *Unconditional Surrender.* New Brunswick, N.J.: Rutgers University Press, 1962.

Aron, Raymond, *On War.* Garden City, N.J.: Doubleday, 1959.

———, *The Imperial Republic: The United States and the World, 1945–1973* Trans. Frank Jellinek. Cambridge, England: Winthrop, 1974.

Bach. G.L., *Making Monetary and Fiscal Policy.* Washington, D.C.: Brookings, 1971.

Bailey, Thomas, *A Diplomatic History of the American People.* Englewood Cliffs, N.J.: Prentice Hall, 1980.

Baker, James A. III, *The Politics of Diplomacy: Revolution, War, and Peace, 1989–1992.* New York: G.P. Putnam, 1995.

Barber, Sotirios A., *On What the Constitution Means.* Baltimore: Johns Hopkins University Press, 1984.

Barlow, Joel, *Advice to the Privileged Orders of the Several States of Europe.* Ithaca, N.Y.: Cornell University Press, 1956.

Beale, Howard K., *Theodore Roosevelt and the Rise of America to World Power.* Baltimore, Md.: Johns Hopkins University Press, 1954.

de Benedetti, Charles, *An American Ordeal: The Anti-War Movement of the Vietnam Era.* Syracuse, N.Y.: Syracuse University Press, 1990.

Bennett, Edward M., *Franklin Roosevelt and the Search for Security: American-Soviet Relations, 1933–1939.* Wilmington, Del.: Scholarly Resources, 1985.

Bensel, Richard Franklin, *Yankee Leviathan.* New York: Cambridge University Press, 1990.

Berman, Larry, *Planning a Tragedy: The Americanization of the War in Vietnam.* New York: W.W. Norton 1982.

Bernstein, Irving, *Guns or Butter: The Presidency of Lyndon Johnson.* New York: Oxford University Press, 1996.

Beschloss, Michael, *The Crisis Years: Kennedy and Khrushchev, 1960–1963.* New York: Edward Burlingham, 1991.

——— and Strobe Talbot, *At the Highest Levels: The Inside Story of the End of the Cold War.* Boston: Little, Brown, 1993.

Blight, James G., and Welch, David A., *On the Brink: Americans and Soviets Reexamine the Cuban Missile Crisis.* New York: Hill & Wang, 1989.

Blue, Frederick, *The Free Soilers: Third Party Politics, 1848–1854.* Urbana: University of Illinois Press, 1973.

Blum, John Morton, *The Republican Roosevelt.* Cambridge, Mass.: Harvard University Press, 1954.

————, *The Progressive Presidents: Roosevelt, Wilson, Roosevelt, Johnson.* New York: W.W. Norton, 1980.

Bornet, V.D., *The Presidency of Lyndon B. Johnson.* Lawrence: University of Kansas Press, 1983.

Bradford, James C. Ed., *The Crucible of Empire: The Spanish-American War and its Aftermath.* Annapolis, Md.: Naval Institute Press, 1993.

Branch, Taylor, *Parting the Waters: America in the King Years, 1954-63.* New York: Simon & Schuster, 1988.

Breisach, Ernst A., *American Progressive History: An Experiment in Modernization.* Chicago: University of Chicago Press, 1993.

Brion, David, *The Problem of Slavery in the Age of Revolution.* Ithaca, N.Y.: Cornell University Press, 1975.

Brookhiser, Richard, "Gravedigger of the Revolution," *The Atlantic,* October 1992, pp. 70-78.

Brown, Michael K. and Erie, Stephen P., "Blacks and the Legacy of the Great Society," *Public Policy,* Vol.29 No.3, 1981, pp. 299-330.

Bryce, James, *The American Commonwealth,* 2 vols. New York: Macmillan, 1911.

Brzezinski, Zbigniew, *Power and Principle: Memoires of a National Security Advisor, 1977-1981.* New York: Farrar, Strauss & Giroux, 1983.

Buckley, William F. Jr., "Veni, Vidi, Victus," *The National Review,* March 17, 1972, p. 258.

————, "Human Rights and Foreign Policy: A Proposal," *Foreign Affairs,* Vol.58. No.4, 1980. p. 792.

Bulloch, John, and Harvey, Morris, *Saddam's War: The Origins of the Kuwaiti Conflict and the International Response.* London: Faber & Faber, 1991.

Burnham, Walter Dean, *Critical Elections and the Mainsprings of American Politics.* New York: W.W. Norton, 1970.

Burns, James MacGregor, *Roosevelt, The Lion and the Fox.* New York: Harcourt, Brace, & World, 1956.

————, *Roosevelt, The Soldier of Freedom, 1940-1945.* New York: Harcourt, Brace, Jovanovich, 1970.

————, *The Workshop of Democracy.* New York: Alfred A. Knopf, 1985.

————, *The Crosswinds of Freedom.* New York: Alfred A. Knopf, 1989.

————, *The Vineyard of Liberty*. New York: Alfred A. Knopf, 1991.

Calvocoressi, Peter and Wint, Guy, *Total War: The Causes and Courses of the Second World War*. London: Allen Lane, 1972.

Cannon, Lou, *Reagan*. New York: G.P. Putnam's 1982.

Caro, Robert, *The Years of Lyndon Johnson: The Path to Power*. New York: Alfred A. Knopf, 1983.

Cashman, Sean Dennis, *America in the Age of the Titans: The Progressive Era and World War I*. New York: New York University Press, 1988.

Chambers, John W. II, "The Big Switch: Justice Roberts and the Minimum Wage Cases," *Labor History*, Vol.10, No.1, 1969, pp. 44-73.

————,*The Tyranny of Change: America in the Progressive Era, 1900-1917*. New York: St. Martin's, 1980.

Cherny, Robert W., *Populism, Progressivism, and the Transformation of Nebraska Politics, 1885-1915*. Lincoln: University of Nebraska Press, 1981.

Clinton, David, *The Two Faces of National Interest*. Baton Rouge: Louisiana State University Press, 1994.

Clinton, Robert Lowry, *Marbury v. Madison and Judicial Review*. Lawrence: University of Kansas Press, 1989.

Cohen, Warren I. and Tucker, Nancy Bernkopf Eds., *Lyndon Johnson Confronts the World: American Foreign Policy, 1963-1968*. New York: Cambridge University Press, 1994.

Combs, Arthur, "The Path Not Taken: The British Alternative to U.S. Policy in Vietnam," *Diplomatic History*, Vol.19, No.1, 1995, pp. 33-57.

Commager, Henry Steele, *Documents of American History*. New York: Appleton-Century-Crofts, 1948.

————, *The Empire of Reason*. Garden City, N.Y.: Doubleday, 1977.

Conkin, Paul, *The New Deal*. New York: Crowell, 1967.

Craig, Gordon A., and Lowenheim, Francis L. Eds., *The Diplomats, 1939-1979*. Princeton, N.J.: Princeton University Press, 1994.

Crawford, Alan, *Thunder on the Right*. New York: Pantheon, 1980.

Dallek, Robert, *Franklin Roosevelt and American Foreign Policy, 1932-1945*. New York: Oxford University Press, 1979.

————, *The American Style of Foreign Policy: Cultural Politics and Foreign Affairs*. New York: Oxford University Press, 1983.

————, *Ronald Reagan: The Politics of Symbolism*. Cambridge, Mass.: Harvard University Press, 1984.

————, *Lone Star Rising: Lyndon Johnson and his Times, 1908–1960*. New York: Oxford University Press, 1991.

Danelski, David J., and Tulchin, Joseph S. Eds., *The Autobiographical Notes of Charles Evans Hughs*. Cambridge, Mass.: Harvard University Press, 1973.

Dauer, Manning J., *The Adams Federalists*. Baltimore, Md.: The Johns Hopkins University Press, 1953.

Davies, Richard O., *Defender of the Old Guard: John Bricker and American Politics*. Columbus: Ohio State University Press, 1993.

Diggins, John, *The Lost Soul of American Politics: Virtue, Self-Interest and the Foundation of Liberalism*. New York: Basic Books, 1984.

Dionne, E.J., *Why Americans Hate Politics*. New York: Simon & Schuster, 1991.

Divine, Robert, *The Illusion of Neutrality*. Chicago: University of Chicago Press, 1962.

————, *Second Chance: The Triumph of Internationalism in America During World War II*. New York: Atheneum, 1967.

————, *Roosevelt and World War II*. Baltimore, Md.: The Johns Hopkins University Press, 1969.

————, "The Cold War and the Election of 1948," *Journal of American History*, Vol.59, No.1, 1972–1973, pp. 99–110.

————, *Foreign Policy and US Presidential Elections, 1940–48*. New York: New Viewpoint, 1974.

————, *The Reluctant Belligerent: The American Entry into World War II*. New York: John Wiley & Sons, 1979.

———— Ed., *Exploring the Johnson Years*. Austin: University of Texas Press, 1981.

————, *The Sputnik Challenge*. New York: Oxford University Press, 1993.

Doyle, Edward P. Ed., *As We Knew Adlai*. New York: Harper & Row, 1966.

Drell, Sidney D., *The Reagan Strategic Defense Initiative*. Cambridge, England: Ballinger, 1985.

Drew, Elizabeth, *Election Journal: Poltical Events of 1987–1988*. New York: William Morrow, 1989.

Dull, Jonathan, *The Diplomacy of the American Revolution*. New Haven, Conn.: Yale University Press, 1985.

Einaudi, Mario, *The Roosevelt Revolution*. New York: Harcourt, Brace, 1959.

Eisenhower, Dwight D., *The White House Years, 1953-1956: Mandate for Change.* Garden City, N.Y.: Doubleday, 1963.

———, *The White House Years, 1956-61: Waging Peace.* Garden City, N.Y.: Doubleday, 1965.

Epstein, Leon, *Political Parties in the American Mold.* Madison: University of Wisconsin Press, 1986.

Evans, Rowland, and Novak, Robert, *Lyndon B. Johnson: The Exercise of Power.* New York: Signet, 1966.

Fairlie, Henry, *The Kennedy Promise.* New York: Dell, 1972.

Fallows, James, "The Passionless Presidency", *The Atlantic,* June 1979, p. 81.

Faulkner, Harold U., *Politics, Reform, and Expansion, 1890-1900.* New York: Harper Torchbooks, 1959.

Feis, Herbert, *Churchill, Roosevelt, Stalin: The War They Waged and the Peace They Sought.* Princeton, N.J.: Princeton University Press, 1957.

Fenno, Richard, *Home Style: House Members in their Districts.* Boston: Little, Brown, 1978.

Ferguson, Thomas and Rogers, Joel Eds., *The Hidden Election: Politics and Economics in the 1980 Presidential Campaign.* New York: Pantheon, 1981.

Ferguson, Thomas, "From Normalcy to New Deal: Industrial Structure, Party Competition, and American Public Policy in the Great Depression," *International Organization,* Vol.38. No.1, 1984, pp. 85-94.

Ferrell, Robert H., *Choosing Truman: The Democratic Convention of 1944.* Columbia: University of Missouri Press, 1994.

Finegold, Kenneth, *Experts and Politicians: Reform Challenges to Machine Poltics in New York, Cleveland, and Chicago.* Princeton, N.J.: Princeton University Press, 1995.

Fleming, Dan B., *Kennedy vs. Humphrey, West Virginia 1960.* Jefferson, N.C.: McFarland, 1992.

Flexner, James Thomas, *George Washington, Anguish and Farewell (1793-1799).* Boston: Little, Brown, 1972.

Foner, Eric, *Free Soil, Free Labor, Free Men: The Ideology of the Republican Party Before the Civil War.* New York: Oxford University Press, 1970.

———, *Reconstruction: America's Unfinished Revolution, 1863-1877.* New York: Harper & Row, 1988.

Franklin, Benjamin, *The Autobiography of Benjamin Franklin,* L.W. Larabee Ed., New Haven, Conn.: Yale University Press, 1964.

Franklin, John Hope, *Reconstruction after the Civil War*. Chicago: University of Chicago Press, 1961.

Fraser, Steve, and Gerstle, Gary Eds., *The Rise and Fall of the New Deal Order, 1930–1980*. Princeton, N.J.: Princeton University Press, 1989.

Freedman, Lawrence, and Karsh, Efraim, *The Gulf Conflict: Diplomacy and War in the New World Order*. Princeton, N.J.: Princeton University Press, 1993.

Freidel, Frank, *Franklin Roosevelt: A Rendezvous With Destiny*. Boston: Little, Brown, 1990.

Gaddis, John Lewis, *The Long Peace: Inquiries Into the History of the Cold War*. New York: Oxford University Press, 1987.

————, *The United States and the End of the Cold War: Implications, Reconsiderations, Provocations*. New York: Oxford University Press, 1992.

Gamble, John Allen, *The Bull Moose Years: Theodore Roosevelt and the Progressive Party*. Port Washington, N.Y.: Kennikat Press, 1978.

Gardner Lloyd, *Economic Aspects of New Deal Diplomacy*. Madison: University of Wisconsin Press, 1964.

Garthoff, Raymond, *Reflections on the Cuban Missile Crisis*. Washington, D.C.: Brookings, 1989.

————, *Assessing the Adversary: Estimates by the Eisenhower Administration of Soviet Intentions and Capabilities*. Washington, D.C.: Brookings, 1991.

————, *Détente and Confrontation: Soviet-American Relations from Nixon to Reagan*. Washington, D.C.: Brookings, 1994.

————, *The Great Transition: American-Soviet Relations and the End of the Cold War*. Washington, D.C.: Brookings, 1994.

Gelb, Lesley and Betts, Richard, *The Irony of Vietnam: The System Worked*. Washington, D.C.: Brookings, 1979.

Gelman, Harry, *The Brezhnev Politburo and the Decline of Détente*. Ithaca, N.Y.: Cornell University Press, 1984.

Germond, Jack, and Witcover, Jules, *Mad as Hell: Revolt at the Ballot Box, 1992*. New York: Warner Books, 1993.

Gerschenkron, Alexander, *Bread and Democracy in Germany*. New York: Howard Fertig, 1966.

Giglio, James N., *The Presidency of John F. Kennedy*. Lawrence: University of Kansas Press, 1991.

Gilbert, Felix, *To the Farewell Address: Ideas of Early American Foreign Policy*. Princeton, N.J.: Princeton University Press, 1961.

Goldman, Marshall I., *Détente and Dollars: Doing Business with the Soviets.* New York: Basic Books, 1975.

Goldman, Peter et.al., *Quest for the Presidency, 1992.* College Station: Texas A&M University Press, 1994.

Goldwater, Barry, *The Conscience of a Conservative.* New York: Hilliman, 1960.

Görtemaker, Manfred, *Unifying Germany, 1989-1990.* New York: St Martin's Press, 1994.

Gould, Lewis L., *The Spanish-America War and President McKinley.* Lawrence: University of Kansas Press, 1982.

Greenstein, Fred I. Ed., *Leadership in the Modern Presidency*, Cambridge, Mass.: Harvard University Press, 1988.

Greider, William, "The Education of David Stockman," *The Atlantic*, December 1981, pp. 27-54.

Griffith, Robert, *The Politics of Fear: Joseph McCarthy and the Senate.* Amherst: University of Masschusetts Press, 1992.

Gunther, Gerald, *Cases and Materials on Constitutional Law.* Mineola, N.Y.: Foundation Press, 1980.

———, *John Marshall's Defense of McCulloch v. Maryland.* Stanford, Calif.: Stanford University Press, 1969.

Hahn, Dan F., "The Rhetoric of Jimmy Carter," *Presidential Studies Quarterly*, Vol.14, No.2, pp. 265-288.

Haig, Alexander, *Caveat: Realism, Reagan, and Foreign Policy.* New York: Macmillan, 1984.

Haldeman, H.R., *The Haldeman Diaries: Inside the Nixon White House.* New York: Putnam, 1994.

Hall, Kermit, *The Supreme Court and Judicial Review in American History.* Washington, D.C.: American Historical Association, 1985.

Hall, Peter A. Ed., *The Political Power of Economic Ideas: Keynesianism Across Nations.* Princeton, N.J.: Princeton University Press, 1989.

Hamby, Alonzo L., *Liberalism and its Challengers, From F.D.R. to Bush.* New York: Oxford University Press, 1992.

Hamilton, Alexander, Madison, James, and Jay, John, *The Federalist.*

Hammond, Bray, *Banks and Politics in America.* Princeton, N.J.: Princeton University Press, 1957.

Harrison, Richard A., "A Presidential Démarche: FDR's Personal Diplomacy and Great Britain," *Diplomatic History*, Vol.5, 1981, pp. 245-272.

Hart, Roderick P., *The Sound of Leadership*. Chicago: University of Chicago Press, 1987.

Hawley, Ellis W., *The New Deal and the Problem of Monopoly: A Study in Economic Ambivalence*. Princeton, N.J.: Princeton University Press, 1966.

Hays, Samuel P., *The Response to Industrialism, 1885–1914*. Chicago: University of Chicago Press, 1957.

Henry, Robert Selph, *The Story of Reconstruction*. Gloucester, Mass.: Peter Smith, 1963.

Herring, George C., *America's Longest War: The United States in Vietnam, 1950–1975*. New York: Wiley, 1976.

Herzstein, Robert E., *Roosevelt and Hitler: Prelude to War*. New York: Paragon, 1989.

Hietala, Thomas R., *Manifest Destiny: Anxious Aggrandizement in Late Jacksonian America*. Ithaca, N.Y.: Cornell University Press, 1985.

Higham, John, *Strangers in the Land: Patterns of American Nativism, 1860–1925*. New York: Atheneum, 1966.

Hinckley, Barbara, *Less Than Meets the Eye: Foreign Policy Making and the Myth of the Assertive Congress*. Chicago: University of Chicago Press, 1994.

Hodge, Carl Cavanagh, *The Trammels of Tradition: Social Democracy in Britain, France, and Germany*. Westport, Conn.: Greenwood, 1994.

Hoff, Joan, *Nixon Reconsidered*. New York: Basic Books, 1994.

Hoffman, Ross J.S., and Levack, Paul Ed., *Burke's Politics: Selected Writings and Speeches of Edmund Burke on Reform, Revolution, and War*. New York: Alfred A. Knopf, 1959.

Hofstadter, Richard, *The American Political Tradition*. New York: Vintage, 1954.

———, *The Age of Reform, From Bryan to FDR*. New York: Vintage, 1955.

———, *Anti-Intellectualism in American Life*. London: Jonathan Cape, 1964.

Hogan, Michael J., *The Panama Canal in American Politics: Domestic Advocacy and the Evolution of Policy*. Carbondale: Southern Illinois University Press, 1986.

———, *The Marshall Plan: America, Britain, and the Reconstruction of Europe, 1947–1952*. New York: Cambridge University Press, 1987.

Horn, Stanley, *Invisible Empire: The Story of the Ku Klux Klan*. Montclair, N.J.: Patterson Smith, 1969.

Hyneman, Charles S., *The American Founding Experience: Political Community and Republican Government*. Urbana: University of Illinois Press, 1994.

Immerman, Richard, *The CIA in Guatemala: A Foreign Policy of Intervention*. Austin: University of Texas Press, 1982.

——— Ed., *John Foster Dulles and the Diplomacy of Cold War*. Princeton, N.J.: Princeton University Press, 1990.

Ippolito, Dennis S., *Congressional Spending*. Ithaca, N.Y.: Cornell University Press, 1981.

———, *Uncertain Legacies: Federal Budget Policy from Roosevelt through Reagan*. Charlottesville: University of Virginia Press, 1990.

Isaacson, Walter, *Kissinger, A Biography*. New York: Simon & Shuster, 1992.

Jamieson, Kathleen Hall, *Packaging the Presidency: A History and Criticism of Presidential Campaign Advertising*. New York: Oxford University Press, 1984.

———, *Eloquence in the Electronic Age*. New York: Oxford University Press, 1988.

Jarausch, Konrad H., *The Rush to German Unity*. New York: Oxford University Press, 1994.

Jeffreys-Jones, Rhodri, *The CIA and American Democracy*. New Haven, Conn.: Yale University Press, 1989.

Johnson, Lyndon Baines, *The Vantage Point: Perspectives on the Presidency, 1963-1968*. New York: Popular Library, 1971.

Johnson, Paul, *The Birth of the Modern: World Society, 1815-1830*. New York: Harper-Collins, 1991.

Jones, Charles O., *The Trusteeship Presidency: Jimmy Carter and the United States Congress*. Baton Rouge: Louisiana State University Press, 1988.

———(ed.), *The Reagan Legacy: Promise and Performance*. Chatham, England: Chatham House, 1988.

Junker, Detlef, *Der unteilbare Weltmarkt: Das ökonomische Interesse in der Aussenpolitik der USA, 1933-1941*. Stuttgart: Klett, 1975.

Karnow, Stanley, *Vietnam, A History*. New York: Penguin, 1983.

Kazin, Michael, *The Populist Persuasion: An American History*. New York: Harper-Collins, 1995.

Kaufman, Burton, *The Presidency of James Earl Carter Jr.*, Lawrence: University of Kansas Press, 1993.

Kearns, Doris, *Lyndon Johnson and the American Dream.* New York: Mentor, 1976.

Keller, Morton, *Affairs of State: Public Life in Late Nineteenth Century America.* Cambridge, Mass.: Harvard University Press, 1977.

Kennan, George, "The Sources of Soviet Conduct," *Foreign Affairs*, Vol.25, No. 4, July, 1947, pp.169–182.

Kennedy, Paul, *The Rise and Fall of the Great Powers.* New York: Fontana, 1989.

Key, V.O., *Politics, Parties, and Pressure Groups.* New York: Thomas Crowell, 1964.

Kimball, Warren, *The Most Unsordid Act: Lend-Lease, 1939–1941.* Baltimore: The Johns Hopkins University Press, 1969.

——, *The Juggler: Franklin Roosevelt as Wartime Statesman.* Princeton: Princeton University Press, 1991.

Kissinger, Henry, *Diplomacy.* New York: Touchstone, 1994.

Koch, Adrienne and Peden, William Eds., The *Selected Writings of John and John Quincy Adams.* New York: Alfred A. Knopf, 1946.

Kohl, Lawrence Frederick, *The Politics of Individualism: Parties and the American Character in the Jacksonian Era.* New York: Oxford University Press, 1989

Kunz, Diane, *The Economic Diplomacy of the Suez Crisis.* Chapel Hill: University of North Carolina Press, 1991.

—— Ed., *The Diplomacy of the Crucial Decade: American Foreign Relations in the 1960s.* New York: Columbia University Press, 1994.

LaFeber, Walter, *The Panama Canal: The Crisis in Historical Perspective.* New York: Oxford University Press, 1989.

——, *America, Russia and the Cold War, 1945–1990.* New York: McGraw-Hill, 1991.

——, *Inevitable Revolutions: The United States in Central America.* New York: W.W. Norton, 1993.

Lapham, Lewis, "Morte de Nixon," *Harper's*, July 1994, p.6.

Ledeen, Michael A. and Lewis, William H., "Carter and the Fall of the Shah: The Inside Story," *Washington Quarterly*, Vol.3, No.1, 1980, pp. 3–40.

Leeman, Nicholas, *The Promised Land: The Great Black Migration and How it Changed America.* New York: Vintage, 1991.

Leffler, Melvyn, *A Preponderance of Power.* Stanford, Calif.: Stanford University Press, 1992.

Leuchtenburg, William E., *Franklin Roosevelt and the New Deal.* New York: Harper & Row, 1963.

————, *In the Shadow of FDR.* Ithaca, N.Y.: Cornell University Press, 1993.

Lincoln, Abraham, *The Collected Works of Abraham Lincoln,* Roy P. Basler Ed., New Brunswick, N.J.: Rutgers University Press, 1953.

Link, Arthur, *Woodrow Wilson and the Progressive Era, 1910-1917.* New York: Harper & Row, 1954.

————, *Wilson: Campaigns for Progressivism and Peace, 1916-1917.* Princeton, N.J.: Princeton University Press, 1965.

Little, Douglas, *Malevolent Neutrality: The United States, Great Britain, and the Origins of the Spanish Civil War.* Ithaca, N.Y.: Cornell University Press, 1985.

Litwak, Robert S., *Détente and the Nixon Doctrine.* New York: Cambridge University Press, 1984.

Lofgren, Charles A. *The Plessy Case: A Legal-Historical Interpretation.* New York: Oxford University Press, 1987.

Lowi, Theodore, *The End of Liberalism: Ideology, Policy, and the Crisis of Public Authority.* New York: W.W. Norton, 1969.

————, *The Personal President: Power Invested, Promise Unfulfilled.* Ithaca, N.Y.: Cornell University Press, 1985.

Lunch, William L., and Sperlich, Peter W., "American Public Opinion and the Vietnam War," *Western Political Quarterly,* Vol.32, 1979, pp. 21-30.

Lytle, Mark Hamilton, *The Origins of the American-Iranian Alliance, 1941-1953.* New York: Holmes & Meier, 1987.

Malcolm, Joyce Lee, *To Keep and Bear Arms: The Origins of an Anglo-American Right.* Cambridge, Mass.: Harvard University Press, 1994.

Maier, Charles S., *In Search of Stability: Explorations in Historical Political Economy.* New York: Cambridge University Press, 1987.

Maitland, Ian, "Only the Best and the Brightest?," *Asian Affairs.* Vol. 3, 1976, pp. 263-272.

Mandelbaum, Michael, *The Fate of Nations.* New York: Cambridge University Press, 1988.

Mason, Alpheus T. "The Federalist, A Split Presonality," *American Historical Review*, Vol.57, No.3. 1952.

May, Ernest, *Imperial Democracy: The Emergence of America as a Great Power*. New York: Harcourt, Brace, & World, 1961.

May, Ernest R. Ed., *American Cold War Strategy: Interpreting NSC 68*. Boston: Bedford Books, 1993.

Mayer, William G., *The Changing American Mind*. Ann Arbor: University of Michigan Press, 1992.

Mayers, David, *George Kennan and the Dilemmas of U.S. Foreign Policy*. New York: Oxford University Press, 1988.

McCoy, Charles A., *Polk and the Presidency*. Austin: University of Texas Press, 1960.

McCoy, Drew, *The Elusive Republic: Political Economy in Jeffersonian America*. Chapel Hill: University of North Carolina Press, 1980.

————, *The Last of the Fathers: James Madison and the Republican Legacy*. New York: Cambridge University Press, 1989.

McCullough, David, *Truman*. New York: Simon & Schuster, 1992.

McKeever, Porter, *Adlai Stevenson, His Life and Legacy*. New York: William Morrow, 1989.

McNamara, Robert S., *In Retrospect*. New York: Times Books, 1995.

McPherson, Harry, *A Political Education*. Boston: Little, Brown, 1972.

McPherson, J.M. *The Battlecry of Freedom*. New York: Oxford University Press, 1988.

Meade, R.D., *Patrick Henry, Practical Revolutionary*. New York: J.B. Lippincott, 1969.

Meany, Neville Ed., *Studies on the American Revolution*. Melbourne: Macmillan, 1976.

Meers, Sharon I., "The British Connection: How the United States Covered its Tracks in the 1954 Coup in Guatemala," *Diplomatic History*, Vol.16, No.3, 1992, pp. 409–428.

Melanson, Richard A., and Mayers, Davis Eds., *Reevaluating Eisenhower: American Foreign Policy in the Fifties*. Urbana: University of Illinois Press, 1987.

Merck, Frederick, *The Oregon Question*. Cambridge, Mass.: Harvard University Press, 1967.

Merrill, Horace Samuel, *Bourbon Leader: Grover Cleveland and the Democratic Party*. Boston: Little, Brown, 1957.

Mervin, David, *George Bush and the Guardiansip Presidency*. New York: St. Martin's Press, 1996.

Millican, Edward, *One United People: The Federalist Papers and the National Idea*, Lexington: University Press of Kentucky, 1990.

Miscamble, Wilson D., *George Kennan and the Making of American Foreign Policy*. Princeton, N.J.: Princeton University Press, 1992.

Moreland, Laurence W. Ed., *The Presidential Election in the South*. Wesport, Conn.: Praeger, 1991.

Morgan, H. Wayne, *America's Road to Empire: The War with Spain and Overseas Expansion*. New York: Wiley, 1965.

Mosher, Steven W., *China Misperceived: American Illusions and Chinese Reality*. New York: Harper-Collins, 1990.

Mowry, George E., *The Era of Roosevelt and the Birth of Modern America, 1900–1912*. New York: Harper Torchbooks, 1958.

Moynihan, Daniel Patrick, *The Politics of a Guaranteed Annual Income*. New York: Random House, 1973.

Muir, William Ker Jr., *The Bully Pulpit: The Presidential Leadership of Ronald Reagan*. San Francisco: Institute for Contemporary Studies, 1992.

Muravchik, Joshua, *Uncertain Crusade: Jimmy Carter and the Dilemmas of Human Rights Policy*. Lanham, Md.: Hamilton Press, 1986.

Nelson, Keith, *The Making of Détente: Soviet-American Relations in the Shadow of Vietnam*. Baltimore Md.: The Johns Hopkins University Press, 1995.

Nieman, Donald, *Promises to Keep: African Americans and the Constitutional Order, 1776 to the Present*. New York: Oxford University Press, 1991.

Neustadt, Richard E., *Presidential Power*. New York: Wiley, 1960.

Niskanen, William, *Reaganomics: An Insider's Account of the Policies and the People*. New York: Oxford University Press, 1988.

Nitze, Paul H., *From Hiroshima to Glasnost: At the Center of Decision*. New York: Grove Weidenfeld, 1989.

Nixon, Richard M., "Asia After Viet Nam," *Foreign Affairs*, Vol.46, No.1, 1967, pp. 111–125.

Nolan, Cathal J., *Principled Diplomacy: Security and Rights in US Foreign Policy*. Westport, Conn.: Greenwood, 1993.

——— Ed., *Ethics and Statecraft: The Moral Dimension of International Affairs*. Westport, Conn.: Praeger, 1995.

Noll, Mark Ed., *Religion in American Politics*. New York: Oxford University Press, 1990.

Oberdorfer, D., *The Turn: From the Cold War to a New Era*. New York: Touchstone, 1992.

Odell, John S., *U.S. International Monetary Policy: Markets, Power and Ideas as Sources of Change*. Princeton, N.J.: Princeton University Press, 1982.

Okun, Arthur, *The Political Economy of Prosperity*. New York: W.W. Norton, 1970.

Onuf, Peter S., *The Origins of the Federal Republic*. Philadelphia: University of Pennsylvania Press, 1983.

Osgood, Robert E. Ed., *Retreat from Empire? The First Nixon Administration*. Baltimore, Md.: The Johns Hopkins University Press, 1973.

Oye, Kenneth A. et. al. Eds., *Eagle Resurgent? The Reagan Era in American Foreign Policy*. Boston: Little, Brown, 1983.

Paine, Thomas, *The Life and Works of Tom Paine*. 10 Vols. William M. Van der Weyde Ed., New Rochelle, N.Y.: Thomas Paine Historical Association, 1925.

Pangle, Thomas L., *The Spirit of Modern Republicanism: The Moral Vision of the American Founders and the Philosophy of John Locke*. Chicago: University of Chicago Press, 1988.

Parmet, Herbert S., *Eisenhower and the American Crusades*. New York: Macmillan, 1972.

———, *Richard Nixon and His America*. Boston: Little, Brown, 1990.

Paterson, Thomas G., *Meeting the Communist Threat, Truman to Reagan*. New York: Oxford University Press, 1988.

——— Ed., *Kennedy's Quest for Victory: American Foreign Policy, 1961–1963*. New York: Oxford University Press, 1989.

Patterson, James T., *Congressional Conservatism and the New Deal*. Lexington: University of Kentucky Press, 1967.

Pesson, Edward, *Jacksonian America: Society, Personality and Politics*. Urbana: University of Illinois Press, 1985.

Peterson, Merill D. *The Jeffersonian Image in the American Mind*. New York: Oxford University Press, 1962.

Polsby, Nelson, *The Consequences of Party Reform*. New York: Oxford University Press, 1983.

———, and Wildavsky, Aaron, *Presidential Elections: Strategies of American Electoral Politics*. New York: Scribner, 1980.

Prange, Gordon W., *At Dawn We Slept: The Untold Story of Pearl Harbor.* New York: McGraw-Hill, 1981.

Pringle, Henry F., *Theodore Roosevelt.* New York: Harcourt, Brace & World, 1956.

Quandt, William B., *Camp David: Peacemaking and Politics.* Washington, D.C.: Brookings, 1986.

Raack, R.C., *Stalin's Drive to the West, 1938–1945.* Stanford, Calif.: Stanford University Press, 1995.

Rahe, Paul A., *Republics Ancient and Modern: Classical Republicanism and the American Revolution.* Chapel Hill: University of North Carolina Press, 1992.

Randall, J.G. and Donald, David Herbert, *The Civil War and Reconstruction.* Lexington, Ky.: D.C. Heath, 1969.

Ranney, Austin Ed., *The American Elections of 1980.* Washington, D.C.: American Enterprise Institute, 1981.

Remini, Robert, *Andrew Jackson and the Course of American Democracy.* New York: Harper & Row, 1984.

Riccards, Michael P., *The Ferocious Engine of Democracy: A History of the American Presidency.* Lanham, Md.: Madison Books, 1995.

Riordon, William L., *Plunkitt of Tammany Hall,* Terrence J. McDonald Ed. New York: Bedford Books, 1989.

Robinson, Donald, *Slavery and the Structure of American Politics, 1765–1820.* New York: Harcourt, Brace, and Jovanovich, 1971.

Romasco, Albert U., *The Poverty of Abundance: Hoover, The Nation, The Depression.* New York: Oxford University Press 1965.

———, *The Politics of Recovery: Roosevelt's New Deal.* New York: Oxford University Press, 1983.

Roosevelt, Franklin, *The Public Papers and Addresses of Franklin D. Roosevelt,* 5 Vols., New York: Random House, 1938.

Rusk, Dean, "The President," *Foreign Affairs,* Vol.38, No.3, April 1960. pp. 353–369.

———, *As I Saw It.* New York: W.W. Norton, 1990.

Rutland, Robert, *James Madison, The Founding Father.* London: Macmillan, 1987.

Sabato, Larry, *PAC Power: Inside the World of Political Action Committees.* New York: W.W. Norton, 1984.

Safire, William, *Before the Fall: An Inside View of the Pre-Watergate White House.* New York: Doubleday, 1975.

Sarasohn, David, *The Party of Reform: Democrats in the Progressive Era.* Jackson: University of Mississippi Press, 1989.

Savage, James D., *Balanced Budgets and American Politics.* Ithaca, N.Y.: Cornell University Press, 1988.

Scammon, Richard M., and Wattenberg, Ben J., *The Real Majority.* New York: Cowerd McCann, 1970.

Schlesinger, Arthur Jr., *The Coming of the New Deal.* Cambridge, Mass.: Houghton Mifflin, 1958.

———, *The Politics of Upheaval.* Boston: Houghton Mifflin, 1960.

———, *A Thousand Days: John F. Kennedy in the White House.* Boston: Houghton-Mifflin, 1965.

———, et. al., Eds., *The History of American Presidential Elections, 1789-1968.* 4 Vols. New York: McGraw-Hill, 1971.

Schoenbaum, Thomas J., *Waging Peace and War: Dean Rusk in the Truman, Kennedy and Johnson Years.* New York: Simon & Schuster, 1988.

Schram, Martin, *Running for President, 1976: The Carter Campaign.* New York: Stein & Day, 1977.

Schrecker, Ellen, *The Age of McCarthy.* Boston: Bedford Books, 1994.

Schultz, George, *Turmoil and Triumph: My Years as Secretary of State.* New York: Charles Scribner's Sons 1993.

Schwartz, John E., *America's Hidden Success: A Reassessment of Public Policy from Kennedy to Reagan.* New York: W.W. Norton, 1988.

Schwartz, Thomas Allen, *America's Germany: John J. McCloy and the Federal Republic of Germany.* Cambridge, Mass.: Harvard University Press, 1991.

Schwabe, Klaus, *Der amerikanische Isolationismus im 20 Jahrhundert, Legende und Wirklichkeit.* Wiesbaden: Franz Steiner, 1975.

Shalhope, Robert E., "The Ideological Origins of the Second Amendment," *Journal of American History*, Vol.69. No.3, 1982, pp. 599-614.

Sheldon, Garret Ward, *The Political Philosophy of Thomas Jefferson.* Baltimore: The Johns Hopkins University Press, 1991.

Sherwood, Robert E., *Roosevelt and Hopkins, An Intimate History.* New York: Harper Brothers, 1948.

Silbey, Joel H., *The American Political Nation, 1838-1893.* Stanford, Calif.: Stanford University Press, 1991.

Sindler, Allan P. Ed., *Policy and Politics in America: Six Case Studies.* Boston: Little, Brown, 1973.

Sklar, Martin J. *The Corporate Reconstruction of American Capitalism, 1890–1916: The Market, The Law, and Politics.* New York: Cambridge University Press, 1988.

Skrowonek, Stephen, *The Politics Presidents Make: Leadership from John Adams to George Bush.* Cambridge, Mass.: Belknap, 1993.

Small, Melvin, *Johnson, Nixon, and the Doves.* New Brunswick, N.J.: Rutgers University Press, 1988.

Smith, Adam, *An Inquiry into the Nature and Causes of the Wealth of Nations.* 2 Vols., W.B. Todd Ed., Indianapolis, Ind.: Liberty Classics, 1976.

Smith, Gaddis, *Morality, Reason, and Power: American Diplomacy in the Carter Years.* New York: Hill & Wang, 1986.

Smith, Joseph. *The Spanish-American War: Conflict in the Caribbean and Pacific, 1895–1902.* New York: Longman, 1994.

Solomon, Robert, *The International Monetary System, 1945-1981.* New York: Harper & Row, 1982.

Sorenson, Theodore C., *Kennedy.* New York: Harper and Row, 1965.

Sparkes, A.W., *Talking Politics: A Workbook.* London: Routledge, 1994.

Stares, Paul B., *Space and National Security.* Washington, D.C.: Brookings, 1987.

Stave, Bruce M. Ed., *Urban Bosses, Machines, and Progressive Reformers.* Lexington: D.C. Heath, 1972.

Stein, Herbert, *Presidential Economics: The Making of Economic Policy from Roosevelt to Reagan and Beyond.* New York: Simon & Schuster, 1984.

———, *The Fiscal Revolution in America: Policy in Pursuit of Reality.* Washington, D.C: AEI Press, 1996.

Stern, Philip H., *Still the Best Congress Money Can Buy.* Washington, D.C.: Regnery Gateway, 1992.

Stevenson, Richard W., *The Rise and Fall of Détente: Relaxations of Tension in U.S.-Soviet Relations, 1953–1984.* Urbana: University of Illinois Press, 1985.

Stockman, David, *The Triumph of Politics.* New York: Harper & Row, 1986.

Stroud, Kandy, *How Jimmy Won: The Victory Campaign from Plains to the White House.* New York: William Morrow, 1977.

Sundquist, James L., *Politics and Policy: The Eisenhower, Kennedy and Johnson Years.* Washington, D.C.: Brookings, 1968.

————, *The Decline and Resurgence of Congress*. Washington, D.C.: Brookings, 1981.

————, *Dynamics of the Party System: Alignment and Realignment of Political Parties in the United States*. Washington, D.C.: Brookings, 1983.

De Tocqueville, Alexis, *Democracy in America*. Trans. George Lawrence, J.P. Mayer Ed., Garden City, N.Y.: Doubleday, 1969.

Trask, David F., *The War with Spain in 1898*. New York: Macmillan, 1981.

Treverton, Gregory, *America, Germany, and the Future of Europe*. Princeton, N.J.: Princeton University Press, 1992.

Utley, Jonathan G., *Going to War With Japan, 1937-1941*. Knoxville: University of Tennessee Press, 1985.

Vance, Cyrus, *Hard Choices: Critical Years in America's Foreign Policy*. New York: Simon & Schuster, 1983.

Van Deusen, Glyndon G., *The Jacksonian Era, 1828-1848*. New York: Harper & Row, 1959.

————, *William Henry Seward*. New York: Oxford University Press, 1967.

Vincent, J., and Burke, Vee, *Nixon's Good Deed, Welfare Reform*. New York: Columbia University Press, 1974.

Vogelgesang, Sandy, *American Dream, Global Nightmare: The Dilemma of U.S. Rights Policy*. New York: W.W. Norton, 1980.

Wall, Irwin M., *The United States and the Making of Postwar France, 1945-1954*. New York: Cambridge University Press, 1991.

Warren, Harris G., *Herbert Hoover and the Great Depression*. New York: Oxford University Press, 1959.

Weed, Clyde, *The Nemisis of Reform: The Republican Party During the New Deal*. New York: Columbia University Press, 1994.

Weinberg, Albert K., *Manifest Destiny: A Study of Nationalist Expansionism in American History*. Gloucester, Mass.: Peter Smith, 1958.

Weinberg, Gerhard, *A World at Arms: A Global History of World War II*. New York: Cambridge University Press, 1994.

Welch, Richard E., *The Presidencies of Grover Cleveland*. Lawrence: University of Kansas Press, 1988.

Werth, Alexander, *France, 1940-1955*. London: Robert Hale, 1956.

White, Joseph and Wildavsky, Aaron, *The Deficit and the Public Interest: The Search for Responsible Budgetting in the 1980s*. Berkeley, Calf.: University of California Press, 1989.

White, Leonard D., *The Republican Era, 1896-1901.* New York: MacMillan, 1958.

White, Theodore, *The Making of the President, 1964.* New York: Atheneum, 1965.

————, *The Making of the President, 1968.* New York: Atheneum, 1969.

Wicker, Tom, "Committed to a Quagmire," *Diplomatic History*, Vol.19. No.1, 1995, pp. 167-171.

Williamson, Chilton, *American Suffrage: From Property to Democracy, 1760-1860.* Princeton, N.J.: Princeton University Press, 1960.

Wilson, Douglas L., "Thomas Jefferson and the Character Issue," *The Atlantic*, November 1992, pp. 57-74.

Wilson, James Q., *The Amateur Democrat: Club Politics in Three Cities.* Chicago: University of Chicago Press, 1966.

Wilson, Woodrow, *The New Democracy* 2 vols., Ray Stannard Baker and William E. Dodd Eds., New York: Kraus Reprint, 1970.

Wood, Gordon S., *The Creation of the American Republic, 1776-1778.* New York: W.W. Norton, 1969.

————, *The Radicalism of the American Revolution.* New York: Alfred A. Knopf, 1992.

Woodward, C. Vann, *Tom Watson, Agrarian Rebel.* New York: Oxford University Press, 1963.

Zelikow, Philip and Rice, Condoleezza, *Germany Unified and Europe Transformed: A Study in Statecraft.* Cambridge, Mass.: Harvard University Press, 1995.

Index

336   Index

Hall, 53; dominance of Democrats and Republicans, 53–54; Greenbacks and Grange, 54; as political holding companies, 115; direct mail fundraising (see also: elections)
Patrons of Husbandry, 55
Peace Treaty of 1763, 6
Pearl Harbor (see Japan)
Pendergast, T.J., 112
Peoples' Party
Perle, Richard, 271
Perot, H. Ross, 285, 286
Perry v. the United States, 98
Persian Gulf War, 206, 277; 279–282
Philadelphia Plan, 235
Phillipines: acquisition of, 64
Plessy v. Ferguson, 59–60
Plunkitt, George Washington, 54–55
Poland: German-Soviet invasion, 125; Soviet repression, 138; Solidarity movement, 270, 272
political action committees (PACs), 254–255, 293, 298; direct mail fundraising, 261–262
Polk, James, 39, 40
populism, 27, 55-57, 117–118, 285, 286
Populist Party, 56–58, 60, 61, 62
post-materialism, 222–223
Potsdam Conference, 149, 163, 167, 184–185
Powell, Colin, 293
President: four-year term, 10; foreign affairs, 10; clerk-in chief, 12; election of, 12–13, 26; executive authority and political profile, 13, 16; Jackson's contribution, 28–29; Lincoln's contribution, 32; *Crittendon Resolution* and war powers 32;

commander-in-chief, 36–37, 40; executive privilege, 37; under McKinley, 64–65; under TR, 70; FDR and modern presidency, 95, 106–112, 118–120, 182,183–184; new assets under Truman, 148, 151, 160; under Eisenhower, 165, 172–173; Kennedy legacy, 179–180; the impossible office, 197–199; under Johnson, 199–200, 201–202, 210, 211–212; under Nixon, 219–220, 220–221, 225, 231–232; embattled office, 222, 239; under Carter, 260; under Reagan, 265–266 271–272, 273–274
primaries, 70, 161; Kennedy nomination, 178; Nixon nomination, 217; McGovern nomination, 233; Carter nomination, 252; undermine Bush reelection, 285; Dole nomination, 294
Proclamation Act, 21
Progressive Party of America, 154
Progressive Party, 69
progressivism, 49, 58–59, 114; diffuse impact, 62, 66; foreign affairs, 62–63; reform agenda of, 66–67; Progressive Party, 69
property: and liberty, 14, 21, 29; slavery and, 14–15; Madison on conflict, 15

Québec Act, 21
Quemoy and Matsu, 172–173
Railroad Retirement Board v. Alton Railroad Company, 98
Rayburn, Sam, 253
Reagan, Ronald, 205, 220, 258; nomination and election